Being-in-the-World

Being-in-the-World

Selected Papers of
LUDWIG BINSWANGER

*Translated and
with a Critical Introduction
to His Existential Psychoanalysis*

BY

Jacob Needleman

BASIC BOOKS, INC.
NEW YORK *Publishers* LONDON

FOR

my mother and father

PREFACE

Ludwig Binswanger's *Daseinsanalyse* is an effort to complement and correct the view of man and human experience implicit in Freudian psychoanalysis. As such, it is eminently philosophical and must be so understood if its relevance to practical psychological and clinical issues is eventually to be appreciated. Unfortunately, the tendency in America has been to approach Binswanger's work primarily as a clinical alternative to Freudian psychoanalysis without careful attention to the philosophical ground of both schools of thought. For, as I hope to have shown in this book, it is there that the battle is joined. Daseinsanalyse cannot but seem impotent and superfluous if it is treated as an *Ersatz* for scientific psychiatry. One must realize that its strength is of a different sort than that of natural science, a strength sorely needed if science is to succeed in taking man as its object.

In this study I have used the term "existential a priori" in order to emphasize what I take to be the Kantian elements in Binswanger's and Heidegger's method of thought. In singling out this one aspect of Binswanger's work, I have underplayed some facets that he himself considers vital: to name but one, the unique conception of love as presented in his *Grundformen und Erkenntnis menschlichen Daseins*. I saw my choice as lying between a faithful exposition and an interpretive focus, and felt that by choosing the latter I would be able to discuss more clearly some of the issues that divide Binswanger and Freud in their philosophical context. If I have succeeded in this, then perhaps whatever distortion by selection is inherent in such an undertaking has been justified.

American interest in Daseinsanalyse has, unfortunately, raced far ahead of the material available in English. Except for the excellent translations in *Existence*,[1] readers in this country have had to settle for secondhand presentations of Binswanger's thought, particularly in its relation to Freudian theory. The attempt to rectify this situation somewhat has been the main principle guiding my choice of translation. But I have also sought to make my study of Binswanger's work and the selections from his writings integral and interrelated. It is to be hoped, therefore, that an English translation of his *Grundformen* will soon be undertaken. This monumental and closely-welded work argues that human existence cannot be understood solely under Heidegger's aspect of "Care" (*Sorge*), and presents an extensive analysis of the equally fundamental ontological mode of *love*. Although Binswanger later claimed this work was based upon a "creative misunderstanding" of Heidegger's philosophy, to my mind it still stands as a valid, necessary, and remarkably far-seeing supplementation of Heideggerean thought.

I should like to thank Dr. Ernest Angel (who must take much of the credit for the first importation of Binswanger's thought to America) for turning over to me his translation of "The Case of Lola Voss," and for helping me navigate certain of the troubled waters of Binswanger's prose. I wish also to express my gratitude to the Samuel F. Fels Foundation, under whose auspices I was able to work in Europe; to Professor Binswanger, whose profound hospitality and conversation in Kreuzlingen showed me the man behind the work I so admired; and above all to Professor John E. Smith of the Yale University Department of Philosophy, who shepherded my ideas when I was working them into the form of a doctoral dissertation.

I am grateful to Max Niemeyer Verlag of Tübingen for granting me permission to include the essay "Extravagance," which appears as Chapter I in Binswanger's *Drei Formen Missglückten Daseins*. "Freud and the Magna Charta of Clinical Psychiatry" ("Freud und die Verfassung der klinischen Psychiatrie"), "Heidegger's Analytic of Existence and its Meaning for Psychiatry" ("Die Bedeutung der Daseinsanalytik Martin Heideggers für das Selbstverständnis der Psychiatrie"), "Freud's Conception of Man in the Light of Anthropology" ("Freuds Auffassung des Men-

[1] Rollo May, Ernest Angel, and Henri Ellenberger (eds.), *Existence* (New York: Basic Books, 1958).

schen im Lichte der Anthropologie"), and "Dream and Existence" ("Traum und Existenz") were all published by A. Francke Verlag, Bern, in the two volumes of Binswanger's *Ausgewählte Vorträge und Aufsätze*. "The Case of Lola Voss" and "Introduction to *Schizophrenie*" were published in Binswanger's *Schizophrenie* by Gunther Neske Verlag, Pfullingen.

August 1963   JACOB NEEDLEMAN

CONTENTS

Contents

Being-in-the-World

INTRODUCTION

In *"Freud and the Magna Charta of Clinical Psychiatry,"* Ludwig Binswanger writes:

It was on a September morning of the year 1927. Having broken away from the Congress of German Neurologists and Psychiatrists that was meeting in Vienna, I hurried to Semmering, full of impatience to return the unforgettable visit he [Freud] had paid me in those difficult times. I was about to leave and we were talking about the old days. Soon, however, the conversation turned to that which twenty years ago had brought us together and which, in spite of clear differences of opinion, had held us together, namely his life's work, his "great idea." With respect to a concrete clinical example—a serious case of compulsion neurosis —that had occupied us both a good deal, I threw out the question as to how we were to understand the failure of this patient to take the last decisive step of psychoanalytic insight and to thus continue in his misery in spite of all previous efforts and technical progress. As a contribution to the solution of the problem, I suggested that such a failure might only be understood as the result of something which could be called a deficiency of spirit [*Geistigkeit*], that is, an inability on the part of the patient to raise himself to the level of spiritual communication with the physician. Thus the patient was barred by his own lack from encompassing and overcoming his unconscious instinctual impulses at the last decisive point. I could barely believe my ears when the answer came: "Yes, spirit [*Geist*] is everything." I presumed that by spirit, Freud meant something like intelligence. But then he continued: *"Man has always known he possessed spirit: I had to show him there is such a thing as instinct.* But men are always unsatisfied, they cannot wait, they always want something whole and finished; *but one has to begin somewhere and very slowly move forward.*" Encouraged by this concession, I went a step further, explaining that I found myself forced to recognize in man something like a basic religious category; that, in any case it was impossible for me to admit that "the religious" is somehow and from somewhere a derivative phenomenon. (I was thinking, of course, not of the origin of a particular religion or even of religion in general but of something which I have since learned to call the religious I-thou relation.) But I had stretched the bow of agreement too far and began to feel its resistance. "Religion arises," so Freud declared, quickly and curtly, "out of the helplessness and anxiety of childhood and early manhood. Indisputably." With that he went to the drawer of his desk: "This is the moment for me to show you something," laid before me a finished manuscript that bore the title "The Future of an Illusion," and looked laughingly and questioningly at me. I easily guessed from the situation what the title meant. Meanwhile the moment of farewell had come. Freud accompanied me to the door. His last words, spoken with a knowing, lightly ironic smile, were: "Forgive me that I cannot satisfy your religious needs." [1]

This reminiscence of Binswanger's is noteworthy not only because it points up an attitude toward religion at variance with Freud's. It is much more significant in that it epitomizes an orientation toward man within psychiatry that, more than any single difference of viewpoint, has set Daseinsanalyse apart from psychoanalysis. In that same year, 1927, Heidigger's *Sein und Zeit* was published and provided Binswanger with the vocabulary and conceptual tools he needed to articulate his approach to psychiatry. His first major work under the influence of Heidegger appeared as a series of articles in the *Schweizer Archiv für Neurologie und Psychiatrie* from 1931 to 1933, a series entitled "On the Flight of Ideas" ("Über Ideenflucht"). Freud's remark, "Man has always known he possessed spirit; I had to show him there is such a thing as instinct," was no doubt in Binswanger's mind when, at the conclusion of this series, he wrote:

[1] Binswanger, *Ausgewählte Vorträge und Aufsätze* (Bern, 1955), Vol. II, pp. 81-82.

Spirit (in its widest sense, by which is not meant the strictly religious, ethical and aesthetic) and instinct are limiting concepts in the sense that "the instincts" remain as residue when man is taken as stripped of spirit and spirit remains when man is totally devitalized. But human existence never goes forth exclusively as spirit or instinct, it is always both. Only theoretically and abstractly can instinct and spirit be sundered. . . . If Nietzsche and psychoanalysis have shown that instinctuality, especially in the form of sexuality, extends its reach up to the highest pinnacles of human spirituality, then we have attempted to show the degree to which spirituality extends its reach down to the deepest valleys of "vitality." We have, in other words, tried to demonstrate how one must speak also of the religious, moral and aesthetic life in those spheres of human existence which till now have seemed dominated exclusively by the vital or instinctual life. Hand in hand with this goes the notion that one speaks of religiosity, morality and aesthetics not only where man has won to a clear self-consciousness of a persistent independent self, but in all those cases where a self— permanent, persistent or otherwise—intends an object (*Gegen-Stand*) which stands over against it. So much for the positive clarification of such a term as "unconscious" spirit.[2]

In 1936 Binswanger delivered his address in commemoration of Freud's eightieth birthday. This paper, entitled "Freud's Conception of Man in the Light of Anthropology," described the extent to which psychoanalysis as the doctrine of *homo natura* oversimplifies and constricts full human reality. While Binswanger saw this oversimplification as a necessary price for the power of scientific explanation, at the same time he proposed that scientific psychology and psychiatry must found themselves on a discipline that includes the ontological problem of man's total being. For only thus could that which is being explained and simplified retain its wholeness as the science progresses.

Binswanger sent a copy of the lecture to Freud, who responded with a warm and amused reaffirmation of his own stand:

Dear Friend! A sweet surprise, your lecture! Those who heard you and reported to me were visibly untouched by it; it must

[2] Binswanger, "Über Ideenflucht," *Schweizer Archiv für Neurologie und Psychiatrie*, Vol. 30 (1932-33), pp. 75-76.

have been too difficult for them. In reading it I rejoiced over your beautiful prose, your erudition, the scope of your horizon, your tact in disagreement. Truly, one can put up with infinite amounts of praise.

But, of course, I don't believe a word of what you say. I've always lived only in the *parterre* and basement of the building. You claim that with a change of viewpoint one is able to see an upper story which houses such distinguished guests as religion, art, etc. You're not the only one who thinks that, most cultured specimens of *homo natura* believe it. In that you are conservative, I revolutionary. If I had another lifetime of work before me, I have no doubt that I could find room for these noble guests in my little subterranean house. . . .[3]

If he were alive today and able to witness the growth of Binswanger's Daseinsanalyse, Freud would doubtless have stronger words against this "reactionary" movement back to the "spirit." But would he be justified in rejecting as reactionary a school of thought that gives the heartiest assent to all his discoveries and that could not even have come into existence without them? To be sure, Daseinsanalyse attempts to reinstate spirit in the science of psychiatry, but it is a notion of spirit that could only have emerged after Freud. No longer is "man's essential freedom" seen as separate from his participation in matter and body; no longer is science seen as warring against freedom and spirit. Rather, science is embraced by the spirit as a movement of spirit, and the instinctuality that it discovers in man is welcomed as *man's* instinctuality. Binswanger does not seek spheres of man's existence that argue against the explanatory power of psychoanalysis. What he asks is a Kantian question: "What is it in man that enables his existence to be explained by psychoanalysis?" When, therefore, Binswanger complains of the reductionism of natural science as applied to man, he is not questioning science's ability to explain, he is rather urging that that which is being explained be kept in mind in its full phenomenal reality. He is not saying to science: "You cannot explain the spirit of man"; what he says is: "Be sure it is the spirit of man you are explaining!"

Whether we call this "spirit" consciousness, freedom, or mind,

[3] Ludwig Binswanger, *Erinnerungen an Sigmund Freud* (Bern, 1956), p. 115.

[4]

there ultimately comes a point in the science of spirit where we are faced with an antinomy or contradiction. For example, the question as to the origin of consciousness, both in mankind and the infant, presents us with two possible answers, neither of which is satisfactory. We seem forced to choose between a mysterious leap in the continuum of nature upon the arrival of consciousness, or we must relegate consciousness to the level of organic nature and with bad conscience maintain that "nothing really new" has emerged. As with the Kantian antinomies, the first alternative is "too large" and the second "too small." Perhaps what is needed here is a new "Copernican Revolution" that will side with neither alternative, but will undercut the legitimacy of the question itself.

In psychology, those antinomies, paradoxes, dilemmas, and blind alleys that are the legacy of a separation of consciousness and its world were first noted by a contemporary of Freud's: the philosopher Franz Brentano. His doctrine of intentionality as defining the essence of consciousness may be seen as a first step in this new Copernican Revolution. Brentano's chief disciple, Edmund Husserl, expanded and extended his teacher's insight into the fundament of a new method of philosophy. Consciousness was now understood as *consciousness-of*, as pure *reference-to*. It was no longer a strange and unprecedented thing or process whose workings were somewhat more puzzling than those of its neighbor objects, the things of this world. Nor was it a distant spectator, alien and sufficient unto itself, moving like a ghost in the earth. Consciousness was "what it intended," it was a going-out-to-something. "We must convince ourselves," Husserl wrote,

> *that the psychical in general in the psychological sense*, that psychical personalities, psychical properties, experiences or states are *empirical* unities, and are therefore as realities of every kind and degree, mere unities of an intentional "constitution"—in their own sense truly existing [*Wahrhaft seiend*]: intuitable, experienceable, and on empirical grounds scientifically determinable— and yet "merely intentional," and therefore merely "relative." [4]

It was but a step—perhaps from a strictly Husserlian point of view an unwarranted one—from the notion of consciousness as

[4] Edmund Husserl, *Ideas*, trans. by W. R. Boyce Gibson (London, 1952), pp. 167-168.

[5]

intentionality to Heidegger's concept of the essentially human as being-in-the-world (Dasein). Heidegger speaks, not of consciousness, but of human consciousness; moreover not in isolation from all else human, but as human *being*. Just as consciousness for Husserl was its intention, so man is his world. Heidegger seeks to bring man out of Cartesian exile from his world by showing how human being in the context of Care structures the being of his world and his known self. Husserl had said "the whole being of the world consists in a certain 'meaning' which presupposes absolute consciousness as the field from which the meaning is derived. . . ." [5] He had, however, added, "But we must note that our aim has not been to present a detailed theory of such transcendental constituting, and therewith to sketch a new Theory of Knowledge in respect of the spheres of reality so constituted. . . ." [6] But with Heidegger the new Copernican Revolution is complete. By moving the Husserlian cargo back "within" the phenomenological brackets, Heidegger has attempted to found a new ontology based on the fiat that man is essentially being-in-the-world. Just as Kant had placed the source of necessary truth within man, so Heidegger placed the source of meaning in general, and hence of Being, within man.

Binswanger took Heidegger's analysis of the structure of human being as it constitutes world and self by being essentially being-in-the-world as the instrument with which to understand the existence of his patients. He saw that science, as a human endeavor, also makes its world as it knows it. He saw, too, that when science as psychology focuses its methods upon its own source, human existence, it brings down upon its head all the paradoxes of the separation of subject and object, consciousness and thing, man and world. By claiming that each individual is his own unique world, he demanded a presuppositionless entering into that world as the precondition for explanation of it. By maintaining that the world and human reality that Freud showed holds human spirit at its mercy, itself depends on that spirit, Binswanger points the way to an enlightened anthropocentrism based in Freud on a chastened awareness of limit and finitude.

[5] *Ibid.*, p. 169.
[6] *Loc. cit.*

PART ONE: A CRITICAL INTRODUCTION TO LUDWIG BINSWANGER'S EXISTENTIAL PSYCHOANALYSIS

I

The Concept of the Existential A Priori

Kant's "Copernican Revolution"

When Descartes severed reality into the isolated realms of mind and matter, he bequeathed to subsequent philosophers the problem of bringing the two sufficiently together again so that our knowledge of nature could be rendered intelligible. Following Descartes' unsatisfactory appeal to God as ultimate guarantor of knowledge, a long line of subtle thinkers tried their hand at answers. The result was that philosophy, as well as its world, has long been split into two irreconcilable regions, which may be called (among other things) rationalism and empiricism. The former had finally to claim that the mind need not come into contact with nature in order to have knowledge of it. The latter claimed, eventually, that the only knowledge we could have of the world would come from the passive and comparatively meager contact with nature provided by our senses. Thus rationalism could offer some certainty of knowledge, but could not guarantee that this was knowledge about nature. Empiricism could speak of the contact with nature provided by the senses, but could not guarantee it to be certain knowledge.

Thus the two axioms that, as will be shown, generate the philosophical outlook of Kant's epoch-making *The Critique of Pure Reason* could only appear equally incompatible to both rationalism and empiricism. These two axioms are: (1) that the mind of itself gives us certain knowledge about nature (synthetic a priori knowledge) and (2) that all knowledge must involve contact with the thing known. For rationalism, the incompatibility

[9]

stems from the view that mind is a substance (*res cogitans*) alien to and separate from nature (*res extensa*). For empiricism, the incompatibility arises from the view that since nature, as opposed to mind, is a fixed order of reality, the only contact possible between mind and nature is that of sensory impressions, i.e., the influence of nature upon mind. Therefore, it is impossible to obtain true knowledge from the mind alone, since its contact with the known is merely passive, waiting upon nature for its objects.

There remained for Kant only one reasonable way to account for his two axioms. He compared his line of thought to the revolution brought about by Copernicus in astronomy. Before Copernicus it was thought that the sun and stars moved around the earth. But Copernicus, in order to explain certain changes in the positions of the heavenly bodies, introduced the hypothesis that the earth itself moved. Before Kant it was thought that our knowledge had to conform to its objects; Kant introduced the hypothesis* that the objects conformed to our ways of knowing. The mind, that is, is *constitutive* of its objects. It creates them in knowing them. By this hypothesis Kant could explain how we could have a priori knowledge of objects. So long as one supposed that knowledge conformed to, or simply copied, objects that were given ready-made in our experience, one could not explain how any a priori knowledge was possible. But if the objects conformed to our ways of knowing, if the mind were constitutive and objects were determined by our faculty of knowledge, then *to the extent* that they were so determined, they might be known even prior to experience.

Thus Kant accounts for the fact that we can have certain and direct knowledge of nature by cutting through the basic presuppositions of both the rationalists and the empiricists. He claims two things: first, that the mind is not utterly separated from nature; and, second, that the kind of contact it has with nature is not limited exclusively to a passive subjection to the influences of nature. In this he is by no means saying that there is *no* influence upon mind by nature. Quite the contrary. What he is saying is that, while knowledge consists of impressions derived from passive contact with nature, it also requires elements supplied by the faculty of knowledge itself. "This leaf is green" is a piece of knowledge. But

* It is actually a fiat; cf. below.

the mere "green" impression of the senses does not represent knowledge until it is organized by ideas of substance (leaf) and quality (green): ideas supplied by the understanding. Our faculty of knowledge, however, cannot work unless it gets its material from sense impressions. Knowledge, then, is a union of the active, organizing (constitutive) function of the mind with its more receptive and passive function called "sensibility." All we can know with certainty about nature is the general way all sense impressions must be organized by the mind. The general ways in which the mind orders its material are called by Kant "categories of the Understanding." One might say that this kind of knowledge is not knowledge about things, but is rather knowledge of how we know things. This is true, but since in knowing things we are at the same time dictating to them some general structure, then such knowledge is also knowledge of the object in general. Such "knowledge" is, in Kant's terminology, "transcendental." That which the mind of itself can supply is *transcendentally* true. It is knowledge of the way things must appear to us if we are to have the kind of experience that we, in fact, do have. Thus such a priori truths as "every event must have a cause" are truths about the way the Understanding orders the manifold of sense impressions in order to make experience possible.

Kant's philosophy delivered a death blow to the deep conviction or hope of traditional metaphysics that it could achieve positive knowledge of reality as it is in itself, independent of our knowledge of it. Since in knowing a thing we shape it, we can never know what it is in itself. Kant is not, however, denying a dualism of mind and nature. Certainly he is not collapsing one into the other, as both Idealism and Materialism tend to do. What he is saying is that we can have certain knowledge of reality only to the extent that we ourselves give it shape. Things as they are in themselves must forever remain hidden from us. In Kant's language: we can know *phenomena*, but we are forever barred from having knowledge of *noumena* (things in themselves). Thus, though the mind is distinct from nature as it is "in itself," it is intimately and essentially related to nature *as humanly known and experienced*.

Here it is important to stress that the Kantian categories of the Understanding (categories of quantity: unity, plurality, totality; of quality: reality, negation, limitation; of relation: substance-and-accident, cause and effect, reciprocity; of modality: possibility, existence, necessity) have no meaning or significance unless we can point to the sensory objects that correspond to them. All the categories must be related to sensory contact (or "intuition"). The Kantian statement that there are categories in the mind that make experience possible should not be taken to mean that such categories "exist" all by themselves "in" the mind empty of any "content," like so many empty pitchers waiting to be filled. The categories *are only* their *use* and *function* of ordering the sensory manifold. They are not ideas that *have* functions and *can* be used in certain ways. They *are* that use. To reason to the constitutive function of the mind is not to hypothesize some state of things existing prior in time to experience. The constitutive functions of the mind are those that make it possible to apprehend things as before or after, as real or not real. They therefore are not possible objects of their own organizing principles.

These categories of the Understanding, then, are entirely limited to the sphere of sense-experience. Since they cannot otherwise describe the real properties and relations of things in themselves, the utmost Understanding can achieve is to anticipate the form of a possible *experience* in general; it cannot give us a priori nontautologous knowledge of *things* in general. There is, however, another function of the mind—which Kant terms *Reason*—that organizes the activity of the Understanding in a way similar to that in which Understanding organizes sense impressions. Just as Understanding orders the manifold supplied by sensory contact (initution), so reason unifies the concepts and judgments of Understanding, thus relating itself to objects not directly but indirectly. Reason may thus be called *pure* in that no sensory data correspond entirely to its organizational principles. The goal of pure reason is to provide principles or unconditioned, absolute starting points for the employment of the Understanding. But the unconditioned is not anything that can be found within experience. Our experience of a cause, for example, does not include experience of an absolutely first cause. The ideas of reason, which may be said to regulate the Understanding, are not *constitutive* because no experience corresponds to them. Philosophy's search for answers to such questions as to whether the world had a beginning or not is thus a misemployment of reason (which cannot in itself tell us about the world) and is the quest of a chimera. The ideas of reason are *transcendent*, i.e., they pass beyond the limits of possible experience. The concepts or categories of the Understanding are *transcendental*, i.e., they are that which makes experience in general possible.

The Concept of the Constitutive Function of the Understanding and the Corresponding New Method of Philosophy

In *The Critique of Pure Reason* Kant asked: what are the conditions that the mind must fulfill in order to account for the fact that we know the world and the laws of nature in the way that we do? [1] Such reasoning to preconditions is a hallmark of the transcendental philosophy as Kant conceived it, a philosophy that asks not primarily "What do I know?" nor "How do I know what I know?" but, rather, "This is what I know and this is how I know it—what conditions are being fulfilled by the Understanding in order for this to be possible?" It is, ideally, a particularly certain form of philosophizing, but a certainty fully dependent on the truth of particular premises. In *The Critique of Pure Reason*, if all experience must have a sensory component and if there are such things as synthetic a priori judgments about the objects of knowledge, then the Copernican axiom follows: the Understanding is constitutive.

The peculiarity of Kant's thought, however, has to do with those very synthetic propositions that he claims exist and that, if they do, necessitate the transcendental approach. These propositions are, if closely examined, found to be *transcendentally* true: that is, they are necessarily true only insofar as their truth is a necessary precondition of experience. For example, if the quantity of matter did not remain unchanged, it would mean either that something absolutely new had appeared, or that something had vanished completely. In either case the unity of experience would never be possible, and thus experience itself would not be possible.

It can be shown that in the perspective of Kant's philosophy these synthetic judgments are such that the "third thing" that con-

---

[1] Immanuel Kant, *The Critique of Pure Reason*, trans. by Norman Kemp Smith (London, 1953), B229.

nects subject and predicate must be this particularly Kantian notion of possible experience. Any other alternative would lead, in the Kantian frame of reference, to one of four unsatisfactory conclusions. First, the judgment in question would not be necessary and universal (i.e., would have an empirical element in it). Or, second, it would be universal, but not directly related to the objects of knowledge (a regulatory principle). Third, it would represent a function of the mind that does not exist (intellectual intuition). Or, finally, it would be merely analytically true (the apparent connecting link being simply another form of a predicate that is contained in the subject).

There is thus a peculiar doubling back in Kant's critical philosophy. If there is a given, sensory component to experience and if there are synthetic a priori judgments about the objects of knowledge, then, for experience to have the unity that it does have, the Understanding must be constitutive. *But* synthetic a priori judgments about the objects of knowledge are the result of the mind's constitutive power, which is what, ostensibly, was to have been "deduced" or "justified."

Kant, therefore, cannot claim as a given fact *that* there are synthetic a priori judgments about the objects of knowledge. He can say only that *if* there are such propositions, then the Understanding is constitutive. Since such judgments are only possible as the result of the mind's constitutive power, the implicative dependence is mutual: if and only if the Understanding is constitutive are there synthetic a priori judgments. Both sides of the implication have to be antecedently true for the statement itself to be true. One side cannot be deduced from the other.

There are only two alternatives here. Either the notion that the Understanding is constitutive is a fiat of sorts, or we must examine the nature of experience from a standpoint independent of that of the critical philosophy. But the latter attempt would mean either seeking necessary laws in the object itself, or seeking necessary laws in the manner in which we experience and know objects. The first alternative, of course, is automatically excluded since it is the most blatant negation of that critical standpoint that we hope to justify. As to the second alternative, we might find through empirical psychology or somehow through a metaphysics of reason the *fact* or disposition of the mind to experience and know its objects under the aegis of categories. However, such an endeavor would have to treat the mind either as an object among objects or as an entity in itself. We should still have to justify the transcendental epistemological status of these categories by recourse, again, to that critical standpoint that we had hoped to justify independently.

The notion of the constitutive function of the Understanding is a fiat, then, and we arrive at the tentative formula: the Understanding can never *find* its own functioning in the world it makes and, making, experiences; nor can it rigorously *deduce* itself as maker. It can know the world, but it can never arrive at the notion of its constitutive power as a conclusion in a strict chain of thought. All of Kant's arguments, therefore—including his notion about the possibility of experience, which springs from his assumption that objects conform to the Understanding—are no more nor less than exfoliations of the basic fiat that the mind makes its world, and of the basic *fact* that experience has and must have a sensory element.*

Kant's transcendental deductions are no more and, again, no less, than the spelling out of the implications of the Copernican Revolution. They are implications in the sense of deducing what must be so if the mind is to be constitutive (e.g., the doctrine of the unity of apperception), and implications as to the structure of the act of knowing (e.g., the sections on the various syntheses of the imagination). The "Transcendental Dialectic" thus appears as not only an implied conclusion of the Copernican Revolution but as its strongest and, in a sense, its only possible *philosophical* support. For, while we cannot with certainty deduce *from* the inherent failure of all metaphysical speculation as to the nature of the world, God, and the self, *to* the constitutive power of the Understanding, yet if we are to continue systematic philosophizing, we shall find the notion of the constitutive function of the Understanding an appealing one.†

---

* The reader will no doubt have noticed the frankly circular nature of Kant's argument as I have presented it. For now let it simply be noted, subject to discussion in a later chapter, that systematic argument is necessarily circular and that far from being a failing, circularity is entailed by the very project of system and explanation. The criterion of adequacy hinges, as will be shown, on the scope and size of the circle.

† Its appeal lies in the fact that it points with much-desired *necessity* to the fail-

I call the concept of the constitutive function of the Understanding a fiat and not a theoretical construct or a hypothesis. A theoretical construct or a hypothesis will relate or unify or interpret given facts or other theoretical constructs and hypotheses. But the notion of the constitutive function of the Understanding offers a new concept of the nature of experience itself and of those facts that are to be explained by theory both scientific and philosophical. It is a fiat in the sense that the cutting of the Gordian knot was a fiat, a refusal to accept the criteria for solution that traditionally were bound up with certain problems of philosophy. It imposes new standards and forces old problems into a different hierarchy, not only because the old standards seemed futile or had not yielded their aim after many years* (this in itself would not justify their abandonment), but because these standards themselves, as Kant believed he showed in the "Transcendental Dialectic," lead to contradiction and are thus not possible as standards of reason, the principle of noncontradiction being the prime canonical structure of reason.

Heidegger: The Notion of Constitutive "Function" and Its Corresponding Method Applied to the Science of the Being of Man

If we have spent some time on Kant's epistemological critique of the older metaphysic—accomplished chiefly through his "constitutive function of Understanding"—it is because Heidegger's argument in *Sein und Zeit* can be taken as an elaborate extension of this same concept of constitutive "function."

What I wish to suggest is that, for Heidegger, Care and its components function in a manner strictly analogous to the Kantian

---

ure of metaphysics and, as we shall see with Heidegger, allows us to overcome, rather than utterly abandon, the previous futile attempts of and at metaphysics.

* Logical Positivism was similar in the sense that it, too, imposed new standards and limits to philosophical speculation, but, it seems, primarily because the old attempts had *not yet* yielded any fruit. It is such a lack of necessity in its aims and structure that places it on a lesser plane than the critical approach. It cannot, as has often been observed, accommodate the unverifiability of its main assumption into its theory. It defines truth in terms of verifiability, but this itself being unverifiable is neither true nor false. The Copernican Revolution, on the other hand, is *in principle* and of necessity unconfirmable. It says only that *if* the mind is constitutive, then . . . etc.

Understanding. Heidegger, to be sure, has not explicitly attempted anything like a Transcendental Deduction of the existentials and yet the entire argument of *Sein und Zeit* can be read as a "justification" (in the Kantian sense described in the "Transcendental Deduction") of the essential Being-in-the-world of the Dasein. That is, it offers no *proofs* in the traditional sense for this ground of being; for, as I have tried to indicate, there can be no proofs: the "self" can neither find itself in its own world nor deduce itself as the maker of that world. All the philosopher can do is to presuppose the constitutive nature of the self by fiat.* And the term "Dasein," which Heidegger elects to use instead of "self," has buried within it this very fiat. Part of the definition of Dasein or human being is that it is already-in-the-world: Dasein does not emerge as Dasein unless it has already constituted its world.

> . . . what then is there left to ask when one *presupposes* that knowing is already [merged] with its world which it was not supposed to get to except by transcending the subject? [2]

> Knowing is a mode of the Dasein founded on its being-in-the-world. This being-in-theworld, as a fundamental structure, requires *antecedent* interpretation.[3]

Being-in-the-world demands an antecedent *interpretation*, not a deduction or explanation. The inherent structure of the Dasein is such that Being-in-the-world is *presupposed;* it is antecedent to all other experiences or modes of being of the Dasein.

But it must now be shown in what sense this *being* of Being-in-the-world is constitutive of world. We may say that for Kant the Understanding is inherently in-the-world insofar as it constitutes the world in becoming aware of it—in emerging in its function of understanding. And, truly, is there any other sense to be attached to saying of the self or of a function of the self that it is inherently in-the-world than that this self constitutes its world to some de-

---

*This characteristic of Heidegger's method of argument was also noted by Sartre: "In his abrupt, rather barbaric fashion of cutting Gordian knots rather than trying to untie them, he gives in answer to the question posited a pure and simple definition." J.-P. Sartre, *Being and Nothingness*, trans. by Hazel E. Barnes (New York, 1956), p. 244.

2 Martin Heidegger, *Sein und Zeit* (Tübingen, 1953), p. 61.

3 *Ibid.*, p. 62.

gree? A relation of self to a *totally other* cannot be conceived as inherent in the structure of self, as definitive of its nature, while still retaining its role as the totally other. Neither does it make sense to accept the only other possible way of understanding the notion that the self is inherently in-the-world—namely, that the world constitutes the self either completely or partially. Not completely because then the self becomes just one being among other beings in a world, and to say, therefore, that the world constitutes the self makes as much sense as to say that the world constitutes a tree or a planet; not partially (although the reciprocal constituting of world and self is certainly not excluded, but only in the sense of self *re*acting and not of world *acting*) because if the self did not go out "of its own accord" to the world, that which the world "constituted" would be only accidental and not essential to the self. Thus to say that the self (or the Dasein, or the Understanding) is inherently and essentially in-the-world is in some sense to endow it with constitutive "powers." Thus if Heidegger is seriously to claim that Being-in-the-world is a "basic structure of the Dasein," he must also claim for the Dasein a constitutive "function."

But what kind of constitutive "function"? Constitutive of what? Constituted *by* what or whom? With Kant the answers are relatively clear. It is not the individual self that makes its world, but rather the Understanding that is at the same time less than the individual (being one function among others and certainly not locatable, for example, in the phenomenal self) and more than the individual (not subject to the inclinations of the individual so far as it is employed properly and also shared by all reasonable beings to the same degree). As to the *kind* of constitutive function in Kant, it is a function of synthesizing under the unity of apperception and, through the categories, the manifold of intuition. And as to what it is constitutive of, the answer is also relatively clear: of the world, nature, the objects of knowledge and science; trees, tables, planets, animals, the object-self, and all objective relations among these things.

Here we find that Heidegger's terms are significantly different from Kant's, although the relationship between them is strikingly similar. Heidegger stresses, not Understanding, but human *being*, Dasein. Moreover the world is not conceived ontically* as the to-

* Ontology is the study of Being as such, and as distinguished from any one

tality of entities that can be present within the world or as the region that at any time embraces these entities, but "world" is conceived as that wherein the Dasein dwells. "World" for Heidegger is that in terms of which the Dasein refers itself; on the strength of which the mode of being of context or bearing (*Bewandtnis*) is possible. The being of World is thus dependent on *Bewandtniszusammenhang* (*frame of reference* or bearing).

It is, therefore, clear that in Heidegger we find no world that apparently is separate from the self, only later to discover, as in Kant, that it is constituted by the self. Rather we find "world" defined in terms of Dasein, and once again we run up against the fiat nature of Heidegger's argument. Yet it is also clear that the Dasein constitutes this world as so defined by Heidegger—for the very notion of *Bewandtniszusammenhang* is derived from the activity of the Dasein: in particular from its understanding. We can only conclude that such terms as "Dasein," "world," and so forth do not (like Kant's conceptions of world, nature, self, and Understanding) represent the end product of Dasein in functioning and activity. Rather they represent the way in which these terms must be understood in order to account for the fact that the Dasein does so function and is active in this way. For Kant, "world" is a concept that is a *result* of the categorical, constitutive nature of Understanding as well as the *result* of the working of the Reason. But Kant does not, like Heidegger, ask what must be the being-of-the-world and of-the-self in order that this very functioning may be possible.

This is the sense in which the work of Heidegger may be called ontologically transcendental or ontologically critical. Heidegger is seeking the ontologically necessary preconditions of all ontic or regional activity and function in man.

The "transcendence problem" cannot be reduced to the question: how does a subject go out toward an object, whereby the totality of objects becomes identified with the idea of world. The ques-

---

being. The term "ontic" is a Heideggerean innovation and refers to the study of particular elements that *have* being. This parallels the distinction between Being (*Sein*) and beings (*Seiende*). The various sciences are, for example, *ontic* disciplines because they deal with beings (animals, light waves, mathematical functions, etc.). There is a sense, then, in which every discipline except ontology is *ontic*.

tion is: what makes it ontologically possible that beings can be encountered in the world and as such objectified? [4]

The transcendental "universality" of the phenomenon of Care and all fundamental existentials have a broadness on which *every* ontic exposition of Dasein is based. . . .[5]

Ontically speaking, the world is not-self. Ontologically speaking, the Dasein is in-the-world in various modes; it constitutes the being-of-the-world by that network of meanings through which the world is disclosed. *Zuhandenheit* and *Vorhandenheit* are two of the modes in which the Dasein constitutes the being-of-the-world. Ontologically, then, for Heidegger, there can be no "self" and no separate, distinct "world," for ontologically these terms represent one mode of Being-in-the-world: *Vorhandenheit*. It is from this very network of meanings that the "individual self" itself emerges. Dasein is thus always already-in-the-world, and the expression Being-in-the-world is an empty formula that says nothing about human beings, but only about human *being*, and about the being-of-the-world ("world" having been already understood as that which it is in the nature of human being to illuminate: in *Bewandtniszusammenhang*).

The meaning-references which define the structure of the world are therefore not a network of forms which a worldless subject casts upon an [unformed] matter. The factistic Dasein moves, rather, . . . from these horizons back to the beings [already] encountered within them.[6]

The being-of-the-world as thus structured by meanings (bearing, context) by the Dasein is the ontological ground (or in the Kantian sense: transcendental-ontological) of the emergence, not only of the world as it is commonly meant and known, but also of the ego or self. Man is thus ontologically conceived not as a being possessing properties, but rather:

The essential determination of man as the understanding of Being implies at the same time that the [theoretically] separable charac-

---

[4] *Ibid.*, p. 366.
[5] *Ibid.*, pp. 199-200.
[6] *Ibid.*, p. 366.

teristics of man can never be on-hand [*vorhanden*] "properties" of on-hand beings which "appear to be" so and so. Rather, the essential structure of man is to be defined as none other than his possible modes of being. The essence of man *is* ever his possibilities, which he "has" not merely in the way an on-hand being has properties. The essential determination of man can therefore never be realized by an account of the factual content of an object [*ein Was*] because the essence of man lies in this: that it has [yet] to be his being as his. Indeed, man's essence is illuminated by himself as being-in-the-world—not through another being, but in such wise that his essence *is* the light. The Dasein carries "within him" his sphere of illumination, his "there" [*Da*], which both as a matter of fact and essentially cannot be abjured. Only such a being could have access to what is on hand in the light and [what is] hidden in the dark. Because man is in such a manner himself the illumination of Being, Heidegger chooses the term "Dasein" as the expression of the Being of this being.[7]

Here we find, fully described by Boss, the final essential element in Heidegger's method and thought. This, as mentioned earlier, is to assume as a *fact* that man is the being whose ontic nature it is to be ontological. "That man's essential structure consists of the understanding of Being is not a theoretical postulate, but a fact." [8] This concern of man as to the nature of Being is fact for Heidegger just as the necessary sensory element of experience and knowledge is fact for Kant.

We may now roughly schematize the relation of fact and fiat in both Heidegger and Kant:

HEIDEGGER:

The fact: Man is the being concerned with Being.
The fiat: Dasein is Being-in-the-world.
The two together: Dasein as "Already-being-in-the-world, in-advance-of-itself, as the Being-concerned-with-beings encountered in the-world." [9]

---

[7] Medard Boss, *Psychoanalyse und Daseinsanalytik* (Bern, 1957), pp. 62-63.
[8] *Ibid.*, p. 61.
[9] Werner Brock, *Existence and Being* (Chicago, 1949), pp. 64-65.

The above formula is Heidegger's expression of what he conceives to be the Ontological A Priori structure of man. To this formula he gives the name "Care."

KANT:

The fact: All knowledge has an intuitional given element in it.
The fiat: The mind is constitutive.
The two together: The Understanding combines the manifold of sense into unitary objects in order that experience or knowledge be possible.

The above formula is Kant's expression of the source and basis of a priori knowledge. This formula expresses the working of the categories.

Heidegger has thus extended to the sphere of Being what Kant did in the sphere of objective knowledge—or, in Heidegger's words, in the sphere of the *Vorhanden*.

> Thus the positive result of Kant's *Critique of Pure Reason* hinges also on his elaboration of that which belongs to a nature in general, and not on any "theory" of knowledge. His transcendental logic is an a priori factual logic of nature, as a field of Being.[10]

What I am trying to emphasize here is that for Heidegger, Dasein, ontologically understood, involves in its essential structure (being) the constituting (through the endowing of meaning) of the *being* of the world and self (also ontologically understood). The parallel with Kant, however, goes farther and extends to the method which Heidegger employs in "arriving at" this position. The method is one of fiat, a method that I have tried to show is peculiarly necessary for just such an argument to constitutive powers (in any sense) of the "self." "Care" and its components, the existentials, function for Heidegger in a manner analogous to the Kantian categories in that they are the forms through which ontic reality can manifest itself to the Dasein.

One important difference must be emphasized, however. These existentials are not forms that create objects to be encountered as not-self in the world, as are the Kantian categories. They are not so much empty formulas as they are *matrices* representing the possible modes in which the Dasein, considered solely *qua* Being re-

[10] Heidegger, pp. 10-11.

lates itself to world, also considered qua Being. I choose the word "matrix" here because it expresses the peculiar role of these "forms" more accurately than "formula." A matrix may be understood as a place in which an organism or thing is developed, a womb. Or it may also mean a set of possible groups of variables defined by an internal relation common to each set of possible groups: a formula referring to formulas. In both senses, Being-in-the-world, Care, and the existentials (*Verstehen, Verfallenheit, Befindlichkeit, Rede*), as well as *Vorhandensein* and *Zuhandensein*, are to be understood as matrices of varied scope and definition. This notion of matrix, particularly as applied to meanings—a meaning-matrix—emerges with considerable significance in the works of Binswanger.

In all that has been said above, we may thus with justice speak of Being-in-the-world and Care as the Ontological A Priori, bearing in mind the Kantian overtones of "a priori" and the Heideggerian overtones of "ontological." The existentials may be termed partial or secondary a prioris since they represent Being-in-the-world in particular modes. In the works of Binswanger we find these Ontological A Prioris treated in the perspective of *individual*, existing Dasein. The manner in which he applies these Ontological A Prioris to Dasein in its concrete existence gives rise to what I will call the concept of the Existential A Priori.

Husserl's A Priori

Both Heidegger and Binswanger are outspoken regarding the extent of their debt to Husserl. Here, however, I shall limit myself to a brief discussion of Husserl's treatment of the a priori within the context of the preceding issues. Two aspects of the question must be kept separate: (1) Husserl's method of arriving at these a prioris, and (2) the function in consciousness which he attributed to them. Regarding the latter, I think it is safe to say that the question of constitutive "function," which Husserl developed later in his career, was not the aspect of his phenomenology that influenced or challenged Heidegger and Binswanger. For Heidegger, the pure Husserlian phenomenology can achieve insights into the essential structures of consciousness as such. But no conclusions can be drawn from these, either as to the relation of consciousness to the objects of scientific knowledge in their status as empirical reality, or as to the being of consciousness and world. Viewed in this light, pure phenomenology cannot and ought not essay any position about the constitutive function of the mind. The very notion of constitutive function would simply be one of many possible qualifications regarding intentionality. To ask whether the self in any way constitutes its world or itself would thus be programatically as irrelevant as to question the reality of the external world.

In this regard, then, Heidegger represents a considerable extension or even alteration of pure phenomenology. For him, phenomenology is a tool for more adequate understanding, not of consciousness, but of human being, and eventually of Being itself.

When we come to discuss Binswanger, we shall find that he follows Heidegger in this respect. While also proclaiming allegiance to Husserl, he extends the method as a tool for understanding "psychic" phenomena in their relation to real existing human beings. Thus the door is opened both in Heidegger and in Binswanger for an effectual functioning of these a prioris that goes beyond pure eidetic description of the phenomena of consciousness as such.

It is, however, in respect to the phenomenological method of arriving at these a prioris that Heidegger and Binswanger wish to remain strictly Husserlian and will on no account admit to being Kantians.

As is well known, Kant distinguishes "a priori forms" both in the sensuous sphere and in the sphere of understanding which "emerges beyond the sensuous." The former are the pure forms of intuition, space and time; the latter are the pure categories of thought or understanding. Here we find the categories of causality, reality, necessity, etc. Pure forms of intuition in the sphere of understanding are not recognized by Kant. In this context we see what is new in Husserl's doctrine. According to him objects of understanding or thought can be *intuited*, objects which thus "emerge beyond the sensuous"; therefore the expression categorical intuition. The acts of categorical intuition thus direct themselves to objects of the understanding. They are not themselves acts of understanding but intuition of a sort not found in Kant.[11]

11 Binswanger, *Ausgewählte Vorträge und Aufsätze* (Bern, 1947), Vol. I, p. 17n.

The essential forms and structures of consciousness are arrived at by intuition, an intuition that carries with it all the stringent demands of the Husserlian phenomenological reduction but is nonetheless intuition. Here we find a clear expression of what I have referred to as the frankly fiat nature of Heidegger's argument, as compared to the more implicit fiats of Kant. It was pointed out above that if Kant failed actually to *deduce* anything at all as to the constitutive function of the Understanding, Heidegger does not even attempt such a "transcendental deduction." Husserl's "first philosophy" of phenomenology thus provides a transcendental philosophy—a philosophy of *necessary fiat*—with an explicit and self-conscious standpoint.

For such a philosophy—which holds by necessary fiat to the notion of the constitutive powers of the self—the ideal method would be one in which neither presuppositions nor conclusions refer to "Reality" in any sense, and which is based on a well-defined discipline of Intuition (*Wesenschau*). For since the self can never deduce itself from nor find itself in the world it makes, it ought not, in philosophy, explain or describe its world from any preferred frame of reference. The reason for this is that of the very notion of a preferred frame of reference implies that the self is not focusing its attention on the *ground* of experience, knowledge, reality, or whatever it is that the self constitutes when it constitutes its world. It is focusing rather on the end product of those very functions that constitute its world. To put it more tersely: to confront the world from a preferred frame of reference is not to understand the world as constituted by the self, but is, in fact, to constitute the world! Therefore, phenomenology is the method *par excellence* of apprehending that which is constituted by self in its immediacy, and therefore the method *par excellence* of apprehending the nature or form of that process of constituting.

Over-all Characterization of the Concept of the Existential A Priori

Binswanger's "Daseinsanalyse" can be seen most generally as an application of the "Daseinsanalytik" of Heidegger to the problems of psychiatric theorizing and therapy.

In thus indicating the basic structure of the Dasein as being-in-the-world, Heidegger places in the psychiatrist's hands a key by means of which he can, free of the prejudice of any scientific *theory*, ascertain and describe the *phenomena* he investigates in their full phenomenal content and intrinsic context.[12]

There are thus two directions open to us to begin this preliminary characterization of the Existential A Priori. Either we can begin with Binswanger's revelations of what he takes as psychiatry's necessarily limited and distorting presuppositions as to the nature of man and human experience—including his attempts, as *Anthropolog*, to balance these limitations that inhere in scientific method itself. Or, we can examine his notion of the a priori or essential potentialities of human existence as a philosophical extension and modification of Heidegger's thought. Actually both directions should be pursued simultaneously, and will be in future chapters; but as a matter of attitude I should like here to throw emphasis on the second or philosophical direction.

Just as Heidegger's notion of Being-in-the-world brought Husserl's "intentionality" of consciousness out of the "thin air" [13] of the Transcendental Ego and into an ontological frame, so Binswanger's Existential A Priori takes the ontologically determined existentials of Heidegger and brings them into the frame of concrete human existence. It is not enough to say simply that Binswanger's Daseinsanalyse is an extension of Heidegger's ontology to the ontic level, for Binswanger's Daseinsanalyse attempts to be ideally the most complete, or, most ideally, the only possible extension to the ontic level of Heidegger's ontology and phenomenology. There is thus implied in Binswanger's work a peculiarly necessary relation to Heidegger's ontology, and although Daseinsanalyse makes ontic statements concerning "factual findings about actually appearing forms and configurations of existence," [14] these statements are at the same time propositions as to the possibility and ground of the experience of particular human beings. Thus, while not ontology, Binswanger's Daseinsanalyse might be said still to be "meta-ontic" in the sense that these same statements as to the possibility of experi-

[12] Binswanger, p. 206 of this volume.

[13] *Loc. cit.*

[14] Binswanger, "The Existential Analysis School of Thought," in Rollo May, Ernest Angel, and Henri F. Ellenberger (eds.), *Existence* (New York, 1958), p. 192.

ence are also and more accurately to be understood as referring to the possibility of real, human existence itself: this is, in fact, one general way of understanding the term "Existential A Priori." In other words, any discipline that concerns itself with the transcendentally a priori essential structures and possibilities of concrete human existence is, strictly speaking, neither ontological nor ontic, but lies, rather, somewhere in between.

We may thus provisionally define the Existential A Priori(s) in this manner: they are the universals or forms that stand to the experience of *each* human being in the same manner that the Kantian categories of the Understanding stand to the objects that we know. The Daseinsanalytic concept of experience, it must immediately be added, is far wider than Kant's. In *The Critique of Pure Reason*, experience was understood by Kant necessarily to refer to knowledge. The famous opening lines ". . . all knowledge begins with experience," can, with the weight of the entire critical argument behind them be read as "all experience begins with knowledge." This strict qualification of the concept of experience, namely, that it is inseparable from knowledge, goes hand in hand with the critical conception of knowledge itself as constitutive of its own objects. For, in the Kantian view, whatever the objects of experience—be they the world itself, its particular objects, or the laws of nature—the objects are to a profound degree the result of our ordering of the manifold of intuition. And again, this ordering of the manifold by the Understanding is knowledge. For Kant, just as surely as we cannot know what we cannot experience, so, in this qualified conception of experience, we cannot experience what we cannot know.

Thus we may say that for Kant experience is a form of knowledge.

> In other words, they [the categories] serve only for the possibility of *empirical knowledge;* and such knowledge is what we entitle experience.[15]

> All synthesis, therefore, even that which renders perception possible, is subject to the categories; and since experience is knowledge by means of connected perceptions. . . .[16]

15 Kant, B148.
16 Kant, B161.

. . . but it is the *a priori* laws that alone can instruct us in regard to experience in general, and as to what it is that can be known as an object of experience.[17]

Experience is an empirical knowledge, that is, a knowledge which determines an object through perceptions.[18]

In Daseinsanalyse, on the other hand, knowledge is a form of experience; knowledge represents one mode of man's Being-in-the-world. To be sure, Binswanger does not imply that, for example, in the experience of mourning the death of a loved one, the Kantian categories are not "at work." Such an issue is, rather, of secondary importance, for the question in Daseinsanalyse is not what am I knowing, but what am I knowing-feeling-willing: how am I existing? The Kantian categories *in toto* represent the conditions of one mode of Being-in-the-world among others—the mode of objective knowledge, or, in Heidegger's language, the mode of *Vorhandensein*. To know an object or event, its structure, its causes and effects, its relation to other objects is, again speaking with Heidegger, to thematize the object, to take it in and for itself. To be sure, this mode of existing is an essential one—but only one. Binswanger can very well admit that the Understanding constitutes the objects of experience even in a profound emotional experience, but for him the question is, rather, how does the whole man stand at that moment to the objects so constituted? In fact, the question is equally relevant, for Binswanger, in the case of the most abstract and "unemotional" states of being—the contemplation, say, of a mathematical problem.

So far there is no real argument with Kant. Kant never meant to equate the working of the categories with conscious judgmental consideration of, say, an academic problem. But he does mean to imply objectivity as a standard for genuine experience and this is understandable in his perspective for the following reason: no matter how broad our notion of what experience is may be, there is always the element of the apparent other-than-self attached to it. We experience *something*. "Subjective experience," then, for Kant would be a useless term, for it would imply that something within the self is experienced as other than self without coming under the

17 Kant, B165.
18 Kant, B218.

aegis of the categories. This is impossible since, for one thing, the very notion of "other" already implicates the categories. There may be, for Kant, subjective knowledge, but not subjective experience. "I feel the book as heavy" is subjective knowledge of the book, but objective experience of a feeling or impression.

In Daseinsanalyse, however, the term "subjective experience" is not rejected. It is not, I repeat, that Daseinsanalyse claims that there are times when the categories are not "at work." It is, rather, that for Binswanger objective knowledge represents an attitude of man, a mode of Being-in-the-world that has no claim to priority, that exists within a meaning-context that opens a man to the world of objects, of the *Vorhanden*. That there is an object "out there" to be experienced (even if it be a feeling of the phenomenal self and "out there" only in the sense of being over against the transcendental I) is already an attitude, a frame of reference, a conferring of a meaning-matrix within the Being-in-the-world of the Dasein, which Being-in-the-world is anterior to the subject-object distinction. In Binswanger subjective experience is not rejected, but it is no longer called "subjective." The term "subjective" (whether applied to experience or to knowledge) itself presupposes a frame of reference. This sort of frame of reference constitutes its world by investing meaning. Thus the attitude that experience must be tied up with objective empirical knowledge constitutes its world just as definitely as the categories constitute the objects, except that there the unit is not *object*, but *object-to-me*.

For Binswanger, then, feeling is as genuine an experience as any and not in the sense that loving someone is an objective and genuine experience of *love*, but, rather, that loving someone is a genuine experience of that person who is loved. The vision of God is a genuine experience; so is the fear of imminent death; and so is the paranoid fear of being pursued by a whole city of people.

Here is a crucial point in understanding the Daseinsanalytic conception of experience. Surely, one asks, the psychotic's vision of the Holy Virgin is not as genuine an experience as the normal man's experience, say, of a partial eclipse of the sun. Binswanger's answer is: yes it is—if we are sure we understand what the psychotic is actually experiencing. And by this qualification he does not mean simply that perhaps the psychotic is not *really* seeing the Holy Virgin, but only thinks he is and that this *in a sense* is as genuine an experience as any normal experience. Rather, for Binswanger, the psychotic *is* seeing the Holy Virgin—the question is, however, what does Holy Virgin *mean* for him? In "normal" experience there is no fact, no pure, absolute perception isolated from a general world-design and outlook. The experience of the eclipse of the sun is not an absolute event that anyone, at any time in history, would experience in a similar way. An ancient Egyptian would not see a *sun* being covered by a shadow; he might see a threatening gesture of a god. And today, when we see an eclipse of the sun we cannot separate it from a world-outlook that places the sun in the center of the solar system and the moon as a satellite of the earth, a world-outlook that isolates the sun and moon as objects in themselves. There is an enormous amount that is *learned*, that is presupposed by the "simple" experience of seeing a partial eclipse of the sun and nothing more. But, even more interesting, there is something that is *chosen;* there is a world-outlook that is adhered to: namely, the world-outlook of natural science.

Similarly with the psychotic. To understand his world is not to explain his seeing of the Holy Virgin by reference to a world-outlook of natural science or a world-outlook of "normal" men. To understand his world is "to exhibit the particular a priori existential structure which makes these phenomena possible . . . ," [19] which phenomena are *clinically diagnosed* as symptoms of psychosis. By the method of phenomenology, which will admit no previous frame of reference as favored in the task of understanding the patient, the various phenomena of the patient's world as they are reported by the patient are described in greatest detail. Nothing is at the outset weighed more heavily in favor of anything else. For the phenomenological psychiatrist it is just as significant that the patient experiences time-sequence in the manner he does as it is significant that he hated his father. Whereas in psychoanalysis, for example, there is an antecedent weighing in favor of the early life-history of the *patient,* for the phenomenological psychiatrist there is no anteriorly favored *kind* of phenomenon that appears to the *man.*

It is after as much data as possible "are in" that the phenomenological psychiatrist, in Binswanger's case, passes over into the "Daseinsanalytiker." For now his task becomes to apprehend that over-all transcendental structure that makes it possible for phe-

[19] Binswanger, *Schizophrenie* (Pfullingen, 1957), p. 464.

nomena to be phenomena for the patient; that which makes it possible for facts to be facts in all regions of the patient's experience: temporal, spatial, personal, social, and so forth. That transcendental structure cannot, therefore, be derived from one sphere of the patient's experience and applied to the others. As will become clearer later in the discussion of the Daseinsanalytical conception of symbols, we cannot subsume all the patient's experience under, say, the category of aggression or overly strong mother ties. Such categories are understandable only as emergent in and from one or two spheres of the patient's world as a whole—the social or the personal (the *Mitwelt* and the *Eigenwelt*). Here Binswanger turns to Heidegger, who has attempted to set forth the ontologically necessary preconditions of human being-in-the-world. That transcendental structure that gives meaning and that thereby constitutes the patient's world must be thought of as that patient's manifestation of Care and its components, the existentials. This transcendental structure Binswanger calls the *Transendentale Kategorie*.[20] The Transcendental Category, representing as it does the patient's manifestation of Care, must be capable with equal force and originality of being expressed not only in personal and social terms, but also in terms of temporality, spatiality, reason, choice, and so forth. It must be such a category that it accounts for the patient's complete world without requiring that one aspect of his world, say the social or the temporal, be the basis of "explaining" the others.

Although ontologically Being-in-the-world is the same and must be the same for all human beings (we will remember that Heidegger's [matrix-] formula is *empty*), meta-ontically they may be quite varied. This Transcendental Category—which is the key to understanding the psychotic in that it represents the meaning matrix in which all phenomena appear as phenomena to the patient, and in that it represents the manner in which the ontologically universal structure of Care actually manifests itself in a particular human being in reference to the affairs and things of his daily life—this Transcendental Category is what I term the Existential A Priori. The world of the patient, insofar as this Existential A Priori constitutes it, is his *world-design*.

[20] Binswanger, "The Existential Analysis School of Thought," *Existence, op. cit.*, pp. 191-213.

II

Systematic Explanation and the Science of Psychoanalysis

The Ideal of Explanation

It is claimed by Binswanger that apprehension of the a priori structures of human existence, the Existential A Priori(s), provides the therapist with a fuller *understanding* of the patient's world than does, for example, psychoanalysis. Binswanger claims that natural scientific method *on principle* is barred from the fullest understanding of the patient, although its ability to *explain* psychological phenomena is, in principle, not open to question.[1] The main purpose of this chapter will be a general examination of natural science, especially psychoanalysis, considered as an explanatory system in contrast with the phenomenological approach upon which Daseinsanalyse claims to rest. The ultimate goal is to establish a frame of reference in which philosophical considerations surrounding psychoanalytic and Daseinsanalytic viewpoints may with less generality be discussed in succeeding chapters.

The distinction between understanding (*Verstehen*) and explanation (*Erklärung*) may, at the outset, be roughly equated with the distinction between phenomenology and philosophical system. One of the things that phenomenology claims differentiates it from philosophical system is its attempt to be presuppositionless. Systems there are that claim undoubtable presuppositions, but none that claim to have no presuppositions at all. We shall see that phenomenology's certainty, as well as its powerlessness, stems from this refusal to presuppose.

[1] Binswanger, *Schizophrenie* (Pfullingen, 1957), p. 142.

In Chapter I the circularity of Kant's argument was noted, and it was there hinted that this does not necessarily indicate a flaw in his thinking. Indeed, the goal of a philosophical system is just this circularity. As Weiss has put it,

> A conclusion which repeats the premiss, conforms neatly to the requirements of the most stringent logic. What is wrong with the circular argument is that it is often uninformative, coming back to its beginning too quickly. But if the circle is all inclusive, if it encompasses all there is, it does all that a philosophic system demands.*

In other words, a system that is not circular is as strong and as week as the strength of its premises. Only when the conclusions are in some sense proof of the premises can a system be complete. The circle must be all-inclusive—that is, it must encompass everything that is. But *what is?* If there were no dispute as to what in fact existed or had being in the universe, the divergence of philosophical systems, all of them circular in a grand sense, would be far less pronounced and would perhaps involve only a matter of emphasis or of a starting point. But, in point of fact, *each philosophical system comes with its own pre-established criterion by which something is recognized as an entity*, as something to be encompassed in the system or as something by reference to which all other entities encompassed can be "explained."

The statement, then, that systematic philosophy is a circular enterprise is not fully illuminating, for a philosophical system must presume in advance the precise "qualitative circumference" of the circle. At the risk of stretching the metaphor, we may say that systematic philosophy begins with a small circle, which then moves in a greater circle whose radius may be taken as the smaller circle's diameter.

The smaller circle represents the unavoidable, primitive presuppositions of any system; it traces out the circumference of the greater circle. If the lesser circle is relatively small, we have a system (greater circle) that is comparatively well-defined and sure of

---

* Paul Weiss, *Modes of Being* (Carbondale, Ill., 1958), p. 193. I might add that the difference between the beginning and the end of the circular system is, perhaps, the difference between the *premiss all by itself* and the *premiss as applied to everything else in the universe.*

itself (i.e., one whose criterion for admitting primitive fact is relatively restricted) but that, in its compass, does not explain a great deal (I would cite original logical positivism as an instance). If the lesser circle is large, we have a system that, while it encompasses much, rests on suppositions that themselves appear* to need further justification.

The lesser circle represents the criteria that are definitive of what constitutes a datum to be explained by systematic connection in the greater circle. The lesser circle represents the standard of *quality* of data to be accepted as such and explained by presupposition and rules of inference in the greater circle. It is a *rule of trans-*

formation in accordance with which the philosopher, moving in the greater circle, accepts certain data as irreducible and primary, and others as derivative and transformable into irreducible, primary data.

Hegel's system, as put forth in *The Phenomenology of Mind* is an example of a system in which the lesser circle is relatively large. The lesser circle in Hegel says: everything in science, history, art, religion, and philosophy that manifests itself has a truth and a reality. The presuppositions of the greater circle (the pre-

---

* I stress the word "appear" here because as the lesser circle grows in size, what is solely a rule of transformation of the phenomena may take on the *appearance* of presuppositions of the system proper (the greater circle). Strictly speaking, however, openness to doubt is no differential criterion.

suppositions of the "system") are: the real is rational, and the rational is real; reason proceeds by an inevitable dialectical process. With these presuppositions, Hegel shows in an enormous and ingenious circular argument how everything can be explained, i.e., ordered into a system. Here we see a clear case of how the large size of the lesser circle necessitates a huge greater circle. In Hegel's system, very little that is encountered is transformed, in itself, into something more "basic." At least, each moment has its reality and does not *change*, but necessitates a counter movement that also has its reality. (Of course, Absolute Spirit is the most real, but this does not affect the point that each moment has some degree of reality, integrity, in itself.)

A major criticism of the Hegelian system must be leveled at the lesser circle, in that it provides too lenient a criterion for reality. Nothing is admitted to be unreal, no view is taken as wholly false—everything in the universe of man is taken and accepted on its own terms, the result being that little or nothing is explained. Here emerges the first major contention of this chapter: systematic philosophic explanation must lie at the mean between two opposing forces of human thought—(1) the reductive tendency, which attempts to reduce all phenomena to a minimum of basic substantialities, and (2) an acquiescent tendency, which accepts every thing or idea on its own terms. The former, carried to improper extremes, results, to take the well-known example, in claiming something like "a Beethoven quartet is nothing but a cat's intestines scraped by a horse's tail." The latter, carried to its extreme, results only in an encyclopedia, not a system of explanation, and thus fails to fulfill the task of systematic philosophy, which is, in a sense, to explain the contents of the encyclopedia.

Logical positivism of the Vienna circle was an example of a systematic philosophical approach that, had it lived long enough to expand into a philosophical system, would have represented an excellent example of the poverty of the small lesser circle, considered in its role as generative of the explanatory greater circle. Here the lesser circle demands empirical, sensory filling for any concept and empirical verification for any proposition. Thus propositions concerning morality, aesthetic value, religious consciousness, and the like, are dismissed as nonsense or *transformed*, reduced to a level of substantiality, which reduction is thoroughly repugnant to men in ethical situations, creative acts, and religious struggle. (An example would be that all three situations—ethical, artistic, and religious—are simply the result of the interplay of molecules in the brain cells.)

But equally repugnant to, say, a devout Catholic is the notion that all religions, from that of the Fijian cannibal to Zen Buddhism, are simply different ways of approaching the same God. The reasonable Catholic will be willing to see how some religions are similar to his and even, in a certain sense, say the same thing—but he will demand that a *convincing explanation* of the history of religion show some religions to be heathenish, barbaric, presumptuous, blind, idolatrous, and so forth. He will not allow that goat-worshipers are coming to Christ via too narrow a sense of the All.

The counterpart of the above in philosophy is a system that claims that all systems are true to some degree, that all ideas refer to some reality, that nothing is wholly false or illusory. The thirsty desert traveler does not receive a convincing explanation of his mirage when he is told that the water he saw was real *for him*, although not "intersubjectively." A convincing explanation must begin and end by saying that the water was totally unreal, was really sand and nothing but sand. A philosophical system must have grist in it, must select and reject, as well as accept, both the truth of some other systems and the entities that constitute the "universe." The systematic philosopher cannot let the greater circle be as large as he pleases. He must restrict the greater circle by careful attention to the lesser circle.

The ideal of explanation must, then, combine two mutually opposing goals: to keep that which is to be explained intact as it appears and at the same time to reduce it as much as possible to that with which we are already familiar, of which we have knowledge, or more generally, that which is considered a basic reality. To ignore the former demand is to fall into the danger illustrated by the example of the Beethoven quartet, a danger that can be formalized as follows: *if* A *is explained by reduction* (*either in the sense of subsuming* A *under "pre-established" laws or breaking* A *up into "acceptable" components*) *as "really" abcd, and if, from* abcd *alone it is not possible, without knowing in advance the manner in which* A *in toto appeared, to return to* A,—*then what is explained was not* A, *but only at best an aspect of* A. In our extreme example of the Beethoven quartet, it would hardly be possible to conclude from the notion of horse's tail and cat's intestines back to anything musical (not to say, a *quartet*) unless it be antecedently known that violin strings and bows are made of such things. The danger here is thus a poverty of differential within the "basic reality" of the world as seen by a system. To ignore the latter demand, on the other hand, is to throw back the phenomena to be explained as they appeared in the first place. Such a mode of philosophizing is the "good-for-nothing brother" of phenomenology, which, perhaps, we might term "phenomenography," [2] and which may become merely explication or disclosure. In such a philosophy there exists a corresponding inability to *argue* a point. For, to argue a point in a philosophical system entails that the denial of the point to be made contradicts presuppositions or propositions derived from presuppositions in the system (the greater circle). But since the large lesser circle traces a system in which, in contrast to that traced by the small lesser circle, we have a surfeit of primitive reality, the tendency exists for all "entities" and propositions about entities to be absorbed intact as they appear, to be "swallowed whole." Argument tends to give way to assimilation. The additional tendency in such a philosophy to become mere disclosure or explication exacerbates this situation, for in such a case we are constantly at a loss as to what are presuppositions and what derived propositions.

Phenomenography comes into being when the lesser circle grows uncontrollably, when the criterion for primitive fact becomes infinitely lax. In such a case, the possibility of the greater circle even emerging at all disappears, and with it disappears the possibility of system even while, at the same time, the attempt at system is being made. The result is encyclopedic, not explanatory. It would seem that phenomenology with its conscious disregard of the attempt at reduction—not to be confused with Husserl's Phenomenological Reduction, which is the name for the method of eliminating the reductive, interpretive element from the examination of phenomena—might open itself to such an accusation. However, there is all the difference in the world between accepting the entity or phenomenon as it appears and methodically seeking the essence of phenomena as they truly appear to human conscious-

[2] Ulrich Sonnemann, *Existence and Therapy* (New York, 1954), p. 344.

ness. It is the difference between, say, accepting God as a being of highest reality and of probing the essence of the phenomena of belief-in-God; again, the difference between accepting the phenomena of belief-in-God as a mundane object and probing the essence of belief or faith as it is experienced by the believer. It is, further, the difference between accepting an entity as a basic reality with all the authority of primitive fact and examining a content of consciousness until the essential phenomenal structure of the entity is revealed. In the former, case investigation is stopped radically soon, the fact that something is *real* being the standard; in the latter, investigation is pursued until "the pure *experience* . . . with its own proper essence" [3] is discerned. "The decisive factor lies before all in the absolutely faithful description of that which really lies before one in phenomenological purity, and in keeping at a distance all interpretations that transcend the given." [4]

We may now formulate the distinction implicit here between "explanation" and "understanding." To understand an entity, phenomenon, idea, or experience, is to approach the object to be understood on its terms, to see in it structures that emerge from *its* side, and not from ours. To understand an object is to participate in it until it yields its own essence to us who are understanding. An essential requirement of such a task is, again, "[to keep] at a distance all interpretations that transcend the given." Both reduction and "phenomenography," systems with both a small and a large lesser circle, cannot accomplish this. The former cannot because by definition it seeks to reduce phenomena to what it believes to be ultimate laws[5] or ultimate reality. The latter cannot for a less obvious reason: it records, along with the phenomenon all interpretations of that phenomenon, so that what it gives us is not the phenomenon that really lies before us, but the phenomenon as encrusted with phenomenon-transcending references and interpretations, i.e., the phenomenon as *already reduced*.

In explanation, the phenomena as they appear are transformed in the sense that they are either subsumed under laws that relate them to other, different phenomena, or they are broken down into parts that somehow are taken as more real than the configuration

[3] Husserl, *Ideas*, trans. by W. R. Boyce Gibson (London, 1952), p. 344.
[4] *Ibid.*, p. 262.
[5] Sonnemann, p. 33.

of those parts that are taken to make up the phenomenon in question. Both senses of explanation may be called reduction in that the phenomena no longer retain intactness, independence, or inviolable wholeness.

It may, perhaps, seem odd to imply that it is possible to explain something fully without understanding it. The sense in which I mean to say this, however, is the following: that which is explained is reduced to that which is previously understood. To be sure, we understand the explained phenomenon, *but only insofar as it is related, reduced, transformed into that which we have previously understood*, perhaps by the same route, perhaps by the original sense of understanding as outlined above.

Natural Science as an Explanatory System

Treated in the context of the above distinctions, natural science can be looked upon as one explanatory system among many in the history of thought, or, to be more accurate, a class of explanatory systems, which class consists of physics, chemistry, biology, and so forth. As an explanatory system, we might call it one in which the lesser circle is small and well-defined. For example, in physics:

> Galileo's first step consist [ed] in an *abstraction*. Only the corporeal aspect of things and of the world at large is taken into consideration. The only subject matter of study are spatial configurations and spatio-temporal events.[6]

Here we see one aspect of phenomena, processes, things, given the privileged position of primitive fact: their spatio-temporal aspect. In physics the lesser circle, the rule of transformation of the phenomena, is such that all phenomena explained by systematic connection in the greater circle (physics proper) are first reduced to their spatio-temporal aspect. This general notion of objective space-time is *itself* a result of another presupposition, not of physics itself, but of natural science as a whole, considered as an explanatory system; that more fundamental presupposition is one that defines *corporeality*.

In the science of biology this concept of corporeality has under-

[6] Aron Gurwitsch, "The Last Work of Edmund Husserl," *Philosophy and Phenomenological Research*, Vol. 16 (1956-1957), p. 391.

gone a further modification. Instead of *things*, we find organisms, which are a peculiar kind of thing, but nevertheless still a thing, i.e., still a phenomenon considered in objective space-time. An organism, for nonholistic biology, is a complex *thing* with process and smaller things within it (again in the sense only of objective space-time). Where in physics we have forces, in biology we have tropisms, instincts, drives; where in physics we have elementary particles, in biology we have genes, and so forth. The lesser circle of biology is a modification of that of physics in this sense: irreducible reality for the purposes of biology is spatio-temporal thinghood insofar as it functions in a living organism, itself a highly complex spatio-temporal thing.

The sciences are members of one great explanatory system in that each separate science represents a specification of a primal lesser circle that defines the explanatory system of natural science as a whole.

Turning to an examination of the lesser circle of this, in modern times at least, hypothetical discipline of science in general, we find, instead of a basic *substance* or stuff, what is almost a methodological dictate serving the role of primitive presupposition and world-constituting rule of transformation of the phenomena. It is not enough simply to classify it as empiricism, or as the command to accept as datum that which is perceived with the senses or which has ultimate reference to sense perception. For the term "sense perception" itself is a highly sophisticated one in modern science, one which by no means can be equated with "perception" as we normally experience it in everyday life. The modern scientific conception of sense perception can best be seen as the result of a more basic dictate, namely the dictate to remove the perceiver as much as possible from that which is perceived in the attempt to gain knowledge of that which is perceived. The roots of such a dictate can be seen not only in Galileo's placing the spatio-temporal processes as the underlying reality that he investigated,[7] but also and more strikingly in Descartes, whose isolation of the realm of consciousness from that of the body and the perceived world leads to a notion of a *pure corporeality* that, while devoid of consciousness, is accessible to mathematical knowledge.

If, after all, we still seek a basic substance to which all phe-

7 *Ibid.*, p. 392.

nomena coming under the sphere of scientific explanation are reduced, it would be this pure corporeality. But it is at least equally important to keep in mind this concept of pure corporeality as the product of a frame of mind, or attitude, or methodological dictate: to keep the self out of its world as it investigates "the" world. I will return to this point in discussing the world-design of science.

As for the "greater circle" of science, science proper, the contents of scientific knowledge, that which science knows—the first question we must ask is if, in fact, it is a circle. For it would certainly appear that science is, above all, an open-ended descipline, a *"progressive historical process* which passes from phase to phase [approximating] an ideal goal, viz., 'nature as it really is in itself.' " [8] What seems, therefore, to argue against calling science circular is that science is not yet complete, perhaps essentially not complete since verification, the backbone of scientific theorizing, refers to a future time. And yet what Sonnemann says in characterizing the astronomer can be applied to all natural sciences:

> The movements and magnitudes of celestial bodies are given the observer *in such a way* that a context of quantitative laws governing the four-dimensional domain wherein the observations are made can be abstracted from, as well as reapplied to them, making verifiable predictions possible.[9] (Emphasis added.)

In other words, only that is abstracted from the phenomena which in principle *can* be reapplied, verified. It is a circular enterprise, this—although not a vicious one. It would be vicious only if the laws abstracted from the data themselves became constitutive of further data and failure to verify became virtually impossible, such as happened, for example, in the development of Ptolemaic astronomy, where only perfect circular* movements were *seen* and looked for in the movements of the planets. We might, rather, roughly characterize the circular enterprise of modern science as reasoning from A (the observations) to B (the laws abstracted) to A' (other observations including A). The demand is that A' be conducted in the same spirit as A without allowing B to influence the selection or recording of A'. It thus becomes a nice problem

[8] *Ibid.,* p. 391.
[9] Sonnemann, p. 42.
* Literal, of course, not metaphorical.

as to what, in verification, is verified: the laws or the observations.

If it is possible to speak of an "open-ended circle" (a spiral?), or a "circle in objective time," we have it here. Facts, of themselves, do not exist except within theory, and are, to a degree, constituted by theory; theory is valid only insofar as it conforms with facts. "In this process there is a constant give-and-take between what we regard as ascertained fact and possible hypotheses. We not only eliminate hypotheses found inconsistent with the facts, but we also employ theoretical arguments to correct the readings of observation or experimental results." [10]

In sum, then, the lesser circle of science demands the reduction of phenomena to fact, fact being understood as phenomena devoid of consciousness and human selfhood. The greater circle ascertains what the facts are in detail by the application and reapplication of theories that themselves in part constitute and illuminate the facts.

The Possibility of Psychology as a Natural Science

Psychology, the science of human consciousness and behavior, thus finds itself in a strained position. On the one hand it would be "objective," would take its place as one of the natural sciences, would find corroboration in and would corroborate other sciences such as biology and chemistry. On the other hand, it would study that which science since Descartes and Galileo demands be ruled out of the field of investigation: the soul, psyche, consciousness.

In psychology the phenomena reduced by the lesser circle of science are also of the same class as the investigation itself.

> Unlike the physicist, the psychologist . . . investigates processes that belong to the same general order—perception, learning, thinking—as those by which he conducts his investigation.[11]

The danger is that scientific method be taken as constitutive of the nature of thinking or perception and thus any thinking or perception that a man claims to give him the truth and that is at variance with scientific thinking, is at once labeled "merely subjective" or "projective," and so forth. For the psychologist cannot

[10] Morris R. Cohen, *Reason and Nature* (Glencoe, Ill., 1953), p. 81.
[11] Sonnemann, p. 15.

admit that his mode of obtaining the truth is supplantable by another mode of thought or perception. If he does so in an attempt to be true to the phenomena he is investigating, he is implicitly admitting that his method may be contradicted and his results negated by another method—say, the artistic, or intuitive.

The psychologist attempts to bring into the field of investigation what Descartes excluded. The objective world, the world of *res extensa* is the world with consciousness and selfhood removed from it. Scientific method cannot reduce that which is doing the reducing, consciousness, thought, perception—self. Psychology cannot explain those processes that are of the same order as that by which it conducts its investigation without dictating at the outset what those processes are like; without dictating to the data in advance. In such a case the circle would be vicious, as in Ptolemaic astronomy.

It would seem, then, that the only possibility for psychology to exist as a natural science is in the form of behaviorism where, in fact, consciousness has been excluded from the field of inquiry. In behaviorism the dictate of natural science is fully adhered to; what the behaviorist explores are entities that are corporeal, in which the perceiver is eliminated. In short the subject matter of behaviorism is one in which self is excluded from the world it investigates. This is perhaps scientific method. But is it psychology? If the self is excluded, if consciousness is labeled meaningless, if all that we experience as "subjective" is not only not explained but rendered out of the field of inquiry, we have no longer a science of the self, no longer a psychology, but a set of theories about human behavior that in principle can be verified only by avoiding the very source of verification, the conscious subject himself.

It does not help to say that science dictates only that the individual subject be eliminated as much as possible from investigation, that consciousness, thinking, per se, can be investigated by a particular individual as long as that particular investigator, *qua* scientist, keeps his own subjectivity out of the investigation. For, to repeat, the psychologist is after the truth about thinking, perception, and so on. To "reduce himself" to a scientist—and only a scientist—who orients himself to his subject matter as the physicist orients himself to his, is automatically to exclude from view certain possible data, among which data are conceptual forms that contradict those toward which he feels his investigation to be leading.[12]

The difficulty may be formulated thus: it is inherently illegitimate to reduce (i.e., transform) phenomena that are of the same general order as those that are the *source* of the systematic structure used to explain the phenomena so reduced. The only way to think about thinking is to observe thinking. But to what can thinking be *conceptually* reduced other than to itself? To explain thinking by transforming it is to lose the phenomena of thinking. But to preserve it intact is to surrender the natural-scientific method that would keep its world free from consciousness, final causes, and so on; to preserve it intact is to violate the lesser circle of natural science and to admit as real that which in science is transformed into something else.

Thus psychology as a natural science fails to explain because of the extreme smallness of its lesser circle in comparison with the contents of its universe. In such psychology we find the same difficulty as encountered in explaining the Beethoven quartet as horse's hair and cat's intestines. We can never return from the explanation to the thing explained without previous knowledge of what it was to be explained.

The dilemma of psychology is similar to that of any discipline whose subject matter is human consciousness and whose wish is to emulate natural science. The radical difference between the subject matter of physics, biology, etc., and psychology, history, literary criticism, etc., is indicated in the following manner: whereas in physics each datum is meaningless until it is brought into connection with other data through a conceptual scheme and hypothesis, in psychology each datum, a human perception, thought, emotion, etc., itself has its own meaning to the perceiver, thinker, feeler—to the human being.

We might put this point in the language of phenomenological psychology: the variation of a light pattern does not of itself point to, refer to, intend of itself something beyond itself—whereas an act of consciousness is essentially intentional, essentially refers beyond itself (Brentano, Husserl). Science, when dealing, as in physics, with the objects of intentional acts, with things, does

[12] *Ibid.*, p. 15.

[44]

right in eliminating intention as inhering in the intended object (strips the world of consciousness). The astronomer does not reduce the act of perceiving the star; he does not reduce the star's beauty, its romance. These qualities he ignores because they represent qualifications of consciousness-of-a-world, of being-in-the-world, of intentional acts.* Object processes in physical space-time thus having no reference beyond themselves are given reference by scientific theory, and the world conceived solely as a thing is then explained. The psychologist, on the other hand, when he emulates science, can only strip consciousness of the very quality that constitutes its essence, its intentionality. To be truly empirical, the psychologist must preserve the "transcendence," the reference beyond itself of conscious processes—in a word, their *meanings* to the self in whom they are taking place.

If psychology can exist as a natural science, it can only do so by preserving the *meanings* of those perceptions and thoughts that it wishes to explain. It may then attempt to link *those* meanings into a conceptual scheme, but its lesser circle, its rule of transformation of phenomena encountered must not fall below the level of meaning-to-a-self. It must, in a word, understand more before it seeks to explain. It must not dictate to the subject, as is often done in psychological experiment, a mode or attitude of perceiving an object, unless all it wants to investigate is perception under experimental conditions.

Gestalt psychology was a move in the direction of studying perception, thinking, learning, in the context of meaning. It too, however, continued to isolate the "perceptual" from the "emotional." And thus the *Gestalten* still represent a subliminal lesser

---

* The psychologist, on the other hand, when he attempts to emulate the natural scientist, does not ignore but transforms the act of perception itself until, as in radical behaviorism, for example, the perception of the star's beauty, its romance, becomes a pattern of movements of a physical object with two legs and arms. The power of physics springs partly from its renunciation of consciousness in its world: the star is not beautiful, not romantic; it is a fourth magnitude nebula surrounded by gases XYZ. The weakness of scientific psychology springs from the very source that lends power to physics: the star is perceived as beautiful, romantic; the *perception* is not a process of synthesizing retinal impressions with learned ocular orientation to perspective and distance, much less a probable pattern of movements or behavior of a featherless biped. Any explanation that utterly loses the perception of the star's beauty cannot be said to have explained the perception. Psychology, if it seeks to deal with retinas, light waves, and the like, is neurology, physiology, or biochemistry—anything but a science of consciousness.

circle where the basic reality, although a meaning-context, is still not the kind of meaning-context in which perception and thinking take place in "ordinary" life and consciousness. It was Freud who, as a natural scientist, accepted phenomena as basal that corresponded to phenomena as lived and experienced in conscious life by human beings. Here, however, we find ourselves no longer in the realm of natural science per se—of science simply as an attempt to explain. We are also with at least equal force in the realm of psychotherapy —a branch of medicine, a brief characterization of which now follows.

The Science of Medicine

We may characterize medicine as that branch of biology of the human organism dealing with biological purpose, norms, values. It must, according to Binswanger, be distinguished from purely natural scientific biology: "Health and illness are value concepts, objects of judgments based on biological purpose . . ." [13] When applied to organisms other than the human or the humanized (pets), the distinction between medicine and biology is not as fruitful, i.e., the explanation of biological phenomena frequently exhausts their consideration as to purpose or value. The appearance, say, of certain microorganisms in the intestines of a shark can be explained by the fact that in the intestines of a shark certain conditions are fulfilled that are most congenial to those microorganisms. The additional fact that the presence of those microorganisms results in a malfunctioning of the shark's digestive system and ultimately in his death, is irrelevant. The value to the microorganism (value understood as referring to that which keeps it alive) of these conditions in the shark's intestines helps to explain its presence there. If we are not interested in keeping sharks alive as long as possible, the fact of the shark's ultimate death is of no importance in this context. Biology, then, is the science of organisms with no emphasis or center being placed on any one species of organism. Medicine is biology with the center of reference on one particular group of organisms. Thus plant medicine, dog medi-

[13] Binswanger, "The Case of Ilse," in Rollo May, Ernest Angel, and Henri F. Ellenberger (eds.), *Existence* (New York, 1958), p. 229.

cine, and the like. Of course medicine as we most often think of it is biology with special reference to man and keeping him alive.

Medicine is thus biology with a specific attitude, center of reference—man. To keep man alive, free from (physical) suffering, medicine reduces man to a natural object, seeks causes in natural objects for his suffering or for the threat to his life and attempts to remove or prevent these causes. "This natural object is the *organism* in the sense of the total context of living and functioning of a human individual." [14]

If we may speak of a lesser circle in what, in comparision with physics, is so unsystematic a science as medicine, we might be tempted to view it as a specification of that of biology: irreducible reality for the purposes of medicine is spatio-temporal thinghood insofar as it functions in or has reference to the human organism, itself a highly complex organism among organisms. Such a description of the manner in which medicine originally confronts the phenomena with which it deals would, however, fail to distinguish it from, say, physiology. What is lacking in such a description is the *value*-context in which medicine, conceived as the science of healing, functions. In medicine, as distinguished from other sciences, phenomena as they appear are not transformed into facts, but into symptoms, determinants of health, disease, malfunction. Symptoms and such determinants may be defined as value-laden biological facts with reference to the functioning of a specific organism, usually man. That is, in medicine, biological facts receive a teleological reference—the health of the organism.

The Science of Psychoanalysis

In the light of the foregoing, I wish now to bring psychoanalysis into focus, indicating the limitations and power that Binswanger sees inherent in it and pointing the way in which Binswanger proposes Daseinsanalyse as its necessary complement.

The dilemma of a natural-scientific psychology (which Binswanger calls a *contradictio in adjecto*[15]) was formulated above in

---

14 *Ibid.*, p. 229.
15 Binswanger, "Freud's Conception of Man in the Light of Anthropology," in this volume.

this manner: while attempting to be an objective science the essence of which we saw was fully to transform phenomena into facts devoid of consciousness or self-generating significance in order to bring those phenomena under the aegis of mathematics, phychology finds at the same time that the subject matter that it investigates is of the same order as that which forms and shapes the investigation itself. To avoid dictating to the data, it would therefore have to abandon its pre-established method—give up its claim as an heir of the natural sciences. Proceeding with scientific method so understood, psychology can only strip the phenomena of consciousness, thinking, perceiving, willing, of their essential nature—intentionality, pointing-beyond the phenomena to an object. That is, it can only destroy the meaning-to-a-self of the phenomena of consciousness that it seeks to explain, in the very act of explaining. At best, it can only reduce those phenomena in advance to such as correspond with those phenomena of consciousness by which it conducts its investigation.

Psychology as a natural science is thus faced with the apparently absurd and self-contradictory task of investigating consciousness as part of the realm of *res extensa,* absurd and self-contradictory because it is of the essence of the Cartesian *res extensa* that it is what appears to consciousness or what exists independently of consciousness; in a word, psychology must strip consciousness of consciousness in order scientifically to investigate consciousness.

It is this seemingly self-contradictory task that Freud accomplished. What is his doctrine of the Unconscious but such an attempt to view the essence of consciousness as that which is essentially in the realm of *res extensa?* *

> Psycho-analytical speculation starts from the impression gained on investigating unconscious processes that consciousness cannot be the most general characteristic of psychic processes, but merely a special function of them.[16]

* It is a question only of terminology to raise the distinction here between conscious and mental. The point at hand is that Freud placed what Cartesian science specifically eliminated from scientific investigation back into the sphere of possible scientific investigation. We call it the mental, consciousness, the soul, etc. See Freud, "The Unconscious," trans. by Cecil M. Baines, in *Collected Papers* (New York, 1959), Vol. IV, pp. 98-100.

16 Freud, *Beyond the Pleasure Principle,* trans. by C. J. M. Hubback, in *The*

Thus, in contrast to such natural scientific psychology as described above, scientific method does not, in Freud, at the outset, run the risk of encroaching on its own data, or of dictating to the data. We will see later that it, too, dictates to the data, but to data of a different sort in its role as medicine and that *this* dictation to the data is not necessarily to be condemned. But for now, be it only noted that as soon as the major part of psychic processes are placed, by definition, out of direct experience of consciousness, they become susceptible to treatment and observation by scientific method—in fact, they appear to become amenable even to mathematics. We need only cite such a passage in Freud to see how inclined he was toward the ideal of mathematics:

> It is as though the resistance to consciousness against them [the derivatives of repression] was in inverse proportion to their remoteness from what was originally repressed.[17]

Thus the first half of the dilemma of psychology as posed above is avoided. The other half is also avoided in Freud. Mental acts, feelings, thinking, perception—in short, all the phenomena of consciousness—are not disembowelled of their meaning-to-a-self. Whereas in such psychologies as behaviorism or Pavlovian psychology the phenomena of consciousness are broken down to "objective" constituents in such a way that their meaning-to-a-self becomes irrelevant to that psychology, in Freud it is just those meanings that are part of the main subject matter of psychoanalysis. This point will become clearer if we examine psychoanalysis as an explanatory system.

Our first task is to apprehend what was described above as the lesser circle of this system, the rule of transformation according to which the phenomena are encountered either as reducible or irreducible. This aspect, incidentally, of explanation in science was noted by Freud himself in the beginning of "Instincts and Their Vicissitudes":

> The true beginning of scientific activity consists rather in describing phenomena and then in proceeding to group, classify and

Major Works of Sigmund Freud (Vol. 54 of *Great Books of the Western World* [Encyclopaedia Britannica, 1955]), p. 646.

[17] Freud, "Repression," trans. by Cecil M. Baines, in *Collected Papers*, Vol. IV, p. 88.

correlate them. [The greater circle.] *Even at the stage of description, it is not possible to avoid applying certain abstract ideas derived from various sources and certainly not the fruit of new experiences only.* [The lesser circle.] [18] (Emphasis added.)

We have already noted that any particular science will have as a lesser circle a modification and specification of the lesser circle of science per se, namely, the removal of self or consciousness from the world. We have also noted that in Freud this demand is carried out with great faithfulness as represented in his doctrine of unconscious psychic processes. However, the notion of the unconscious is a postulate that exists in the systematic structure of psychoanalysis proper, the greater circle; it is a hypothesis that helps to connect certain *facts* about dreams, hypnosis, and the like.[19] What we are after here is something even more fundamental, something that circumscribes the manner in which the facts themselves are *ascertained*. The doctrine of the unconscious, being a hypothesis of the greater circle, must itself spring from a more basic assumption, one which even more blatantly takes consciousness and self out of the field of investigation and which therefore even more radically hews to the fundamental demand of Cartesian science, "objectivity."

We need go no further than Freud himself to find a clear and explicit statement of this most fundamental assumption which we term the lesser circle: "In our method, observed phenomena must take second place to forces that are merely hypothesized." [20] These *Strebungen* are the *drives*, the *instincts* ". . . whose elemental nature is the same in all men and which directs him to the satisfaction of certain primal needs." [21] Thus psychoanalysis is a science that explains psychic phenomena by reduction of these phenomena initially to their instinctual component. The lesser circle of psychoanalysis transforms phenomena as it encounters (describes)* them into their function in relation to drives and needs.

[18] Freud, "Instincts and Their Vicissitudes," trans. by Cecil M. Baines, in *Collected Papers*, Vol. IV, p. 60.

[19] Freud, "The Unconscious," p. 99.

[20] Freud, quoted by Binswanger in "Freud's Conception of Man," this volume, p. 156.

[21] *Loc. cit.*

* An example of how in psychoanalytic theory the lesser circle transforms phenomena as it encounters (describes) them may be found on page 213 of *In-*

Here it is essential to note that this basic reality of psychoanalysis, the drives or instincts, although a concept arising strictly from the science of biology, is a purposive, intentional reality. An instinct intends an object; it is not, like the objective processes, say, of physics, something in itself possessing no meaning or reference beyond itself and needing the theorizing of the physics to relate it conclusively with other data. An instinct points beyond itself to its satisfaction. The phenomena that are explained in psychoanalysis are therefore never reduced below the level of intentionality, something that previous natural-scientific psychologies cannot claim.*

Thus in Freud, phenomena of consciousness, themselves intentional, are reduced to instincts, also intentional. It would not be possible to reduce these phenomena to another set or species of conscious phenomena—to say, that is, that all psychic acts are based on transformations of a psychic tendency whose essence involves consciousness and the possibility of self-consciousness. For then simply self-observation by any human being would, in principle, be enough to prove or disprove the hypothesis. The instincts must have their source in the nonconscious in order to fulfill their explanatory role of reducing the phenomena and thereby allowing them to be ". . . absorbed by the hypothesized forces, drives, and the laws that govern them." [22]

And yet, in order to keep the lesser circle from growing too small, the "basic reality," the instincts, must be of the same genus as the reducible phenomena of consciousness. To complete, therefore, an adequate explanatory system in which justice is done to

---

stinct in Man by Ronald Fletcher (New York, 1957): "In concluding this account of the 'mental mechanisms,' it must be emphasized that, as presented above, these mechanisms are not intended as *explanations* of the process whereby the individual accommodates himself to the demands of the environment, but are simply *descriptive concepts* indicating the particular ways in which this process of accommodation takes place."

* An interesting point here is that the concept of instinct is itself derived from the greater circle of another science, biology. The concept of instinct in biology is a hypothesis that connects and brings into unity certain phenomena of the highly complex thing, the organism. It would be rewarding, I think, through outside the scope of this book, to draw parallels of such a nature in the development and interdependence of other sciences, where elements pertaining to the greater circle, the theoretical structure, of one science, become definitive of the lesser circle of another.

[22] *Loc. cit.*

both tendencies of explanation, Freud posits mental acts that are unconscious. The problem that now arises is to ascertain the distinction between a conscious and an unconscious intentional act, mental process. The temptation to assume that since all acts of this sort must have an "agent behind" them and then draw the distinction by claiming that the agent of the unconscious mental act is different from that of the conscious act must be avoided for it can only involve us in the difficulties of formulating the concept of an agent that is not a self and that yet performs functions that a self performs. The distinction between conscious and unconscious mental acts must, rather, be drawn more broadly in this same direction: an intentional act with no agent is unconscious; one "emanating" or having essential reference to an agent would be conscious.

Thus we may define instincts (*Triebe*) in this context as intentional acts having no original essential reference to an agent-self. This is the more precise specification of the lesser circle, the rule of transformation of the data as they are encountered. I have spoken above of the necessity of preserving meaning-to-a-self as an irreducible datum in explaining the phenomena of conscious life. If we understand meaning, very broadly in the phenomenological context, as intention or reference of the act beyond itself (i.e., thinking is of something, perception is perception of something), we see that what Freud's lesser circle does is to preserve meaning, but not meaning to an *individual* self. The psychoanalytic theory of man, stressing as it does the similarities of men and mental phenomena, can speak of the meaning of mother-love, of a knife as a symbol of phallus, of fatherhood. There thus arises a set of meanings that are explained and unified in the greater circle and that are used as a standard by which individually appearing meanings, meanings to the patient, are reduced. That is to say: the essential reference of intentionality to an agent-self is erased by postulating in its stead a form of intentionality (instinctuality) for which the reference to an agent-self is not constitutive. Intentionality, meaning, is preserved; the individual self is "robbed" of its uniqueness.

To sum up this section, psychoanalysis is an explanatory system that remains true to the primitive demand of science since Galileo and Descartes in that it removes the self and consciousness from the field of investigation. Its subject matter being the "self" and consciousness (intentional phenomena), the phenomena that it encounters and explains must to a degree be preserved in their intactness. The lesser circle, or most primitive presupposition of psychoanalysis, thus becomes a rule for reducing the phenomena to a kind of intentionality in which no essential reference is made to an agent-self. Both reduction and preservation of the phenomena are accomplished in this "lesser circle of medium size." This kind of intentionality comes out of a concept of biological theory, the concept of *instinct*.

Binswanger's View of Freud

The foregoing helps to explain why Binswanger looks upon Freud as the first thinker ever *thoroughly* to propound the idea of man as *homo natura*. (This is the dominant theme of Binswanger's essay "Freud's Conception of Man in the Light of Anthropology," included in this volume.) "Thoroughly" because far from an extensive set of *aperçus* relating man to organic nature, Freud's theories link the reduced phenomena of psychic life by a systematic connection corresponding to what I have described above as the greater circle of science. Freud's theories as to the structure of the psychic apparatus, pleasure principle, wish fulfillment, repression, constitute this greater circle. Speaking, for example, of the relation of the dream-work to wish, Binswanger says:

> That the dream-*work* . . . can be set in motion only by means of a wish stimulus is as much a necessary postulate of the psychic apparatus as it is a fact of experience. Whoever sees a vicious circle here has not understood scientific method in general. Just as the notion of the psychic apparatus is a theoretical epitomization of the actuality of experience, so "experience" is a theoretical verification of that epitomization. *All of natural science exemplifies this circle.*[23]

A comparatively more detailed examination of the contents of this greater circle, psychoanalysis proper, and its relation to the notion of the Existential A Priori, will concern us in subsequent chapters. What I wish here to indicate is the radical extent to

[23] *Ibid.*, p. 164.

which Freud, as Binswanger understands him, reduces man and explains him as *homo natura*, a creature of organic nature.

Binswanger first presents an interesting parallel between Frued and Locke.[24] Where Locke asks how far man's capacity for knowledge extends, Freud asks how far man's capacity for civilization, culture, extends. Where Locke seeks the method of correct knowledge, Freud seeks the method of living correctly with respect to civilization. Where Locke proceeds from the doubt as to whether the goal of all-embracing knowledge is attainable, Freud proceeds from the doubt as to whether the goal of a complete capability for culture is attainable in man. For both, the psychic life is a "movement" according to laws of its simpler elements, in Locke images and in Freud instincts. Both are strictly psychological empiricists and are rooted as far back as Descartes. Both reject metaphysical hypotheses as prejudicial. Both are oriented predominantly, sensualistically, and nominalistically, and so on.

The parallel between Locke and Freud is summed up by Binswanger by applying to Freud a rephrasing of the Lockean "nihil est in intellectu, quod non feurit in sensu." For Freud, "nihil est in homine cultura, quod non feurit in homine natura."

Binswanger draws the parallel most decisively when he speaks of the Freudian *tabula rasa*. The important qualification that Freud gives to the notion of *tabula rasa*, however, lies in the fact that for Freud "in the newly born infant there is already a certain biological etching on this tablet, a blueprint according to which subsequent cultural *development* takes place.[25] This *Zeichnung* (blueprint) is, of course, sketched by the instincts, the notion of which, as has already been noted, forms the most basic substructural presupposition of psychoanalysis. The reduction of all aspects of man's psychic life to the biological, to instincts, is not in itself condemned by Binswanger. "This is the geniune natural-scientific spirit," he writes. "Natural science never begins with just the phenomena, indeed, its main task is to divest the phenomena of their phenomenality as quickly and as thoroughly as possible." [26] Also viewed as genuine scientific method is

[24] *Ibid.*, p. 154n.
[25] *Ibid.*, p. 154.
[26] *Ibid.*, p. 156.

. . . the *tendency* of Freudian theory to level or equate the several aspects of man's essential being by bringing them to the level of "general" exigencies or needs and the psychic significance of these needs.[27]

The extent of this leveling or reductive-explanatory process is nowhere more clearly visible than in Freud's notion of the Id, the deepest, most primitive psychic reality. The basal structure of the "individual" is no more than a swarm of agentless processes or intentional acts.

Deep down, the individual life, too, is chaotic, dark, inaccessible, and only negatively describable in negative comparison with and in contrast to the "organized" ego. It is like a "cauldron of seething excitement." [28]

Thus the leveling of man to *homo natura* structures him as most essentially amoral, unfree, irrational, and unhistorical—morality, freedom, rationality, historicity, be it noted, being those qualities that the lesser circle of science since Descartes and Galileo removes from the universe when it removes consciousness and attends merely to *res extensa*.

It has been discussed how the intentional acts, meanings, that are the phenomena of psychic life as they appear are reduced to another brand of intentional act, instinct. Although emanating essentially from no organized self-agent, the object intended by an instinct is explicitly formulated by Freud as *Lust,* pleasure. Thus, meanings as they are experienced and lived by man are reduced in Freud's scientific theory to one kind of meaning, the wish.[29]

Medical Psychology: Psychopathology

Binswanger sees Freud's main service to science as Freud himself saw it: [30]

He did not attribute major significance to the "practical task" of interpreting symbols, but rather to the "theoretical" task of *ex-*

---

27 *Ibid.,* p. 159.
28 *Ibid.,* p. 161.
29 *Ibid.,* p. 164.
30 *Loc. cit.*

plaining the supposed "operations" of the particular modes of functioning of the psychic apparatus.[31] (Emphasis added.)

Furthermore,

. . . what singles Freud's doctrine out is just the goal of showing *what follows with mechanical necessity from the given conditions of the natural organisation of man and the encounter of these conditions with factors of the environment.*[32]

With this "disclosure of a mechanism" we are, according to Binswanger, in the realm of medical psychology and psychotherapy.

Here necessity everywhere usurps the place of freedom, mechanicalness the place of reflection and decision. And with this we find ourselves in the territory of medicine. "For," says Lotze in his famous treatise on instincts, "how poorly our health would in fact fare were reflection, rather than mechanicalness, its protector." [33]

Referring to the discussion above, we need only introduce the value-concept of mental health into the lesser circle of psychoanalysis as already described to see how shift from a theoretical structure to a practical discipline is effected. Instinct intends pleasure. Failure in this goal results in pain, anxiety, and the like. Health thus becomes the ability to satisfy the goals of the instincts as much as possible within a civilization whose essence involves the thwarting of primal satisfaction of the instincts.[34] Psychological facts become symptoms, just as in somatic medicine physiological facts become symptoms.

It is as medicine where the distorting of the data, so condemned in itself above in reference to nonpsychoanalytic psychology, becomes definitory of the very task of medicine. The world as it appears to the patient must be altered, for it is by reference to this very world, meanings as they are lived by the patient, that sickness manifests itself.

In somatic medicine the value terms health, symptom, illness

[31] *Ibid.*, p. 165.
[32] *Loc. cit.*
[33] *Loc. cit.*
[34] Freud, *Civilization and Its Discontents*, trans. by Joan Riviere, in *Major Works* (Vol. 54 of *Great Books of the Western World*), pp. 767-806.

are fully expressible in a nonvaluational context of physiology, anatomy, neurology, with reference to life, pain, death, malfunctioning of the organism. That is, every medical fact is completely transformable into a fact of the biology of man, what is lost being the *attitude* of the scientist, the doctor, toward the facts. In somatic medicine, therefore, the value terms of health and illness, for example, are guides to procedure, as it were, regulative ideas—that do not, ideally, constitute the data, but only influence emphasis in ascertainment of the data, in attention, and control.

But in medical psychology the notions of (mental) health, normality, and so on, are not referrable to such "objectively" unambiguous states of the physical organism such as life, death, organic malfunction. To allow this would be to fall into the error of allowing the lesser circle to admit unintentional acts as the primitive reality, the error of nonpsychoanalytic psychology. On the other hand, the objects intended by instincts or drives are objects of value, desired, wanted, needed; in other words, biological purpose becomes the criterion of judging the "normality" of purposes, desires, and values as they are experienced in their phenomenality. In a word, if I may so express it, values themselves are evaluated, whereas in biological medicine processes themselves unintentional are evaluated.

As a theory of explanation, psychoanalysis may be justified in reducing phenomena of psychic life to drives and needs and thereby structuring these phenomena into a system of facts. As medicine, however, where it attempts to influence the course of psychic life, its own valuational structure is seen to be of the same genus as that which it influences. That is, whereas in nonpsychoanalytical psychology, as just discussed, the problem stemmed from the fact that the method of inquiry was of the same genus as the object of inquiry, in medical psychology or psychotherapy the basis of the method of influence and control is of the same genus as that which is to be influenced. It is in such a frame of reference that such questions can be directed at psychoanalysis: Is suffering necessarily a sign of abnormality—and if not, when not? Is guilt always pathological? Is maladjustment to social demands a symptom of emotional disorder?

If there is forthcoming a justification of the biological standard of evaluating values themselves, it will be practical, rather than scientific-theoretical. Science cannot justify a value as it justifies a theory. And although it may turn out that the "distorting" of the patient's world (something condemned by "pure" phenomenological psychiatrists such as Van den Berg)[35] is the essence of psychotherapy, and that certain kinds of psychotherapy (such as psychoanalysis) *work* as judged by standards of mental health derived from their own explanatory systems, psychological medicine cannot, indeed does not attempt to, justify its valuational assumptions purely biologically. It must without privileged status enter into the general arena of value systems.

[35] J. H. Van den Berg, *The Phenomenological Approach to Psychiatry* (Springfield, Ill., 1955).

III

The Symbol in Psychoanalysis and *Daseinsanalyse*

In the following three chapters I propose to bring the notion of the Existential A Priori more clearly into focus by juxtaposing Daseinsanalyse and psychoanalysis in the following contexts: (1) the nature and interpretation of symbols, (2) the status of the "unconscious," (3) psychopathology. This is perhaps the place to emphasize that Daseinsanalyse does not stand as a counter depth-psychology in relation to Freudian psychoanalysis in the manner of the work of, say, Jung or Adler. It should be kept in mind that in Binswanger's perspective Daseinsanalyse, without such techniques and theorizing as is found in psychoanalysis, is clinically almost impotent, but also that psychoanalysis without Daseinsanalyse is in danger of biased distortion of the patient's world—even where it is clinically most "successful." In this connection, the following note of Binswanger's must also be kept in mind:

> We are speaking here of the role of psychopathology within the total frame of psychiatric medical research. We do not neglect the fact that in the psychoanalytical investigation, as well as in every purely "understanding" psychopathology, germs of existential-analytical views can always be found. But they indicate neither a methodical scientific procedure nor a knowledge of why and in what way existential analysis differs from the investigation of life-historical connections and from an "empathic" or "intuitive" entering into the patient's psychic life.[1]

[1] Binswanger, "The Existential Analysis School of Thought, in Rollo May, Ernest Angel, and Henri F. Ellenberger (eds.), *Existence* (New York, 1958), p. 212n.

The Symbol

The Freudian concept of symbolization is summarized by Robert Fliess as

> the exchange of an element of a sexual nature, including those of an infantile sexual one and in a few cases of an incest object, for an element or object of a nonsexual nature.[2]

Sandor Ferenczi's formulation serves, however, as an important qualification:

> Only such things [or ideas] are symbols in the sense of psycho-analysis as are invested in consciousness with a logically inexplicable and unfounded affect, and of which it may be analytically established that they owe this affective over-emphasis to *unconscious* indentification with another thing [or idea], to which the surplus of affect really belongs. Not all similes [or allegories, metaphors, allusions, etc.], therefore, are symbols, but only those in which one member of the equation is repressed into the unconscious.[3]

Taken together these two quotes can be said to constitute the nucleus of the Freudian notion of symbolization. The first point to be noticed is that only the horizontal dimension of symbolism, as it is normally understood, seems to receive attention. By the horizontal dimension I mean the reference involving two members of the same genus, a leading from the concrete to the concrete, from the image to the image. Such a symbolic equation from concrete to concrete cannot, however, be made without at least implying a universal exhibited by both the symbol and the symbolized. When, for example, a writer likens the eyes of his beloved to two precious gems, gems symbolize eyes because, among other things, they both have brilliance, luster, and inner light.*

---

[2] Robert Fliess, "On the Nature of Human Thought," in *Readings in Psychoanalytic Psychology*, edited by Morton Levitt (New York, 1959), p. 216.

[3] Sandor Ferenczi, *Selected Papers* (New York, 1950), Vol. I, pp. 277-278.

* Of course, psychoanalytic literature is not lacking in instances where the vertical dimension of symbolism seems to be treated. Herbert Silberer's famous hypnagogic experiments contain many examples of this—where, for instance, after reflecting upon the idea of transsubjectivity, he begins to grow tired and in a

The second point concerns the irreversibility of the symbolic equation. Ernest Jones writes:

> As energy flows from them [the primary interests] and never to them, and as they constitute the most repressed part of the mind, it is comprehensible that symbolism should take place in one direction only. Only what is repressed is symbolized; only what is repressed needs to be symbolized.[4]

There is thus no room made for what may be called reciprocal modification between symbol and symbolized. A nation that chooses the eagle as its symbol lends dignity to the bird as well as receives it. Does the king choose trumpets to announce him because they are regal, or are they regal because they announce the king?

Third, and closely related to the above, the reductive, explanatory nature of the science of psychoanalysis demands that the conditioned in a symbolic equation is always the symbol of the condition. The following, also cited by Roland Dalbiez, illustrates this perfectly:

> The river which waters and irrigates India springs from the hair of Shiva. That is clearly a fabulous notion, a myth. On the other hand, there is a well-known fountain in Brussels, the "Manneken-Pis," in which the stream of water flows from the natural passage of a little boy, who appears to be urinating. These two cases contain a single fundamental notion from which the artist drew his inspiration: the flow of liquid from the human body. But in which of the two is this notion expressed with least distortion? When have Hindu painters or poets seen a jet of water coming from a head of hair? Never, surely. The nearest realization of their myth which they may, consciously or unconsciously, have experienced (and which they later distorted in their own fashion,

---

state of semisomnolence sees before him the image of a large balloon with many human heads in it. However, in such cases where psychoanalytic literature treats the representation of an idea by an image, it is the case either that (1) the symbolized need not have been suppressed but is so only because rational operations, according to Freud, are not realizable in dreams, or (2) the idea is only an elaboration or sublimation of that of which the image is more adequately symbolic.

[4] Ernest Jones, quoted by Roland Dalbiez in *Psychoanalytical Method and the Doctrine of Freud*, trans. by T. F. Lindsay (London, 1941), Vol. I, p. 109.

in creating their work of art), could not be so very different from that which inspired the designer of the fountain at Brussels.

. . . it seems to us legitimate as honest scientists, to connect symbolic expressions with their most natural and simple significance.[5]

Or, in Binswanger's paraphrasing: *nisi est in homine cultura, quod non feurit in homine natura.* The issue that this raises concerns the legitimacy of the term "symbol," as opposed to "sign." In the above quotation, Theodore Flournoy is seeking the source of symbols in their psychic *causes*, as does Freud in *The Interpretation of Dreams.* As Dalbiez points out, "the ordinary symbol implies no direct causal relation with what it symbolizes." [6] Carl Jung's well-known criticism of Freud's use of the term "symbol" makes the same point:

Those conscious contents which give us a clue, as it were, to the unconscious backgrounds are by Freud incorrectly termed symbols. They are not true symbols, however, since according to his teaching, they have merely the role of signs or symptoms of the background processes.[7]

THE COMMON UNIVERSAL / The above three issues, which arise from the Freudian conception of intrapsychic symbols, are three aspects of one problem, namely, the problem as to the meaning to the patient of the symbol to be interpreted or explained.

Turning to the first point, we see that in psychoanalysis the common universal, which connects the two items in the symbolic equation, is frequently allowed to remain implicit. Otto Fenichel, however, is one psychoanalytic writer who, at least in the typical example of money as the symbol of feces, makes every effort to be explicit. According to Fenichel, this symbol arises from the child's experience of not being allowed to put into his mouth a very precious part of his own body, his feces. This leads to the concept of possession, which comes, therefore, to mean "things that do not

[5] Theodore Flournoy, quoted by Dalbiez, Vol. I, p. 111.

[6] Dalbiez, Vol. II, p. 102.

[7] Carl Jung, *Contributions to Analytic Psychology*, trans. by H. G. and C. M. Baines (London, 1928), pp. 231-232.

actually belong to the ego, but ought to; things that are actually outside, but symbolically inside."

> What money and feces have in common is the fact that they are deindividualized possessions; and deindividualized means necessarily losable. Thus money, in the same way as feces previously, is estimated and watched over as a possession which is in constant danger of losing its ego quality.[8]

Thus the basis of this symbolic equation centers about childhood sensations that are taken as irreducible. The common universal, "deindividualized possession," is taken to emerge from the basic experience of the child's relation to feces.

Now the universal that both Daseinsanalyse and psychoanalysis seek is not the universal in the sense in which it is normally understood. Neither seeks the common properties of objects considered "apart from our experience of them." Considered "detachedly" as objects, that is, in reference merely to, say, Lockean primary and secondary properties, money and feces have no more in common than any two objects in the world chosen at random. Both Daseinsanalyse and psychoanalysis seek the properties of objects insofar as they are related to the self—"subjective" properties. The Freudian view maintains that these properties, or universals, arise from childhood sensations and urges, in this case the sensations of pleasureableness associated with putting things inside the mouth, or with the pleasurable sensations that arise during defecation. Daseinsanalyse, on the other hand, maintains that those sensations are not received in a vacuum but are experienced within some kind of meaning-matrix. In order, for example, for the child to experience the hoarding and retaining of feces as pleasurable in the first place, the child must be in some sense "empty" and must experience this "emptiness" as unpleasurable. In Binswanger's words:

> "Filling" is the a priori or transcendental tie that allows us to combine feces and money through a common denominator. It is only this that provides psychoanalysis with the empirical possibility of considering money-addiction as "originating" from the

[8] Otto Fenichel, *The Psychoanalytic Theory of Neurosis*, (New York, 1945), p. 281.

retention of feces. But by no means is the retaining of feces the "cause" of stinginess.[9]

The psychoanalyst who objects that pure physiological pleasure sensations in erogenous zones do not require any kind of anterior "preparation" to be experienced as pleasurable must then account for the fact that these various pleasure and unpleasure sensations somehow together form a personality, or a world-outlook—in our example, that of the anal-erotic. In "The Case of Ellen West" Binswanger observes:

> Existential analysis cannot admit that pleasure sensations during defecation, that is, the fixation of the anal zone as erogenous zone, can build up the picture of a hole-, grave-, or swamp-world, just as in general no world can be constructed from sensations and urges. That view belongs entirely to a former time, the time of Positivism. Rather, existential analysis is of the opinion that, conversely, only when a design of the world as hole-world is present, at a certain stage of childhood or with certain forms of "spiritual (*geistig*) decomposition," the being-a-hole, the being-filled and being-emptied, or the retaining is experienced as "pleasurable." This "Copernican switch" is basic to all existential analysis. Hence, anality in the psychoanalytical sense is only a segment of the total hole-world, the segment which is restricted to the bodily share in the *Eigenwelt*.[10]

The universals "filling-emptiness" are thus categories in a sense analogous to Kantian categories. They are transcendental categories in the sense that without them the experience in question could not emerge. In Binswanger's works, to speak of a transcendental category or of its products, the world-design, is to refer to a patient's matrix of possible experience that, in the sense of giving them meaning, creates the objects of experience as it encounters them. The similarity to Kant's Copernican Revolution is clear. The source of meaning and hence the source of pleasure and unpleasure, anxiety and realization are, in Binswanger's view, placed in the Dasein that, in a sense to be discussed later, "selects" what is pleasurable, meaningful, traumatic, and so forth *in that* the Dasein (and

[9] Binswanger, "The Existential Analysis School of Thought," *op. cit.*, p. 210.
[10] Binswanger, "The Case of Ellen West," in R. May *et al.* (eds.), *op. cit.*, p. 317.

not the body, physical sensations, reflexes, or such) *is* the context in which and over against which pleasure, anxiety, fear, *emerge*.

It is not that we are "philosophers before we are babies," but:

> This world-design did not manifest itself before the traumatic event occurred; it did only on the *occasion* of that event. Just as the a priori or transcendental forms of the human mind make experience only into what experience is, so the form of that world-design had first to produce the condition of the possibility for the ice-skating incident in order for it to be experienced as traumatic.[11]

Psychoanalytic theorists resolutely maintain that it is the primary sensations that are, ultimately, the symbolized. The common universal shared by the symbol and the symbolized thus can be looked upon, in psychoanalytic terms, as itself a symbol.

> . . . whereas ordinary symbolism links the objects represented, psycho-analytical symbolism links the representations themselves . . . the psycho-analyst only studies dereistic, objectless psychic products. He therefore regards representations as derived from one another according to a strict causal relationship. He will systematically call the derived representation the symbol, and the primary representation the symbolized.[12]

Thus, in Fenichel's example, "deindividualized possession," which we might think was the source of the symbolic equation of feces-money, itself is merely the psychoanalytic symbol of pleasure and unpleasure sensations in childhood. *The Existential A Priori* (*transcendental category*), *on the other hand, is the source of both sides of the equation and not a derivate or sublimation of one side.* The common universal, as psychoanalysis implies it, is no more than a theoretical expression of the sensational, instinctual basis of all symbolism. And, indeed, insofar as psychoanalysis seeks to ascertain the causal relation between the instinctual demands and sensations connected with defecation and the image of money as it appears in dreams or in neurotic symptomology, we cannot demand a common universal in the same way that we can demand it of a symbolic equation between two objects or representations in

11 Binswanger, "The Existential Analysis School of Thought," *op. cit.*, p. 205.
12 Dalbiez, Vol. II, p. 104.

the same genus. And yet when psychoanalysts attempt to explain why the appearance of a certain image in a dream is caused by, say, childhood trauma, they are not content to remain with purely inductive generalizations. They rather, as Fenichel does, seek a common universal. That is, according to psychoanalysis there exists a distinct symbolic method whereby certain images in, for example, the manifest content of dreams, are of invariably the same symbolic significance. We then find psychoanalytic literature referring to "objective" properties—such as the long shape that such things as sticks, snakes, or knives have in common with the phallus; the plasticity that softish materials such as clay or mud have in common with feces. In order, therefore, to justify its interpretation of symbols, psychoanalysis either (1) adopts the purely inductive method, which we saw yields no genuine common universals as the connecting link between the members of the symbolic equation and opens itself to the charge of dealing not with symbols but with effect-signs, or (2) claims certain objective properties, properties with primary reference to communal (objective), rather than individual "reality," as the connecting link or common universal in the symbolic equation. We will treat the first alternative presently; what now demands attention is the specific manner in which the Existential A Priori serves as this common universal.

We have already spoken of the Existential A Priori (transcendental category) as the meaning-matrix within which events are experienced and which, in that sense, is the condition of the possibility of experience, traumatic and otherwise. In "The Case of Ellen West," Binswanger writes:

> Existential analysis shows that in this case no one-sided meaning or symbolic relationship of one side of the equation to the other is before us, but that both sides, on the basis of belonging to the same significance in respect to the world, have a common meaning.[13]

What psychoanalysis takes as conditioning factors—instinct, childhood sensations, and so forth—are, for Daseinsanalyse, already representations of a basic world design. It is not that Daseinsanalyse wants to push back the causal chain, but rather that the causal chain itself, as described in scientific depth-analysis, must be viewed as a

[13] Binswanger, "The Case of Ellen West," *op. cit.*, p. 316.

whole, which whole has no privileged reference point in terms of which all else is to be explained. Such explanation in terms of a privileged reference point assumes a theory, and a theory assumes a world-outlook—in this case the world outlook of natural science. Daseinsanalyse cannot, therefore, use the past to account for the present; indeed the past of a patient exists in the present in that the world-design, within which a particular event in the past "conditioned" a present neurosis, *is* the patient. The present, therefore, or the "conscious," or the manifest content of dreams and the manifest verbal expressions all point to a unity or category(ies) that is basic to the patient's world. In other words, since a self cannot experience a "pure" event outside of a meaning-context,[14] even if that self be that of a child, it is that source of meaning-context that Daseinsanalyse seeks to ascertain. It does not look for the particular meanings that, say, the child gives to certain events and of which he may or may not be aware at the moment; Daseinsanalyse seeks, rather, the mode of being-in-the-world that can be said to govern those meanings. The Existential A Priori is not a Kantian category in the sense that it is the direct condition for the perception of objects, but only in the sense that it is the condition for the experiencing of meanings.

If Martin Heidegger's existentials represent the being of man, then the Existential A Priori, which represents the being of this particular man as he exists in his particular world, cannot be viewed as the *cause* of this meaning or that of this traumatic event or that pleasure-laden experience. Rather the Existential A Priori is the translation of the "empty" ontological formulas of Heidegger into a formula capable of receiving content. The content of such a formula are meanings—"mother loves me," "I hate brother," "I fear father," and so forth. Thus we term the Existential A Priori a *meaning-matrix*. Whether there be an unconscious mind or not, that which was repressed into that "unconscious" was first experienced; and if it was at all experienced, it formed and forms part of the world of the patient as he experiences his world.

I hasten to add that Binswanger never speaks of a self, but of a Dasein. The term Dasein refers to a being whose essence is to be-in-the-world. Meanings and experiences that are the subject matter of psychoanalysis are conceived by psychoanalysis as, for example,

14 Binswanger, *Vorträge*, Vol. II, p. 292.

an ego confronted by the world or by demands or commands, or instinctual urges being thwarted by external conditions. But the Dasein of which Binswanger writes is the Dasein as already-in-the-world. This Dasein is thus the background upon which the "self" in fact emerges and is always emerging. It may be termed the *Gestalt* within which the self differentiates itself from its world while at the same time being in its world. Just as the Kantian categories are those within which articulated and differentiated knowledge of the world and the phenomenal self arise, so the Existential A Priori of a patient is the ground of those experiences and meanings that psychoanalysis links causally.

True to the Husserlian spirit, Daseinsanalyse limits itself to "the analysis of what is actually present, i.e., immanent, in consciousness." [15] Like Edmund Husserl too, Binswanger is careful to distinguish the phenomenological method of Daseinsanalyse from psychological description. According to Husserl, the psychologically oriented phenomenologist, however much he limits himself to immanent conscious acts always views these acts as actual processes that he cannot conceive of apart from a real human being (*einem realen Naturgeschöpf*). The pure phenomenologist, on the other hand, brackets out any judgments, however implicit, as to the reality of the self or acts of that self. On this point Binswanger stands somewhere between the pure phenomenologist and the descriptive psychologist. The a priori structures that Daseinsanalyse seeks serve in the world of the patient as the transcendental (in the Kantian sense) condition of total experience, of concrete being-in-the-world.

How does Binswanger bridge the gap between the Husserlian pure eidetic structures of consciousness and "categories" that condition the possibility of experience, the Existential A Priori that seems, in a word, to be a *universal with power?* As we have seen, Binswanger is not content to call the transcendental category of a patient nothing other than a generalization, however pure, as to the theme of the patient's history and experience. Binswanger writes:

> Everything that makes the world significant is submitted to the *rule* of that one category which alone supports her "world" and being.[16] (Emphasis added.)

[15] Binswanger, *Vorträge*, Vol. I, p. 25.
[16] Binswanger, "The Existential Analysis School of Thought," *op. cit.*, p. 203.

. . . so the form of that world-design had first to *produce* the condition of the possibility (of the incident) . . . in order for it to be experienced as traumatic.[17] (Emphasis added.)

What is involved here are not chance combinations, but unshakable a priori existential structures.[18]

In "The Case of Lola Voss":

But why do just garments—clothes, underwear, shoes, hats. play so prominent a role in Lola's case? To answer this question we would have to conduct a biographical investigation. . . . But the question of how it is possible that garments *can* play so prominent a part is, indeed, a problem for existential analysis.[19]

Existential analysis is not interested simply in facts pertaining to linguistic science, that in metaphor "the meaning of a word is transferred from one particular region to another," but rather in the *existential grounds of the possibility of such a transferring.*[20]

The above passages clearly indicate that the a priori existential structures (which I have called the Existential A Prioris) represent not only essences or universals that are apprehended phenomenologically, but also effective, conditioning, determining categories. To understand more specifically in what sense the Existential A Priori is a universal with power is also to understand the manner in which Daseinsanalyse approaches the "vertical dimension" of symbolic equations.

Special care must be exercised to prevent the notion of causal efficacy from determining our thinking in seeking the relationship between the Existential A Priori and the world as it is experienced by the patient. The Existential A Priori without a corresponding world-design and hence without a corresponding world is, for Binswanger, unthinkable, contradicting, as it would, the very notion of *transcendental* category. Just as it makes no sense to speak of the Kantian categories of the Understanding as "existing" previous to knowledge of the world, so it makes no sense to speak of

17 *Ibid.*, p. 205.
18 Binswanger, *Vorträge*, Vol. II, p. 289.
19 Binswanger, "The Case of Lola Voss," p. 300 of this volume.
20 Binswanger, *Vorträge*, Vol. II, p. 290.

Binswanger's Existential A Priori as "being there" previous to experience. Like the Kantian categories, the definition of the Existential A Priori is exhausted in an account of its functioning and its functioning is only theoretically separable from its intended objects. For example, Binswanger describes a case in which a young girl at the age of five suffered an attack of anxiety and fainting when her heel separated from her shoe after being stuck in her ice skate. His analysis of the case revealed that "What serves as a clue to the world-design of our little patient is the category of continuity. . . . Everything that makes the world significant is submitted to the rule of that one category." [21] Binswanger does not mean to say that the category of continuity "working through her" somehow *caused* the anxiety and fainting, an expression that would be almost senseless in any context. He does mean, I think, that the being-in-the-world of this patient is so constricted that all her perceptions and experiences in order to be assimilated, that is, in order to be perceptions and experiences, must satisfy a certain criterion. The criterion in this case is best expressed, for Binswanger, by the term "continuity."

To say that the being-in-the-world of this Dasein is restricted to the category of continuity-discontinuity is to say that all perception and experience of the individual is selective in a certain way. It is also, and more fundamentally, to say that the world of the individual is grounded in this category. Thus the category of continuity-discontinuity is that which expresses the individual's self-determination within time, space, the *Mitwelt* and the *Eigenwelt*.

Binswanger as phenomenologist holds, with Hegel, that

> Individuality is what its world, in the sense of its own world, is. Individuality itself is the cycle of its own action, in which it has presented and established itself as reality, and is simply and solely a unity of what is given and what is constructed—a unity whose aspects do not fall apart, as in the idea of psychological law, into a world given *per se* and an individuality existing for itself.[22]

As Daseinsanalytiker, he holds with Heidegger that "world" means a "whole of significance." [23] And as a "Kantian":

[21] Binswanger "The Existential Analysis School of Thought," *op. cit.*, p. 203.
[22] Georg Hegel, *The Phenomenology of Mind*, trans. by J. B. Baillie (London, 1949), p. 336.
[23] Martin Heidegger, *Sein und Zeit* (Tübingen, 1953), p. 151.

Its task is to single out the uniqueness of the a priori *existential structure* which *makes possible* all the unique phenomena which we clinically diagnose as schizophrenic *symptoms* and as schizophrenic *psychosis* in general.[24]

The "power" of the Existential A Priori lies in the Dasein itself as an actually existing being. The existentially a priori structure that Binswanger seeks in the Daseinsanalyse of a particular case is: the possible modes of being of the Dasein, the existentials of Heidegger, become actual. This sum total of an actual manifestation of the ontologically a priori characteristics of the Dasein is the Existential A Priori of a particular individual. The Dasein is not the individual; it is the background upon which the individual emerges. When Binswanger, therefore, maintains that, for example, continuity is the transcendental category of a particular individual, although he may have arrived at his insight phenomenologically, he is giving us transcendental knowledge about this particular individual. Each case, therefore, is, in a sense, a "transcendental deduction" whereby the possibility of experience of a particular individual is accounted for. It is equally correct to say not only that the world of the individual is grounded in his Existential A Priori, but also that the individual himself is so grounded. We are here thrown back on more "strictly" "existentialist" doctrine, a point that will be treated later. For now, let us simply note that we are faced with an *act* of the Dasein standing behind the very possibility of individual and world, something that may possibly be regarded as a Kierkegaardian choosing of oneself or failure to choose oneself and something that also must be carefully compared with the Sartrean original project. These are points that must be reserved for a later chapter.

In seeking to understanding the Existential A Priori as a "universal with power" we have found that this power is located not in a universal, nor in the self, but in the Dasein. Expressible as a particular kind of universal, a transcendental category, the Existential A Priori points not to an idea, or rule, but to an existence, an existence that is transcendentally prior to the self/not-self distinction in experience. Representing, as it does, the concrete manifestation of Care, it must be equally articulable in each possible

24 Binswanger, *Schizophrenie*, p. 464.

aspect of the world of the Dasein. Continuity, for example, is equally understandable and applicable in reference to time (continuity of event vs. the sudden and unexpected), space (contiguity), the *Mitwelt* (ties, e.g., oedipal ties, continuity of relationships), the *Eigenwelt* ("inner" continuity, continuity of feelings, affections). For an "anal-erotic" whose Existential A Priori may be that of filling-emptiness, we have time being filled up or spent: spatial filling in the containment of hands or money-bags, or the filling of the body in eating, as with Ellen West; in the *Mitwelt* the openness or lack of it to other people; in the *Eigenwelt*, the problem again of eating or taking in to oneself.

This Existential A Priori is thus truly the "common universal" —it is the meaning-matrix within which both members of the symbolic equation take on relevance for the individual. How, then, does Daseinsanalyse interpret symbols and dreams? In fact, it does not "interpret" the symbols, but, rather, stakes out the circle for clinical, scientific interpretation (reduction):

> That the existential-analytic interpretation, however, can stake out the circle for what may be interpreted psychoanalytically in the dream becomes apparent when we see how psychoanalysis would regard this dream. The psychoanalytic interpretations then reveal themselves to be special [Freudian] symbol-interpretations on the ground of fundamental existential-analytical understanding.[25]

> It is well known that in dreams flying and falling often are manifested as hovering and sinking of our own bodily form. These dreams of flying and falling are sometimes thought to be connected with the bodily condition, especially breathing, in which case we are dealing with the so-called body-stimuli dreams; sometimes with erotic moods or purely sexual wishes. Both are possible and we do not wish to dispute either assumption, since in our case it is a matter of uncovering an a priori structure of which the body-stimuli [and body schema in general] as well as the erotic-sexual themes are special secondary fillings.[26]

The common universal that psychoanalysis uncovers is of a quite different order. In the first place it is usually a universal that

[25] Binswanger, "The Case of Ellen West," *op. cit.*, p. 323.
[26] Binswanger, p. 228 of this volume.

has primary reference to only one area of human existence. When, for example, a knife is said to be the symbol for phallus, the psychoanalyst is too often content to justify this interpretation *theoretically* simply by calling attention to similarity of shape. In such a case, of course, he must seek evidence as to why this particular patient used the knife and not, say, a building or a snake, as the phallic symbol. As the case progresses further and his knowledge of the patient grows deeper, he may come to the conclusion that the knife is a symbol of phallus because it is a tool of aggression. Aggression, however, as it is usually understood (in "communal reality"), means disposition to injure another and therefore refers primarily to only one mode of being of the Dasein, being-with-others, and, hence, to only one aspect of the total world of the individual, the *Mitwelt*. One would be hard put to understand aggression as the constitutive determination of, say, a man's relation to his future or his relation to himself as exemplified in his attitude toward death. And certainly there seems no obvious way of expressing aggression in temporal or spatial terms without somehow bringing in notions derived from the concept of being-with-others. The full "meaning" of a symbol is thus attenuated, a priori, by limiting its context to only one aspect of the patient's world.

A second and at least equally important question concerns the meaning of these psychoanalytically ascertained common universals: the question, namely, as to *their* meaning in the world of the patient. The phenomenologist will ask, for example, what does "aggression" mean in the world of this individual? His answer will not consist in relating what is ordinarily taken as aggressive behavior to a postulated striving that is checked, sublimated, or diverted by an equally postulated subconscious dynamism. For the phenomenologist "to injure another" is not ultimately reducible to a transindividualistic instinct, such as a "death-instinct." Rather, "injury to another" will reveal its *sense* only in connection with the Existential A Priori of the individual. In the case above, for example, where the Existential A Priori was the universal continuity-discontinuity, injury to another might be a way of warding off a threatening break in the continuity, rather than a sublimated sexual or death wish. Furthermore, what constitutes "injury to another" for an individual may vary. The "psychotic" who is wrecking the authority of hospital officials by tying his shoelaces a certain way is being aggressive just as much as the maniac who hurls objects at nurses.

Universals such as "aggression," "possession," and "submission" are either reduced in psychoanalytic theory to the natural scientific frame and absorbed into the system of explanation, in which case they are no longer the common universals that we seek; or they dissolve into variables that themselves need reference to another universal in order to understand their sense. The Existential A Priori may be viewed as the third thing relating the common universal, say aggression, with the two objects subsumed under aggression (e.g., phallus and knife). Phallus and knife are symbols of aggression insofar as they are tools for aggression. But the reality of which they are a part is the world-design of the patient and the clue to this world-design lies in the uncovering of the Existential A Priori. Aggression itself must be understood in the context of a world-design governed by the Existential A Priori.

Once this Existential A Priori is uncovered, the "circle is staked out" for reductive, systematic interpretation and diagnosis. That is, once the meaning-matrix of the individual, that which is the ground of his experiencing the world, is laid forth, the particular manner in which this matrix has been "filled" can be explained. Overly strong mother ties in childhood, for example, may be said to be the *cause* of certain anxiety attacks in later life only after that which first makes possible the overly strong ties is revealed. The accent here, it must be stressed, is not in the past. The Existential A Priori is that which *makes* possible these overly strong mother ties, not that which *made* it possible. Psychoanalysis will speak of a sequence of experiences: incest wishes, castration-anxiety, leading to strong oedipal ties, leading later to anxiety, and so forth. Daseinsanalyse, on the other hand, speaks of an *experience of sequence:* the entire causal chain of psychoanalysis is possible only by virtue of this Existential A Priori.

REVERSIBILITY / Turning now to the second aspect of psychoanalytical symbolism, namely the irreversibility of symbolic equations, one need not look further than the nature of scientific method itself as applied in psychoanalysis for its *raison d'être*. The notions of reducible and irreducible as discussed in the previous chapter would lead us to expect such an irreversibility. The repressed, the instincts, the primal urges, constitute the most "real," the irreducible; while the conscious representation, the symbol, is that which is to be reduced, explained, interpreted. We find in all cases of psychoanalytic interpretation and explanation that what we have delineated as the lesser circle of psychoanalysis serves as the point beyond which explanation does not go. Daseinsanalyse, on the other hand, cannot accept such a unidirectional reference. What psychoanalysis calls the symbol is for Daseinsanalyse, just as primary a reality as the "repressed" or symbolized. The full meaning of the symbol (the manifest dream and verbal structures) in the world of the individual determines the meaning of the symbolized, not merely to the analyst in his attempts to interpret the symbol, but for the individual himself.

If knife is said to be symbol of phallus, understanding of the patient falls short if it is not further asked: what does the phallus mean to the individual? The full phenomenal meaning of the knife in the world of the patient must be laid forth before the analyst can understand what phallus means to the patient. In psychoanalysis, however, the question is: what does the knife mean? And the answer, the phallus, presupposes that all meaning-direction emanates from a biological need. This ignores the possibility that these biological needs are themselves enmeshed in a larger meaning-matrix and, therefore, themselves point to something beyond themselves. It also, if the analyst is not careful, presupposes a *fixed* notion of what phallus means to any individual.

For Daseinsanalyse, symbol and symbolized modify each other. The following long selection from Boss's work on dream analysis exemplifies an important aspect of the attitude of Daseinsanalyse toward symbols:

Freud thought he had found an unequivocal proof for this conception [of dream symbolism] in Schroetter's experiment. Schroetter [1912] had ordered his hypnotized subjects to dream of coarse sexual processes during their subsequent hypnotic sleep. In the dreams all those things which Freud designates as sexual symbols appeared in the relevant places. Once, for instance, a woman was ordered during hypnosis to dream of homosexual relations with a girl-friend. In the dream she met this girl-friend carrying a suitcase with the label "For Ladies Only." From this Schroetter and

Freud concluded that the suitcase could only be a symbolic representation of the girl-friend's genitals.

However, such a conclusion is very flimsy since it neither explains the full meaning of sexual intercourse nor all the connotations of a suit-case in the actual life of the dreamer. What if sexual intercourse meant more to her than the mere contact of sexual organs—if, for instance, we agree with Herbert Silberer and Jung, who under certain conditions see in sexual intercourse a symbol of interconnecting and bridging the most different things, even such that do not belong to the sexual sphere at all? Who would indeed, deny that healthy sexual activity is not a solitary affair, but implies the coming together of two people bound by love; that this, in fact, is of its very essence? Thus the hypnotist by his suggestion of homosexual intercourse had prepared his experimental subject for a loving human relationship, even though he had limited it to a female. Possibly for this reason in the dream not only the "symbolic genitals" but an entire person appeared who was nothing else but this very girl-friend and a suit-case. Had the luggage only symbolized her genitals, why then was it a *suit-case* and not, for instance, an evening bag, which would surely have belonged more clearly to an erotic sphere? What inherent connection is there between travelling, which is unmistakably indicated in this dream, and female genitals? Not the slightest. Travelling, however, can bring people closer together and can also separate them. Surely this large suit-case was much more likely to indicate the fact that it contained many other things besides those merely relating to the genital organs: objects of everyday life, perhaps even books, valuable jewellery, and some family keepsakes. These things would not be so closely related to the girl-friend's genitals as to her entire personal history, thoughts and feelings.[27]

That is, that which determines the attitude of the patient toward the suitcase is the same as that which determines the attitude toward sexual intercourse. It is not simply that the meaning of sexual intercourse is expressed in selecting the suitcase as the symbol, but also that sexual intercourse symbolizes a meaning-context that

[27] Medard Boss, *The Analysis of Dreams*, trans. by Arnold J. Pomerans (New York, 1958), pp. 91-92.

can only be understood by a full phenomenological examination of the significance of suitcase to the patient.

Jones, like Flournoy, writes that lightning was first conceived as divine semen,[28] that the sun is first conceived as a mighty eye[29]— all in accordance with the psychoanalytic presupposition that "All symbols represent ideas of the self and the immediate blood relatives or of the phenomena of birth, love, and death." [30] What he and other psychoanalytic theorists fail to consider with due care is the possibility that the notion of what, say, semen, is, is as much derived from the relation of the primitive to lightning. The primitive mind does not separate the object "semen" and unconsciously relate his feelings to this object with a new separate object "lightning." Rather, what, for us who are examining the process, is a reciprocal modification takes place wherein the primitive's relation to lightning conditions his relation to semen as well as vice versa. The psychoanalyst may then raise the question as to why the primitive chose lightning from among all the natural phenomena as relating to semen. But we may justly return the question as to why he chose semen from among all "bodily" phenomena to relate to lightning.

And so, we may well admit that all symbols refer to the self, immediate blood relatives, love, death, and birth—but we must add that the conception of these is determined as much by the symbols as the symbols are determined by the primitive mind's conception of them.

Being an explanatory system, psychoanalysis cannot "go this far," or, cannot "rest content" with such a notion of reciprocal modification. It seeks an irreducible, a basic reality in terms of which other phenomena are to be explained. This basic reality, or lesser circle, we have seen to be the biological conception of instinct. In order to explain or interpret symbols, psychoanalysis seeks to reduce the symbols to instinctual components and claims that these symbols are symbolic *of* these instinctual bases of psychic life. We have already observed that the sense in which, for psychoanalysis, these symbols are symbolic of the instinctual bases is a dubious one. The question as to the common universal, or

---

[28] Ernest Jones, *Papers on Psychoanalysis* (New York, 1913), pp. 134-135.
[29] *Ibid.*, p. 134.
[30] *Ibid.*, p. 102.

ground of similarity between the symbol and the symbolized, as I have tried to show, is not adequately handled by psychoanalytic theory. We must therefore ask if there is not another sense in which the term "symbol" is being used by psychoanalysis, a sense that does not have necessary or primary reference to the kind and degree of similarity between the symbol and the symbolized. This brings us to our third point, the question as to whether psychoanalysis deals with symbols or with effect-signs.

SIGN AND SYMBOL / Jones tells us that there is a "strict sense" in which psychoanalysis employs the term "symbol." [31] According to him, the characteristics of true symbols are (1) representation of unconscious material, (2) constant meaning, (3) independence of individual conditioning factors, (4) evolutionary basis, (5) linguistic connections, and (6) phylogenetic parallels. Of these six characteristics, Jones lists the first as "perhaps the characteristic that most sharply distinguishes true symbolism from other processes to which the name is often applied." [32] And the key point that Jones makes in delineating representation of unconscious material is that "the affect investing the concept [the symbol] is in a state of repression." [33] To be noted here is the fact that Jones's main stress falls not on considerations as to the similarity between symbol and symbolized, or on the power of the symbol to express the symbolized, but rather on the cause-effect relation between symbolized and symbol. The principle standard, in short, that, for Jones, defines the true symbol allows that the relationship between the symbolized and the symbol be external and even adventitious to the essential, *sui generis* structure of the symbolized. Jones's standard is one of efficient causality in which the symbol refers to the symbolized, but does not necessarily lead to a conception of it.

It appears, then, that the "strict sense" in which Jones uses the term "symbol" is the sense usually attached to the term "sign," or, to be more precise, "effect-sign." Ferenczi writes:

> . . . it is more prudent not to assume that the conditions under which symbols arise are identical with those for analogy-forma-

[31] *Ibid.*, pp. 87-142.
[32] *Ibid.*, p. 97.
[33] *Ibid.*, p. 97.

tion in general, but to presuppose for this specific kind of analogy-formation specific conditions or origin, and to search for these.[34]

It may be remarked that in any endavor to seek out the essential structures of intrapsychic symbolism, the search for some type of causality must be naturally of primary importance. But clearly this is so only where meaning to an individual is conceived of as subsequent to motivation. If we limited ourselves only to consciousness, such a proposition would be close to nonsense—motivation and meaning being in consciousness inextricably interwoven. However, as soon as we posit such a thing as unconscious motivation, it is possible to speak of motives that occur *before* meaning is given to certain representations. In fact it is *only* when we posit some kind of unconscious psychic process that we can meaningfully ask about an individual's motives for *perceiving* or relating himself to an image or event in a certain way. If we limit ourselves to consciousness, then the way in which an individual manifestly perceives or understands an object, image, or event exhausts all doubt as to his motives. Even the obsessive-neurotic has a phenomenal field of meaning for his "irrational" acts or fears. For consciousness, the perceived object itself lends us the "motivation" for perceiving it in the way we do. Snakes are fearful because they are poisonous; I love this woman because she is beautiful, and so forth.[35] A full phenomenological exfoliation (utilizing, among other things, the method of free-association) of my feeling and understanding of snakes may reveal tie-ins with such things as sex, tie-ins of which I was not thetically aware. But this does not necessarily imply that my fear of snakes is motivated or caused by that which is so revealed. It may be that my particular fear of snakes is representative of a larger fear that profoundly defines my character (or existence). And both the fear of snakes and the associated fears and desires may be said to be symbolic of the larger fear. We might say then that snake is for me a symbol, or more accurately, that my fear of snakes is a symbol.

Insofar, however, as we seek to *explain* certain perceptions, emotions, images, rather than "merely" lay forth their complete

[34] Ferenczi, Vol. I, p. 278.
[35] Compare D. Snygg and A. W. Combs, "The Phenomenological Approach and the Problem of 'Unconscious' Behavior," *Journal of Abnormal and Social Psychology*, Vol. 45 (1950), pp. 532-538.

meaning within consciousness, the laws that govern the relation of symbol to symbolized cannot lie within the conscious structure of the meaning of an image as it presents itself to the individual—that is, *he* cannot "really" explain his fear of snakes, he can offer only "rationalizations." The explanatory laws cannot even be of the same kind as those that the individual is aware of as governing the association of images and objects. For the explanation lies not in the full elaboration of the meaning-phenomena as they are experienced, but in the reduction to elements and laws that are their necessary condition. Explanation cannot be satisfied with a quantitative extension of those components that make up the lived and conscious structure of meaning-phenomena, for such an elaboration would, theoretically, place the source of explanation in the source of the meaning-phenomena, the individual. Since it is just this that psychoanalysis, a priori, cannot allow without its own intervention, the totality of meaning-phenomena themselves are delimited, and a qualitatively different ground of their being is established. The cause-effect relation adequately satisfies this criterion of explanation. The image and its meaning to an individual are seen as caused by a force or "affect" of which the individual is unaware. Nothing in the phenomenological content of the meaning-phenomena or their structural laws (in the case of symbols, those laws being either similarity between symbol and symbolized, power of expression) points to this cause; it is "unconscious."

> . . . one was formerly inclined to believe that things are confounded because they are similar; nowadays we know that a thing is confounded with another only because certain motives for this are present; similarity merely provides the opportunity for these motives to function.[36]

Before proceeding further in this vein, it is advisable briefly to sketch in the context of this discussion a distinction between the terms "sign" and "symbol." It is important to bear in mind that we are moving here intrapsychically—both symbol and symbolized, sign and signified being "located within" the psyche, or, in Daseins-analytic terms, within the *Eigenwelt*. In science, literature, art, religion, mathematics, both symbol and symbolized are, at least os-

[36] Ferenczi, Vol. I, p. 281.

tensibly, external to the individual to whom they are present. Perhaps in art or religion a symbol may at times be subjective and personal, but the symbolized at all times extends beyond the borders of what the individual considers himself. In psychology, however, the symbolized must of necessity be viewed as part of the self or "within" the psyche.

Now, as to the distinction between sign and symbol, we recognize in literature the distinction between "mere" allegory and symbolism. Allegory is frequently distinguished from symbolism by the arbitrariness of its representations; symbols, on the other hand, are known by their epitomization of and participation in the reality of which they are a symbol. Allegory demands of the reader that he know beforehand what meaning is being represented; symbolism, ideally, carries its meaning in itself. Allegory is substitution, symbolism expression. The structure of the symbol, taken in itself, is, essentially, the structure of the symbolized. In religion, we recognize the difference between the seer's reading of the entrails of a bird and a natural phenomenon such as thunder and lightning as a symbol of the Deity. In such a case the seer reads *signs* that do not carry on their face the meaning that he attributes to them, whereas thunder and lightning are a symbol of, say, power, because of their immediate phenomenal effects—might we not even say that the notion of power springs from just such things as thunder and lightning? In mathematics we may say "let P stand for pressure, V for volume, T for temperature of an ideal gas." P, V, and T are signs or arbitrary designations. But the *equation* expressing the fact that V is directly proportional to T and inversely proportional to P, simply because it expresses an observable factual truth, is a symbol.

Although it might be argued that the sign-symbol distinction as implied above is relative to the degree of knowledge of the confronted individual and that what for one is a sign for another is a symbol, the point at hand is that such a distinction in fact is to be made no matter where, in particular cases, one chooses to draw the line. All of the above considerations as to literature, religion, and science have in common that the reference of both signs and symbols is to something extrapersonal, something other than the confronted individual. The difference between sign and symbol, expressed phenomenologically, is that whereas the symbol expresses and partakes of that of which it is a symbol, the sign refers to that which is qualitatively different from it—and, this being the case, it therefore does not and cannot express the signified.

We therefore reach the conclusion that, *phenomenologically, experientially, an intrapsychic sign is an impossibility*. That is, one cannot *experience* something as a sign of an inner state or emotion. There is no sense to be made of inward referring of one state or emotion to another without that state in some respect resembling and expressing the other. If the "signified" is unknown (or "un-conscious"), it also makes no sense phenomenologically to speak of an "inner sign," since, as pointed out above, the signified must be known or suspected for a sign to be at all possible. My fear of harmless kittens, which I cannot justify as I would a fear of poison-ous snakes, insofar as I see it as referring to a larger fear, is, by virtue of similarity, a symbolic expression of that larger fear. The psychoanalyst may tell me that it is a "symbol" of a need for affec-tion, but I cannot experience it as such without altering the very nature of my emotion of fear.

The point here is that the essence of a sign, as distinguished from a symbol, does not involve the meaning structure of the signified, but only refers to the signified. The sign serves either as a substitute or pointer in relation to the signified. In all cases the function of the sign is replaced or overridden by the presence of the signified. In this sense, the sign is a "stepping stone" to the sig-nified. Speaking phenomenologically, we posit the presence of the emotion, meaning, or object that is intrapsychically represented—this presence as *experienced* by the individual. There can be no experience of an intrapsychic sign because that which is to be signi-fied is always already present.

The following example might be adduced as an objection: I am climbing the stairs of a strange house and before I enter one of the rooms I note that my palms are perspiring, my heart is beat-ing faster, my throat is dry. Are these not signs of an intrapsychic phenomenon—fear? We need not enter the complexities of the James-Lange theory of emotions to dispose of this objection. The condition of my palms, heartbeat, and throat are not intrapsychic phenomena—for the way the objection is phrased implies a state where the body is being observed as other than the "mind." In the experiencing of fear, we do not experience signs of fear, signs that are of qualitatively a different order than what they signify. Let me, however, entering this same house, hear a rustling at the top of the stairs, and I fear a ghost, a bandit, and so forth. The fear of a ghost in this case represents a larger, more general fear of this strange house—but it expresses it, it partakes of the reality that it represents; it *symbolizes* it.

Returning now to the main stream of the discussion, we recall that "the Freudian symbol is essentially and by definition an effect of what it symbolizes." [37] We also recall that the cause-effect relationship adequately fulfills the criteria of an explanatory system where the phenomenal, experienced meaning contents must be reduced to something qualitatively different, in the case of psychoanalysis this something being a repressed instinctual affect. From the distinction drawn above of the difference between a sign and a symbol, namely that the sign is qualitatively different from the signified, we see the necessity of psychoanalysis' dealing mainly with effect-signs, rather than symbols insofar as it explains the patient's world. What is phenomenologically a symbol is scientifically a sign.

I have tried to indicate the phenomenological impossibility of intrapsychic signs, but this does not imply their scientific impossibility. From the point of view of an explanatory system, an intrapsychic sign is perfectly feasible—as long as it is not claimed that the sign is experienced as such. We understand the term "intrapsychic sign" as referring to the instance where both sign and signified lie "within" the self. There must, therefore, be an aspect or part of the self that is in principle unexperienceable—the unconscious—wherein the signified is to be found.

[37] Dalbiez, Vol. II, p. 102.

IV

The Unconscious

In the preceding chapter I have shown how the natural-scientific, explanatory nature of psychoanalysis precludes it from ascertaining the meaning to the individual of symbols, but, rather converts the experienced symbols into effect signs. This meaning or "common universal" we have seen was to be found in the Existential A Priori or fundamental meaning-structure that is the transcendental condition of the emergence of self and its "opposed" world together with that world's *particular, specific* meanings. I have further shown that the psychoanalytic notion of intrapsychic sign is possible only on the supposition that a part of the psyche is in principle unexperiencable—unconscious. In Chapter II it was pointed out how psychoanalysis, in order to be an *adequate* explanatory, scientific system whose object was the self or psyche that Cartesian science ruled out of the field of investigation, was led to posit unconsciousness as the essence of consciousness. In this chapter I shall indicate how the notion of the unconscious, although necessary scientifically is unacceptable from Binswanger's point of view and how the Existential A Priori is the phenomenological ground of that which, from the point of view of natural science, refers to an unconscious mind.

We have already noted that the concept of the unconscious is one of the main presuppositions of what has been called the greater circle of the science of psychoanalysis. That is, the notion of the unconscious is a theoretical construct that serves to unify and therefore explain certain psychic phenomena.

> All these conscious acts [parapraxes, dreams, etc.] remain disconnected and unintelligible if we are determined to hold fast to the claim that every single mental act performed within us must be

consciously experienced; on the other hand, they fall into a demonstrable connection if we interpolate the unconscious acts that we infer. A gain in meaning and connection, however, is a perfectly justifiable motive, one which may well carry us beyond the limitations of direct experience.[1]

Most clinical descriptions found in Freud employ the inferential construct of the *unconscious*. Freud considers the assumption of unconsciousness as necessary because the data of consciousness are "exceedingly defective." [2]

As a scientific system of explanation, psychoanalysis represents a specification of the lesser circle of science in general, the dictate to remove consciousness from the field of investigation and its corresponding "substantialization," the notion of pure corporeality. I have indicated how this leads to an approach to psychic phenomena exemplified in Freud's notion of psychic apparatus. The concept of instinct, borrowed from biology, specifies the main force of this psychic apparatus and thereby serves as the lesser circle or data-constituting concept of the system as a whole. Behavior, emotions, thoughts are all approached and initially *seen* as "the transformation of certain instinctual desires." [3] The notion of the unconscious serves the function of explaining how instincts act where they are not perceived as acting. The unconscious provides a way of ascertaining efficient causality among phenomena that, at face value, do not exhibit this causality. Not only are the gaps in the sequence of conscious acts[4] thus patched according to a preconceived notion of how the psyche ought to work,* but also the

---

[1] Sigmund Freud, "The Unconscious," trans. by Cecil M. Baines, in *Collected Papers* (New York, 1959), Vol. IV, p. 99.

[2] Else Frenkel-Brunswik, "Psychoanalytic Concepts and Theories," in Morton Levitt (ed.), *Readings in Psychoanalytic Psychology* (New York, 1959), p. 31.

[3] A. C. MacIntyre, *The Unconscious* (London, 1958), p. 27.

[4] Medard Boss, *Psychoanalyse und Daseinsanalyse* (Bern, 1957), p. 21.

* "William James dealt faithfully in *The Principles of Psychology* with those who wish to postulate an unconscious mind on account of such occurrences as temporary forgetfulness or the fact that the solution to a problem may spring to mind effortlessly some time after our preliminary brooding on the problem had been abandoned for want of success. For it may be that this is just how things happen in consciousness: happenings such as these only seem to stand in need of explanation if we are able to assume that we ought to have expected them to happen otherwise. And we have no inherent right to make this assumption." MacIntyre, p. 7.

"correlation of earlier . . . experiences with such symptoms [as well as parapraxes, dreams, etc.] [5] is explained.

It appears, then, as if the concept of the unconscious functions in a manner similar to the way the concept of the electron functions in physics. Freud, however, claims more for the unconscious than the physicist claims for the electron. The physicist does not assert the existence of the electron; he merely uses the hypothesis of the electron to explain. But Freud also wants to maintain that the unconscious exists, and it is therefore incumbent upon him to produce evidence that it is a real existent.[6] Since, however, the unconscious is *ex hypothesi* unobservable, what possible scientific evidence of its existence could be forthcoming?[7] The difficulties inherent in treating the unconscious as though it were a real existent lead most psychoanalytic writers to stress that what are being talked about are processes, not a discrete thing—processes that are not wholly separable from conscious processes (secondary processes).

> Freud does *not* conceive of an "unconscious mind" as a separate, unchangeable entity somehow inhabiting our mortal flesh . . . intricate patterns may be formed at the unconscious level which function to some extent as a dynamic unit and which combine in a variety of ways with the secondary processes as they take shape during the course of life . . . the unconscious is a process—or better, processes. . . . "The unconscious" must not be considered to imply a directly separable entity.[8]

And yet, even if the unconscious be viewed as process, the difficulty remains as to its status: are the processes "merely" theoretical constructs, or are they as real as the processes for which they serve as an explanatory basis? There is no doubt that the unconscious (be it a process or a thing) is often viewed by psychoanalysis as a real existent—but then only when it has supposedly become *observable*.

> Of course, such "unconscious dispositions toward affects" are not theoretical constructions but may be observed clinically in the

[5] MacIntyre, p. 24.
[6] *Ibid.*, p. 71.
[7] *Loc. cit.*
[8] Ruth L. Munroe, *Schools of Psychoanalytic Thought* (New York, 1955), pp. 35-37.

[86]

same way that unconscious ideas may be observed: they, too, develop derivatives, betray themselves in dreams, in symptoms, and in other substitute formations.[9]

Clearly, however, what is observed in such a case is not the unconscious as such but only those things for which the unconscious was supposed to serve as an explanatory basis. Indeed the same author, Fenichel, admits earlier that

. . . the existence of the unconscious is an assumption that forced itself upon psychoanalytic research when it sought a scientific explanation and a comprehension of conscious phenomena.[10]

This ambiguity as to the "real existence" of the unconscious must, I think, be resolved by saying that what is most basic (most "real") for psychoanalysis is the biological nature of man, his instincts, and that the assumption of an unconscious is necessary to explain the relation between conscious acts that are not *apparently* instinctual and the instincts themselves. In a word, the notion of instinct constitutes psychoanalysis' particular lesser circle, and the notion of the unconscious is a presupposition of the greater circle.

Nevertheless it may be objected that the distinction drawn above between the psychoanalyst and the physicist is not legitimate, that the physicist does not claim that the electron does not exist, and is only and no more than a theoretical construct. That is, it may be objected that the hypothesis of the electron is the *correct* hypothesis and that therefore the electron exists—that, namely, existence can be inferred. I reply that the physicist, if he concludes to the existence of the electron, does so because of what the hypothesis of the electron explains, whereas the psychoanalyst seems often to conclude to the existence and reality of phenomena because of the assumed existence of the unconscious. However, it may well be that this is an instance of the above-mentioned "good" circularity of a science, and similar instances may be cited from physics in support of the psychoanalyst; and it may also be that each science, as it grows, passes through phases, one being the alteration of its field of investigation under the aegis of its theoretical constructs.

[9] Otto Fenichel, *The Psychoanalytic Theory of Neurosis* (New York, 1945), p. 17.
[10] *Ibid.*, p. 7.

Binswanger's criticism of the notion of the unconscious is only rarely explicit, and even then it is comprised only of hints and fragments. He is content, for the most part, to assume that his criticism of the reductive, explanatory nature of psychoanalysis as a whole implies his criticism of the more specific aspects of psychoanalytic theory.* And yet, his whole position is, in a sense, a criticism of such a notion as the unconscious—since what he is after is the structure of the world of the individual as it appears to the individual, and since the unconscious has no world.[11]

In contrasting the Existential A Priori with the Freudian unconscious, we approach the issue from the following points of view: (1) The Existential A Priori is to be understood as the *horizon* of consciousness, a concept that we may use phenomenologically "in most instances where psychoanalysis will speak of the unconsciousness of a certain experiential content." [12] (2) The Existential A Priori refers to a Dasein, whereas the unconscious refers to a being.[13] (3) The Existential A Priori is a manifestation of the Heideggerean Ontological A Priori (as described in Chapter I), whereas the unconscious represents the Dasein in only one of its "existentials," that of "thrownness" (*Geworfenheit*).

The Existential A Priori as the Horizon of Experience

The term "horizon," from the Greek *horos*, meaning boundary or limit, is, in contemporary usage, differentiated from the notion of boundary in general by its primary reference to a particular purview. That is, a horizon is a horizon *for* someone. To speak of the horizon of an experience is to speak of the limit of meaningfulness that arises from the experience itself considered apart from any larger, more inclusive experience. I do not refer here to the horizon of the *object* of my experience, which, in the case, say, of perception is a dimly apprehended depth or fringe of indeterminate

---

* It must be remembered that Binswanger views Daseinsanalyse as complementary to a scientific explanatory system, and so his criticism of such things as the notion of the unconscious involves their claim to finality, not their restricted application and practical effectiveness.

[11] Binswanger, *Schizophrenie* (Pfullingen, 1957), p. 149.

[12] Sonnemann, *Existence and Therapy* (New York, 1954), p. 195.

[13] Binswanger, *Schizophrenie*, p. 149.

perception.[14] The horizon of an object of experience is an indeterminate object. The horizon of an experience is an undetermined
meaning. If I run to a tree for shelter from a sudden rain, the tree
that I experience is "partly pervaded, partly girt about" [15] by the
dim perceptual experience of other objects—the hills in the distance, the automobile parked along the road, even, perhaps, the
rain itself. The tree is the focus of the experience, and *its* horizon
is also that of which the experience is an experience, however incompletely outlined that horizon must necessarily be. If we speak,
however, of the horizon of the experience itself and not of its objects, the point must be phrased differently. The tree means shelter
to me, and the experience of being sheltered by the tree has its own
particular kind of horizon that must be distinguished from the
horizon of the object that is the tree. This experience is also "partly
pervaded, partly girt about" by the experience of, perhaps, being
sheltered by an umbrella, a roof; being sheltered from the sun or
the wind; being *protected*, being *covered*, and so forth. We may,
therefore, speak of an objective horizon and an experiential horizon.

Sonnemann presents another aspect of the notion of horizon:

> Horizonlike, however, is not only the contour of the field of
> vision as our focus encounters it [phenomenal horizon], but its
> lateral contours in their remoteness from the focal axis, towards
> which the field of vision gradually dims out, as well. The horn
> rims of our glass, which our focus by-passes, are, in this sense,
> horizonlike precisely in their nearness; even more horizonlike [as
> well as nearer] to our vision is the contour of the eye itself.[16]

What Sonnemann tells us here is that if we understand horizon
as the limit of a particular purview, then the essential unalterable
limit, that which cannot possibly be focused upon, is the structure
of that which makes the purview possible. Our phenomenal focus
may shift; what was once horizon may become the focus and, frequently, what was focus may become horizon. But that which
makes vision itself possible cannot become the focus of vision. In
The Critique of Pure Reason, time is the horizon, in this sense, of

14 Husserl, *Ideas*, trans. by W. R. Boyce Gibson (London, 1952), p. 102.
15 *Loc. cit.*
16 Sonnemann, p. 195.

intuition, and the transcendental schemata are the horizon of experience. Not the Kantian categories, for they are forms of thought and correspond, in the metaphor of the eye, to the eye itself. It is the transcendental schemata that correspond to the "contour of the eye," since they are necessary determinations of the categories with respect to time. We may speak of an individual's horizon, thus understood, as transcendental in that it represents the limit of experience in the sense of determining the possibilities of experience for the individual.

These two aspects of the notion of horizon are combined in the Existential A Priori, which may be termed the "transcendental experiential horizon." This somewhat forbidding expression simply means that the ultimate limit of the experience of an individual is that grand meaning-context that makes his experience possible. This grand meaning-context is the Existential A Priori. A specific comparison with the Freudian application of the notion of the unconscious is now in order.

As an example of psychoanalytic procedure in this context, we may cite, in a highly schematized and simplified manner, that group of neurotic reactions in which a present disturbance is linked causally to a past traumatic experience. We limit ourselves here to those cases where the event is experienced as traumatic because certain impulses hitherto repressed threaten to break into consciousness, this being a special case of those experiences where unmastered and unmasterable quantities of inner excitation force a breakdown of equilibrium. Already we see how Daseinsanalyse complements such psychoanalytic description. For Daseinsanalyse, a traumatic experience is one in which the meaning to the individual of an event contradicts or, "goes beyond" the transcendental experiential horizon; that is, the overarching meaning-context that is the Existential A Priori makes possible an experience that leads to its own negation. Binswanger's example of the skating incident illustrates this.[17] In this case the Existential A Priori is the category of continuity; "Everything that makes the world significant is submitted to the rule of that one category." [18] The loss of the heel in the skating rink is experienced as a break in continuity, and thus

[17] Binswanger, "The Existential Analysis School of Thought," in Rollo May, Ernest Angel, and Henri F. Ellenberger (eds.), *Existence*, p. 203.
[18] *Loc. cit.*

the Existential A Priori (which *is* this particular Dasein) leads to its own contradiction, and therefore to the negation and contradiction of its world, and, therefore, to the closing off of that world, to fainting.

According to psychoanalysis this traumatic experience causes a phobia in which the patient suffers an uncontrollable spell of anxiety whenever the heel of her shoe appears loosened or whenever anyone touches her heel or even speaks of heels.[19] (Her own heels have to be nailed firmly to her soles.) At such times, if she cannot run away in time, she faints. The causal link for psychoanalysis, between the early skating incident and the present phobia, lies in the unconscious. *A*, the skating incident, is the cause of *B*, the present phobia. The phobia connected with heels arises from an unconscious identification, early and late, of the skating incident with the fear of separation from the mother. Memory of the traumatic event is thus, perhaps, repressed; and the present anxiety attacks and fainting spells are explainable only by recourse to the notion of the persistence of this memory in the unconscious.

Daseinsanalyse would, however, put it thus: the narrowness of the transcendental experiential horizon cannot admit the *meaning* that this very horizon lends to the skating incident. What is "repressed," therefore, is not the memory of that event, but its *meaning*. The horizon in which the patient now lives still cannot admit such a meaning, break in continuity; and thus the shutting off the world by fainting continues to be the only way of preserving that horizon without giving up whatever freedom remains within that horizon. It is thus not that *A* is the cause of *B*, but rather, that the present horizon is no less restricted than the past, and so the meaning of *A* still cannot be accepted. The skating incident is traumatic because of what is *now* the horizon; and it is therefore *B*, the patient's present state, which is the cause of *A*.

The link between the past incident and the present phobia is, indeed, unconscious, but only in the same sense that the "person who raids the icebox at night . . . is . . . unconscious of what an observer may term his voraciousness. . . ."[20] The Existential A Priori of continuity in the patient is lived and is therefore, like the horizonlike contour of the eye, not in the focus of attention.

[19] *Loc. cit.*
[20] Sonnemann, p. 194.

What the category of continuity "brackets-in" is at the focus of attention, while the category itself is so near to her as knower that precisely as long as her being-in-the-world is defined by this category as her conceptual focus, her focus of attention, always requiring a certain sense of otherness in order to be the object of focal attention, must bypass—shoot beyond—this category as the possible beholding of her thought.[21] Only by the establishing of a new, larger horizon can this meaning become conscious, a therapeutic goal that departs from the classic psychoanalytic emphasis on bringing the unconscious to consciousness as itself the effective "cure."

What does this "philosophical" notion of horizon add to understanding the neurotic? Its immediate effect is to underline the dubiousness of strict past-to-present causal relationships that psychoanalysis originally stressed. For the horizon is in time, and what from an observer's point of view was in the past is present within the transcendental experiential horizon. *The Existential A Priori makes possible the effect of the past on the present; the relation of the present individual to his past is not itself determined by that past, but by the horizon within which he experiences both present and past.*

> The difficulty, now, is precisely the one met with in the case of the psychoanalytic usurpation of the principle of strict causalism: in order to claim to know that B is the effect of A, one must be able to deduce from an objectively given A that its effect *will be* [rather than *has been*] B, a requirement psychoanalysis never meets since its whole interpretation, even its "knowledge," of A is, vice versa, determined by its knowledge of B *as a datum*. As partaking in the patient's present state $[B]$, his own mnemonic knowledge of A *objectively belongs* to that datum; but this means that just objectively the knower and the known can never be disentangled. What causally is never reducible to any states of its past, the referent of his own inner life history, the *who* of an existence, registers, pre-reflectively, what amounts to a reversal of "causality"—a reversal of the objective functional order of genetic evolutions *qua processes:* in phenomenal time, not a childhood trauma A is the cause of an adult symptom picture B, a connection which only mnemonic reflection can establish here as

21 Paraphrased from Sonnemann, p. 195.

phenomenal causality with all its misleading implications that we reviewed before. On the contrary, what *A is* is wholly determined by the present state of the existence [*B*]; for *being* presupposes *presence*, and what *is* present here of *A* but a memory that, as such, belongs totally to *B? [22]*

More positively, this notion of horizon enables us to speak about the *original* "cause" of traumatic experience itself while still remaining true to the phenomenological dictate that we allow no presupposed theories to shape the data. The psychoanalyst must account for the original trauma by recourse to a theory of instinctual needs and frustrations in early childhood. Daseinsanalyse, on the other hand, approaches such a problem in this manner:

> We should, therefore, not explain the emergence of the phobia by an overly strong "pre-oedipal" tie to the mother, but rather realize that such overly strong filial tie is only possible on the premiss of a world-design exclusively based on connectedness, cohesiveness, continuity. Such a way of experiencing "world"— which always implies such a "key" [attunement, *Gestimmtheit*]— does not have to be "conscious"; but neither must we call it "unconscious" in the psychoanalytical sense, since it is outside the contrast of these opposites. Indeed, it does not refer to anything psychological but to something which only makes possible the psychic fact.[23]

Neither the loss of the heel nor the womb and birth fantasies are "explanations" of the emergence of the phobia. Rather, they became so significant because holding on to mother meant to this child's existence—as is natural for the small child—having a hold on the world. By the same token, the skating incident assumed its traumatic significance because, in it, the world suddenly changed its face, disclosed itself from the angle of suddenness, of something totally different, new, and unexpected. For that there was no place in this child's world; it could not enter into her world-design; it stayed, as it were, always outside; it could not be mastered. In other words, instead of being accepted by the inner life so that its meaning and content could be absorbed, it appeared

22 Sonnemann, p. 233.
23 Binswanger, "The Existential Analysis School of Thought," *op. cit.*, p. 204.

and reappeared over and over again without having any meaning for the existence, in an ever-recurring invasion by the Sudden into the motionlessness of the world-clock.[24]

The notion of horizon gives us the possibility of speaking phenomenologically about that which Husserl termed a phenomenological Nothing. It gives us this possibility by indicating, from the point of view of consciousness, the relationship of experience to that which makes experience possible, the relationship of a particular meaning to that which is the ground of that meaning.

The notion of horizon by no means can replace the notion of the unconscious. If it should masquerade as an explanatory principle, it would rightly be condemned as an ineffectual paraphrasing of a powerful theoretical insight. But if we seek to understand the world of the individual as he himself experiences it; and if we find, as we do, that an essential element of this world must of necessity escape the focus of experience in the way that a transcendental ground must a priori escape the focus of experience, the metaphor of a horizon admirably depicts the manner in which this transcendental ground is experienced.

Denotation of "Unconscious" and "Existential A Priori"

It is clear that the concept of horizon as delineated above does not preclude a usage of the term "unconscious" as adjectival, as *descriptive* of an aspect of experience. We may say with MacIntyre that this descriptive aspect represents

> . . . Freud's additions to the catalogue of mental events whereby unconscious wishes, anxieties and the like appear as well as conscious ones. Here Freud extends ordinary language, but ordinary language provides a foundation for his work. And his work at this point is a work of description.[25]

Our concern here, however, is with what is called the "specific psychoanalytic meaning" of the concept of unconsciousness.[26] In

---

[24] *Ibid.*, pp. 204-205.
[25] MacIntyre, p. 48.
[26] James C. Miller, *Unconsciousness* (New York, 1942), p. 42.

cases where Freud describes his work as "the scientific method by which the unconscious can be studied," [27] he is implying a concept of the unconscious that goes beyond the merely adjectival; when he speaks of the unconscious as discriminating and censoring, he is implying a concept that goes beyond the function of a theoretical, explanatory concept. It is this strict psychoanalytic meaning of the concept of the unconscious that Binswanger opposes to his own views:

> Hence Freud did not at first speak of an "ego" in regard to the unconscious, but of an "id"; later, however, he lent support to the popular conception of the unconscious as a second ego or a second person by the assertion that "parts of the ego and super-ego," too must be recognized as unconscious.

> In the light of all this, existential analysis must state that the unconscious in the strict psychoanalytic sense [i.e., not in the sense of nonattention or forgetting] may point to a being but by no means to an existence.[28]

Insofar, then, as Freud is introducing a concept of the unconscious that radically differs from the manner in which that term had been used up to his day (both by psychologists and "imaginative writers," [29]) the unconscious refers either to real *being*, or to a "second person." Binswanger allows that the unconscious may refer to a being, but not an existence (Dasein), and by this he means the unconscious can have no world and no relation to itself through a world. Yet, it may represent part of the being of the Dasein, a manifestation of one existential (thrownness). However, insofar as it represents a part of the Dasein, it is the Dasein that relates to it and determines it at least as much as it finds itself (*sich befindet*) determined *by* it. In a word, when we termed the Existential A Priori a "universal with power" and referred this power back to the Dasein itself, we implied that the locus of self-determination of an individual lies in the mode in which the Dasein manifests the fundamental ontological a priori of Care. Binswanger cannot, therefore, allow what he would consider the Freudian no-

---

[27] MacIntyre, p. 44.

[28] Binswanger, "The Case of Ellen West," in R. May *et al.* (eds.), *Existence*, p. 326.

[29] MacIntyre, p. 44.

tion that one aspect of Care determines the Dasein. Such a notion would be incompatible with the (Kantlike) transcendental freedom in the Heideggerean view of man. There can, in sum, be no causal efficacy (in the natural-scientific sense) determining the Existential A Priori.

We must turn to Jean-Paul Sartre for the spelling-out of that criticism only implied in Binswanger's writings—the criticism, namely, of a position that allows the determination of the whole self by a part of the self, or, in Binswanger's terms, a position that allows beings, *Seiende*, to determine Dasein. Sartre's attack on this position takes the general form that self-determination by a part of the self must implicitly reintroduce a whole self as the part, leading thus either to an infinite regress or to the subversion of the initial part-whole distinction. The well-known chapter on "Bad Faith" in *Being and Nothingness* presents the argument that the unconscious censor must be conscious of that which it represses in order to be unconscious of it.

> But it is not sufficient that it [the censor] discern the condemned drives; it must also apprehend them as *to be repressed*, which implies in it at the very least an awareness of its activity. In a word, how could the censor discern the impulses needing to be repressed without being conscious of them? How can we conceive of a knowledge which is ignorant of itself? To know is to know that one knows, said Alain. Let us say rather: All knowing is consciousness of knowing. Thus the resistance of the patient implies on the level of the censor an awareness of the thing repressed as such, a comprehension of the end toward which the questions of the psychoanalyst are leading, and an act of synthetic connection by which it compares the *truth* of the repressed complex to the psychoanalytic hypothesis which aims at it. These various operations in their turn imply that the censor is conscious [of] itself. But what type of self-consciousness can the censor have? It must be consciousness [of] being conscious of the drive to be repressed, but *precisely in order not to be conscious of it*.[30]

We need not elaborate on the Sartrean context of Bad Faith in order to see the relevance of this argument in our own perspective.

[30] Jean-Paul Sartre, *Being and Nothingness,* trans. by Hazel E. Barnes (New York, 1956), pp. 52-53.

Consciousness, which was to be "accounted for" is reintroduced on the level of the so-called unconscious. Translated into Heideggerean terms, the Dasein must be viewed as ontologically and transcendentally prior to its determination or "parts."

Another part of Sartre's argument highlights this point equally decisively. Sartre starts with the observation that, by the distinction between the "id" and the "ego," Freud has cut the psychic whole into two:

> I *am* the *ego*, but I *am not* the *id*. I hold no privileged position in relation to my unconscious psyche. I *am* my own psychic phenomena in so far as I establish them in their conscious reality. . . . Thus psychoanalysis substitutes for the notion of bad faith, the idea of a lie without a liar; it allows me to understand how it is possible for me to be lied to without lying to myself since it places me in the same relation to myself that the Other is in respect to me; it replaces the duality of the deceiver and the deceived, the essential condition of the lie, by that of the "id" and the "ego." *It introduces into my subjectivity the deepest intersubjective structure of the Mit-sein.*[31] (Emphasis added.)

Hence we are faced with an infinite regress as long as we posit a part of the self that, while being inaccessible to consciousness, still causally determines consciousness.

The above serves to indicate more explicitly Binswanger's views on the unconscious. He sees its power as an explanatory hypothesis, but from the perspective of Daseinsanalyse, the experiential data that it accounts for represent one aspect of the Dasein, that which Heidegger terms thrownness.

The Unconscious and "Thrownness"

Before pursuing this last point further, I want to make clear that where Sartre speaks of consciousness, Heidegger and Binswanger speak of Dasein; neither look upon the basic existential reality of consciousness as over against, say, emotion or will. Consciousness, in this latter sense, is itself open to a Deseinsanalytic *placing* or interpretation within the Dasein. Thus Binswanger:

[31] *Ibid.*, pp. 50-51.

While psychoanalysis, as we know, interprets the unconscious from the perspective of consciousness, it is clear that a doctrine, which rather than taking its departure from the intentionality of consciousness shows how this [consciousness] is grounded in the temporality of the human Dasein, must also interpret the distinction between consciousness and unconsciousness temporally and existentially.[32]

The temporal-existential "placing" of "unconsciousness" is the (Heideggerean) existential of thrownness:

The point of departure for this interpretation cannot, therefore, be consciousness. It can, instead, only be the "unconscious," the thrownness and determinateness of the Dasein.[33]

The thrownness of the Dasein, its facticity, is the transcendental horizon of all that scientific systematic psychiatry delimits as reality under the name of organism, body (and heredity, climate, milieu, etc.), and also for all that which is delimited, investigated and researched as psychic *determinateness:* namely, as mood and ill humor, as craziness, compulsive or insane "possessedness," as addiction, instinctuality, as confusion, phantasy determination, as, in general, unconsciousness.[34]

For Heidegger the existential of *Befindlichkeit* expresses that constitutive aspect of the Dasein that emphasizes the *Da*, the *fact* of being *there*, placed in a world in which countless articulations of the non-Dasein influence and give shape to the futurity and projectedness of the Dasein. *That* the non-Dasein of necessity so reveals itself to the Dasein is expressed by Heidegger's term, *Angewiesenheit* (disclosing persistent reference).* Dasein's attitude toward itself within the context of *Befindlichkeit* is termed thrownness. The Dasein finds itself determined, limited, placed in time and space; it finds in itself what on reflection would appear to be elements of the non-Dasein; in a word, it encounters itself as facticity, as that which already has been determined and fixed without, so to speak, its own consent. This sense of passivity, of having-been-

[32] Binswanger, p. 219 of this volume.
[33] *Loc. cit.*
[34] *Ibid.*, pp. 212-213.
* Brock's translation.

determined is what is primarily expressed by the term *Geworfen-heit*, being-thrown.

Binswanger terms this throwness the transcendental horizon of all that psychiatry investigates under the name of body, organism, mood, depression, insanity, compulsion, instinctuality, etc.— in sum, unconsciousness. From the above discussion of the notion of horizon, we can conclude that for Binswanger that which makes possible the experience of being determined by that which lies within the self is that ontologically a priori structure of the Dasein to which Heidegger gives the name *Geworfenheit* (throwness). We may therefore also conclude that for each individual the Existential A Priori manifests itself partially under the aspect of facticity, being-determined by "drives," "moods," *the past*, all of which are *found there* ("within" the self). That this aspect of facticity is ultimately to be viewed as caught up in a larger *freedom*, in the Existential A Priori as a whole with its other aspects of pro-ject (*Entwurf*), understanding (*Verstehen*) and openness (*Erschlossenheit*) need not blind us to seeing the relevance of Heideggerean *Befindlichkeit* as throwness to the experiential data and theoretical orientation of the science of psychoanalysis.

Thus Binswanger does not *deny* psychic determinism, or the facticity of the body and its chemistry, or the needs that *drive* the compulsive. He is ready to agree with Lindner that the instincts are "just there," [35] or with Madame Sechehaye, who notes that the body, as definition and determination, is a priori necessary for the *existence* of what we call and define as ego or self.

> The consciousness of "being a body" seems indispensable to the differentiation of the ego and the non-ego. . . . Since it constitutes at once part of both subject and object, the body serves the function of linking the ego to the outer world.[36]

> . . . The ego is nothing without its own body and without an awareness of the universe which would be impossible except for the body. Not that the body produces it [the ego] by a mysterious epiphenomenon, but in order for consciousness to exist, we

[35] Robert Lindner, *Prescription for Rebellion* (New York, 1952), pp. 30-31.
[36] M. Sechehaye, *Autobiography of a Schizophrenic Girl* (New York, 1956), pp. 144-145.

must differentiate ourselves from the world and consequently realize our body's limitations.[37]

What Binswanger, it seems to me, wants to emphasize is that
thrownness is an a priori constitutive element of (in) the Dasein
and hence, constitutive of the self to a degree. He wants, therefore,
to stress the *prior* unity of the Dasein as Care while at the same
time acknowledging one of its manifestations as facticity, symbolized by the body, the unconscious.

> It is Heidegger's great merit to have summed up the being of the
> Dasein under the all too easily misunderstood title of Care
> [=caring for], and to have phenomenologically explored its
> basic structures and make-up. Thrownness, in the sense of the
> facticity of the Dasein's answerability to its that-it-is, is only *one*
> component ["existential"] of this structure. . . . Thus what in
> psychiatry is irreversibly separated into discrete realities of fields
> of study, namely, the finite human Dasein, is here presented in its
> basic structural unity.[38]

The Existential A Priori must therefore be viewed as accom-
modating the causal necessity that psychoanalysis describes as lying
in the unconscious and as sourced in the instincts. The emergence
of the self on the background of the Dasein (the *Jemeinigkeit* of
Heidegger) transcendentally presupposes the encounter of Dasein
with its own facticity. As the concrete manifestation in the individual of the ontologically a priori structure of Care, the Existential A Priori as thrownness expresses the individual's sense of his
own finitude, character, needs, and history, these latter elements
and their interrelation being what psychoanalysis *explains* by the
postulation of the unconscious.* Further investigation of this con-

---

[37] Louis Lavelle, in Sechehaye, pp. 145-146.

[38] Binswanger, p. 213 of this volume.

* The natural-scientific reduction process that introduces causal necessity under
the rubric of unconsciousness, organism, psyche, therefore finds its support, for
Binswanger, in the "nature of the case."

> We can say of the psyche as well as of the organism that they belong to
> the hidden, but *as hidden* "disclosed" ontological character of the *facticity*
> of *thrownness* of the being we call man in his thereness (*Da*). (Binswanger,
> *Vorträge*, Vol. II, p. 299.)

We must be careful, however, to distinguish this facticity, which is a *Seinscharak-
ter des Daseins*, from the *factuality* that natural science investigates. The Heideg-

cept of thrownness is best placed within the context of the psychoanalytic and Daseinsanalytic treatment of psychopathology, to
which we now turn.

---

gerean notion of facticity expresses that the Dasein finds it has *seinen Grund
nicht selbst gelegt*" (*Vorträge*, Vol. II, p. 299), but is nevertheless "surrendered
over to it" (*ihm überantwortet*). It is simply the that-it-is which is revealed
(*erschlossen*) to the Dasein; *why* the Dasein is as it is, is hidden (*verborgen*)
in this original encounter. The Dasein, therefore, does not encounter its own facticity as it encounters an object in the world (*eine Vorhandene*); its facticity is a
determination of its own essential being.

> *That* it factually is may, as far as *why* (it is), be hidden; the "that" itself,
> however, is revealed to the Dasein. (Heidegger, *Sein und Zeit*, p. 276.)

Binswanger treats this *why* of the Dasein before its own facticity as the source
of science.

> The existential concept of science is carried by the question "why?" When
> this question is directed by the Dasein solely to the hidden ground of its
> that-it-is, then we find ourselves in the science of *life*, of biology, genetics,
> biological psychology and psychopathology. (*Vorträge*, Vol. II, pp. 299-
> 300.)

The Dasein, seeking to know the *why* of its facticity uncovers laws, explanations,
causal necessity: in a word, *factuality*.

> The "why" in the sense of facticity of answerableness of the Dasein to its
> ground is changed, as science, into the "why" of the *fact* of its "being-alive"
> as an innerworldly being. (*Vorträge*, Vol. II, p. 300.)

The Existential A Priori is the unitary manifestation of Care and its existentials,
among which is that one that Heidegger calls *Befindlichkeit, Geworfenheit*, and
Faktizität. Factual is the content of the mode of existence called Facticity. The
particular causes, needs, drives, and meanings that psychoanalysis deals with and
explains do not constitute facticity, but it is the facticity of the Dasein that makes
possible and that necessitates the asking-why of science.

V
Psychopathology

In Chapter II the biological concept of instinct was singled out as that which constitutes the lesser circle of psychoanalysis considered as an explanatory system. Within the context of that chapter instincts were defined as intentional acts having no original essential reference to an agent-self. By maintaining this minimal intentionality as its lesser circle, psychoanalysis, it was observed, is able to draw the mean between the overreductive tendencies of non-Freudian scientific psychology and a nonreductive, nonexplanatory descriptive psychology. Meanings are preserved as the most primitive reality in the system, meanings that have no essential reference to an individual self, the latter being that which is reduced by explanation.

Prior to this, medicine was characterized as that branch of biology of the human organism dealing with biological purpose, norms, and values—as biology with a specific attitude and center of reference: man. We therefore spoke of medicine as the introduction of a valuational attitude into the lesser circle of biology. After a discussion of Freud's conception of man as *homo natura,* we thereby arrived at the point where we could speak of medical psychology or psychopathology in the Freudian sense as the introduction into the lesser circle of psychoanalysis of the value-concept of mental health. The problem then arose that—whereas in biological medicine the value terms of health, symptom, illness, etc., are fully expressible in a nonvaluation context of physiology, neurology, etc.—in medical psychology the notions of (mental) health, normality, etc., are not referrable to such "objectively" unambiguous states of the physical organism such as life, death, organic malfunction.

This problem arises only *because* the notion of instinct forms the lesser circle of psychoanalysis. That is, for psychoanalysis the primitive reality is an intention; the instincts intend objects and these objects are correspondingly valued, desired, needed, *wished for*. In biology the concept of instinct lies in the greater circle and serves as a theoretical construct that, among others, unites data that are the result of a *prior* transformation of the phenomena in accordance with the Cartesian demand that intentionality (consciousness) be removed from the field of inquiry, the *res extensa*. Viewed out of the historical context of its development (which, to be sure, is the context of practical medicine), the science of psychoanalysis, while exhibiting the desirable mean between the acquiescent and reductive tendencies of reason, pays a price for its explanatory adequacy when it becomes medical, a price exacted by the nature of its subject matter.

When biology is viewed as medicine, processes themselves unintentional are evaluated, referred, placed in a framework of relatively unambiguous value, organic health. When psychoanalytic psychology is viewed as medicine, however, processes themselves intentional such as values, meanings to a self, are evaluated—evaluated according to the criterion of biological purpose. The point I am making here is that such evaluating of values themselves is inevitable as long as the intentionality of instinct remains the lesser circle of psychoanalysis—as it must remain if psychoanalysis is to avoid the pitfalls of overreduction exhibited by such schools as behaviorism. All these considerations led us further also to conclude in Chapter II that where psychoanalysis avoids the dilemmas that arise when the method of inquiry is of the same genus as the object of inquiry, it encounters them again as medicine, where the basis of influence and control is of the same genus as that which is to be influenced. The price of evaluating values or of attempting to endow meanings with meaning is an overriding ambiguity as to the nature of the therapeutic goal: normality. For science cannot justify a value as it justifies a theory—unless it can potentially reduce this value to "fact" as can biological medicine simply by transforming every medical fact into a biological fact with the loss only of an evaluating attitude. Again, it is just this that psychoanalysis cannot do, for its theoretical heart (the lesser circle) is the concept of instinct—and an instinct intends and values an object. Psychoanalysis can perhaps justify the notion of instinct by indicating its explanatory power, but it cannot in the same way justify the value of that which instinct intends or that, therefore, which the psyche, *viewed as a biological structure*, "needs."

Because the notion of instinct forms the *lesser* circle of psychoanalysis, values (of individuals) in their phenomenality are transformed so that by the time they are *data* they are already seen as vicissitudes of instincts—as more or less indirect modes of realizing the goal of instinct, in Ernest Schachtel's words, "detours on the path to gratification of basic biological needs." [1]

When we focus our attention on just *what* it is that instinct intends, we come upon a significant difference between the psychoanalytic formulation and the formulations of biology. As a rule an instinct in biology involves an adaptation, a purposive action in the sense of a theoretically posited intentionality buried in a unit force that works upon the organism as a whole with efficient causality.

> The instinct action is characterized by the fact that an organism carries out some complicated movements which appear very purposeful, *either for its own life or for the life of its offspring*. This is done without previous experience, independently of training, and often without any possibility of knowing in advance something of the success which is to be achieved.[2]

The emphasis in this quotation is mine, for the point I wish to make here is that the biological notion of instinct directly involves the biological-medical concept of health in the sense of continuance of existence (*successful* adaptation to environment, *efficient* total function, etc.).

In Freud, however, we find the following:

> The power of the id expresses the true purpose of the individual organism's life. This consists in the satisfaction of its innate needs. No such purpose as that of keeping itself alive or of protecting itself from dangers by means of anxiety can be attributed to the id. That is the business of the ego, which is also concerned with discovering the most favorable and least perilous method of obtaining satisfaction, taking the external world into account. . . . The

[1] Ernest G. Schachtel, *Metamorphosis* (New York, 1959), p. 274.
[2] Kurt Goldstein, *The Organism* (New York, 1939), p. 183.

forces which we assume to exist behind the tensions caused by needs of the id are called *instincts*.[3]

In a word, the Freudian notion of instinct is such that instinct does not by any means necessarily intend what biological medicine understands as health. The instincts intend, rather, pleasure that, apparently at least, may or may not contribute to biological health. That such a divorce between psychological and biological values is inevitable once instinct is treated psychologically is a point made by Lloyd Morgan[4] and implicitly accounted for by Mortimer Ostow[5] as due to the transition from viewing behavior from without (biology) to viewing psychic function from within (psychology). Morgan, however, points out that

> The two sets of values—survival values and satisfaction values—are, however, so often and of necessity so predominantly consonant—their interrelations are so many and so close—that we are apt to forget that they are logically distinct.[6]

This remark of Morgan's would tend to trivialize my observation that the Freudian instinct is not necessarily involved with health by implying that no instinct, viewed psychologically (from "within") essentially relates to health. But Morgan's point refers only to one and the same processes (instincts) viewed from different perspectives. Viewed biologically (from without) an instinct serves the "vital program of the individual and the species," [7] while viewed from within the *same* instinct intends its own gratification (pleasure). This cannot be said of the Freudian instincts, split off as they are from the ego, which alone serves the purposes of self-preservation. Since, further, for Freud, the "power of the id (instinct) expresses the true purpose of the individual organism's life," biological health must be seen as merely an ancillary adjunct to the realization of pleasure. The ego, therefore, must serve the Id's "value scheme." Failure to do so results in neurosis:

[3] Freud, "Outline of Psychoanalysis," *International Journal of Psychoanalysis*, Vol. 20 (1940), p. 31.
[4] Ronald Fletcher, *Instinct in Man* (New York, 1957), p. 38.
[5] Mortimer Ostow, "The Biological Basis of Human Behavior," in Silvano Arieti (ed.), *American Handbook of Psychiatry* (New York, 1959), Vol. I, p. 63.
[6] Fletcher, p. 38.
[7] Max Nachmanson, "Versuch einer Abgrenzung und Bestimmung des Instinktbegriffes," *Schweiz. Arch. f. Neur. u. Psych.*, Vol. 40 (1934), p. 179.

Psycho-analytic work has furnished us with the rule that people fall ill of a neurosis as a result of *frustration*. The frustration meant is that of satisfaction for their libidinal desires. . . . That is to say, for a neurosis to break out there must be a conflict between the libidinal desires of a person and that part of his being which we call the ego . . .[8]

All our analyses go to show that the transference neuroses originate from the ego's refusing to accept a powerful instinctual impulse existing in its *id* and denying it motor discharge, or disputing the object towards which it is aimed. The ego then defends itself against the impulse by the mechanism of repression; the repressed impulse struggles against this fate, and finds ways which the ego cannot control to create for itself substitutive gratification (a symptom), which is forced upon the ego in the form of a compromise; the ego finds its unity menaced and injured by this interloper, pursues against the symptom the struggle it had formerly maintained against the original impulse, and all this together produces the clinical picture of a neurosis.[9]

All classical psychoanalytic definitions of mental health, explicitly and implicitly, in the end involve instinctual satisfaction as the health-goal of the psyche and view "neurosis as essentially a consequence of pathologic operation of instinctual forces." [10] *

What the above discussion serves to point out is the manner in which value is written into the heart of psychoanalytic theory. Further evaluation of the data from the perspective of medical biology becomes almost superfluous, for the lesser circle of psychoanalysis in "constituting" its *facts*, its *data*, has already structured them on a value scale. Instinctual gratification is the domi-

[8] Sigmund Freud, "Some Character-Types Met With in Psycho-Analytic Work," trans. by E. Colburn Mayne, in *Collected Papers*, Vol. IV, pp. 318-344.

[9] Freud "Neurosis and Psychosis," trans. by Joan Riviere, in *Collected Papers*, Vol. II, p. 251.

[10] Mortimer Ostow, "Virtue and Necessity," *American Imago*, Vol. 14 (1957), p. 254.

* "Neurosis is an illness, and thus a form of suffering which disturbs the functioning of the pleasure principle. It prevents the direct satisfaction of libidinal drives and affords the ego a secondary benefit. Treatment, therefore, is an attempt to restore the primacy of the pleasure principle." (De Saussure, "The Metapsychology of Pleasure," *International Journal of Psychoanalysis*, Vol. XL (1959), pp. 88-89.

nant value in human life; all others are essentially a transformation of it.

I have pointed out in Chapter II that medicine represents a valuational attitude toward biological facts. The obvious analogy *within* the science of psychoanalysis of a body of psychological facts on the one hand, and an evaluative medical attitude on the other, cannot be drawn. That is, psychoanalysis does not evaluate the values intended by the instincts. To do so, I repeat, would be either to slip below the minimal level of intentionality represented by the lesser circle of psychoanalysis—or, paradoxically, to confute its own lesser circle by taking that which, by its own viewpoint, is derivative from the instincts (a "noninstinctual" value) and reapplying it to the instinctual values themselves.

Neurosis, then, is an internal state where nonsatisfaction of instinctual demands is perpetuated. Psychoanalysis cannot allow itself to adduce further independent reasons for calling such a state neurotic. It cannot say, for example, that because such a state is unproductive or socially deleterious, unpleasant (to the ego!), etc., it is neurotic or pathological. Only if these reasons refer ultimately to the perpetuated nonsatisfaction of the instinctual drives, are they psychoanalytically valid; but then, of course they are no longer "independent" reasons. The instincts do not intend productiveness of the individual, nor social or moral value, nor such ego pleasures as prestige—all these involve mainly the ego as it relates to the world in the service of the instincts. In other words, that the satisfaction of instinctual demands is healthy is, within the framework of psychoanalysis, an analytic statement.

It also is an unrealistic statement and next to useless except from the most abstract, theoretical point of view. The psychoanalytic notion of health must be reformulated if it is to accommodate the fact of the existence of the ego and super-ego and the renunciation of instincts upon which human civilization, according to Freud, is built. It is here that the overriding ambiguity as to the nature of normality shows itself. The definition of health becomes a negative formulation in which it represents the negation of a rather precise definition of neurosis. The reason for this is that if psychoanalysis cannot limit its definition of health to the bare satisfaction of instinctual demands, a value-context superseding that of the instinctual aims must be introduced. Again I point out that it is because the lesser circle of psychoanalysis is constituted by a notion involving the intention of an object, and hence a value, that any further introduction of value in a medical sense is excluded. Witness, therefore, the difficulties that psychoanalytic theorists encounter when they attempt to cite, for example, the *freedom* of an act as indicative of its health and the candor and consistency of the founder, Freud, who maintained that all that psychoanalysis can do in therapy is to provide the patient with the *illusion* of freedom.

We can, I think, from the above discussion conclude the following: Psychopathology, within the Freudian framework, presents us with a view of man as a Cartesian mechanism of intentions, values, meanings. This mechanism is called into play by the fact that the basic value (instinctual satisfaction) is unrealizable. In other words, if the satisfaction of the instincts could have been perpetuated, the psychic mechanism peculiar to man would never have emerged. Since the initial, basic value is unrealizable, the goal of a realistic medical psychology can refer only to the mechanism, to the mechanicalness of man. It is not, therefore, that psychoanalysis looks to the ultimate gratification within civilization of instinctual demands, but, rather, that it seeks to eliminate the mechanical, deterministic *manner* in which the psyche seeks gratification within a culture that prevents this gratification. It is not surprising, therefore, to find one of the more sophisticated contemporary theorists on this matter renouncing all health-criteria that refer to the content of psychic acts.

> Thus the essence of normality is flexibility, in contrast to the freezing of behavior into patterns of unalterability that characterizes every manifestation of the neurotic process, whether in impulses, purposes, acts, thoughts, or feelings. Whether or not a behavioral event is free to change depends . . . upon the nature of the constellation of forces that has produced it. No moment of behavior can be looked upon as neurotic unless the processes that have set it in motion predetermine its automatic repetition irrespective of the situation, the utility, or the consequences of the act.[11]

[11] Lawrence S. Kubie, "The Fundamental Nature of the Distinction between Normality and Neurosis," *Psychoanalytic Quarterly*, Vol. 23 (1954), p. 182.

. . . on pragmatic grounds we are justified in calling "normal" any act in the determination of which the alliance of conscious and preconscious forces plays the dominant role, . . . whereas on the same grounds we are justified in calling abnormal or unhealthy or neurotic any act in the determination of which unconscious processes are dominant . . . because such forces will predetermine its automatic repetition irrespective of its suitability to the immediate situation or its immediate or remote consequence.[12]

We have now, I think, the appropriate context in which to view the Daseinsanalytic stand on psychopathology. The theoretical structure of the science of psychoanalysis is such that its fulcrum is constituted by a concept involving intentionality, the valuation of that which is intended. Its data, therefore, represent structures of valuation and meaning, and hence further "independent" evaluation of the data, from the point of view of somatic medical biology, becomes inadmissible. Since, for psychoanalysis, a necessary condition of the emerging of the psychic mechanism peculiar to man is the thwarting of the same basic instinctual value, it cannot realistically emphasize the fulfillment of instinctual goals as the standard of mental health. Since it also cannot, within its own presuppositions, introduce values that are to be conceived as independent of the instinctual values, it can speak only of the *manner* in which the psyche *in toto* seeks gratification, rather than of the *content* of the psyche's strivings, as the standard of normality.

For Lawrence Kubie, the word *repetition* most adequately characterizes the psychopathological constellation of neurotic acts, and, more precisely, *automatic* or *mechanical* repetition. We have seen, further, that for Kubie the predisposition for such automatic repetition is occasioned when the act is determined predominantly by unconscious forces. The reason that the latter leads to the former is given by Kubie as inhering in the nature of the symbolic process leading from the unconscious to the conscious mind.

. . . whenever the unconscious system (or perhaps an alliance between the preconscious and the unconscious systems) predominates, the resultant action must be repeated endlessly. This occurs

[12] *Ibid.*, pp. 184-185.

because its goals are predominantly unconscious symbols and unconscious symbolic goals are never attainable.[13]

Although this is an unfortunate phrasing, Kubie's point is, I think,
clear enough. What is, for Kubie, attainable by action determined
predominantly by the unconscious, is just and only the symbolic
goal. That of which it is a symbol, however, is not attainable, and
it is this that provides the motive force for the repetition.

Our discussion of symbols in Chapter III leads us to expect
just such a formulation. Because, as was there argued, psychoanalysis means most essentially "sign" where it says "symbol," it is
possible for it to speak of the symbol not only as not expressing or
epitomizing or partaking in the symbolized, but actually of the
symbol as disguising or masking the symbolized. We expect, therefore, that Binswanger would reject (or supplement) such an account, and not only on the *general* principle that it lies within a
reductive, explanatory system—but on the specific ground that
just such an account epitomizes the failure of the psychoanalytic
system to do justice to experiential phenomena that, as genuine
symbols, express the meaning of the symbolized by virtue of the
Existential A Priori. What role, then, does psychopathology play
in Daseinsanalyse?

At first glance, apparently none:

> *Daseinsanalyse* distinguishes itself from psychopathology not only
> in that it does not proceed with objective-discursive and induc-
> tive methods to examine an ensouled organism, but rather seeks a
> phenomenological interpretation of existential forms and struc-
> tures. It also differs in that it assiduously ignores the biologically
> oriented distinction between sick and healthy. The task of psy-
> chopathology is therefore to assimilate the material offered to it
> by *Daseinsanalyse,* to categorize it, to test it and to articulate it.[14]

That is, Daseinsanalyse views itself as examining the individual and
his world *prior* to any evaluative distinction between illness and
health. The fact is, however, that Binswanger's major studies concern *that which* the science of psychiatry would classify as pathological. What Binswanger attempts, therefore, is that which we

[13] *Ibid.*, p. 183.
[14] Binswanger, *Schizophrenie* (Pfullingen, 1957), p. 269.

have just observed is not possible within the science of psycho-analysis: he is attempting to present human phenomena (meanings to a self) prior to transformation by a systematic lesser circle into data, and which therefore may independently be explained and valued by a scientic psychopathology. For Binswanger, the Heideggerean "categories," the existentials, do not, as does the notion of instinct considered as the lesser circle of psychoanalysis, transform the phenomena of human existence as they encounter them, but, rather, *indicate the essential modes in which the Dasein itself receives, transforms, constitutes world.*

> Thus the central concept here is that of the *Dasein* as world-design, "world" in the sense of the mode and manner in which beings are accessible to the Dasein. In this light mental illness appears as a modification of the fundamental or essential structure, as a metamorphosis of this being-in-the-world.[15]

The modification of the essential structure of the Dasein must, therefore, be understood as a modification of the manner in which world is accessible to the Dasein. Psychopathology, in Binswanger's terms, is thus the study of those modifications of the essential structure of the Dasein that result in a "narrowing," "constricting," or "flattening" of world.

> Transcendence thus means something much more basic than knowledge and, indeed, intentionality, since world is first and foremost made accessible (*erschlossen*) through mood (*Stimmung*). Keeping in mind the definition of being-in-the-world as transcendence and viewing our psychiatric *Daseinsanalyse* in its light you will notice, first, that in this frame of reference we are able to grasp and examine the psychoses also; second, we must see in them certain *modifications* of transcendence. Insofar as we do, we say . . . : in the mental illnesses we are faced with modifications of the fundamental or essential structure and structural parts of being-in-the-world as transcendence. It belongs to the task of psychiatry to examine and confirm these modifications with scientific precision. . . .
>
> In insanity, in what is termed psychotic forms of being-in-the-world in general, we found till now modifications of the world

[15] Karl Konrad, "Die Gestaltanalyse in der Psychiatrischen Forschung," *Nervenarzt*, Vol. 31, No. 6, p. 268.

picture (*Weltbildung oder Weltlichung*) in the sense of "leaping" (ordered flight of ideas) and "whirlpool" (disordered flight of ideas) on the one hand, and on the other hand modification in the sense of demundanization (*Ver-Weltlichung*) of the Dasein, that is the "withering" of its world its simultaneous shrinking, stagnation and moldering.[16] *

What estranges us from the "mentally ill," what makes them appear to us as alien, are not single perceptions or ideas, but rather the fact of their imprisonment in a world-design which is enormously restricted because it is ruled by one or a very few themes.[17]

The emptier, more simplified, and more constricted the world-design to which an existence has committed itself, the sooner will anxiety appear and the more severe will it be.[18]

What Binswanger is saying is that that which makes existence and experience possible, that which is *existentially a priori* has been "constricted" and "narrowed"; that is, existence is *ruled* by only one or a very few categories. The meaning-matrix within which all phenomena appear and take on relevance for the Dasein and within which both world and self are constituted is dominated (in extreme cases) by only one theme. We express this by saying that there is only one Existential A Priori.

In the above-mentioned case of the ice-skating incident, the Dasein was ruled completely and only by the Existential A Priori of Continuity:

What serves as a clue to the world-design of our little patient is the category *continuity*, of continuous connection and containment. This entails a tremendous constriction, simplification, and depletion of the "world content," of the extremely complex totality of the patient's contexts of reference. Everything that makes

[16] Binswanger, *Existence, op. cit.*, pp. 194-195.
* Cf. Goldstein, p. 491. "The low level of existence in the sick, as compared to the normal level, can be characterized, first, by shrinkage of world, privation of personality through limitation of degrees of freedom."
[17] Binswanger, *Schizophrenie*, p. 401.
[18] Binswanger, "The Existential Analysis School of Thought," in Rollo May, Ernest Angel, and Henri F. Ellenberger (eds.), *Existence* (New York, 1958), p. 205.

the world significant is submitted to the rule of that *one* category which alone supports her "world" and being.[19]

Binswanger's studies of schizophrenia present us with individuals whose being-in-the-world is ruled in just such a way. The world-design of Ellen West is governed by the existentially a priori polarity of ethereal vs. tomb-world; that of Jürg Zünd by the Existential A Priori of push and pressure; that of Lola Voss by the Existential A Priori of familiarity and unfamiliarity (uncanniness); that of Susanne Urban by the Existential A Priori of danger.[20] In all these cases, mental illness (*Geisteskrankheit*) is viewed as the over-powering of the Dasein by one world-design, and psychosis is seen as the sharpest expression of this.[21]

Before pursuing this train of thought further, we may pause now to see what light this throws on the issue that emerged in reference to psychoanalytic definitions of mental illness. When there is only one Existential A Priori governing the world-design of the individual, all perceptions as well as all concrete meaning-situations fall under its rubric. This one Existential A Priori thus becomes the "common universal" (cf. Chapter III) of all the individual's experience, past, present, and future. With the girl in the ice-skating incident, for example, nothing can appear to her except under the category of continuity; things and happenings either preserve or threaten continuity. The breaking of the heel threatens the collapse of her world and produces anxiety;* temporally, any-thing sudden produces the same effect by a disruption in the con-tinuity of "time-flow." The healthy individual realizes that some-thing that happens suddenly may be good or bad, pleasant or unpleasant; its suddenness is not necessarily an essential determi-nation of its relevance to him. But the sick individual in this case abstracts from all phenomena only that which corresponds to the transcendental conditions of his world, in this case a world defined completely by the Existential A Priori of continuity. To say that the sick individual abstracts thusly is not to say that he finds him-self confronted with certain phenomena and then abstracts from

[19] *Ibid.*, p. 203.

[20] Binswanger, *Schizophrenie*.

[21] *Ibid.*, p. 308.

* Cf. Goldstein's definition of anxiety as world loss, cited in Rollo May's *Meaning of Anxiety* (New York, 1950).

them; this would imply that he perceives and then abstracts from his perception. What is meant is what has been stressed all along— in Binswanger's words,

> What we perceive are "first and foremost" not impressions of taste, tone, smell or touch, not even things or objects, but rather, meanings.[22]

The one Existential A Priori thus governs *all* experience— down to the most immediate; and so in our example we are not speaking of events and situations that are, *among other things*, sudden and that therefore provide some "objective" ground for such one-sided abstraction. Rather, it is the Dasein as such that "temporalizes itself" (*sich zeitigt*) in the mode of suddenness.[23] For such a Dasein, everything that happens happens suddenly, and therefore any event has an anxiety-producing potential; and the Dasein must exert itself to subsume all events under a condition of always-having-been. Time is thus brought to a "standstill," there is no "existential ripening" [24] possible.

In this general context we may now describe mental illness in terms of a pervasive uniformity of experience, as the widespread homogeneity of symbolic reference. By this is meant that all experience, perception, knowledge, etc., participate in and epitomize the one Existential A Priori.

What we have here is an indication of what we may term the transcendental conditions of the possibility of abnormality as defined above by Kubie. Repetition, in Kubie's sense, is existentially possible only where all experience has the same symbolic value, not in the sense of a sign-reference to an unconscious cause, but rather in the sense of an expression of the Existential A Priori, the "common universal" of *both* the cause and the effect (and, therefore, that which is the transcendental ground of both cause and effect). The reader is referred to Chapter III for a more detailed spelling-out of this point. Let us simply note that Kubie's sense of repetition is inevitable in a Dasein in which a meaning-

---

[22] Binswanger, *Grundformen und Erkenntnis Menschlichen Daseins* (Zürich, 1953), p. 290.
[23] Binswanger, *Schizophrenie*, p. 261.
[24] *Ibid.*, p. 260.

context is so pervasive as to be the necessary condition of all experience.

What emerges here also is a sense of the existential "cash-value" of the term throwness. The major Dasein-analytic criterion of mental illness is the degree in which the freedom of the Dasein is surrendered over to the power of another. In the neurotic, this surrender is only partial; although his being-in-the-world is overpowered and ruled by one or a few categories, he is constantly struggling to hold on to his own power of self-determination. This struggle takes the form of the Dasein renouncing certain of its potentials in order to ward off the threat of dissolution of that world that has been so restrictedly constituted under the aegis of one dominant meaning-context, and hence, dissolution of the self. But since it is just this renouncing of potentials of existence that represents the beginning of the dissolution (flattening, narrowing, emptying) of the self, all such efforts lead to their own negation, and the neurotic finds himself caught in a bind. The attempted solution of his problems results in their reinforcement. The psychotic goes one step further and surrenders himself completely over to the power of another. The price he pays for the lessening of the experience of anxiety is the loss of his own self-determination. In psychosis the Dasein is completely surrendered over to one definite world-design.*

> In all these cases the Dasein can no longer *freely* allow the world to be, but is, rather, increasingly *surrendered over* to *one* particular world-design, possessed by it, *overpowered* by it. The *terminus technicus* for this state of being surrendered over is: *Throwness*.[25]

We recall, however, from the previous chapter that throwness is a mode of merely *one* of the Heideggerean existentials, *Befindlichkeit*. And yet here it seems to loom up as the most dominant among them. The reason for this will emerge now that

---

* In this context, Erwin Straus's observations suggest an approach to a conception of sleep as also the surrender to the world as structured by the Existential A Priori. "In sleep, we do not withdraw our interest from the world so much as we surrender ourselves completely to it. We abandon ourselves to the world, relinquishing our individuality. We no longer hold our own in the world, opposed to it." "The Upright Posture," *Psychiatric Quarterly*, Vol. XXVI (1952), p. 535.

[25] Binswanger, p. 284 of this volume.

we have reached the point where we can specify, from the Heideg-gerean perspective, just what the modifications (*Abwandlungen*) of the essential structure of Dasein in mental illness consists of.

> Freedom consists in the commitment of the Dasein to its Thrown-ness as such.[26]

Freedom, then, implies the ability of the Dasein to stand over against the brute fact of what it sees itself as being, the unalter-ability and causal efficacy of its past, etc., and through Com-prehension (*Verstehen*) project itself into the future while at the same time willing a responsible relation to its own throwness. In mental illness, the Dasein is surrendered over to a world-design and hence to a world of beings to which it does not actively relate itself and for which it assumes no responsibility. The tran-scendental condition for such a state of affairs is an Existential A Priori that manifests Care primarily in the mode of throwness and that thereby renders inauthentic the other existentials. Neurosis and psychosis are therefore to be viewed as one manner in which the Dasein exists inauthentically, a manner defined by the dispro-portionate place of the existential of throwness. The cash value of the term throwness can thus be expressed in terms of repe-tition. In mental illness, this repetition is, from the Heideggerean perspective, inauthentic.* In Binswanger's words:

> The Dasein no longer extends itself into the future, is no longer in advance of itself, but rather turns round in a narrow circle into which it is *thrown*, in a meaningless, and that means future-less, fruitless, repetition about itself.[27] †

Schematic: (1) Dasein constitutes its world through the meaning-context of the Existential A Priori; (2) Dasein *finds* its world and its Self so constituted (*Befindlichkeit*); (3) Dasein

---

[26] *Ibid.*, p. 321.

* For a description of authentic repetition as choosing oneself or relating in freedom to one's facticity, see Kierkegaard's *The Sickness Unto Death* and *Either/Or*, Vol. II.

[27] Binswanger, *Schizophrenie*, p. 267.

† In "Extravagance" the unfreedom takes the form of the attempt to deny facticity, throwness. The Dasein is defined thereby. It is thus just as much ruled by its facticity. Compare Kierkegaard's concept of the despair of possibility as due to the lack of necessity in Chapter III of Kierkegaard's *The Sickness Unto Death*. See also p. 321 of this volume.

either (a) com-prehends its world and its Self by a free open (*Weltoffen*) relation and projects itself toward future (*Sein-zum-Tod*), having at the same time realized the necessity of its here and now facticity (the mode of thrownness) or (b) abandons itself to its world, to facticity (*Verfallenheit, Verweltlichung*) and is ruled *as if from without* by its own mode of constituting world (*Ausgeliefertsein*); (4) energy expended to maintain self-determination by depletion of existential potential (progress toward inauthenticity) = neurosis; (5) total renunciation of freedom of self = psychosis. Over-all pattern: pervasive, homogeneity of symbolic reference to one Existential A Priori = repetition.

For Heidegger, the existential mode of thrownness entails the relation of the Dasein to the fixed, determined facticity that is an essential component of human existence. When this mode overshadows all others, it follows that the Dasein may appear to be fully understandable by reference to that which is necessary and fixed in his existence. Ontologically, then, psychoanalysis, with its doctrines of psychic determinism, the causal efficacy of the past, the influence of biological forces on ideation, valuation, etc., is to be viewed as the science of Dasein in the mode of thrownness.

It has all along been maintained that Binswanger's Existential A Priori is the manifestation of Care, its expression in a particular, existing human being. From the preceding inquiry into neurosis and psychosis, the impression may have been given that the Existential A Priori may in some sense be conceived as separable from and somehow more basic than one or another or all of the Heideggerean existentials. It may have seemed that one or another kind of existentially a priori category, such as continuity, by virtue of something inherent to the category itself may itself influence the structure of the particular Dasein. It must therefore be stressed again that the Existential A Priori represents the basic wholeness of the total-structure of the particular Dasein ("die ursprüngliche Ganzheit des Strukturganzen des Daseins" [Heidegger]). It is not the case that in neurosis and psychosis one of the existentials rules out all others, for, in fact, the Heideggerean existentials do not and cannot "function" in isolation. Each implies the others.

Understanding (*Verstehen*), for example, Dasein's central way of existing, would be impossible without that basic presence to the things-that-are, natural to Dasein from birth. Likewise, there could be no such *Befindlichkeit* if it were not of the very essence of Dasein to stand-in by interpreting, i.e., understanding.[28]

The modification of the essential structure that is known as mental illness is a modification of the structural whole of Care in that the Dasein no longer freely relates (through *Verstehen*) to its own facticity. The Dasein, as *Verstehen* and *Rede* thus becomes subservient to that mode of being-in-the-world termed thrownness. It is, in Binswanger's words, a "self-chosen unfreedom." [29]

When we specify the particular Existential A Priori of an individual, a concept such as "continuity" describes the manner in which the Dasein constitutes and relates to its world, and this means the manner in which understanding relates to that which of necessity is, the manner in which language expresses, grasps, and shapes the world, the manner in which space is structured meaningfully, the manner in which future, present, and past as such are experienced. We are also, and perhaps more fundamentally, pointing to a freedom in the Dasein through which the Dasein has so structured its world and its self. *What is lost in mental illness is this freedom.* To say of an individual that his Existential A Priori is, say, continuity, is not, of itself, to say that he is "sick." To say, however, that in order for him to experience the world as he does experience the world, he must have surrendered, to a degree, his freedom of understanding over to the world, *is* to say he is "sick." The world over to which he has surrendered his freedom, is not "the" world, but a world structured by the Dasein itself. This paradox of self-chosen unfreedom, of surrender over to a world of one's own structuring is what, for Binswanger, most essentially characterizes the dynamic vicious circle of neurotic anxiety. The resolving of the paradox by complete surrender and perpetuated loss of freedom characterizes the psychotic. Thus a category such as continuity, when used to characterize the Existential A Priori in the mentally ill, points to a languishing, struggling freedom (neurosis) or to freedom as a transcendental condition of existence that is no longer being fulfilled (psychosis) as well as to the

---

[28] Thomas Langan, *The Meaning of Heidegger* (New York, 1959), p. 23.
[29] Binswanger, *Drei Formen Missglückten Daseins* (Tübingen, 1956), p. 61.

transcendentally necessary meaning-context that structured that world.

It follows that Binswanger's primary emphasis is not primarily on the *number* of existentially a priori categories, but on the manner in which the Dasein relates to its self and world as manifested in and through these categories. The Existential A Priori is not an object before consciousness, but, as was pointed out in the previous chapter, the horizon of existence, the matrix within which being, world, and self become accessible to the Dasein. The freedom of the Dasein does not mean standing over against a concept or category, but points to a mode of the Dasein's relating itself to that world and self that emerges in the context of the Existential A Priori. Freedom in this sense implies, then, a constant openness to things and to the self and a readiness of the Dasein to creatively understand or recreate that which is.

When Binswanger speaks of the "tremendously varied contexture of references and compounds of the healthy" [30] he refers to the plurality of existentially a priori categories that condition the world of the healthy. Both here and in Chapter III, it has been pointed out that the "power" of these existentially a priori categories lies in the Dasein itself as freedom. This multiplicity of existential a priori categories that characterizes health for Binswanger must be understood as the necessary concomitant of existential freedom. Any one of these categories can define a neurotic or psychotic individual as soon as the power that posits it disappears. The varied contexture of references of the healthy represents the freedom and power of the Dasein as understanding to re-experience and recreate that which is, while at the same time willing itself as responsible and committed to the world and self thus experienced and thus created.

I conclude by noting that we have not changed our definition of the Existential A Priori as the concrete manifestation of the ontologically a priori structure of care. What we have done, however, is to emphasize the presence or absence of freedom as an essential qualification.

[30] Binswanger, *Existence, op. cit.,* p. 205.

VI

The Dasein as Constitutive:
Binswanger, Heidegger, Sartre

Kant and Heidegger

In Chapter I the point was made that, for Heidegger, Care and the existentials function in a manner strictly analagous to the Kantian categories of the Understanding. The question was then raised as to the sense in which the Dasein is constitutive and as to what it constitutes. The answer given was that frame of reference—*Bewandtniszusammenhang*—was that through which the Dasein constitutes the being of its world and self. It is important now to emphasize that there is a great difference, for Heidegger, between saying that the Dasein constitutes the objects and saying that the Dasein constitutes the being of the objects. Heidegger on no account wants to say the former, but he does claim the latter.

Again, we may go to Kant to clarify this point. It will be remembered that Kant calls himself both a transcendental idealist and an empirical realist. By this he means to say that he is an idealist insofar as he regards the objects of knowledge as appearances or representations of things-in-themselves, and that time and space are therefore only sensible forms of intuition.[1] He is a realist insofar as he insists that the objects in space and time are as real as the succession of our ideas.[2] In other words, that which the Understanding constitutes is a representation *of* an external in-

---

[1] I. Kant, *The Critique of Pure Reason*, trans. by Norman Kempt Smith (London, 1953), A 369.

[2] H. J. Paton, *Kant's Metaphysics of Experience* (London, 1951), Vol. II, p. 375.

dependent reality. Things are not in the mind, for Kant, but they are known and shaped by the mind.

Heidegger presents us with a kind of reasoning and a distinction that are strikingly similar. We may, I think, put it this way: Heidegger is an ontological idealist but an ontic realist. That is, for Heidegger, the Dasein constitutes Being, but not beings. It is therefore possible for Heidegger to speak of truth as *gegenstehenlassen von . . .*[3] (allowing over-againstness of . . .) and as *des Seinlassen von Seienden*[4] (the letting-be of beings) without compromising his position that the Dasein as Care (and temporalization) is the ontological ground of the possibility that beings can be encountered.[5] Indeed, just as Kant's empirical realism is necessarily bound up with transcendental idealism, so Heidegger's ontological "idealism," rightly understood, implies this ontic realism.

The analogy between Kant and Heidegger suggests that, for Heidegger, ontology is a transcendental discipline on the order of Kant's method in *The Critique of Pure Reason,* and, correspondingly, that Kant's critical method, which seems to be "merely" epistomological, is actually, for Heidegger, an effort in ontology. I have pointed out in Chapter I the idiosyncratic reasoning to preconditions, which is the hallmark of the critical philosophy as well as one of the most salient characteristics of Heidegger's method. The point to be made now is that, for Heidegger, it is just this kind of reasoning to preconditions that is definitive of ontology, as opposed to those disciplines that, while bearing the same name, have since Plato been concerned with beings, rather than with Being.[6] Langan, in explicating Heidegger's ontic-ontological distinction, makes this same point:

> To grasp something "ontically" is to grasp it in its full determination as a concrete phenomenon. To grasp it "ontologically," i.e., in its full Being, one must think behind the phenomenon to grasp the ground of its possibility—what it is that makes it possible for the phenomenon to be as it is.[7]

[3] Martin Heidegger, *Kant und das Problem der Metaphysik* (Bonn, 1929), p. 71.
[4] Heidegger, *Vom Wesen der Wahrheit* (Frankfurt, 1954), p. 14.
[5] Heidegger, *Sein und Zeit* (Tübingen, 1953), p. 366.
[6] William Barrett, *Irrational Man* (New York, 1956), p. 189.
[7] Thomas Langan, *The Meaning of Heidegger* (New York, 1959), p. 74.

In the Heideggerean perspective, then, what Kant did when he showed that time is the sensible form of all intuition was to show that the meaning of beings lies within the Dasein and therefore, that time is the horizon of Being. The point to be stressed here is, put baldly, that for Heidegger, to endow meaning is to endow being—and, therefore, the Dasein, as the unique source of meaning in the world,[8] is the unique ground of Being.

The question that naturally springs to mind, by way of objection, would be to demand of Heidegger some justification of this equation of meaning and Being. Such a question, however, presumes the possibility that Being may be conceived as independent of meaning, and, for Heidegger, this means independent of the Dasein. The question, in effect, presumes the subject-object split that Heidegger's notion of the Dasein as being-in-the-world is intended to undercut. Once again we run into the fiat nature of Heidegger's (and the critical) argument. One cannot ask of Kant how the categories come into existence, what causes them to function, for the job of the critical philosophy is to reason to that which makes possible the nature of this kind of question. Likewise Heidegger claims that the Dasein exists in the way it does only on the ground of its being essentially in-the-world as the endower of meaning, reference, bearing (*Bewandtnis*). All questioning, for Heidegger, is possible only on the ground of Dasein's being-in-the-world conceived in this way.

To ask what is it that the Dasein constitutes when it constitutes Being, is to ask what is Being. Since Heidegger does not want the question of Being to slip into the traditional mode of seeking "out there" for *a* being (i.e., *ens realissimum*), he can begin to answer only by saying that Being is the ground of beings, in the sense that Being is that which makes possible that beings (the *Vorhanden*) as such emerge. The Dasein is the context in which beings emerge as concrete phenomenal beings. This context is a meaning-context to which Heidegger gives the name Care. Care is not one possible meaning-context among others, but rather meaning-context itself, the transcendentally a priori basis of human existence as it *in fact* manifests. What does the Dasein constitute when it constitutes Being? The answer is that it constitutes the possibility of beings. It does this by letting the beings be what and as they are. And since

[8] *Ibid.*, p. 28.

beings cannot be except within the context of Care, it turns out, by an unprecedented dialectical twist, that for the Dasein to constitute Being means that it does not constitute beings.* "Our mode of cognition," Heidegger says, speaking of Kant, "is not ontically creative." [9]

What I term Heidegger's ontological "idealism" and ontic "realism" is his response to the problem that, in his study of Kant, he so explicitly states:

> How can a finite human *Dasein* in advance pass beyond (transcend) the essent [being, as opposed to Being] when not only has it not created this essent but also is dependent on it in order to exist as *Dasein?* [10]

To reiterate what was said in Chapter I, Heidegger's position is that, ontically speaking, the world is not-self. Ontologically speaking, the Dasein is in-the-world (*auf das Seiende angewiesen*) and constitutes the being of the world by a network of meanings through which the (ontic) world (*das Seiende*), is disclosed, revealed (passively, receptively). The Dasein, as the ontological ground of beings and as that which constitutes Being is, it seems to me, the sense of Heidegger's repetition (*wieder-holung*) of Kant's Copernican Revolution:

> Ontic truth, then, must necessarily conform to ontological truth. This is the correct interpretation of the meaning of the "Copernican Revolution." By this revolution, Kant thrusts the problem of ontology to the fore. [11]

What is the role of phenomenology in this connection? In Chapter I it was pointed out that phenomenology would be the method par excellence for a philosophy that holds by necessary fiat to the notion of constitutive powers of the "self." The reason given there was in sum that, granted this constitutive function, to confront the world from a preferred frame of reference or explanatory system is not to understand the world as it is con-

---

* It may also be that Heidegger is attempting to provide the root of sensibility and understanding that Kant, in A15, B29, says is unknown. See Heidegger, *Kant*, p. 33.

[9] Heidegger, *Kant and the Problem of Metaphysics*, trans. by James S. Churchill (Bloomington, Ind., 1962), p. 76.

[10] *Ibid.*, p. 47.

[11] *Ibid.*, p. 22.

stituted by the self (Dasein?), but, in fact, to constitute the world. For Heidegger, ontology is the reasoning to the preconditions of beings *qua* beings in order to apprehend the essence of Being. Phenomenology, therefore, since it is the most accurate mode of access to the possibility of beings (considered as not-self), is, for Heidegger, the main tool of the ontologist: "Ontology is only possible as phenomenology." [12] *

Binswanger's Relation to Heidegger

As was stated in Chapter I, it is not quite accurate to say simply that Binswanger's Daseinsanalyse is the extension or application of Heidegger's ontology to the ontic level. If Heidegger's restatement of Kant's Copernican Revolution consists in placing the Dasein as Care as the ontologically a priori condition of beings,

[12] Heidegger, *Sein und Zeit*, p. 35.

* Now that Heidegger's *Kant and the Problem of Metaphysics* has appeared in an excellent English translation, the Kantian elements of his philosophy may become better appreciated. For it is, of course, in this work, rather than in *Sein und Zeit*, that the Kantian element is made quite explicit. For example:

"Hence, what makes the relation to the essent (ontic knowledge) possible is the precursory comprehension of the constitution of the Being as the essent, namely, ontological knowledge." (p. 15)

"However, ontic knowledge by itself can never conform 'to' objects, because without ontological knowledge it cannot have even a possible 'to what' (*Wonach*) of the conformation." (p. 18)

"This totality composed of pure intuition and pure understanding, united in advance, 'constitutes' the free-space within which all essents can be encountered." (p. 81)

"Does it not follow, then, that ontological knowledge, which is achieved in the transcendental imagination, is creative? . . . Not only does ontological knowledge not create the essent, it does not even relate itself directly and thematically to the essent . . . But to what does it relate itself, then? What is known in ontological knowledge? A nothing. Kant calls it an X and speaks of an 'object.' . . . By a Nothing we mean not an essent but nevertheless 'something.' It serves only as 'a correlate,' i.e., according to its essence it is pure horizon. . . . Consequently, this something may not be the direct and exclusive theme of an intention. . . . If ontological knowledge discloses the horizon, its truth lies in letting the essent be encountered within this horizon. . . . [This] knowledge . . . is 'creative' only on the ontological level and never on the ontic." (pp. 125-128)

"All projection—and, consequently, even man's 'creative' activity—is *thrown* (*geworfener*), i.e., determined by the dependence of the Dasein on the essent in totality, a dependence to which the Dasein always submits." (p. 244) then what we have termed Binswanger's Existential A Priori must represent ideally the most complete or only possible extension of Heidegger's thinking to the ontic level. Although Binswanger's studies are ontic in that they concern particular individual human *beings*, they are more than ontic in that as far as each individual studied is concerned, his analyses refer to that which makes possible the experience of the particular individual. We have, in Chapter I, called such a discipline (which concerns itself with the transendentally a priori essential structures and possibilities of a concrete human existence) neither ontological, nor ontic, but "meta-ontic." The question we now ask is how far do Binswanger's investigations on the meta-ontic level fit into the Heideggerean scheme?

Medard Boss, whose psychiatric writings in many ways show agreement with Binswanger, is nevertheless the most vociferous critic of what he sees as Binswanger's misunderstanding of Heidegger. Referring to Binswanger's view that neurosis and psychosis can be treated as modifications of the essential structure of the Dasein, Boss says:

> Transcendence as that one factor which defines the essence of being human and its being-in-the-world in Heidegger's sense never means a kind of relation, realized through a primary immanence, which can be "modified" to this or that mode of the Dasein. Transcendence and being-in-the-world in [Heidegger's] analysis of Dasein are, rather, names for the same thing: that unmodifiable and basal essential structure of the Dasein which lies at the basis of all relations.[13]

Boss understands the Heideggerean notion of Dasein as the in-itself, unobjectifiable receiver of objects; one could almost say that Boss sees the Dasein as the "pure subject." When Binswanger, in his essay "Dream and Existence" speaks of a rising and falling Dasein, Boss objects:

> As Dasein, that is as the completely unobjectifiable illumination of Being, . . . it can neither rise nor fall.[14]

13 M. Boss, *Psychoanalyse und Daseinsanalytik* (Bern, 1957), p. 93.
14 *Ibid.*, p. 94.

As Boss understands Heidegger, the Dasein as Being-in-the-world, is in no sense a reflective, bipolar structure. Boss limits the Heideggerean concept of Dasein to a pure outgoing endower and receptacle. In no case, for Boss, can *that which is encountered* be spoken of as part of the essential structure of the Dasein. Thus Boss criticises Binswanger's concept of the Dasein as *Welt-Entwurf*, for Boss understands the notion of *Entwurf* to imply an object-pole as assimilated within the structure of the Dasein, thus tainting the ontological structure of the Dasein with a kind of contingency and variability reserved only for ontic structures.

> Just as it does not lie within the conceptual horizon of [Heidegger's] analysis of Dasein to speak of "modifications" of being-in-the-world, so we cannot view neurotics or psychotics as having special and unique world-designs [*Entwürfe*]. . . . Indeed from Heidegger we hear that the concept "world-design" [used] in his analysis of Dasein is to be understood as world-design*ing* Welt-*Er*wurf because it is the light which proceeds from Being. But if the concept of world-design*ing* signifies the essence of man in [Heidegger's] analysis of Dasein, an essence which is the non-objectifiable light and revealer of Being, then one cannot characterize world-design with properties such as specific spatiality or temporality; materiality or consistency.[15]

The issue that Boss raises is, in our context, a crucial one. It involves the possibility of individual variations of the ontologically a priori structure of Care. What Boss is claiming is that on Heideggerean terms the formal structure of Care is invariable and that all individual differences are to be viewed as falling within the strictly defined a priori rule of the interrelation of existentials to which the name of Care is given. Boss is taking Heidegger's claim that Care is an "empty formula" in its strictest sense. In other words, for Boss, the dichotomy of ontological-ontic is exhaustive. What Binswanger views as conditioning or constituting the individual's world, Boss would claim is the conditioned. To put it in terms repugnant to this entire school of thought, we might say that what Binswanger views as emanating from the subject, Boss claims is objective. For Boss, the Dasein, as Care, illuminates Being by receiving beings in the ontological meaning-context strictly de-

[15] *Ibid.*, pp. 95-96.

fined by Heidegger. All further specification of meanings are to be viewed as emanating from beings, not from the Dasein. Binswanger, on the other hand, claims that the ontological structure of Care can vary in individuals and that the particular Dasein thereby determines or constitutes his world to a greater degree and in more detail. For Binswanger the over-all structure of Heidegger's ontology is mirrored in each individual. Boss can make no room for a distinction between an ontological and an existential a priori, and in his psychiatric writings he stops just short of such a point of view. He does not admit the legitimacy within a Heideggerean framework of the concept of an existential a priori. In a word, he rules out what I have termed the meta-ontic level of inquiry, the reasoning to transcendental preconditions of a given, concrete world.

From the standpoint of Heidegger's avowed purpose in *Sein und Zeit*, Boss's criticism of Binswanger seems to me a just one. What the concept of an Existential A Priori does, in effect, is to render "existentialistic" a doctrine that purports to be mainly a study of Being and not of man. Binswanger, for example, does not speak of this or that *self*, but of this or that particular Dasein, whereas Heidegger limits himself to speaking of *the* Dasein. The implication is that there is something in the *being* of a concrete human individual that the Heideggerean account of Dasein omits. This something can only be the particular Existential A Priori and the particular world-design. This is not to say that viewed from Binswanger's perspective, Heidegger has omitted either the individuality of the Dasein or the multiplicity of the Dasein's manifestations in the world. His notion of the *Jemeinigkeit* (each-to-his-ownness) of the Dasein is an attempt to treat the former; and as for the latter, it cannot be his task as an ontologist, metaphysician or simply philosopher to enumerate or make room for the specific particularity of human beings. Is it not rather the specific degree of power that the Dasein in its freedom exhibits that is Heidegger's omission as seen in the context of Binswanger's works?

My point here is this: If Binswanger's works were solely an application to the ontic level of Heidegger's ontology, then, as we have seen in the above discussion of Heidegger's ontological idealism and ontic realism, Binswanger's task would involve *mere* eidetic-descriptive phenomenology; all implications as to the constitutive function of the Dasein would have to be studiously avoided. At most, Binswanger's "structural a priori categories," which we have termed the Existential A Prioris, would be viewed as no more than Husserlian essential structures. That this is not Binswanger's position—that rather these a priori categories function in a manner analogous to the Kantian categories of the Understanding, which constitute the world as known—it has been the burden of the previous chapters to demonstrate.* That is, a faithful application of Heidegger (as I understand him) to the ontic level would not deal with the Dasein as constitutive, this being reserved for the strictly ontological level. The application to the ontic level would, rather, entail a discipline of phenomeno-logical apprehension of essences of emotion, desire, conflicts, etc. The Heideggerean element in such an attempt would probably re-sult in the apprehension of categories similar to those of Binswanger, with the essential difference that no sense of these categories as constitutive of world would emerge. In this sense, it is Boss, rather than Binswanger, who is faithful to Heidegger. In the Heideggerean frame of reference, Boss's level of inquiry is ontic; Binswanger's is meta-ontic. Binswanger has, in this regard, taken a fundamentally Heideggerean framework and moved more in the direction of Sartre than Binswanger himself would, perhaps, care to admit.

Binswanger and Sartre

In Maurice Natanson's interpretive critique of Sartre's ontology we find a chapter devoted to what Natanson calls Sartre's "Coper-nican Revolution."

* "The phenomenological analysis of experience . . . works . . . predominantly with the various kinds of psychological understanding and empathy. Its goal is to accumulate as many single psychological observations as possible in order to be able to read off and demonstrate as clearly as possible the form or species of the experience in question. We, on the other hand, seek in the first place neither the specification of the factual experience nor that of the process of experiencing, but, rather, that something which stands "behind" or "above" both. We seek, namely, the mode of being-in-the-world that makes possible such experience, that, in other words, makes such experience understandable." (Binswanger, *Schw. Archiv.*, Vol. 29, pp. 215-217.)
"Distinguished from the phenomenological analysis of act and experience is the method of analysis of constitutive a priori structural elements which at the time build the total world of the particular being-in-the-world and determine its na-ture." (*Ibid.*, p. 217.)

> Sartre's "Copernican Revolution" is essentially the attempt to formulate at the ontological level what Kant attempted to show at the epistemological level. . . . The basic similarity between Sartre and Kant . . . is that for Sartre the "molding" of phenomenal reality is at the ontological level derivative of and dependent upon the activity of the *pour-soi*, which both "exists" reality and exists *in* reality.[16]

This appears to coincide essentially with what has been said about Heidegger in the foregoing pages. However, and this is the first point I wish to make here, seen from Heidegger's position, Sartre's investigations are *not* ontological. Sartre starts by understanding Being as the in-itself, as the self-sufficient, nonintentional, opaque plenum unto itself.[17] For Sartre,

> This is equivalent to saying that being is uncreated. But we need not conclude that being creates itself, which would suppose that it is prior to itself. . . . Being is *itself*. This means that it is neither passivity nor activity.[18]

From Heidegger's standpoint we might make two points: First, no matter how original a formulation it is, Sartre's description of Being as the in-itself still points to a kind of *ens realissimum*, an epitomization of that which is true of beings, rather than Being. At the most, it can be taken as the description of a special kind of being, but which still has in common with beings that it is not *human* being. Second, Sartre's Being cannot be viewed as the ground of beings; it is more to be understood as *de trop*,[19] as neither related nor unrelated to beings that are essentially, for Sartre, appearances. Thus, in Sartre, reasoning to preconditions of phenomena cannot lead to Being and is therefore not ontology in Heidegger's sense.

For Sartre, the transcendental condition of beings, of world, of human reality, is the freedom (or nothingness) of the *pour-soi*, consciousness, human being. But for Sartre the *pour-soi* is not the

---

[16] Maurice Natanson, *A Critique of Jean-Paul Sartre's Ontology* (Lincoln, Neb., 1951), p. 93.

[17] J.-P. Sartre, *Being and Nothingness*, trans. by Hazel E. Barnes (New York, 1956), pp. lxiv-lxix.

[18] *Ibid.*, p. lxiv.

[19] *Ibid.*, p. lxvi.

source of Being. In Heidegger, it is the Being of the world, the Being of things and self that is constituted by the Dasein, which thus provides the matrix for the emergence and passive letting-be of beings. For Sartre, on the other hand, each individual human being constitutes the meaning of his world and therefore his world is a being for which he is responsible. There is, for Sartre, no general structure of human being, such as Care, that defines and constitutes Being as such. Rather each individual chooses his own world, a world that is thereby mightily lacking in the self-sufficiency and opacity that, for Sartre, characterize Being. For Sartre the *pour-soi* —and that means each individual—cannot escape this freedom of choosing his world or of being responsible for his world, much as he yearns for the self-sufficiency of Being-in-itself. But Being escapes man, he can only "hew beings out of it"; he cannot constitute Being, which means for Sartre that he cannot be both free and not lacking, both plenum and void. Thus, in speaking of Sartre, we may reverse what we said about Heidegger: for Sartre the *pour-soi* cannot constitute Being because it is condemned freely to create, constitute, beings.

> We are taking the word "responsibility" in its ordinary sense as "consciousness [of] being the incontestable author of an event or of an object." In this sense the responsibility of the for-itself is overwhelming since he is the one by whom it happens that *there is* a world; he is also the one who makes himself be.[20]

At this point we may ask: to what degree is Sartre's notion of original project comparable to Binswanger's Existential A Priori? It would seem at first glance that no meaningful comparison of Sartre and Binswanger on this score could get beyond the apparently overwhelming disparity of the two in their views as to the degree and kind of freedom in man. I have already quoted a typical passage of Sartre in this respect, the kind of passage that has led some critics to see Sartre as the champion of a freedom so absolute as to be scarcely distinguishable from the most radical subjective idealism. In Binswanger, on the other hand, we find the following:

> The Dasein, although it is essentially for its own sake, has not itself laid the ground of its *being*. And also as a creature "come into

[20] *Ibid.*, p. 553.

existence" it is and remains, as *thrown*, determined, i.e., enclosed, possessed and compelled by beings in general. Consequently it is also not "free" in its world-design.[21]

From this it follows that world-designs also should be thought of as thrown designs and in no case as "free acts of an absolute ego." [22]

What I wish to show is that the disagreement here is only apparent and that actually both Binswanger and Sartre have a view of human freedom that in many respects is almost identical. Sartre's views as to the absolute freedom of the original project have to be understood with a qualification that Sartre himself provides and that is too often bypassed by his critics.

I start out on a hike with friends. At the end of several hours of walking my fatigue increases and finally becomes very painful. At first I resist and then suddenly I let myself go, I give up, I throw my knapsack down on the side of the road and let myself fall down beside it. Someone will reproach me for my act and will mean thereby that I was free—that is, not only was my act not determined by any thing or person, but also I could have succeeded in resisting my fatigue longer, I could have done as my companions did and reached the resting place before relaxing. I shall defend myself by saying that I was *too tired*. Who is right? Or rather is the debate not based on incorrect premises? There is no doubt that I could have done otherwise, but that is not the problem. It ought to be formulated rather like this: could I have done otherwise without perceptibly modifying the organic totality of the projects which I am; or is the fact of resisting my fatigue such that instead of remaining a purely local and accidental modification of my behavior, it could be effected only by means of a radical transformation of my being-in-the-world—a transformation, moreover, which is *possible?* In other words: I could have done otherwise. Agreed. *But at what price?* [23]

This "at what price?" is Sartre's way of expressing that all particular acts must be viewed within the framework of the larger, vaster

[21] Binswanger, p. 212 of this volume.
[22] Binswanger, *Ausgewählte Vorträge und Aufsätze*, Vol. II (Bern, 1955, p. 287.
[23] Sartre, pp. 453-454.

project. Granted the original project, granted its freedom—all particular acts and motivations follow of necessity from that project. For Sartre, man is free at any moment to alter the original project, but this does not mean that any particular act, in its particularity is autonomous.

> Hence it becomes evident that we can not suppose that the act could have been modified without at the same time supposing a fundamental modification of my original choice of myself. . . . This does not imply that I must *necessarily* stop (on the hike) but merely that I can refuse to stop only by a radical conversion of my being-in-the-world; that is, by an abrupt metamorphosis of my initial project—i.e., by another choice of myself and of my ends. Moreover this modification is always possible.[24]

We see, therefore, that Sartre's notion of original project has this in common with the Existential A Priori: it is to be taken as inclusive, all-embracing, universal—it is not to be taken as on the same level as those choices, situations, or confrontations of which it is the foundation. It is, in a word, a *matrix* in the general sense described in Chapters I and III.

This notion of matrix is also what prevents the concept of Existential A Priori from leading to a doctrine of "free act(s) of an absolute ego." That which emerges within the context of the Existential A Priori has a brute fact quality, a facticity that, while it refers ultimately back to an original freedom, is, in its particularity, a *given*. Thus, both Binswanger and Sartre, in order to maintain the freedom of man as self-determination, resolutely deny the freedom of man as indeterminateness, as haphazard, instantaneous arbitrary will.

Thus Sartre:

> In addition we must not think of the original choice as "producing itself from one instant to the next"; this would be to return to the instantaneous conception of consciousness from which Husserl was never able to free himself . . . we must conceive of the original choice as unfolding time. . . .[25]

And thus Binswanger:

24 *Ibid.*, p. 464.
25 *Ibid.*, p. 465.

On the other hand the freedom of world-designs is also not "absolute" insofar as they must stand to one another in an a priori continuity. "We cannot," says Szilasi, "voluntarily interrupt the conditioned consequences of an horizon of understanding, for that would mean that the voluntary world-design is completely unmotivated and senseless. It would appear to us . . . to have come out of thin air.[26]

The Existential A Priori and the Original Project are similar, then, in that each represents a matrix within the context of which world and self emerge. We have further qualified the concept of the Existential A Priori by explicating it as a *meaning*-matrix. That Sartre's Original Project is also to be understood in this way is evidenced when he says

> We choose the world, not in its contexture as in-itself but in its meaning.[27]

Sartre is saying that the original project informs or constitutes reality by providing a framework of meaning within which reality takes on its form for each individual.

> . . . it is this original choice which originally creates all causes and all motives which can guide us to partial actions; it is this which arranges the world with its meaning, its instrumental-complexes, and its coefficient of adversity.[28]

Thus, for Sartre, as for Binswanger, it is an original, a priori *meaning*-matrix that provides the framework and the possibility that beings shall emerge—that provides the accessibility of beings.

To continue the comparison we bring into focus another problem posed by Natanson:

> It is one thing to assert that the *meaning* of experience is dependent on the meaning-giver: the *pour-soi;* it is quite another thing to hold that the object itself is constituted by the *pour-soi.*[29]

Here Natanson, after establishing a fundamental similarity between Sartre and Kant, is trying to differentiate Sartre's Copernican Revolution from Kant's. He does this by reminding us that for Sartre

---

[26] Binswanger, *Vorträge*, Vol. II, p. 287.
[27] Sartre, p. 463.
[28] *Ibid.*, p. 465.
[29] Natanson, p. 94.

the *en-soi* does have a facticity which is independent of and prior to the individual *pour-soi*, but the meaning of the *en-soi* is determinable only through the *pour-soi*. Thus, Sartre's Copernican Revolution establishes two points: (1) that reality is a function of the *pour-soi* although it is not the phenomenal world of Kant; it is the dialectical reality which the *pour-soi* "exists"; (2) that the facticity of things has a realistic status, but that the meaning of this status depends on the interpretation it receives from the *pour-soi*.[30]

But it seems to me that Sartre's position is starker than Natanson would have us believe. Natanson errs, I think, not so much in presenting the *en-soi* as a kind of thing-in-itself (an impression that, much as Sartre struggles against it, still remains at the end of *Being and Nothingness*), but, rather, in seeing the Kantian phenomenal world as a world that while accessible to the *pour-soi* is independent of the meaning-structure with which the *pour-soi* endows its world. The danger here is of relegating Sartre's position to one in which the old distinction of primary and secondary qualities becomes the standard of distinguishing between human and extra-human reality. The point is that for Sartre, as well as for Heidegger, the objective phenomenal world of Kant—the world of objects, itself—is possible only on the ground of a particular meaning-context, or choice of being-in-the-world, just as for Binswanger scientific objects emerge only to a Dasein with a particular world-view. Now it is true that we find such passages in Sartre:

> Freedom implies . . . the existence of an environment to be changed: obstacles to be cleared; tools to be used. Of course it is freedom which reveals them as obstacles, but by its free choice it can only interpret the *meaning* of their being. It is necessary that they be there, wholly brute, in order that there may be freedom.[31] (Emphasis added)

But it would be incorrect to conclude from such passages that Sartre is referring to an objective world that exists before or independently of the *pour-soi*.

[30] *Ibid.*, pp. 95-96.
[31] Sartre, p. 506.

It would be absolutely useless to seek to define or to describe the "quid" of this facticity "before" freedom turns back upon it. . . . The question itself is unintelligible, for it involves "before" which has no meaning; it is freedom, in fact, which temporalizes itself along the lines of a "before" and "after." Nevertheless the fact remains that this brute and unthinkable "quid" is that without which freedom could not be freedom.[32]

This means that we apprehend our choice as not deriving from any prior reality but rather as being about to serve as foundation for *the ensemble of significations which constitute reality.*[33] (Emphasis added.)

Thus, we may agree with Natanson that there is a difference between the meaning of an object or experience and the object itself, but only if we do not understand object as being an articulated structure. The counterpart of this qualification is that we must not understand meaning solely as derivative from the object. As with Binswanger, Sartre is saying that the over-all meaning-matrix, the original project, provides the framework within which objects in their otherness can appear. These objects, in turn, have particular meanings for the individual. But these objects are always to be viewed as being constituted by the overarching meaning-matrix. Object, considered as an articulated structure, independent of meaning, has no place in either Binswanger or Sartre. Indeed our whole point in comparing Binswanger and Sartre with Kant is to point out that the "human" factor in the structure of objects refers not only to the understanding considered as separated from the emotions, but that human being as a whole is the precondition of a structured world, of reality.

The issue that Natanson poses must, then, be paraphrased if it is to illuminate Sartre's stand: "It is one thing to assert that the *meaning* of experience and objects (beings) is dependent on the meaning-giver: the *pour-soi;* it is quite another thing to hold that meaning is Being and that Being itself is constituted by the *pour-soi.*" Expressed in this way, we see that Sartre's position is the converse of Heidegger's; that he wants to keep Being as an independent, self-sufficient *quid* about which nothing can be said, known, or experi-

---

[32] *Ibid.,* p. 494.
[33] *Ibid.,* p. 464.

enced, and that beings are what is constituted by the *pour-soi* by appropriation. The dualism in Sartre's thought, it therefore seems to me, is expressible not only as the dichotomy between *pour-soi* and *en-soi*, but also as the radical separation of Being and beings.

Binswanger, who is no metaphysician, does not deal with such issues, having left them to Heidegger to resolve. Yet, as I have tried to show, his manner of treating each concrete individual as mirroring the Heideggerean ontological structure of the Dasein is not just a simple "application" of Heidegger. It is rather a position that, by the very nature of its application has forced Heidegger's notion of the Dasein's passive receiving of beings into a harder mold. For Binswanger is not merely examining the phenomena of experience in his patients when he speaks of *existenziell einheitlichen Bedeutungsrichtungen*[34] or *apriorische Daseinsstruktur die alle . . . phänomene ermöglicht.*[35] If he can be said to be faithfully applying any philosophical system, he is, *as far as constitutive function of the Dasein is concerned*, closer to Sartre than Heidegger.

Sartre begins his discussion of *existential psychoanalysis* with the general criticism that psychological explanations have the fault of referring to an inexplicable given, of reducing an individual to that which cannot and does not serve as the basis of meaning of the individual's life and world. "What we are demanding," says Sartre,

> . . . is a *veritable* irreducible; that is, an irreducible of which the irreducibility would be self-evident, which would not be presented as the postulate of the psychologist. . . . This demand on our part does not come from that ceaseless pursuit of a cause, that infinite regress which has often been described as constitutive of rational research. . . . This is not the childish quest of a "because," which allows no further "why?" It is, on the contrary, a demand based on a preontological comprehension of human reality and on the related refusal to consider man as capable of being analyzed and reduced to original givens, to determined desires (or "drives"). . . . This unity (which is sought) which is the being of the man under consideration, is a *free* unification, and this unification can not come *after* a diversity which it unifies.[36]

[34] Binswanger, *Vorträge*, Vol. I, p. 146.
[35] Binswanger, *Schizophrenie* (Pfullingen, 1957), p. 464.
[36] Sartre, pp. 560-561.

Point by point, this is as clear a statement of the role of Existential A Priori as could be wished. (1) Sartre seeks the source of meaning —the Existential A Priori is the overarching meaning-matrix; (2) Sartre seeks not a final link in a causal chain, but the ground of the causal chain—the Existential A Priori has been described as just such a ground; (3) Sartre seeks a unity that does not come after the diversiy that it unifies—the Existential A Priori is the transcendental ground of the individual's world.

That Sartre further understands the original project as the "common universal" in the sense detailed in Chapter III is evidenced when he says:

> It is . . . by a *comparison* of the various empirical drives of a subject that we try to discover and disengage the fundamental project which is *common to them all*—and not by a simple summation or reconstruction of these tendencies; each drive or tendency is the entire person.[37] (Emphasis added.)

> Existential psychoanalysis seeks to determine the original choice . . . [which] brings together in a prelogical synthesis the totality of the existent, and as such *is the center of reference for an infinity of polyvalent meanings*.[38] (Emphasis added.)

The Existential A Priori as horizon:

> But if the fundamental project is fully experienced by the subject and hence wholly conscious, that certainly does not mean that it must by the same token be *known* by him; quite the contrary.[39]

What Sartre is proposing is an ever-regressing search for the preconditions of the world of an individual. The question is always to be: what is it that makes this world possible, what is it that makes it possible for *A* to be the cause of *B*, what makes it possible that *X* is a symbol of *Y* for this individual. In short, Sartre is proposing a meta-ontic discipline as the proper basis for psychoanalysis. Like Binswanger, Sartre objects to a reductive, explanatory, "lesser circle" that decides in advance what is the primitive, basic reality—that in terms of which all else is to be explained.

[37] *Ibid.*, p. 564.
[38] *Ibid.*, p. 570.
[39] *Ibid.*, p. 470.

Sartre's existential psychoanalysis differs fundamentally from the Freudian in that Freudian psychoanalysis "had decided upon its own irreducible instead of allowing this to make itself known in a self-evident intuition." [40] Existential psychoanalysis is not looking for causes or basic drives as psychoanalysis does. *It looks for that in the individual which makes it possible that these causes and basic drives have the efficacy that Freudian psychoanalysis ascertains them as having.* And this, as will be recognized, is precisely the point of Binswanger's Daseinsanalyse.

> The results thus achieved—that is, the ultimate ends of the individual—can then become the object of a classification, and it is by the comparison of these results that we will be able to establish general considerations about human reality as an empirical choice of its own ends. The behavior studied by this psychoanalysis will include not only dreams, failures, obsessions, and neuroses, but also and especially the thoughts of waking life, successfully adjusted acts, style, etc. This psychoanalysis has not yet found its Freud.[41]

I suggest that in Binswanger it has.

[40] *Ibid.*, p. 571.
[41] *Ibid.*, p. 575.

Conclusion

Power and Powerlessness
(Macht und Ohnmacht)

The foregoing comparison of Binswanger and Sartre made within the confines of the question as to constitutive function need not blind us to one of Binswanger's most vital themes: that also the *denial* of certain possibilities bestows upon the Dasein its power over against its world. It is this theme that I should like to serve as the concluding note.

The *leitmotiv* of this study has been what I have termed Binswanger's notion of the Existential A Priori, a notion that expresses the Dasein's dominating contribution to the experienced phenomena of its world. It has been pointed out that Binswanger's Daseinsanalyse is the effort to ascertain in each individual that which makes his experience and the phenomena of his world possible. Binswanger employs the phenomenological, rather than the reductive, explanatory method to this end—to ascertain the essential structures of the individual's world as it is experienced by that individual. The diagram of the circles was introduced in order to illustrate the manner in which systematic explanation, in particular scientific explanation, transforms the phenomena it encounters and subsequently explains. In this respect science can be viewed as a world-design, as rooted in a human orientation toward phenomena much in the way that the individual Dasein is viewed by Binswanger as constituting its world *via* the meaning-matrix of the Existential A Priori.

The reader has doubtless noticed the parallel here between

human existence and scientific explanation. Just as the Dasein was viewed as constituting its world under the aegis of a dominant category or categories, so explanation in general and scientific explanation in particular was viewed as transforming its world *via* the lesser circle as it confronted its world. I do not now mean to imply that we may speak of the lesser circle of an explanatory system as an "Existential A Priori" in any strict sense. It will be remembered that the lesser circle was defined as a rule of transformation in accordance with which the philosopher (and I now take the liberty of using this term to include the scientist), moving in the greater circle, accepts certain data as irreducible and primary and others as derivative and transformable into irreducible, primary data. The point was made that in explanation the phenomena as they appear are transformed in the sense that they are either subsumed under laws that relate them to other, different phenomena, or they are broken into parts that are taken as more real than the configuration of those parts that make up the phenomena in question. Strictly speaking, then, the lesser circle cannot be spoken of as an Existential A Priori since without the lesser circle there still remain the phenomena, whereas without the Existential A Priori no appearance of phenomena is possible to the Dasein. This distinction is all the more necessary when we speak of the existing, individual philosopher to whom the phenomena are not only theoretically, but experientially, antecedent to explanation.

Taken in a looser sense, however, the parallel is a fruitful one. Just as, for Binswanger, the freedom of the Dasein consists in its choosing responsibility toward its thrownness[1] (In Sartre's words: ". . . freedom is the apprehension of my facticity"), and just as health was understood Daseinsanalytically as the ability to reexperience and recreate that which is, while at the same time freely choosing the world thus experienced and thus created, so systematic explanation must be able to stand detached from the world that it has structured, aware of the relativity of its suppositions while remaining committed to them. In this regard, may we not say that phenomenology is the "health" of explanation, its guarantee of freedom, its source of vigor?

That this is especially true for the sciences of psychology and psychiatry is one of Binswanger's guiding principles. But, he warns

[1] Binswanger, p. 321 of this volume.

us, this freedom to stand outside a frame of reference that is so essential to the groundwork of science cannot of itself give us the power over our world that scientific explanation proper gives us. In a like manner the individual Dasein may stand over against his world, he may be in a readiness creatively to understand or re-create his world, but this readiness in itself is not sufficient for mastery over the world. The tremendous scope of possibility with which the Dasein is confronted as it stands in openness to its world must be narrowed if there is to be an actualization of possibility. Here we recognize the well-known existentialist theme, first em-phasized by Kierkegaard, that human existence proceeds by de-cision, by the cutting off of possibilities.

> The "powerlessness" of the Dasein here shows itself in that certain of its possibilities of being-in-the-world are *withdrawn* because of commitment to and by beings, because of its facticity. But it is also just this withdrawal that lends the Dasein its *power:* for it is this that first brings *before* the Dasein the "real" graspable possi-bilities of world-design. Transcendence, we thus see, is not only a striding or swinging beyond of the Dasein toward world, but at the same time, withdrawal, limiting—and only *in* this limiting does transcendence gain power "over the world." [2]

When, a few pages later, Binswanger speaks of "realizing the necessary limitedness of psychiatry's world-design, which, like all world-designs, owes its power precisely to the *withdrawal* of other possibilities . . ." [3] he is not only focusing on the parallel between human existence and scientific explanation, but stressing its par-ticular significance in reference to the power of the Dasein over against its world. How, within the framework of the problems considered in preceding chapters, is this to be understood?

It will be remembered that the ideal of an explanatory system was characterized as the bringing together of two mutually op-posed goals: to keep that which is to be explained intact as it appears, while at the same time to reduce it as much as possible to what is taken as the basic reality. The dangers of overreduction and its opposite, "phenomenography," were then cited. The anal-ogy with the contrete, individual Dasein is suggested by the dis-

[2] Binswanger, p. 212 of this volume.
[3] *Ibid.*, p. 217.

cussion in Chapter V of the Daseinsanalytic conception of psycho-pathology. There I quoted Binswanger's epitomization of the psychopathology in his case studies of schizophrenia:

> In all these cases the Dasein can no longer freely allow the world to be, but is, rather, *surrendered over* to *one* particular world-design, possessed by it, *overpowered* by it. The *terminus technicus* for this state of being surrendered over is: *Thrownness.*[4]

and his characterization of the girl in the ice-skating incident:

> Everything that makes the world significant is submitted to the rule of that *one* category which alone supports her "world" and being.[5]

May we not, therefore, draw the analogy between what we described as the homogeneity of symbolic reference in the mentally ill and the dangers of overreductionism in explanatory systems? In both cases we find ourselves faced with an impoverishment of world, a price paid by the psychotic for the lessening of feelings of anxiety and paid by the overreductive system of explanation for comparative certainty. In both cases this impoverishment of world can be viewed as a loss of freedom: the psychotic is surrendered over (*ausgeliefert*) to his world-design, he is ruled as if from without by a world of his own essential structuring ("projection"); the overreductive system cannot return to the phenomena that it has reduced; it finds itself committed to a world that no longer is the one it sought to understand; it cannot "let the world be." Both cases, in a word, represent a loss of power: the psychotic does not act but is only acted upon; the overreductive system can no longer explain phenomena but only the aspect of phenomena to which it theoretically can return. In this sense, then, phenomenology is the art of "letting the phenomena be" and may with justice be spoken of as the "health" of explanation, its guarantee of freedom.

Our interest in this study has been primarily with the problems involved in overreduction because of their relevance to natural-scientific explanation. However, we might briefly speculate as to

---

[4] Binswanger, p. 115 of this volume.
[5] Binswanger, "The Existential Analysis School of Thought," in Rollo May, Ernest Angel, and Henri F. Ellenberger (eds.), *Existence* (New York, 1958), p. 203.

how the parallel fares when drawn in the other direction. Phenomenography, we recall, comes into being when the lesser circle grows uncontrollably, when the criterion for primitive fact becomes infinitely lax. In such a case we have a surfeit of reality, a bloated system in which the tendency exists for all "entities" and propositions about entities to be accepted as they appear and "swallowed whole." Since such a system records, along with the phenomena all interpretations of the phenomena, what it gives us is not an essential analysis or a faithful description of the phenomena in which all interpretation that transcends the phenomena are ruled out, but, rather, the phenomena as encrusted with phenomenon-transcending references and interpretations, i.e., the phenomena as already reduced. Nor does it give us adequate explanation, but, rather, throws back the phenomena to be explained as they appeared at the outset. The tendency, therefore, of phenomenography is to hold that all phenomena have reality, all are more or less basic, all systems have some truth. We might speak here of, as it were, a "manic" tendency of systematic explanation:

> . . . in a fundamental-ontological sense . . . we can say of the existential unsureness of the manic depressive that it is a matter of the thrownness of the Dasein insofar as he, whether for short or long, is thrown into unambiguous, but oppositional stances toward world—or, more accurately expressed, unambiguously determined, if also mutually opposed, possible modes of interpreting world.[6]

In contrast to the "overreductive" psychosis that Binswanger treats in *Schizophrenie*, we have here in his "Über Ideenflucht" just the reverse. The manic-depressive springs from one world-design to another, thrown into each one, yet not actually freely committing himself to any. The manic-depressive is "possessed" by his manifold and often contradictory worlds just as the schizophrenic is possessed by one world. Just as phenomenography grants the truth and basic reality of all phenomena, so the manic psychotic is plunged into sundried worlds each of which at the moment is full reality. Just as the manic psychotic never comes to himself,[7] never wins to a final stance, so phenomenography produces en-

---

[6] Binswanger, *Schweiz, Archiv. f. Neur. u. Psych.*, Vol. 29, p. 206.
[7] *Ibid.*, p. 243.

cyclopedic, rather than systematic "explanation." And, like the manic, phenomenography has no power over its world that never changes, but merely reappears as it was first encountered.

Thus for the individual and for the system, commitment to a world is the condition for power over that world. If phenomenology as the art of unbiased apprehension of phenomena is the "health" of systematic explanation, then judicious reduction as the *art of presupposing*, is the actualization of that "health." If the standing apart from the world it has constituted and "letting it be" is the meaning of freedom of the Dasein, then chosen commitment to that same world is that freedom realized.

The ideal of explanation as the mean between overreduction and phenomenography is approachable through the phenomenological venture that strikes to the essence of phenomena as they are experienced. But power, considered as the ability to change or alter the world, cannot spring solely from an attitude that seeks only the essence of experience, as does phenomenology. Phenomenology cannot act or do as science can. But it can provide the source and ground of effective explanation and action in which the loss of possibility is fully compensated by the gain of actuality.

Here the parallel stops. The freedom of the individual Dasein, unlike phenomenology, cannot stand as separable from its use. The individual must constitute his world through the meaning-matrix of the Existential A Priori; indeed, the individual from the first *finds* his world so constituted. Thus *thrown* into a world of its own structuring, the Dasein can renew its freedom by the readiness to experience its world afresh, while exercising its power by resolute commitment to the world which it structures.

Science, as compared with any other system of explanation in the history of philosophy, has a unique kind and degree of power. It has achieved this because, more than any other system, it has succeeded in distancing man from what he encounters and has thereby led to the fruition of what Herbert Marcuse[8] cites as the will to subjugate nature. Only since the birth of our science has man been so completely alienated from his world while at the same time being steered back toward that world as the sole reality. Religions and philosophies since the beginnings of our civilization

[8] Herbert Marcuse, *Eros and Civilization* (Boston, 1955), p. 110.

have attempted the former; the addition of the latter was reserved for our times. But only in our century has this attitude extended to the self. Scientific psychology has brought man himself into the realm of nature and in so doing has produced one of the most spectacular paradoxes of our history, the distancing of man from himself, the theme of self-alienation. What is there left, then, but the ghost of a ghost, the shadow of the Cartesian *cogitans?* And what is the gain? Can we point to the power for which, in our natural science, we paid the price of the alienation of man from nature? Or have we not rather reached the point in our science of self where the precondition of power is no longer alienation of knower from known, where the whole notion of object as something which stands over *against* us must be abandoned in the foyers of our thought?

We have spoken loosely of the parallel between system and existing individual. The crisis of our time to which existentialism and Daseinsanalyse reacts is the danger that the parallel will grow stricter, that man will belong to science rather than science being man's, that the lesser circle of science will become man's Existential A Priori, that—in a deep and cruelly literal sense—man will lose his mind.

PART TWO:
SELECTED PAPERS OF LUDWIG BINSWANGER

Freud's Conception of Man in the Light of Anthropology*

To capture in a fleeting hour the essence of the scientific work of a long life of effort and labor, one must delve into the source from which it sprang, the Idea that inspired it. *The idea behind a scientific work combines the unique personal-psychological and cultural-historical conditions that made it possible with the timeless mission it has to accomplish in and for the world, namely, the*

[* TRANSLATOR'S NOTE: Regarding Binswanger's use of the term "anthropology": in *Existence* (R. May *et al.*, eds., p. 191) it was pointed out that "Binswanger uses this word not in its usual American meaning, which is cultural anthropology, the comparative study of races, mores, etc., but rather in its more strictly etymological sense, that is, anthropology as the study of man (*anthropos*) and specifically . . . the study of the essential meaning and characteristics of being human."

Perhaps the best characterization of what Binswanger means by the word is provided by Heidegger: "'Anthropology' denotes the science of man. It comprises all the information that can be obtained about the nature of man as a being composed of a body, a soul, and a mind. The domain of anthropology includes, not only those given verifiable properties that distinguish the human species from plants and animals, but also man's latent abilities and the differences of character, race, and sex. And inasmuch as man appears not only as a natural being (*homo natura*) but also as a being that acts and creates, anthropology must also seek to know what man as an active being can and should 'make of himself.' His powers and obligations depend finally on certain basic attitudes that man as such is always capable of adopting. These attitudes are called *Weltanschauungen*, and the 'psychology' of these includes the whole of the science of man. Since anthropology must consider man in his somatic, biological, and psychological aspects, the results of such disciplines as characterology, psychoanalysis, ethnology, pedagogic psychology, the morphology of culture, and the typology of *Weltanschauungen service of Truth.* The Idea holds the secret of productivity. Its task, to use a profound phrase of Goethe's, is none other than *to fulfill the divine mission to be productive.*

The Idea of Homo Natura

The Idea that governed the unquenchable productivity of the man whom we are now considering with esteem and gratitude, the Idea in whose realization he saw his mission, stemmed from his conception of man, a conception diametrically opposed to a thousand years of tradition. The essence of man for Freud is neither *homo aeternus,* or *coelestis,* nor the "universal" historical man, *homo universalis;* quite the contrary. Indeed, equally opposed to Freud's standpoint is the contemporary ontological-anthropological conception of man as, in a pregnant sense, a "historical" being, *homo existentialis.* For Freud, rather, what is involved is the scientific concept of *homo natura,* man as nature.

A productive idea reflects its divine mission in that it is driven by a specific *faith,* faith in the capacity *to discover something concerning the reality of existence* and to shape the world accordingly. Not only religious, artistic, and moral ideas draw their vigor from this faith but also the very idea that life is something that has to be thought about, fought through, and suffered for its own sake. The scientific man, as a rule, wishes to deny that it is a faith that gives wings to his ideas, but Freud is the exception. In one of those many places in his writings that owe their trenchant force to the power and conciseness of his Idea, he expresses his basic belief: "We believe," he says, in *The Future of an Illusion,* "that it is possible for scientific endeaver to come to know something of the reality of the world, something which can increase our power and according to which we can direct our lives." [1] Every truly productive faith contains a *mysterium tremendum,* an element of awe-stricken wonder, even terror, before the immense unknown. I speak of that unknown that binds Freud's *homo*

---

must converge in it." (M. Heidegger, *Kant and the Problem of Metaphysics* [Indiana, 1962], pp. 215-216.)

Heidegger goes on to suggest that anthropology must be rooted in ontology as he conceives it. Binswanger, of course, agrees with this, and his anthropology is itself rooted in Heidegger's ontology.]

natura to the primal source of all life and that, more than any other biological conception of man, distinguishes and stamps Freud, namely, the instincts. "We have always had the feeling," he still writes in his seventy-sixth year, "that behind these multitudinous little instincts, something grave and powerful is buried, something that we wish to approach cautiously. The theory of instincts is, as it were, our mythology; the instincts are wonderfully vague mythical beings. In our work we cannot take our eyes off them for a moment, yet at the same time we never see them clearly." [2]

Here we see the unceasing awe of the natural scientist before the gravity and power of life and imminent death, the awe before a life in which, as Freud thought, "we all suffer heavily," [3] suffering for which there is no compensation or consolation, but whose toleration remains the "first duty of all living beings." [*] It is possible to fulfill this duty only if we orient ourselves toward death: "Si vis vitam, para mortem"; for life becomes "more endurable" only if we give to *truthfulness* more weight, especially truthfulness in the face of death: "What is painful may none the less be true." [4] In truthfulness Freud saw man's geniune *awareness in his position*. Nothing offended him more about a person—friend, foe, or even mankind in general—than when he discovered him living "psychologically beyond his means," [5] making psychic luxury out of psychic want, seeming virtue out of actual need. In this, Freud, like Nietzsche, discerned the inroads of individual and cultural hypocrisy. No less radically and passionately than Nietzsche, he carried out his unique mission but, instead of Nietzsche's scorching, aphoristic thunderbolts, he systematically, empirically, scientifically, worked out the gigantic structure of his *technique of unmasking*, and became the first to lift the veil from the riddle of the sphinx known as neurosis. In answer to the question: "What is it?" he gives the eternal answer: man. Thus, added to and indeed born out of Freud's arch theme of "life and death" is the theme of "true and untrue" as an epitimization of mankind's own arch theme of "good and evil." To Freud, these are opposite poles that modify,

---

[*] S. Freud, *Gesammelte Schriften* X, 345 f. Compare XII, 114: "I therefore do not have the courage to stand before my fellow men as a prophet, and I bow before their reproach that I can offer them no consolation. For, at bottom, that is what they all demand—the wildest revolutionaries no less passionately than the most virtuous believers."

rather than exclude, each other. What Freud speaks of in *Beyond the Pleasure Principle* as the embattled marriage of life and death holds (with, to be sure, an important qualification) for good and evil. He saw in evil the prerequisite for the existence of good; in the "sadist's" will to destroy he saw the prerequisite for altruism and culture; in hate he saw the precondition of love; in enmity, friendship; in sadness, joy, etc. But his doctrine never allows that this relation be reversed.

Concerning the positive value of evil, evil considered as an active ontological force, Freud stands in strict opposition to Augustine and Fichte, who see in evil only that which is limiting and negative. He stands more in the tradition of Jacob Böhme, Franz von Baader, and Schelling (one thinks also of Goethe's *Mephistopheles* and of Nietzsche). Indeed, Freud's work can be properly evaluated only after it is contrasted with those doctrines that teach the duality of life-principles and the consequent struggle between growth and constriction. It then becomes clear that amid all the similarities of viewpoint concerning man's fundamental participation in the antagonistic forces of creativity, Freud's idea of *homo natura* presents a basic, elemental divergence. What I have in mind is not simply the difference in method between, for example, Schelling's philosophical deductions from metaphysical potencies and Freud's scientific induction from experience—two intellectual orientations that, moreover, according to Heraclitus' insights about the way up and the way down, must ultimately lead to a harmonious coming together. I am thinking, rather, of the manner in which these philosophers see evil *and* good as effective ontological forces, something that one could never say of Freud.

Here we find ourselves before a fact of highest significance: Freudian doctrine is diametrically opposed to the teachings of Augustine and Fichte in that in it the "good," the ethical, is nothing but a negative, i.e., a limiting, constricting, condemnatory and oppressive force that possesses no essentially positive, i.e., liberating or creative, effectiveness.* All "metamorphoses of the

---

* According to Freud, the primitive instinctual impulses are "in themselves neither good nor bad." Yet he must admit that all the impulses which society condemns as evil are of this primitive kind. In addition, many instinctual impulses appear almost from the first in pairs of opposites, and a human being is rarely altogether "good" or "bad." In any case, experience shows "that the pre-existence of powerful 'bad' impulses in infancy is often the actual condition for an unegoistic in social instincts" and thus, properly said, all metamorphoses of evil into good drives and dispositions, occur, according to Freud, under *compulsion*. "Originally, i.e., in *human history* [such transformations occurred] only under external compulsion, but they [occurred] through the bringing into the world of hereditary dispositions for such transformations and also through their perpetuation and reinforcement 'during the life of the individual himself.' " [6] Indeed, this whole "development" takes the direction in which external compulsion is introjected, and which, in the case of the human Super-ego, is completely absorbed. This transformation occurs, as we know, "by the admixture of *erotic* components": "we learn to value being loved as an advantage by virtue of which we may do without other advantages." [7] Culture is thus "attained through the renunciation of instinctual gratifications and furthered by every new development which serves the purposes of renunciation." [8]

In all this, we stand before the pure specimen of *homo natura*: bodily instinct, the gaining of pleasure (sacrificing a lesser for a greater gain), inhibition because of compulsion or pressures from society (the prototype being the family), a developmental history in the sense of ontogenetic and phylogenetic transformations of outer into inner compulsions, and the inheritance of these transformations. (Here I must ignore certain particulars of this theory such as the postulate of the inheritance of acquired characteristics and the notion of the introjection of external compulsion. Such lines of thought bypass, without solving, problems of ethics and mores, raise difficult issues regarding the reduction of historicity to natural history, and somewhat dubiously substitute empirical and biographical facts about human development for essential and a priori human potentialities, etc.) In this theory, we have to distinguish between *homo natura* in the sense of the primitive "natural" man of human history, and *homo natura* in the sense of the primitive natural man of the individual's history, the newly born infant. Just as Goethe's primal plant is not an actual plant, but—as Schiller in his famous conversation with the astounded Goethe pointed out—is, rather, an idea, so is the Freudian primal man not an actual man, but an idea. It is not, to be sure, the result of an

mistakable inclination toward 'good' in the adult." S. Freud, *Gesammelte Schriften* (Vienna, 1924-1934), X, 323 f.

ad hoc intuitive insight into nature, but rather it arises from a hardheaded, discursive examination into the mechanics of nature. This primal man is not the source and fount of human history, but is, instead, a requirement of natural-scientific research.

The same holds true for *homo natura* in the sense of the newly born infant. Here, too, what we have is not an actual man, but an idea; not an actual beginning, but a necessary requirement of scientific, biological reflection and reduction. Both biological ideas treat man—with regard to his genuine historicity, his *capacity* for ethics, culture, religion, art—as a *tabula rasa*. The only qualification of this notion of *tabula rasa* is that in the newly born infant there is already a certain biological etching on this tablet, a blueprint according to which subsequent cultural *development* takes place. At this point we must, however, realize that scientific knowledge speaks of a *tabula rasa* only when it confronts a certain limit. Such was the case with Locke and such is the case with Freud.* The notion of a *tabula rasa* is never something that comes first in scientific thought, but something that comes last. It is the end result of a scientific dialectic that limits and reduces the

---

* The parallel between Locke and Freud is most instructive. Where Locke asks how far man's capacity for knowledge extends, Freud asks how far man's capacity for civilization, culture, extends. Where Locke seeks the method of correct knowledge, Freud seeks the method of living correctly with respect to civilization. Where Locke proceeds from the doubt as to whether the goal of all-embracing knowledge is attainable, Freud proceeds from the doubt as to whether the goal of an over-all capacity for culture is attainable in man. The method of both is an approach to the composite as arising from the simple, the general as derivative from the particular. For both, the psychic life is a "movement" that proceeds according to the laws of its simpler elements (images, for Locke; instincts, for Freud). Both begin (or, rather, end) with the symbol of the *tabula rasa*. Both are strict *psychological* empiricists and are rooted as far back as Descartes. Both reject metaphysical hypotheses as prejudicial. Both are predominantly oriented toward sensualism and nominalism, etc. There are also, of course, considerable differences, particularly those stemming from the fact that Freud, being a natural scientist, was purely an empiricist, whereas Locke was not only an empirical, but also a *critical* philosopher. We might sum up the parallel between them in the following way: Where Locke says, "Nihil est in intellectu quod non feurit in sensu," Freud says: "Nihil est in homine cultura, quod non feurit in homine natura." Just as, with respect to Locke's proposition, we must keep in mind Leibniz' adjunct, "nisi intellectus ipse," so we must add to our Freudian formulation: "nisi homo ipse." It would therefore read: "Nihil est in homine cultura, quod non feurit in homine natura, nisi homo cultura ipse." But this "homo cultura ipse" is the epitome of all a priori cultural forms of human being, just as "intellectus ipse" is the epitome of all a priori forms of cognitive reason.

totality of human experience to one particular kind of experience. Dialectically, this notion serves as an indication that knowledge has come up against a limit beyond which it is not able to go. Seen from the vantage point of the totality of human experience, the *tabula rasa* is thus a symbol of a particular negation, the expression of a dialectical boundary line.

If we now make this symbol into a reality and treat it as a real beginning of human history, then we witness the highly instructive scientific spectacle of a complete reversal of the historical connections of nature, history, and myth. Where we find myth in the earliest periods of human history, where we see history emerge from the husks of hieratic and mythical traditions and biography and see how late in this history the science of nature arises, we now find natural science turning the tables completely, inserting the product of its own constructions—the idea of *homo natura*—at the beginning, converting its "biological, natural development" into history and then taking this nature and this history as the basis upon which myth and religion are to be "explained." Thus, the essential significance of the idea of *homo natura* is that it clamps man in between instinct and illusion. And from the tension that arises between these two forces art, myth, and religion arise.

When I refer to Freud's *homo natura* as *only* an idea, this should not be understood as a disparagement. Science, after all, works as a rule only with ideas. Where, for example, the idea of a primal plant unveils the "vegetative" creations of nature and illuminates individual plants in the light of this revelation—while leaving it for research to provide subsequent, detailed empirical verification—with the theory of *homo natura*, one can work not only scientifically, but also practically. One can, that is, *do something* with the idea, namely, *make* people *healthy*.

The Development of the Idea of Homo Natura *into a Natural Scientific Theory and Its Significance for Medical Psychology*

The reductive dialectic used by Freud to construct his theory of man is, to the last detail, that of natural science. In it, his faith that he is discovering something about the reality of the world finds its proper support, and with it his sense of awe before the

[155]

mystery and power of life tirelessly spurs his work forward. Freud was not one to limit his concern merely to the direct object of his investigations without at the same time being profoundly aware of the intellectual tool that was his method. He himself has given us an excellent description of its most essential prerequisites. He speaks of seeking identity beneath differences. Psychoanalytic investigations show "that the deepest essence of man is instinctual impulse, whose elemental nature is the same in all men and which directs him to the satisfaction of certain primal needs." [9] ". . . the most important and most obscure element of psychological research [is] the organism's 'instincts.' " [10] He speaks "chemistically" of the great qualitative differences between substances being "traced back to quantitative variations in the proportions in which the same elements were combined." [11] By elements, Freud means the individual instincts and instinctual components. We find him confessing "that all we have are merely scientific hypotheses," which cannot "provide final solutions to these doubtful problems" and which merely "provide the proper abstract ideas that, when applied to the raw material of observation, allow order and clarity to emerge." [12] But above all, we find that one statement of Freud's that most concisely articulates the scientific method of psychoanalysis: *"In our method, observed phenomena must take second place to forces that are merely hypothesized"* ("Die wahrgenommenen Phänomene müssen in unserer Auffassung gegen die nur angenommenen Strebungen zurücktreten").[13]

This is the genuine natural-scientific spirit. Natural science never begins with just the phenomena; indeed, its main task is to divest the phenomena of their phenomenality as quickly and as thoroughly as possible.[14] This, as we know, was the main reason Goethe could never accept or appreciate Newton's theories of light and color. Natural science, like history, speaks in the perfect tense. But where the historian asks how things really *were*, the natural scientist asks how things have *become* what they are. Psychology, on the other hand, as an autonomous science in the deepest sense of the word, speaks mainly in the present tense,[15] for the psychologist must ask only what a thing really *is*, an "is" in which the polarity of self-world and past-future is absorbed and preserved in the "present tense."

Wherever Freud speaks of knowing the world, of experience,

research and reason, he means this natural-scientific kind of knowledge. He maintains, "that there is no other source of knowledge of the universe but the intellectual manipulation of carefully verified observations—that is, what is called *research*—and that no knowledge can be obtained from revelation, intuition, or inspiration." [16] Science thus seeks neither to frighten nor console;[17] it recognizes no "tendentiousness" in itself.[18] As such, science is an irresistible force. "In the long run, nothing can withstand reason and experience." [19] "There is no appeal beyond reason." [20] Freud is perfectly aware that what is involved is an "attitude toward the world." In one of the few places in his writings where he uses the word "spirit," he says: "The scientific spirit engenders a particular attitude toward the things of this world." [21] Indeed, he goes so far as to recognize that scientific terms belong to a "language of images" that thus in no way directly grasp and give back the reality of the world.

We can now characterize the idea of *homo natura* more precisely by saying that it is a genuine natural-scientific, biopsychological idea. It is a natural-scientific construct like the biophysiological idea of the organism, the chemist's idea of matter as the underlying basis of the elements and their combinations, and the physicist's of light, etc. The reality of the phenomenal, its uniqueness and independence, is absorbed by the hypothesized forces, drives, and the laws that govern them.*

Notwithstanding all the limitations to knowledge that they express, the above citations are still in keeping with Freud's scientific epistemological optimism, however subdued and disciplined this optimism may appear when compared to that of his teacher, Meynert. It is the optimism of the natural scientist of the last half of the nineteenth and the beginning of the present century. It is this scientific epistemological optimism that forms the protective soil of Freudian doctrine, and to which it owes its world-conquering power. *Homo natura* is the scientific problem in which Freud proved his genius. Without opposing his humane and humanistic dispositions—indeed, quite the contrary—the idea of *homo natura*

---

* What distinguishes the Freudian *homo natura* from Nietzsche's conception is not so much the contrast between eros and the will to power as it is its character of being a strict, natural-scientific, empirical construct. This is also what sets it apart from the *homo natura* of J. J. Rousseau, "Novalis," and Klages.

stands as the scientific edifice that Freud, with amazing integrity and energy, built out of the inconstant stuff of human life.

Proceeding a step further, we ask how it really affects our total understanding of man to interpret him as *homo natura* and to take instinctual impulses as the basis of this interpretation.

Formally, as we have already seen, this interpretation is based on equivalences among classes and species in the natural-science sense; materially, it is based on imperative human needs, termed sexual instincts, and later known as life-instincts (eros), and the ways in which they can be satisfied, substituted, or renounced. "Sexuality," for Freud, always included the erotic. The fact that it occupies so prominent a position stems primarily from Freud's experience with neurosis, which—and the more I see of neurosis, the more I must agree—is rooted in the enormous "somatomorphic" intricacy, complexity, and, above all, "historicity" of the sexual instinct and its by-products. I shall speak later of the somatomorphic meaning of sexuality. As to its historicity, I refer not only to the extreme complexity that Freud first showed to be characteristic of the biological and physiological development of sexuality. What I am primarily referring to is the power and significance of sexuality that, in shaping our relations to other human beings, shapes our *inner life-history*.* Hunger and thirst do not, in this sense, have the power to shape our life-histories.

Where hunger affects "history," it affects world-history and not that of the individual human being (as, for example, in the French Revolution or in a polar expedition). Neither has hunger itself a significant history of its own—not, at least, outside the physiologist's laboratory. (Concerning thirst, we need not deal with those cases where there is already a certain "harmonious" relationship between the drinker and "his" wine.[22]) For the rest, it was precisely hunger that Freud used to illustrate the leveling, equalizing power of the instincts: "Suppose a number of totally

---

* With regard to this term, cf. L. Binswanger, "Lebensfunktion und innere Lebensgeschichte" (*Ausg. Vort. u. Aufs.*, Vol. I). The main significance of sexuality and the erotic for the inner life history is easier to understand in individual cases if we consider the particular relations of sexuality to the experience of time and space (extension and momentization, broadening and shortening of existence), the experience of change and continuity, of the creative and the new, of repetition and fidelity, of drivenness, on the one hand, and resolve and decision, on the other, etc.

different human beings were all equally exposed to hunger. As their urgent need for food mounted, all the individual differences would disappear and in their place one would see the uniform manifestations of the one unappeased instinct." [23] Thus, for Freud, the "physical significance" or "value" of an instinct grows apace with its frustration, but it seems questionable to him whether the satisfaction of an instinct is, in general, accompanied by a comparable lessening of its psychic significance. But in any case Freud holds it necessary to consider the possibility that "something in the nature of the sexual instinct itself is unfavorable to the realization of complete satisfaction." [24] This quite plausible hypothesis serves to substantiate the contention that sexuality plays a greater role than the other drives.

Be that as it may, the main point for us is the *tendency* of Freudian theory to level or equate the several aspects of man's essential being by bringing them to the level of general exigencies or needs and the psychic significance of those needs. This level is, as we know, that of the *body* or *vitality*, and we might also describe Freud's *homo natura* as *homo vita*. Now, Rousseau tends to see his *homo natura* as an angelic creature dropped from the arms of a benign Nature into a paradisical utopia—an, as it were, *homo natura benignus et mirabilis*. Novalis' notion of *homo natura* leans to a magical idealization of the bodily sphere and a magical mundanization of spirituality. But the *homo natura* of Nietzsche and Klages occupies the same level as that of Freud. That is, the body is given unconditional authority in determining man's essential being. "A few hours mountain climbing," says Nietzsche, and Klages concurs, "makes a scoundrel and a saint the same man." As if, Löwith[25] rightly remarks, before the climb the saint and the scoundrel were not bodily essentially the same. Here, then, bodily fatigue and exhaustion are added to the urgency of the sexual and nutritive need. However profound and varied the physical and psychic "significance" of sexuality may be as compared with the nutritive and "ergetic"-vegetative sphere, all three are similar in that they all *proceed* from the needs of the body.

One should not, of course, overlook the importance and value attributed to the body by Plato and by the highest stages of ancient Greek civilization, a value whose denigration began in Neoplatonism and culminated with the arrival of Christianity. But if physical needs are given authority over the whole of man's being, then the image of man becomes one-sidedly distorted and onto-logically falsified. For then the only thing that will be seen, experienced, felt, suffered, and missed as real and actual becomes that which man is *qua* body, i.e., what he feels "in" or "from" his body, what he perceives with his body and, eventually, what he expresses "with" his body (Klages). Everything else becomes, of necessity, a mere "superstructure"—a "fabrication" (Nietzsche), a refinement (sublimation), an illusion (Freud), or an adversary (Klages).[26] For Klages, to be sure, the soul stands between body and spirit (will) as does experience for Nietzsche, and the psychic apparatus for Freud. But this does not mean that corporeality is not seen generally as the proper *motivational basis* in the understanding of man. These new, original insights must, however, still be accommodated within the totality of man's knowledge of himself—they must, that is, be *anthropologically* clarified. This is especially true for the highly original manner in which Freud's genius classified and delimited the governing sexual motive. I refer to the *regional motives*—the oral and anal, the phallic and vaginal, the ocular and manual, the pectoral and ventral, etc. Although certain great minds from Plato to Franz von Baader, Schelling or Nietzsche—to name but a few—have realized how somatomorphic even the subtlest, most spiritual aspects of human experience are, it was Freud who first gave us a genuine *somatography* of experience based on natural-scientific observations and constructs. This is an accomplishment whose anthropological significance cannot be sufficiently highly esteemed.[27]

Klages views bodiliness from the pathic and expressive point of view; Nietzsche sees it within the framework of the particular situation (*Befindlichkeit*) (cf. the above aphorism); for both, bodiliness lies within the aegis of the fullness or poverty of life. For Freud, bodiliness lies under the aegis of the unconscious or the Id, the unbridled chaos of needs, drives, affects, and passions—in a word, the *pleasure principle*. Freud's *homo natura* is not *only* will to power (though it most decidedly is that too!), but, rather, "will" to *something*, of which the will to power represents only a special case: the will to pleasure, i.e., to "life" and the heightening of life by the preservation of "unknown, ungovernable forces"

that are *responsible* for life. The basis of man's being is thus bodiliness; that is, he is the product and passive plaything of those
powerful, invisible mythical entities called instincts that stand out
against the background of the unfathomable stream of cosmic life.

The myth of a universal life (force) here takes the form of a
highly complex, scientific, and empirically based theory of *individual*
life, "individual" human beings and their bio-physiological, onto-,
and phylo-genesis. Deep down, the individual life, too, is chaotic,
dark, inaccessible, and only describable in negative comparison with
and in contrast to the "organized" Ego. It is like a "cauldron of
seething excitement"; it is "somewhere in contact with somatic processes," and "takes over from them instinctual needs and gives them
mental expression," though we cannot say in what substratum this
contact is made. "These instincts fill it [the Id] with energy, but it
has no organization and no unified will, only an impulse to obtain
satisfaction for the instinctual needs, in accordance with the pleasure
principle. The laws of logic—above all, the law of contradiction—
do not hold for processes in the Id. Contradictory impulses exist
side by side without neutralizing each other or drawing apart; at
most they combine in compromise formations under the overpowering economic pressure toward discharging their energy. There is
nothing in the Id which can be compared to a negation . . ." [28];
nor is there anything corresponding to the idea of time, and "no
alteration of mental processes by the passage of time." "Naturally, the Id knows no values, no good and evil, no morality. The
economic or, if you prefer, the quantitative factor, which is so
closely bound up with the pleasure principle, dominates all its
processes. Instinctual cathexes seeking discharge—that, in our view,
is all that the Id contains. It seems, indeed, as if the energy of these
instinctual impulses is constituted differently to that which is found
in the other regions of the mind. It must be far more fluid and
more capable of being discharged, for otherwise we should not
have those displacements and condensations, which are so characteristic of the Id and which are so completely independent of the
qualities of the object—in the Ego we would call it an *idea*—with
which it is cathected. What would one not give to understand these
things better!" [29] Freud's fully developed notion of the Id contains,
therefore, all those characteristics that he had described in his

earlier formulations, as pertaining to "the unconscious," plus some elaborations. In addition, parts of the Ego and the Super-ego were also recognized as belonging to the unconscious.

Perhaps now we have clarified what we meant when we said that for Freud bodiliness lies under the aegis of the Id. It is the chaotic reservoir of the instincts (the instinct is, in fact, the "conceptual borderline between the somatic and the psychic" and always has its "psychic representation" or significance), which pass over into the psychic. Here one could equally well say either that the soma is already psychically conditioned, or that the psyche is already somatically conditioned. But still the essence of the organism, itself, remains unexplained. For Freud, it is more than bodily functions or instinctuality; it includes physique, especially the organs of perception and motility. As opposed to the Id, these organs possess the closest ties to the "organized," "personified" Ego of the conscious personality, which, in the course of civilization, has arisen out of the Id. Bodily functions or instinctuality are therefore related to the vegetative sphere, and the corporal body to the animal sphere (these terms are used in the sense given them by the Zürich physiologist, Hess). Both, as just indicated, pass over into the psychic apparatus and are closely related to it. Here, then, emerges yet another aspect of Freud's preanalytic period: the *neurobiological*. Of this, let it only be remarked that it, too, plays its role in Freud's construction of the psychic apparatus. Does he not, in *The Interpretation of Dreams*, say that the psychic apparatus "is also known to us in the form of an anatomical preparation"? [30] However much he warns us against the temptation to localize psychological functions in any anatomical fashion, his findings concerning aphasic disturbances and his experience with the linguistic apparatus constructed in connection with them tend to confirm his theoretical speculations.

I do not wish to go into any further detail here in discussing Freud's concept of the psychic apparatus. But one thing must still be said: Freud's psychic apparatus seems, at first glance, comparable to a diagrammatic representation of a bodily organ, a diagram such as those used by lung or heart specialists to indicate their clinical findings. But such a specialist needs only a pencil and paper in order to represent the organ schematically. Freud, however, had first to conceptualize the organ itself on the basis of much experience and painstaking thought, for diagrams end where the psyche begins. The psychic apparatus is thus both organ and clinical diagram, on the one hand an epitomization of "topical" systems and instances, their *dynamic* workings and *economic* functions, and on the other hand, a schema for investigating the psychic life and its anomalies. For Freud, a mental disturbance has not been properly examined or theoretically investigated until its relations to the entire schema have become clear. His treatment of anxiety is an example.[31] The same is true of repression, which he does not treat as a general psychological concept—something others before him had already done in a sporadic or aphoristic fashion—but as a function or mechanism. To have worked out the complicated mechanistic details of repression stands as one of his great scientific achievements. No one at all familiar with the problems he dealt with can fail to realize what an enormous concentration of scientific research and thought was required before even one sentence in the language of *mathematical functional equations* could be formulated concerning the psychic life of human beings.

Freud once said it was false to maintain that repression kept all the derivatives of the repressed out of consciousness. For if these are far enough removed from the repressed instinctual representation—whether owing to the process of distortion or by reason of the number of intermediate associations—they have free access to consciousness. He summarizes this contention in the following "mathematical" formula: *It is as though the resistance of consciousness against them (the "derivatives") were a function* of their remoteness from what was originally repressed.*[32] Compared to a mathematical formula such as this, which is the result of an enormous compression of empirical facts (in the area of free association, resistance, symbolic expression, etc.), Herbart's mathematical formulae concerning the "dynamics of images" seem to be idle armchair entertainments. One might even formally express Freud's whole life work by stating that the idea of *homo natura* can lead to the possibility of expressing psychic processes in a mathematical functional equation. Freud succeeded in demonstrating mechanism at work in what was apparently the freest reaches of the human mind, thereby creating the possibility of mechanically "repairing"

---

* There seems to me no doubt that this expression must be understood not only in a dynamic but also in a mathematical sense.

the mind (with the psychoanalytic techniques of unmasking and annuling repression and regression by means of the transference mechanism). Thus, in an undreamed of way, Freud confirmed Lotze's[33] claim about the *unqualified universality of mechanism.*

The entire mechanism of the psychic apparatus is set in motion from the depths, the Id, by means of the psychic representation of all instinctuality, the *wish*. Wishing is the only context within which the Freudian *homo natura* is directed. But even this is merely an *explanatory construct* emanating from a general sundering of human being, primitive and otherwise. For in actuality man, and certainly primitive man, does not strive for pleasure as such, but for the possession or experience of a particular thing that brings him pleasure. Here, therefore, we are within the sphere of meanings and their particular specifications. Only a being that can *only* wish may be thought of as stretched between instinct and illusion. And, conversely, only when we posit such a being can such basic modes of human existence as the religious, the ethical, and the artistic be *explained* as illusion or derived from the need for illusion. Wishing is not constitutive of mankind as such, however constitutive it may in fact be for the psychic apparatus built into *homo natura*.

What *at bottom* sets this apparatus and its particular mechanisms in motion is a wish. Freud developed this concept with astounding consistency, particularly with regard to the mechanisms of dream work. That dream *work* (not the manifest dream and not the latent dream thoughts or the previous day's residue) can be set in motion only by means of a wish stimulus is as much a necessary postulate of the psychic apparatus as it is a fact of experience. If this appears to be a vicious circle, then scientific method in general has not been understood. Just as the notion of the psychic apparatus is a theoretical epitomization of the actuality of experience, so "experience" is a theoretical verification of that epitomization. All of natural science exemplifies this circle. That this wish *must* be unconscious is clear from what has been said of the Id. This, however, does not imply that the notion of the unconscious dream-wish was fabricated "for the sake of theory." On the contrary, the theoretical manner in which experience is approached is such that between theory and experience there exists an open, mutual correspondence. Freud correctly estimated that this theory

was his main service to science. He did not attribute major significance to the "practical task" of interpreting symbols but rather
to the "theoretical" task of explaining the supposed "operations"
of the particular modes of functioning of the psychic apparatus.
Of course, both the practical and the theoretical had to be
"wrought *de novo*," for the one task is inconceivable without
the other. But the scientist's special pride in the latter is unmistakable and thoroughly justified. "The process of dream-work," we
read in the 29th Lecture,[34] "is something quite new and strange, the
like of which has never before been known." But even in *The History of the Psycho-analytic Movement* he said of Jung's analysis
of schizophrenia that "the most important point has been, not so
much the possibility of interpreting the symptoms, as the psychical
mechanisms of the disease." [35]

The various revisionist psychoanalytic movements that have,
with great ease, cast off this theoretical nucleus of psychoanalysis
have also forfeited their right to be mentioned in the same breath
with Freud. For what singles out Freud's doctrine is his attempt to
demonstrate *what follows as a mechanical necessity from the given
conditions of man's natural organization and the impact between
these conditions and environmental factors*. This is what we term
the discovery of a mechanism at work. Here necessity usurps the
place of freedom, mechanicalness the place of reflection and decision. And with this we find ourselves in the sphere of medicine.
"For," says Lotze in his famous treatise on instincts, "how poorly
our health would, in fact, fare were reflection, rather than mech-
anization, its protector." [36] What we have described as the theory
of *homo natura* prides itself not only on having demonstrated
the mechanism that guarantees and "protects" the normal course
of psychic events, but also on having demonstrated just those mechanisms that can serve to explain how psychic disturbances "follow
as a mechanical necessity from the given organizational conditions"
(the mechanisms, that is, of neurosis and psychosis). Finally, it
takes pride in having demonstrated those mechanisms (transference mechanisms) that can be used to repair the disturbance and
protect the newly acquired health of the organism. Here we stand
upon the firm ground of what is called *medical* psychology and
psychotherapy. It was Freud who conquered this whole territory
for natural science. Since Freud, no scientist can work in this area

without, in one way or another, dealing with his theories. However much these theories may later change and develop, they will remain the touchstone of our scientific conscience and ingenuity.

But medicine, and psychiatric medicine as well, comprises only one domain of human civilization, that which is concerned with the protection of health by means of biological and psychological mechanisms. Health is doubtless one of man's greatest goods and its protection one of the noblest tasks of civilization. But man has even more to protect than his physical and mental health. The many-sidedness of his being must be adequate to the many-sidedness of his struggles; the natural-scientific insight into the "unqualified universality" of mechanisms must be matched with the anthropological insight into the limitations of this significance for the totality of human-being.

The Idea of Homo Natura in the Light of Anthropology

The main result of our investigation has been to establish that Freud's idea of *homo natura* is a scientific *construct* that is only feasible if it is based on a *destruction* of man's experiential knowledge of himself—a destruction, that is, of anthropological experience. As I have elsewhere tried to show,[37] this is as true of *homo natura* in clinical psychiatry and psychopathology as it is of every so-called objective psychology. Anthropological investigations and criticisms are quite relevant to all these ideas of *homo natura*: what is involved is a protection of human existence in general, as opposed to the purely medical protection of the health of this existence and the purely natural-scientific preservation of its relation to nature. The task of anthropology is to break down such specialized concepts of man, to retrieve them into the totality of human existence, and to determine their "place" and significance therein.

But anthropology would be throwing the baby out with the bath if, as a result of current attempts to define and interpret man not *as man*, but as *nature*, as *life*, as *will*, as *spirit* (*pneuma*), etc., it were to discard the specialized concepts of man entirely. One extreme is as dangerous as the other, both for the specialized humanistic sciences and for anthropology. We shall, therefore, try to establish at least *four* senses in which the Freudian idea of *homo natura* and its scientific elaboration are significant for anthropology.

First: construing man, as it does, on the basis of psychobiological mechanisms, Freud's theory of *homo natura* is also a most important *methodological organizing principle* for anthropology. It shows how order and system can be brought into our knowledge of man by subsuming all regions of his being under one unitary, organizing principle. With this instrument of organization, natural-scientific knowledge is able to make great strides in advance of anthropology, which, for its part, is first and foremost based upon the multiplicity, individuality, and essential interconnection of "observed" phenomena, and which, therefore, must take the form of *phenomenology*. In this regard, natural-scientific knowledge does the pioneer's job of staking off entire areas and delimiting particular regions, of surveying and weighing, the job of selection and preliminary classification. This work is governed by the principle of profitable applicability and of hard, rigorous natural-scientific necessity. What it results in scientifically is the ascertainment and knowledge of abstract forces* and powers, *by* which man is *ruled*, to which he is surrendered, and which regulate and serve the machinery of his life. But at the same time we must always remember "that the machinery which brings forth the image of a phenomenon is not identical with the meaning of the image," [38] that, therefore, man is more than an *homme-machine* in Lamettrie's sense.

The *second* way in which mechanism is significant for anthropology concerns precisely the fact that it shows man to be *more* than a machine, in that he can relate himself in some way to his mechanism. The reverse side of absolute mechanism, of iron necessity, is unquestionably the notion of absolute freedom. The more mechanically we interpret man, the more freely he is seen to rise *above* mechanism. "La plus intime liberté," writes an important French contemporary to whom we owe much, "consiste dans la conduite d'un homme à l'égard de son caractere." [39] This, in fact, is anthropologically the most significant function of mechanisms. Without it, we could not understand the anthropological tension

---

* "Forces refer to no experience, they are a supplement of thought." R. Lotze, *Kl. Schr.*, I, 153.

that exists between "nature and spirit," necessity and freedom, between (in the passive sense) being liv*ed*, being overpower*ed*, being driv*en*, and the spontaneity of existence.

Insight into the mechanism of *homo natura* allows, *third*, for the discovery of "rifts in the fabric of everyday life" (Löwith) that through the process of unmasking, show mental well-being to be a conglomerate of patched-over needs. The idea of *homo natura* and the ascertainment of psychobiological mechanisms are the least fallible measures against which man can test and examine his existential posture in the world. Mechanism always says "No"; the *onus probandi* of the "Yes" lies on the side of freedom, on the side of existence. Where mechanism enters the field, there must existence, its adversary, prove itself. Nothing can withstand the compelling force of mechanism as well as existence. It, and it alone, can *undermine* mechanism.

Fourth: the idea of *homo natura* epitomizes instinctuality, i.e., the drivenness of human existence, a drivenness conceived according to the principle of mechanical necessity. This general notion of a pure, vital life force has, for anthropology, the significance of a unitary "morphological" or formal principle, precisely in the way in which a leaf is a unitary morphological principle for botany. Instinct as conceived by Freud is the primal shape or form underlying all anthropological metamorphosis or transformation. Goethe believed that, in the metamorphosis of a plant, the primal form of the leaf vanished into its modifications, which were the blossom, the stamen and pistil, the calyx, the seed and the fruit, and that the primal form, as such, persisted only as a formal idea. Freud, on the other hand, sees in all human metamorphosis or change always the same basic form of the instinct itself persisting as an indestructible, ever-present *operational* factor. In this respect, Freud's doctrine, as opposed not only to Goethe, but also to Nietzsche, does not lead to a concept of genuine change. Goethe's statement that our *"whole feat consists in giving up our existence in order to exist"* [40] could never have been written by Freud. In Freudian "doctrine," the main stress is placed not upon existence as change, but upon that which persists and remains amid change, the instinct. But anthropology must attend to both the unitary primal form within change *and* the multiplicity of change as genuine meta-morphosis. For change, after all, essentially requires the *metá* of *morphose,* the *trans* of *transformatio,* the passing over from one shore of being to the shore of a *new* being.

It was, on the other hand, Goethe himself who wrote this sentence, which is so reminiscent of Plato's *Timaeus: "if nature in its lifeless beginning had not been so basically stereometric, how could it have finally attained to life in all its incalculability and immeasureability?"* [41] Here again we see the accent placed upon the *unchangeable* principle of form and, as in the *Timaeus,* we find Goethe capturing the stable principle behind the techniques of nature.

Applied to Freud, this sentence could be paraphrased: *"If man in his lifeless beginning were not so basically instinctual-mechanical, how could he have finally attained to the life of the mind in all its incalculability and immeasureability?"* Here, too, we see Freud as natural scientist, indeed as philosopher of nature, seeking to *explain* the multiplicity of life by *one* or (if we include the form-destroying principle of the death-instinct) *two* unitary principles. But, as has already been noted, man is not only mechanical necessity and organization, not merely world or in-the-world. His existence is understandable only as being-in-the-world, as the projection and disclosure *of* world—as Heidegger has so powerfully demonstrated. To this extent, his existence already embodies the principle of the possibility of separating necessity and freedom, "closed" form and "open" change, the unity of the formal structure and its abandonment and change into new formal structure.

First, however, we must spell out what this means and how we come to oppose mechanism to freedom, *"homo natura"* to existence, and natural science to anthropology.

In every psychology that makes man, as such, into an object— particularly those psychologies founded by natural scientists such as Freud, Bleuler, von Monakow, Pavlov[42]—we find a rift, a gap through which it is clear that what is being scientifically studied is not the whole man, not human-being as a whole. Everywhere we find something that overflows and bursts the bounds of such a psychology. (This "something," which is not given even a passing glance by natural-scientific psychology, is precisely what, in the eyes of anthropology, is most essential.) Limiting ourselves to Freud, we need only open one of his works at random to come upon this "something." We see him, for example,[43] writing of the construction and operations of *our* psychic apparatus, of *our* psyche as that precious instrument by means of which we maintain our lives; we see him writing about *our* psychic life, *our* thoughts.

With all these *possessive pronouns*, what is being spoken of is a being that is presupposed as self-evident and that is just as self-evidently being bracketed out, namely, *existence as ours*. The same is true, of course, of the *personal pronouns* in such phrases as: "I think, I am inclined, he declares, he reports, he recalls, he forgot, he resists, I ask him, he replies, we establish, we trust the future, we were agreed," etc. Here, too, what is being spoken of is an existence as *mine*, *his*, and so forth, and an existential communication, an interhuman or we-relationship, a relationship, that is, between a person and someone *like him*, namely, another person. When this *my* or *our*, this *I* or *he* or *we* are bracketed out, the result is that psychology becomes "impersonal" and "objective," while losing, at the same time, the scientific character of a genuine psychology and becoming, instead, natural science. Freud investigates human beings with the same "objectivity," the same existential surrender "to the object" that characterized his researches on the medulla of Ammocoetes-Petromyzon[44] in Brücke's laboratory, except that instead of an eyesight sharpened by the microscope, he attends with an ear sharpened by his incorruptible sensorium and his natural genius for understanding "human concerns." [45] In place of a reciprocal, "personal" communication within a we-relationship, we find a one-sided, i.e., irreversible, relationship between doctor and patient, and an even more impersonal relationship between researcher and object of research. Experience, participation, and confrontation between human beings in the present moment gives way to the "perfect tense" of theoretical investigation. In this way, Freud reached his tremendous *scientific insight* into man as a creature divided in himself, suffering, struggling, self-concealing and self-revealing—an insight, by means of which he contributed more to the (natural) science of man than anyone before him, and probably than anyone after him.

But we now know that natural science does not comprise the whole of man's knowledge of man. Insofar as it brackets out person and communication and, as we shall see, self and meaning—insofar, in a word, as it brackets out existence—it can never enlighten us as to why a man takes upon himself the divine mission to be productive in the search for scientific truth, why he makes this mission into the guiding light and meaning of his existence, why he suffers and struggles in its name and perceives therein a personal duty heroically to be fulfilled against all the resistance of an apathetic world.

What we have called the rift or gap is thereby widened. Just as natural-scientific psychology—a *contradictio in adjecto*—systematically ignores the most basic anthropological fact that Dasein is always *mine, yours,* or *ours,* and that *we ourselves* always stand * in relation to the abstraction of soul † as well as to the abstraction of body, so, too, it ignores the entire structure of ontological problems that surrounds the question as to the genuine *who* that so relates itself, the question as to the human self. When this self is objectified, isolated, and theorized into an ego, or into an Id, Ego, and Super-ego, it is thereby driven out of its authentic sphere of being, namely existence, and ontologically and anthropologically suffocated. Instead of following Heraclitus in *seeking*[46] himself, and St. Augustine in *returning into himself,* Freud and all other scientists we have named pass by this problem of the self as though it were something too obvious to warrant attention. Precisely in regard to this issue, it becomes plain that there are two ways to practice psychology. The one leads away from ourselves toward theoretical determinations, i.e., to the perception, observation, and destruction of man in his actuality, with the aim in mind of scientifically *constructing* an adequate picture of him (an apparatus, "reflex-mechanism," functional whole, etc.). The other leads "into our self," but not in the mode of *analytic-psychology* (which would again make us into objects), nor *characterologically* (which would objectify us with regard to our individual psychological "class"). The second way is that of anthropology, which concerns itself with the conditions and potentialities of the Dasein *as ours,* or—what comes to the same thing—that concerns itself with the possible kinds and modes of our existence.

---

* Regarding our relationship "to the body," i.e., in anthropological terms, our existence *as bodily,* its spatial and temporal characteristics, its relation to *forgetting* and *repression,* etc., cf. my "Über Psychotherapie."

† Soul is either a religious, metaphysical, natural-scientific, or, at most, objective-psychological concept, but not a *genuine* psychological concept.

This path "into our self" here refers first and foremost to the self of the scientist's own particular existence. It refers to that ground upon which he stands, that which is most authentically his own. It refers to the Dasein that he assumes as his own *within the element of the worker in science,* the seeker, shaper, and spokesman of scientific truth *in* and *for* the world. All this is the self-evident supposition of every scientist. In fact, however, of all things it is the least self-evident, but rather that which is sought out and questioned by any psychology that does not attempt to be just a natural science, but a genuine *psycho*-logy.

Perhaps what I mean will be made clearer if, with Freud's permission, I may be allowed to quote a passage from one of his letters to me: *It has always seemed to me that ruthlessness and arrogant self-confidence constitute the indispensable condition for what, when it succeeds, strikes us as greatness; and I also believe that one ought to differentiate between greatness of achievement and greatness of personality.*[47] Here Freud expresses just what we mean: that there exists a general human potentiality of being *one's* (self's) *own master,* and of having confidence in *one's self* (a potentiality, of course, that also embraces its opposite of un-self-sufficiency). We see further that this potentiality can be either self-evident or not self-evident. Here Freud is being more anthropological than he ever is in his scientific doctrines, for he is describing a certain mode of human existence, which always means a certain mode in which man assumes and lives *his Dasein as a self.*

When the scientist succeeds in viewing his own kind of existence or being-in-the-world as *his* type of selfhood, he cannot, at the same time, help but see that many other kinds of selfhood are possible and are, in fact, lived through. We recall that, "The scientific spirit engenders a particular attitude toward the things of this world." But along with this spirit, there also exist other kinds of "spirit" that are *just as basic* and that "engender" still other sorts of "attitudes" toward the things of this world. Those, however, who are completely permeated with the notion of the *primacy* of science and the scientific spirit will not see the truth of this.

Certainly science, and particularly natural science, is not and ought not to be prohibited from illuminating all regions of being, including human being. It must, however, realize that all modes of human existence and "experience" are autonomous, are—in Ranke's words—"immediate to God." That is: all modes of human existence and experience believe they are *apprehending* something of the reality of being, in the sense of *truth*, and do so, indeed, in accordance with their own proper "forms of reason," which are not replaceable by or translatable into other forms. Freud tells us that the truth cannot be attained except by scientific reason; Augustine says, "Non intratur in veritatem, nisi per charitatem," and Pascal agrees with him: "On n'entre dans la vérité que par la charité" (one cannot penetrate truth except through love). Plato (in the *Phaedrus*) is convinced that the path to the highest good must lead through divine madness, mania, while Nietzsche-Zarathustra "rides" the dionysiac metaphor to every truth. Indeed, as Kant's three great critiques of reason, the modern critiques of historical and mythological forms of reason (Dilthey, Heidegger, Cassirer, etc.), and Nietzsche's and Klages' efforts toward a critique of "life" all show, every form that reason takes may be exposed to criticism. That, however, is the task of philosophy.

Each of these modes of apprehending being represents an essential form of human existence. When one form takes on the role of judge over all the others, then the essence of man is leveled or reduced to one plane. Even though, therefore, the picture of man formed by natural science encompasses all regions of human being, it is unable to give *unmediated* articulation to the intellectual and linguistic forms peculiar to these regions and is thus unable to express the way man lives within each of these regions. (This is the task of anthropology, considered as the totality of man's experience of himself in *all* his modes of existence.) The natural-scientific method, in which the observed phenomena take second place to the merely assumed drives, furthers this levelling process. Thus, the more the idea of *homo natura* is permeated with scientific reason, the less room it leaves for the idea, not only of mythical, religious, and artistic man, but *also* of scientific man, just as the purely religious idea leaves little room for that which is peculiar to the scientific and artistic. The same is true of the artistic with respect to the scientific or the purely ethical, and likewise for the ethical with respect to the artistic, etc. But it would be a great error to conclude from this that "everything is relative." Such a conclusion would overlook the main thing, namely, the *existence* which opts for one of these modes (whether it just accepts a particular mode as its fate, or at the same time wills *to take it upon itself as its own*). With respect to these "relativities" existence is ever the absolute.

These forms of reason do not hang suspended in the air. Science, art, ethics, religion are not abstractions. They are types and modes in which the Dasein exists, and in which it understands, interprets, and expresses *itself*. The fact that all these forms of existence are possible reveals to us the *historicity* of the human Dasein; their actual realization reveals its *history*. The genuine antipode to Freud is, therefore, that which permeates the work of Herder, Goethe, W. von Humboldt, Lotze, Dilthey and, in our times, Heidegger, or Ziegler: the notion that what man is can only be learned from his history. As far back as 1883 Dilthey[48] wrote: "Man, considered as a fact preceding history and society, is a function of genetic explanation." "The individual always experiences, thinks, and acts within a historically conditioned communal sphere." This is but a corroboration of what we already knew, namely, that the *construction* of every scientific picture of man must begin with a destruction of his historicity, i.e., with that which man, as historical Dasein in the "structural context" of experience, expression, understanding, and meaning, can objectify.

Nowhere is this destruction more careful and thorough than in the natural sciences. Thus, the natural-scientific idea of *homo natura* must "destroy" man to the degree that he is taken as living and as being understandable in only one of his manifold meaning matrices (*Bedeutungsrichtungen*). It must work through the natural-scientific dialectic until only the dialectical reduction-product, the *tabula rasa*, remains. In this process, all that makes man into a man, and not an animal, is obliterated. Moreover, all those who seek to "deal" scientifically and practically with man must and do begin from this point. Only when man "as he lives" is thus destroyed, can one begin to *construct* him according to a particular principle or idea, be it Nietzsche's *Will to Power* as holding the possibility of making man's tortured life meaningful again, or be it Freud's *pleasure principle* as having the power to preserve and heighten life.

All this corresponds to the method of natural science in general, which first reduces the world to an event bare of meaning in order

subsequently to allow man to interpret this same artificially objective event "subjectively"—even while the world has already
been encountered (as it ever is) as "laden with meaning." [49] So,
too, "man" is reduced to a meaningless event, a creature driven
and overwhelmed by blind forces, in order to interpret what it is
in human life that goes beyond these forces—namely, meaning—
as poetic fiction (Nietzsche), or as illusion, consolation, or beautiful semblance. Now it is one thing to think it possible to use this
kind of destructive-constructive procedure in order completely to
unmask all of humanity's belief in meaning. This attitude is known
as *nihilism*. But it is quite another thing to attack the hypocrisy of
a particular cultural epoch, or group of people, or individual person, and, in fact, expose them as living "beyond their means." It is
this latter role in which both Freud and Nietzsche demonstrated
their genius. To confuse the unmasking of a *particular* hypocrisy
with the destruction of the meaningfulness of human existence in
general is to fall into the grave error of *interpreting a priori or
essential potentialities of human existence as genetic developmental
processes, the error, in short, of interpreting existence as natural
history*. It results in "explaining" the religious mode of existence
by the anxiety and helplessness of childhood and early manhood,
the awareness of God by the father complex, the ethical mode of
existence by external compulsion and introjection, the artistic by
the pleasures of beautiful semblance,* etc.

This anthropological critique is also, of course, directed to the
theory of *sublimation*. Here, too, we are faced with a confusion of
two things. We have, on the one hand, the indubitable fact of the
"transition" of an instinctual impulse from a lower to a higher
form—or, in other words, a "transition" from directedness toward a
"lower" to a "higher" meaning-content. The trouble is that this
fact is confused with the assumption of a "derivation" of higher
forms with their own particular meaning-contents *out of* the lower.
We must emphasize that no criterion for *judging* a form as lower or
higher can be mined out of instinct or the pleasure principle as such.
For pleasure is just as much of an abstraction as force or power.

Here we can but repeat what Lotze wrote in his review of

---

* Concerning art, Freud in this respect is markedly methodical and cautious.
Cf. his *Leonardo*, his studies of Dostoevsky (*Ges. Schr.*, XII, 7 ff.) and his study
of the Moses of Michelangelo (X, 286).

Fechner's *On the Highest Good* for, in this context, too, Fechner was Freud's scientific prototype. Lotze criticizes Fechner's "maximum of pleasure" as "formless" and containing "in itself *no* further *morphological principle*." He argues that it involves a "nameless, unnamed pleasure" that "allows *no qualitative content to shine through*," and that this maximum "*seems to be the pinnacle of an* additive scale." * This pleasure, furthermore, represents merely "*accumulation and quantity*," instead of being scaled "*according to its meaning*." Such pleasure is an "abstraction," an "inadequate life principle"; its (pleasure's) true value will always seem to us contingent upon its *object* or *content*." "Truthfulness, diligence," etc., are not simply means to the end of attaining the most pleasure, but, rather, *forms* "within which the height of pleasure can first blossom forth," "means by which the *qualitative pinnacle* of pleasure can first be attained." [50] (Emphasis added.)

We can, at this point, speak of the "relation of *pleasure* to human existence." We have only to make the objective *principle* and mechanisms of pleasure anthropologically retroactive, i.e., to retrieve into the Dasein what phenomenologically is fundamental to it. We see then that what Freud, following Fechner's model, elevated to the pleasure principle is *one* and *only* one particular mode of human existence or being-in-the-world. It was this mode that Heraclitus singled out and defined anthropologically as man's existence in the *"idios"*-cosmos, as the reversion to the private world.[51] Sleeping, dreaming, the surrender to passion and sensory pleasure are what Heraclitus cites as instances of this form of being. What is involved here is a form of selfhood in which the self in its historicity is not yet presentationally apparent (cf. Kierkegaard's concept of repetition), but is merely "momentarily" arrested and caught up. What is involved, in other words, is a form of being that can be characterized as being-overcome or being-overpowered. It is thus a form of passivity, the passive givenness of human beings to their momentary being, Klages' "pathic must." This by no means implies that one cannot speak here of a human self. For human passivity, the human "must," is not simply and merely reactivity, being-done-to (*Widerfahrnis*). Essentially, it is a particular way in which the self re-

* Here Lotze has anticipated Erwin Straus's (*The Primary World*) critique of atomistic psychology.

lates itself, which may be characterized as the *self-having*-to-let-itself-be-overcome. Instead of a self grounded in itself, sufficient unto itself, a self that can mature only *via* a *working* encounter with the world, we have here a self that is not autonomous, a self swept along by its images, wishes, and drives. Freud succeeds in constructing *homo natura* by generalizing this *one* cosmos, this *one* anthropological mode of being, into an objective principle and an absolute life and death power. When, furthermore, he succeeds in discovering the face of *homo natura* as ever lying beneath that of *homo cultura*, the anthropological significance can only be that we can never *entirely* give up, or *completely* rise above life in the *idios*-cosmos, the private world. This, however, only means that the various modes of human existence are not simply interchangeable, but are, rather, immanent in each other. If this is so, the same must also be true for the *koinós*-cosmos, for the movement into the spiritual-historical community, the participation in and the sharing of reason, ethics, art, and religion. Nor can life in either of these *cosmoi* ever be completely nil, for man is as much a communal as he is an individual being; he navigates his life back and forth *between* them.

If Freud repeatedly finds that mankind, like the individual, "lives beyond his means," this does not mean that the pleasure principle dominates human life in its entirety, but only that man in his everyday life takes his existence *too lightly*, that the Dasein *makes light* of itself. This unseriousness, this shirking of difficulties, manifests itself, as Freud revealed to mankind, in the neuroses, those adult forms of infantile, i.e., dependent, life, that cling to the moment and continue to cling to it without insight. The actual mode of such an existence, determined by and confined to the moment, is *wishing*, wishing "beyond" real fate: reckless phantasy. Opposed to this is living in the truth, and doing and saying the truth, as they are exemplified in Freud's own life. The "Western command to act," of which Thomas Mann once spoke, is truly the command to seek and to proclaim scientific and artistic truth. This command was uttered and heeded for the first time in the age of the Greeks; it was uttered, for the second time, more shrilly and imperatively in the age of the first natural scientists; but most shrilly, most urgently and most distressingly in our own age, the age of scientific technology.

But Western man does not live in the house he has thus labored to build; he finds no home, no realized goal. Instead, the more he follows this command to act, the more he is set adrift. "Since Copernicus," says Nietzsche, "man has been running from the center into X." * Wishful thinking could not arrest his flight, nor can flight put an end to his wishful thinking; the more fate has tried to accustom man to measure, number and weight, the more reckless has been his wishful thinking. As Nietzsche has said, man is like a tree: "The more he strives upwards toward the heights and toward light, the more powerfully his roots strive earthward, downward, into darkness and depth—into evil." Only the productive man, the man who loves and seeks the *truth*, the man—in other words—*capable of change:* only this man to whom the command to act is not an order and a whip, but a task and mission "unto life and unto death," the *explorer* and the *artist*, only he can "hold out," suspended between good and evil, rising and falling, balanced between wishing and fate, and endure this life of suffering.

Thus Freud, in his historical existence, stands before us as the paradigmatic man of this century. At the other extreme, we see the many, the all-too-many—the unproductive ones and deserters from the truth, those unredeemed and cowed by pain, those fettered and incapable of change, the too-good and the too-evil, who fear either to rise or to fall, who have run aground because of their unbridled wishes and who have been wrecked by a fate that commands moderation—the neurotics and the fanatics, whom Freud studied and through whom he conceived and developed the idea of *homo natura*.

It is clear that as mankind as a whole has been running away from the center into X, the number of individuals who have themselves found no center has inevitably grown immense. It is equally

* Freud recognizes *three* such "blows to human narcissism": First, the *cosmological* by Copernicus; second, the *biological* by Darwin: "Man is not a creature different from animals or superior to them; he himself is of animal descent, more closely related to some species and more distantly related to others. His later acquisitions have not succeeded in effacing the evidence, both in his physical structure and his mental dispositions, of his parity with them. This is but the second, the *biological* blow to human narcissism . . ." (*Ges. Schr.*, X, 352); third, the psychological by Freud himself, which consists in his showing man that "the ego is not master in its own house" (*Ibid.*, p. 355).

clear that at present psychology must take the place of theology, health of redemption, symptom of suffering, the physician of the priest, and that instead of the meaning and substance of life, pleasure and unpleasure have become the major problems of life. In Nietzsche, the "philosopher with a hammer," and in the physician Freud, the century has found both its taskmasters and its educators. Nietzsche defined the unknown X, into which mankind is running, as the cycle of the eternal return of the same—a solution that his contemporaries neither desired nor could accept—and thought that he had found a measure and a center[52] in "the striving beyond man," in the *superman*. Freud, on the other hand, defined the unknown X as the outcome of the struggle between eros and death,[53] and believed he had discovered a measure and a center in his insight into a human nature that, even as it "develops," remains fundamentally the same, and in man's wise submission to the laws and mechanisms of this nature.

But as an explorer of nature, he could not rest content with merely pointing out the goal. He also worked laboriously to indicate the path, the "method" by means of which the individual might reach that goal. As a physician, he helped the individual to follow that path with untiring patience. In his own human existence, he lit the way for mankind, teaching us to respect the hidden forces in life, to trust the power of scientific reason, to face the truth in ourselves and in the inexorability of death.

Notes

1. S. Freud, *Gesammelte Schriften* (Vienna, 1924-1934), Vol. XI, 465.
2. *Ibid.*, XII, 249 f.
3. *Ibid.*, XI, 464.
4. *Ibid.*, XI, 292.
5. E.g., *ibid.*, X, 345; XI, 231.
6. *Ibid.*, X, 324.
7. *Loc. cit.*
8. *Loc. cit.*
9. *Ibid.*, X, 322 f.
10. *Ibid.*, VI, 223.
11. *Ibid.*, XI, 168.

12. *Ibid.*, XII, 235.

13. *Ibid.*, VII, 62.

14. Cf. H. Rickert, *Die Grenzen der naturwissenschaftlichen Begriffsbildung;* L. Binswanger, *Einführung in die Probleme der allgemeinen Psychologie;* T. Haering, *Philosophie der Naturwissenschaft.*

15. Cf. R. Honigswald, *Denkpsychologie* (2nd ed.), and Erwin Straus, *The Primary World.*

16. *Ibid.*, XII, 319.

17. *Ibid.*, V, 211.

18. *Ibid.*, V, 207.

19. *Ibid.*, XI, 464.

20. *Ibid.*, XI, 436.

21. *Ibid.*, XI, 448.

22. *Ibid.*, V, 209.

23. *Loc. cit.*

24. *Loc. cit.*

25. Löwith, "Nietzche im Lichte der Philosophie von L. Klages," *Reichls Philosoph. Almanach*, IV, 310.

26. Cf. Klages, *Die psychologischen Errungenschaften Nietzsches*, as well as the above-cited article by Löwith. I have learned much from both. But Löwith's corrections of Klages' conception seem necessary to me.

27. See also "Dream and Existence" [this volume].

28. Freud, XII, 228.

29. *Ibid.*, XII, 239.

30. *Ibid.*, II, 456.

31. Cf. 32nd *Vorlesung, Ges. Schr.*, XII

32. Freud, V, 470.

33. R. Lotze, *Kl. Schriften*, III, 310.

34. Freud, XII, 165.

35. *Ibid.*, IV, 435.

36. Lotze, I, 228.

37. Binswanger, *Über Ideenflucht* (Zürich, 1933). But see also "Freud and the Magna Charta of Clinical Psychiatry" [this volume].

38. See Lotze's polemic against the atomic theory of his old friend Fechner, *Kl. Schriften*, III, I, 229.

39. René Le Senne, *Obstacle et Valeur.*

40. Goethe, "Maximen und Reflexionen," *Schriften der Goethegesellschaft*, XXI, 57.

41. Goethe, XII, 156.

42. For a critique of Pavlovian psychology, see Erwin Straus, *The Primary World;* F. Buytendijk and H. Plessner, "Die physiologische Erklärung des Verhaltens," *Acta Bibliographica*, Series A (1935), I, 3.

43. Freud, XII, 416 f.

44. *Ibid.*, XI, 121.

45. *Ibid.*, XI, 120.

46. Cf. Frg. 101, Diels.

47. April 14, 1912.

48. See Freud, VII, x.

49. With regard to this, see my controversy with Erwin Straus in "Geschehnis und Erlebnis," *Ausg. Vort. u. Aufs.*, Vol. II.

50. Lotze, II, 282 f.

51. See "Dream and Existence" [this volume] and my "Heraklitus Auffassung des Menschen," in *Augs. Vort. u. Aufs.*, Vol. I.
52. See Löwith, *Nietzsches Philosophie der ewigen Wiederkunft des Gleichen*, 1935.
53. See Freud, *Beyond the Pleasure Principle*.

Freud and the Magna Charta
of Clinical Psychiatry

*A great idea fills the man of genius
and protects him from everything
except his fate.*   HOFMANNSTHAL

It was on a September morning of the year 1927. Having broken away from the congress of German neurologists and psychiatrists that was meeting in Vienna, I had hastened to Freud in the Semmering, impatient to return at last the unforgettable visit he had paid me at an unhappy time in my life. Now I was about to leave and we were talking about the old days. Soon, however, the conversation turned to what, twenty years earlier, had brought us together and, in spite of considerable differences of opinion, had held us together —his lifework, his "great idea."

Using as a concrete clinical example a very severe case of obsessional neurosis that had greatly preoccupied both of us,* I raised the question as to how we were to understand the failure of such patients to take the last decisive step of psychoanalytic insight, which the physician expects of them, and instead, persist in their misery in defiance of all efforts and technical progress made so far. As a contribution toward answering this question, I suggested that such a failure might be understood as the result of something that could only be called a "deficiency of spirit," that is, an inability on the part of the patient to raise himself to the level of "spiritual communication" with the physician. Only on the basis of such communication, I said, could they gain insight into the "unconscious

[* TRANSLATOR'S NOTE: See Binswanger's note about this in his *Freud: Reminiscences of a Friendship* (Grune & Stratton, 1957).]

instinctual drive" in question and be enabled to take the last decisive step toward self-mastery. I could hardly believe my ears when I heard him say, "Yes, spirit is everything." I presumed that by spirit, Freud meant something like intelligence. But then he continued: *"Mankind has always known that it possesses spirit; I had to show it that there are also instincts.* But men are always unsatisfied, they cannot wait, they always want something whole and ready-made; *but one has to begin somewhere and only very slowly move forward."* Encouraged by this admission, I went a step further, explaining that I found myself forced to recognize in man something like a basic religious category; that, in any case, it was impossible for me to admit that "the religious" was a phenomenon that could somehow be derived from something else. (I was thinking, of course, not of the origin of a particular religion, nor even of religion in general, but of something that I have since learned to call the religious I-thou relationship.)

But I had stretched the bow of agreement too far and began to feel its resistance. "Religion originates in the helplessness and anxiety of childhood and early manhood," Freud curtly said. "It cannot be otherwise." With that, he went to the drawer of his desk: "This is the moment for me to show you something," and he laid before me a completed manuscript that bore the title, "The Future of an Illusion," and looked at me with an inquiring smile. From the trend of our conversation I easily guessed what the title meant. It was time for me to go. Freud walked with me to the door. His last words, spoken with a shrewd, slightly ironic smile, were: "I am sorry I cannot satisfy your religious needs." Never was it more difficult for me to take leave of my great and revered friend than it was at that moment when, in full awareness of the "great idea" that culminated his gigantic struggle and had come to be his destiny, he held out his hand to me.

The most important, the most *authentic* problem that must be faced in interpreting Freud's work is this: Does his work signify only a "slowly progressing" beginning, that is, a torso that may legitimately be thought of as part of "the whole"? Or is his "great idea" about the instinctual nature of mankind of sufficient compass to stand in no need of any "enlarging"? If we deny the latter, then we are obliged to view Freud's great idea as not being the last word that can be spoken about man. And we thereby find ourselves confronting a further alternative that is crucial in that it places the interpretation of Freud in a genuinely historical setting: Is this "enlarging" to be undertaken *with* Freud himself or must it be attempted *without* him? In other words: if, for us, "understanding Freud," means "going beyond Freud," how far does Freud go with us and how far must we be prepared to go without him? The conversation I have just quoted indicates that we ought not to identify Freud's theories with the whole of his spiritual or intellectual existence. I have not found one place in all of Freud's monumental writings where he places "the mind" or "spirit" side by side with the instincts, not one place where he recognizes it as basic and contents himself with speaking "also" of the instincts. Everywhere in his writings human spirituality "arises out of" instinctuality. This is perhaps most clearly evident where he derives the ethical from narcissism.

Freud's remark that mankind has always known it "possessed spirit," though it perhaps stands as a singular admission, expresses something that is implicit in many of Freud's statements. He writes, for example, to Romain Rolland on the latter's sixtieth birthday: "Unforgettable man, to have soared to such heights of humanity through so much hardship and suffering!" Even this one sentence expresses a deep awareness of man's spirit. For, if soaring to such "heights of humanity" through hardship and suffering does not refer to spirit, to man's basic, autonomous spirit, then I should like to know what else spirit may mean.* Deep it is, this awareness, because, in Nietzsche's words, it is an awareness of great suffering as the last emancipator of the spirit. Even more than his struggles with his great idea, this "painful" awareness seems to express the total existence of the man whose genius Swiss psychiatry first recognized and whom even today, a full generation later, it still proudly views as one of its greatest champions and leaders.

* I am, of course, perfectly aware that Freud thought "the impulse to perfection observed in a minority of human beings" could be understood "quite easily as a result of instinctual repression." But apart from the fact that such a "sublimation" *into* the spiritual signifies something quite different from a "genesis" of the spiritual, it is precisely Freud's *admiration* that is a spiritual act. *The problem of spirit is, in general, not a problem of origin or genesis, but of content.* It is the "content" that the repressed assumes in its *return* that decides a man's worth and the degree to which we admire him.

In suggesting that we must not identify Freud's doctrine with the whole of his spiritual existence and that his awareness of man's spirit is not contained and encompassed by his great idea, we must of course face the objection that "theory and existence" are in any case never congruent, that Idea and Existence or, as a modern French writer puts it, *détermination et valeur* are, despite their "affinity," still incommensurable. Our view, however, gains a special significance just *because* this objection is correct; for Freud's doctrine is, in his own words, "simply psychology, certainly not the whole of psychology, but rather its substructure, and perhaps its general foundation.[1] However, should it become necessary, under any circumstance, for the total existence—not merely one facet thereof, however important—to become manifest, then it lies within the foundations of psychology. For here it is a question of attempting to understand man in the totality of his existence. But that is possible only when based on the perspective of our total existence. It is possible, in other words, only if with our total existence we can articulately recall to ourselves the "what" and "how" of being human. Only then can a hypothetical construct, bound and limited by its time, its intellectual environment, and its particular goal, be replaced by a real self-understanding "of humanity," by an insight into man's most basic ontological potentialities—by, in sum, a genuine anthropo-logy.

Of all disciplines, it is above all psychology that should be rooted in anthropology. Since, as we have just illustrated, existence can never be absorbed in the idea or in thought, and since psychology, on the other hand, seeks to be a science, a system of true propositions based on logic, we find ourselves faced with the alternative of either giving up the hope of a science of psychology or, on the other hand, of allowing our existence as much purchase as possible in our psychological thought, of thinking existentially. This is not the place to show that this is possible or how psychology as a *science* can actually be pursued *via* existentials. Nor, indeed, is it necessary any longer to do so. For in the grandiosely consistent one-sidedness of understanding man from the perspective of only one region of his being and only one categorical aspect, namely as a part of nature, as "life," *Freudian thought coincides with that of clinical psychiatry*. If, therefore, a discussion of Freud and clinical psychiatry's founding charter can limit itself to that thought, then we can attain the necessary distance and the possibility of historically understanding that thought only if we approach it within the horizon of an awareness that man is more than "life."

The establishment of clinical psychiatry, its actual Magna Charta upon which its basic conceptual categories and its character as medical science rest, dates from the year 1861, the year in which the second edition of Griesinger's *Pathologie und Therapie der psychischen Krankheiten* appeared. Griesinger's place as the drafter of clinical psychiatry's Magna Charta is based not upon his famous statement that mental diseases are diseases of the brain, a view that had already been at least intimated by both French and German alienists, and that was to be fully utilized by Meynert, Wernicke and his school, down to Kleist. Nor is it based upon the psychiatric understanding of the clinical material of the time, an accomplishment in which Griesinger was assisted by the French school and, among the Germans, primarily by Jacobi's friend, Zeller. It is due, rather, to the fact that, in his own words, he used "the light of empirical psychology" to understand psychic and psychopathological phenomena, explaining that psychic phenomena, because of their "organicity," ought only to be "interpreted" by natural scientists. His purposes were thereby well served when he hit upon a psychology that permitted psychic phenomena to be described in a way that enabled the psychologist to understand and interpret them as functions of an organ, the brain—a psychology, therefore, that reduced human psychic life to quantitatively variable, dynamic elementary processes taking place in objective time. Griesinger, himself, conceived of these processes after the analogy of "reflex action in the nervous system." In the sense, that is, of "motor-sensitive" cerebral reflexes that, however, were governed in manifold ways via the "intermediary zone" of imaginary representation.[*]

Actually, this was Herbart's[2] psychology corrupted into a mathematical game by linking it with the profoundly speculative Leibnitzian notion of "unconscious representations." Behind this psychology stood a metaphysical realism that was easily transformed into a scientific materialism. Only then was the way made clear

---

[*] The theoretical part of Freud's interpretation of dreams as well as his whole doctrine of "the genesis" of the reality principle out of the pleasure principle is based on such a view.

for the birth of a psychiatric theory or declaration of principles brought forth in the spirit of natural science, culminating in the proposition that "madness is only a symptom-complex of various abnormal cerebral conditions." The following passages indicate, however, how soberly and cautiously Griesinger advocated his materialism, as compared with those who have succeeded him to this day. "What, now, is to be said to a flat and insipid materialism that would throw over the most valuable actualities of human consciousness merely because it cannot lay its hands upon them in the brain? Insofar as empiricism treats the phenomena of sensation, imagination, and will as activities of the brain, it not only leaves untouched the actual content of the human psychic life in its whole richness and expressly clings to the fact of free self-determination, it also leaves open the metaphysical questions as to *what* it may be which enters into these relations of sensation, imagination, and will as psychic *substance*, and as to the form psychic existence assumes, etc. It must patiently await the time when questions as to the connection between the content and form of human psychic life become problems of physiology, rather than metaphysics." "The fanatics and pietists of materialism might do well to consider a point that I think has not been sufficiently emphasized in previous discussions. The elementary processes in neural matter are probably identical in all men, particularly if these processes are thought of as essentially electrical and therefore, of necessity, extremely simple, consisting of pluses and minuses. How, then, could these processes directly and exclusively give rise to the infinite multiplicity of representations, feelings, and goals not only of an individual man, but of a whole century?" [3]

We see, then, that this Magna Charta of clinical psychiatry by no means clings obstinately to the "direct and exclusive" validity of one principle serving as the guide-line for the understanding of man. Insofar as it views the free self-determination of man and the actual content of human psychic life in all its richness as lying outside its proper sphere, it leaves the door open for a "descriptive and analytical" or *verstehende* psychology. Such a psychology, which proceeds precisely from this richness of content, was later inaugurated—in almost the same words—by Dilthey, only to suffer violent attacks by experimental psychologists of the time, and to suffer indeed, as was true of Freud, not only attacks, but ostracism. But

Griesinger himself approaches the position of a *verstehende* psychology when, for example, he explains: "Almost all fixed ideas are at the very start expressions of a prejudice or a satisfaction of the individual's own emotional interests. Exclusive attention to them as though they were the principal element in insanity always leads, therefore, to a one-sided and limited understanding. Treatment and understanding in particular cases can be based only upon insight into the psychic conditions that lie at the root of their emergence." [4] We know that Freud himself calls on Griesinger as chief witness in *The Interpretation of Dreams*[5] where he speaks of his "acute observation" in showing "quite clearly that ideas in dreams and in psychoses have in common the characteristic of being fulfillments of wishes." Griesinger is also invoked in the *Two Principles*,[6] where Freud speaks of certain cases of hallucinatory psychosis in which the event that precipitated the psychosis is denied. We thus see that psychiatry's original charter left enough leeway for the bloodless colonization of at least one of Freud's basic tenets. But today this charter shows signs of having become so dogmatically rigidified that many of its advocates deem any measure proper that would condemn and excommunicate those scientists who seem to hold opposing views.

Griesinger's theory of the Ego, to which, even today, our psychiatric textbooks often give word-for-word assent, also offers enough points of contact with Freud's conceptions of Ego, Ego and Super-ego, and Ego and Id. For that doctrine was so structured that it could, if necessary, re-interpret dynamic conflict, and thus also ethical conflict, in dynamic-pathological terms. Be that as it may, Griesinger is, at it were, "more modern" than Freud in that he understands what is "unassimilated" by and oppositional to the Ego not as an *Id* (an *it*), but, rather, "as a human *thou*," whereby the genuine dialogical character of psychic conflict is much more strictly preserved.* Otherwise, the ego for Griesinger is also an

---

* It is interesting to note that where Freud wishes to represent the *dialogical* character of psychic conflict, he takes care to abandon the role of the theoretician and relates a fairy tale. See the story of the good fairy and the little sausage, in the *Vorlesungen* (*Gesammelte Schriften*, VII, 221 f.). Only once, so far as I am aware, does he present the Ego as conversing with the Id: "When the Ego assumes the features of the object, it focuses itself, so to speak, upon the Id as a love-object and tries to make good the loss of that object by saying, 'Look, I am so like the object, you can as well love me'" [11] (*Ges. Schr.*, VI, 375).

"abstraction" [7] in the sense that it is "that firm unyieldingly persistent nucleus of our individuality in which the results of our entire psychic history have combined." [8] Griesinger, too, speaks of a diminished "power and energy of the ego" in the sense of "its representational complexes *being held back*," something that occasions a "particularly painful psychic condition most tormenting and oppressive in its nebulousness," * whereby "the newly emergent pathological representations and drives engender a mental bifurcation, the feeling that the personality is disengaged, and threaten to overpower the ego." [9]

All of the above are cited not only to indicate parts of the psychiatric charter that can fit in with at least some of the essential elements of Freudian theory, but above all to indicate the most important characteristic of this charter, namely, the *depersonalization* of man. This depersonalization has by now gone so far that the psychiatrist (even more than the psychoanalyst) can no longer simply say, "I," "you," or "he" wants, wishes, etc.—the only phrases that would correspond to the phenomenal *facts*. Theoretical constructs dispose him, rather, to speak instead of *my, your,* or *his* Ego wishing something. In this depersonalization we see at work that aspect of psychiatry's founding charter that is most at odds with every attempt to establish a *genuine* psychology. An explanation of this baleful influence need go no further than the clearly recognized task that psychiatry, since Griesinger, has set itself—namely, to create a psychology that, on the one hand, serves to bring a reified functional complex into relation with a material "organ," but that, on the other hand, allows this organ itself to be divided into and understood in terms of its functions. To be convinced of the latter, i.e., to see how much the scientific "image" of the brain varies with changes in *psychological* theory, one has only to compare, say, Meynert's "brain" with that of Goldstein. The former's is a sort of infinitely complex amoeba with "pseudopoda" or "feelers" extending to the outside world; the latter's is an "organ of selection," depersonalized, highly refined, and thoroughly equal to the most varied situations and tasks.

In the life of nations, the most enduring and fruitful constitu-

---

* Here we have the positive phenomenal signs of the sustained effects of "unconscious" complexes, such as would be indispensable for a yet unwritten "Phenomenology of the Unconscious."

tions and civil codes are those that steer clear of political extremism and juridical one-sidedness. The same is true for the life of science. What in almost a flash gave Griesinger's project the character of a durable psychiatric charter was not least that he steered clear of biases and overemphasis of particular tenets without compromising himself. He had, in addition, an extremely sharp eye for *what was and what was not possible at the time* and, above all, a clear vision of what was beneficial to the over-all task of psychiatry. Therein lies his main genius. We see this with particular clarity in the position he took on the subject of brain pathology. Though he allowed himself to believe in a future merging of psychiatry with brain pathology, it nevertheless seemed to him that, "at present every attempt to effect such a fusion is premature and completely unfeasible." "If the basic inner connection with brain pathology is but kept in mind, and if here, as there, the same proper method (as anatomic-physiological as possible) is but followed, then the highly monographic working out of such symptomatically structured diseases will help, not harm, brain pathology. Such a fusion, however, is even less likely since psychiatry will have barely established its place as a part of brain pathology, and since many practical sides of psychiatry [problems as to the function of a mental institution, relation to forensic medicine, etc.] give psychiatry its own particular scope and problems and require it under all circumstances to retain a great deal of autonomy even as part of cerebral pathology." [10]

In these lines the drafter of psychiatry's Magna Charta speaks to succeeding generations as their enlightened leader and taskmaster. But not for long; his warning voice is soon to be drowned out by the intoxicating impression of rapid progress in brain anatomy and localization of functions. Indeed, Meynert pithily declared: "I lead our psychiatric knowledge back to Esquirol and know how to value the model which Griesinger gave him." * And yet Meynert violently upset Griesinger's finely poised balance between psychological and brain-anatomical conceptions and terminology, allowing the cellular and fibrous structure of the brain so much theoretical weight that psychology was degraded not only to an appendage of brain anatomy and pathology, but to a mere translation of the same into a second language. It could thus—as it did in the work of

* T. Meynert, *Klinische Vorlesungen über Psychiatrie*. For Meynert, too, reflex process is primary, and consciousness only secondary.

the great von Monakow—come to a direct juxtaposition of "brain and breeding," * and it became possible to think of the "higher" parts of the brain as the "workshops of the good," to explain religion and myth by reference to "proximal association," to speak of an "apparatus of spiritual processes," and to endow individual cortical cells with the ability to be "ensouled." In this and later more moderate speculation about cortical cells and localization, one sees clearly the dangers in undertaking to introduce number and quantification into psychology. A particularly good example of this danger is shown in Meynert's statement that the mind cannot be a monad because there are two hemispheres which in their totality are endowed with consciousness.[11] What Rokitansky valued so highly in the young Meynert, namely his earnest striving "to impress the character of scientific discipline upon psychiatry by founding it upon anatomy" had come to grief in the "immoderacy" of this striving, in his lack of Griesinger's unsurpassed vision for the whole of psychiatric endeavor and the *harmony* of partial goals that it defined and furthered. Like any medical science, clinical psychiatry can tolerate just so much theory. And whoever even slightly exceeds this amount will not be admitted into its legislative assemblies. This is the answer to the question as to why Griesinger is thus admitted and not, for example, representatives of earlier psychic, ethical, somatic, or "eclectic" theories—why Griesinger and not Ideler, Heinroth or Fleming, Jacobi or Nasse; why Kraepelin—and not Meynert or Wernicke; why Bleuler—and not Freud.

We venture now to say that of all these, the most encompassing theoretical psychiatric mind belonged to: Wernicke. Even his teacher, Meynert, said of his own work that he sought to consider mental disturbances "not merely from the standpoint of therapeutics, a standpoint that sees psychic phenomena in relation to their ramifications and ends without trying to penetrate to their roots—without, indeed, even touching the ground in which these roots lie, namely, brain-anatomy." Rather, "theories of mental illness must be raised to a comparable scientific level." [12] In this way, the concept of psychosis already becomes something quite different from what it is for "therapeutics." The same is true of Wernicke. Though he was also an outstanding clinical observer and investiga-

* See the collection of popular scientific lectures.

tor, though he took account of enormous amounts of empirical, clinical material, and though we owe to him exceptional and, in part, completely new descriptions of individual psychopathological conditions, his main interest was not the therapeutics of his day as such—not, that is, the descriptive and classificatory medical science of mental disturbances and their anatomic and biological bases. It was, rather, something with an entirely different significance—a *theory* of mental illness in the sense of a psychopathology of brain functions. As Liepmann, his student, never tired of saying: "Wernicke, with magnificent consistency and single-mindedness, always wished to have psychiatry merged with brain-function neuropathology"; he sought "to make the psychic into a neuropathological object," and he found the pathology of an idea—e.g., a megalomanic idea—not in the *content* of an idea, but in its dynamic significance. For him psychosis was not, as it was for Kahlbaum and Kraepelin, a name for a "sickness" that had a definite cause and followed a definite course. It was, rather, "the totality of psychic aberrations proceeding from a disturbance of basic neural functioning." [13]

That his influence upon clinical psychiatry is much greater and more lasting than Meynert's stems, in my opinion, not only from his more advanced knowledge of brain structure and function and his more precise techniques of observation and research. It stems, rather, from the greater conciseness and consistency of his theory, as well as in his frequent and uneven efforts to reduce psychology to physiology. For example, despite, or, rather, precisely because of the progress made in brain localization, he gives less weight to the kind and number of anatomical elements of the brain than he does to the kind, intensity, and tempo of the physiological functions of the brain. Most striking is the consistency with which he applies this point of view to the entire area of the symptomatology of particular pathological conditions, so that, to cite one example, he succeeds in bringing the flight of ideas, the compulsive busyness, and the "characterological idiosyncrasies" of the manic under one and the same term—*leveling**—and derives this from a single functional disturbance.

The further developments of the charter of clinical psychiatry,

* See, for example, his division of the psychic process into a psychomotor, intrapsychic, and psychosensory "tract."

insofar as it is not influenced by Wernicke but is associated with the names of Kahlbaum, Kraepelin, and Bleuler, is too well known to require further elaboration here. What strikes us as new in this further development is, as we know, the genuinely medical, clinical concentration of interests upon the grouping or classification of diseases according to pathological-anatomical states found to be associated with them, their symptomatology, and their historical course within the total life-history of the individual. With this, goes the distinction between patterns of clinical *states* or "habitual forms" (Hoche's syndromes) and genuine forms or processes of *disease*. What is decisive here is clinical knowledge of the typology, the presence or the absence of anatomical brain pathology, knowledge of the cause and course of the disease, and observation of the patient extending sometimes over the course of his whole life—and above all, the extension of clinical interest beyond the particular individual to his familial background.

If, now, mental illnesses are still understood as brain diseases, it is nonetheless true that observation, investigation, and treatment reach far beyond the sphere of neurological psychiatry and extend to the whole of the organism. Clinical psychiatry now becomes a branch of general and specialized biology, of, that is, the doctrine of total organismic function. It is thus clear that interest has been diverted from the relationship between psychic phenomena and processes in the brain, and that, in any event, this relationship is no longer the center of observational interest. The role of "medical psychology" accordingly becomes quite different. Instead of trying to determine the interrelationships between the structure and functions of the brain, it is now concerned with events "in the organism," which are defined, in part, from a psychological point of view. Psychology now becomes a "branch" of biology. The clearest examples of this are the biopsychological theories of von Monakow and Paulow. The *instincts* are no longer, as with Griesinger, especially "intense" sensations and feelings, but are, rather, special concentrations of partial manifestations of events in the organism, among which are to be reckoned mental phenomena, because of their transformation into the biological-neurological "psychism." Sensation, feeling, image, thought, inference, in short *psychism* as a whole now takes a place *alongside* the *chemism, physicalism,* and *mechanism* of the organism. Instead of, if it may be so expressed, a *neurological* materialism, we witness the triumph of a crass *biological* materialism. Clothed therein is the "great idea" of modern psychiatry: it, too, is based upon the old charter, undisturbed by and blind to the fact that man is more than "life." For it—according to its official program and the greater number of its proponents—morality, culture, religion, and even philosophy have, in like manner, the rank of "biological facts."

Over against this stand the tentative efforts at anthropological investigations in psychiatry in which man is not pigeon-holed by categories (natural-scientific or otherwise) but is understood from the perspective of his own—human—*being*, and which seek to describe the basic *directions* of this being. "Mental illness" is thus lifted out of the context of either the purely "natural" or "mental" and is understood and described within the context of primal human potentialities. What is revealed thereby is not only that the mentally ill "suffer from the same complexes as we," but also that they move in the same spatio-temporal-historical directions as we —though in different modes and ways. Here mental illness is not explained in reference either to disturbances of brain *function* or biological *function* of the organism, nor is it understood in reference to *life-history*. It is, rather, described with regard to the mode and manner of the particular being-in-the-world concerned.

If we wish to evaluate the *significance of Freud's doctrine for clinical psychiatry* according to objective criteria rather than on the basis of personal acquaintance and disposition, then what I have described as the Magna Charta of clinical psychiatry and its historical development must be kept in mind. In what follows I shall speak of Freud's significance only with regard to this Magna Charta.

I have already hinted that Freud's "great idea" intersects with the "great idea" of clinical psychiatry in the endeavor to explain and understand human beings and mankind from the perspective of "life." Both in Freud's doctrine and in the charter that clinical psychiatry laid down for itself there breathes the same spirit, the spirit of biology. For Freud, too, psychology is a (biological) natural science. "The most important, as well as the most obscure, elements of psychological research" are the "instincts of the organism." [14] Instinct is "the conceptual border between the somatic and the psychic." The psychic component is not something autonomous or presentational, but merely representational, "representing organic forces," [15] i.e., "effects stemming from within the body and carried over to the psychic apparatus." [16] For Freud it is the physiological and chemical processes that are properly presentational or present and that we must describe "in the pictorial language of psychology," because we still lack the "simpler" language for it. "The shortcomings of our description would most likely disappear if for psychological terms we could substitute physiological or chemical ones. They, too, only constitute a pictorial language, but one familiar to us for a much longer time and perhaps also simpler." *

Psychology is thus a preliminary undertaking, a necessity from which biology will some day free us. None of this contains anything that runs counter to the psychiatric Magna Charta. Though the insights of the man who drafted this charter were, as we have seen, much more "broad-minded," they were quickly interpreted by his successors in a much narrower, neurological or biological sense—as I have shown to be the case with Meynert and Wernicke, and as we know to be the case with von Monakow, Bleuler, Kretschmer, and many others.

To understand Freud's great ideas correctly one must not, therefore, proceed from psychology—a mistake that I myself made for a long time. For otherwise one does not do him justice and stumbles at every point against the thoroughly unpsychological concept of a psychic *apparatus*, against its topographically overlapping structure of well-defined "systems" related *dynamically* and *economically* to each other. But if these notions are—as Freud wished—understood biologically, they then fit easily into psychiatric thought that, like Freudian theory, accommodates both Fechnerian theories (topics, pleasure-pain principle, quantification of the psychic, psycho-physics) and Herbartian theory (dynamics and conflicts of representations).

This, however, is only the beginning. Much too little attention has been paid to the fact that Freud never disavowed his physiological (Brücke) and, especially, his neurological and neuropatho-

---

* *Ges. Schr.*, VI, 253. This passage also throws some light on Freud's metaphysics. Here he seems to see in scientific language images or symbols of an unknowable, indescribable *reality* standing behind them.

logical (Meynert, Wernicke) background. We see it still in his study of the Ego and the Id (1923) in the highly interesting discussion (Vol. II) about the relation between the Ego, the system *Pcs,* the system *Pcpt-Cs,* and *verbal images.* Freud's "systematization" of the psychic into a psychic apparatus not only finds its precedent in Meynert's "mental apparatus," but must also be understood "neurologically," i.e., with reference to brain physiology and physiopathology.* In this context, Freud's research on aphasia is extremely useful. Neither a historical nor a hermeneutic understanding of Freudian doctrine is possible without a thorough acquaintance with it—and not only because it was the theory of aphasia that first allowed the construction of a *neurological* (in the true sense of the word) psychic apparatus, limited though it was to the neurological basis of language and speech. It is, rather, because of the fact that here Freud encounters a researcher who introduced a decisive new idea—one alien to Wernicke—into aphasia theory: Hughlings Jackson.† With the notion of biological involution and disinvolution (or: potentiation and depotentiation), which was later to be so fruitfully worked out by Goldstein, Jackson effected a connection between neurology and biology of functions. It is upon this connection that Freud's thought is based. The greatness of his conceptions and his destiny rests, in the last analysis, upon the fact that he extended this kind of thinking to the entire psychic life of individual, society, and mankind in general—and pursued and developed it through painful decades of ceaseless, patient labor.

Development thinking is also contained in the original charter of clinical psychiatry, not only with respect to the evolution of the brain on the scale of animals leading up to man, but also with respect to the "temporal metamorphoses" of age: "In these temporal metamorphoses, these progressions from gradual growth to

---

* In contrast to Meynert, he avoids the temptation of brain *localization:* "I shall entirely disregard the fact that the mental apparatus . . . is also known to us in the form of an anatomical preparation. . . ." See *Ges. Schr.,* II, 456.

† Freud, *Zur Auffassung der Aphasien: Eine historische Studie* (Leipzig and Vienna, 1891). This work, which is often cited today because of the distinction it draws between asymbolic and agnostic aphasic disturbances, has an air of the modern about it not because Freud was saying even then that "the significance of the element of localization for aphasia has been greatly overestimated" (p. 107), but rather because there he recognized the particular importance of Hughlings Jackson's theories for the study of aphasia.

the peaks of maturity to deterioration, brain activity parallels all other organic functions and reveals itself as also subject to the developmental laws of the organism." [17] Jackson extended the notions of development and retrodevelopment to include *pathological* disturbances of psychophysical brain function, and Freud went even further in including pathological disturbances of total human psychic development. While this undertaking, attempted by Freud, permits a connection with the structure and functions of the brain, in its entirety it beggars a projection onto the brain. Even, indeed, in aphasia, relationships are infinitely more complex than could be suspected from the famous projection schemata. With regard to this, Freud, as opposed to Meynert, exercised wise theoretical restraint in constantly stressing the speculative nature of his efforts to connect brain structure and function. He had already learned from Jackson that the brain is able to react as an entity to a lesion that incompletely destroys the language apparatus. He learned, that is, "that the partial loss is the expression of the general functional degradation" or "weakening" of this apparatus: *"it answers the incompletely destructive lesion with a functional disturbance which could also arise through non-material damage."* [18] This last sentence—which Freud himself underlined—seems to me of the highest importance for the development of his theories! In appraising the function of the language apparatus under pathological conditions, Freud gave precedence to Hughlings Jackson's statement "that all these modes of reaction represent cases of *functional dis-involution* of the highly organized apparatus and correspond accordingly to earlier conditions of its functional development." [19] He cites the statement of the great English scientist, in which the tempo peculiar to each disturbance is stressed: "Different amounts of nervous arrangements in different positions are destroyed with different rapidity in different persons." *

What Freud knew about the physiological and physiopathological function of "the brain" and its complex mechanisms was at his disposal before he made his special study of the neuroses. And we may see in it the bridge that leads to his insights into the way

* Freud, *Zur Auffassung der Aphasien*, p. 102. Here he links himself also with Jackson's *critical* psychophysical parallelism. At the same time, he reveals himself as being under the influence of J. S. Mill's *Logic* (p. 80). Like most psychiatrists, Freud remained at bottom a positivist and psychologist in Mill's sense.

the brain reacts to "non-material damage," insights that can easily fit in with his experiences regarding hypnosis and suggestion. As he progressed beyond this area and grew more and more familiar with the life-*historical* element of neurosis in general and of the *infantile* portion of the life-history in particular, with the growing insight into the role of sexuality and of defense or repression—with, in fine, his growing awareness of the role of psychic conflict in neurosis and with the corresponding increase of insight into the *historical* genesis of neurotic symptomatology, the element of biological *development* occupied more and more of a central place for Freud, the biologist. For development is the only historical principle that biology recognizes. His main goal, therefore, was to trace everything he encountered of history and historicity back to biological development and to project it upon this element.* Griesinger's views about "temporal metamorphoses," about the growth and deterioration of brain activity were now far from sufficient. It was now necessary to begin further back with regard to his *developmental laws of the organism* (which also "embrace the psychic activity of the brain"). But, as indicated above, for Freud "organism" means the sum total of instinctual processes embracing the psychic, chemical, and physical events within a biological individuality. It means, in short, "the instincts" and their specification in individual tasks and performances. Normal and pathological development of the organism was for him equivalent to normal and pathological development of "the instincts" and their functional interplay. But here, too, we never find such a thing as "partial" instinctual damage. It is, rather, the whole organism that always reacts to partial damage, to a *falling* or being *driven* back of an individual instinct or instinctual component. The result of this highly complex life process is the neurotic symptom as an expression of a degraded or "weakened" total functioning of the organism. It relates itself to the injury just as do the speech or brain apparatuses themselves. It seeks to accommodate it, to master it by falling back to a lower level of functioning. Since Freud, then, we speak of neuroses and psychoses when there occurs in the brain apparatus a disturbance that is "not wholly destructive" and that in most (purely functional) cases leaves its material completely intact,

* The over-all task of psychiatry is not thereby exhausted; see my "Lebensfunktion und innere Lebensgeschichte."

but that compels or induces the apparatus to reach *back* (regress) to earlier modes of functional reaction (which in the meantime have been somewhat escalated). Since what we have here are disturbances that, in contrast to genuine brain lesions, leave intact the material structure of the apparatus, the organism can content itself with reaching back to levels that it has already contained in the course of its individual development. *This life-event, embracing, in its entirety, the disruptive, developmental, and retro-developmental factors, and taking place at a particular time with a particular tempo in a particular person is termed by Freud neurosis* (or *psychosis*). Much more so than the Wernickean concept of psychosis, it is a concept whose many biological aspects set it apart from clinical psychiatry but that, nevertheless, contains nothing that contradicts the original charter. Its most important aspect, however, is indusputably the notion of *regression*, which, though similar to dis-involution, refers far beyond it into the psychic by virtue of its "active," "oppressing" tendency, and which embraces both the life function of remaining and falling behind (fixation) as well as the life-historical forces of restraint ("repression").* It is the degree and extent of this "backward" movement that, as we know, determine the *form* of neurosis and psychosis as well as their entire symptomatology.

The role this aspect plays in Freud's theory of sexuality is too well known to bear repetition here. Freud's theory of sexuality was desgined to gain a basis for the whole of the evolutionary and revolutionary system; it is a theory in which one sees the magnificent further development of his special insights about the pathology of brain function into a conceptual edifice embracing man, world, and human experience.

To recognize this is also to recognize that the interpretation and naming of individual instinctual vectors is of secondary importance for psychiatry. What Freud, in a very broad sense, un-

---

* Freud has contributed more to the understanding of inner life history than any single person before him. We, however, distinguish our position from his in that we see the life-*historical* element as the fundament of "anthropology," while Freud sees therein only a "pictorial language" for biological *events*. The concept of regression as it recurs in *The Interpretation of Dreams* (degeneration of thoughts into images) is by no means as encompassing as the one we encounter later with particular clinical clarity in, for example, the "Psychoanalytischen Bemerkungen über den Fall Schreber" (*Ges. Schr.*, VIII).

derstands by sexuality is not contained in what the physiologist understands by the sexual drive, and especially not in what the psychologist, philosopher, or theologian understands by love. We need think only of how immensely far apart are Freud's notion of self-love in the sense of narcissism and, say, Aristotle's self-love in the sense of philautia or self-love in the Christian sense.* What Freud strove for was always to translate the pictorial language of psychology into "simpler" and—we may add—more uniform, coarser, chemical and physical "images" that, for him, seemed closer to reality. Freud does not concern himself with "pansexualism," especially not during the period of his highest development, which began with the writing of *Beyond the Pleasure Principle*. His final recognition of two *kinds* of instincts—the life and the death instinct—which he expressly[20] owed to the "reliance upon biology" (Hering's, among others), illuminates what Freud understood by sexuality and sexual instincts: certainly nothing psychological, and certainly nothing similar to the physiological, but, rather, a tendency in the basic biological processes—those processes, namely, that are involutive and assimilatory or "constructive," as opposed to those that are disinvolutive and dissimilatory or "destructive." †

* It is not simply that what is lacking is a phenomenological description of what he understands by love, but rather—and this is even more important—what is missing is any interpretation and description of what he understands by "self." As sensitive to this lack as is anthropology, among whose basic concepts is that of the self, so insensitive to it is official psychiatry, which assiduously avoids a phenomenological description and interpretation of the meaning of its psychological concepts. Wernicke's distinction between somato-, *auto-*, and allopsychic mental disturbances is simply an especially crass example of this neglect. These and many other such distinctions are merely like occasional great beacons. They can never form the basis of concept construction for psychopathology.

† The use by Freud of the expressions *Aufbau* [construction] and *Abbau* [destruction], which correspond best to the terms used by Jackson as well as Haering is to be noted above all—save for *Beyond the Pleasure Principle*—in the following summary: "The widely ranging considerations as to the processes which make up life and lead to death seem to necessitate that we recognize two kinds of instincts corresponding to the antagonistic processes in the organism of construction and destruction. The one kind, which works silently toward the goal of leading the living creature to its death, deserves, therefore, the name of the 'death instinct.' It manifests itself outwardly, by the cooperation of the numerous multicellular organisms, as *tendencies* of *destruction* [*Destruktion*] or aggression. The other group of instincts are the analytically more familiar libidinous sexual or life instincts, best understood collectively as Eros, whose goal it is to form ever greater unities out of living substance so that life may be perpetuated and brought to

The same is true of the "unconscious." It represents primarily a developmental system in the psychic apparatus and serves only secondarily as an expression in the pictorial language of psychology. The same is also true of the oral and anal stages, etc., and of the terms "Ego," "Id," and "Super-ego." With regard to the latter, for Freud the *individual* is "an unknown and unconscious Id, upon whose surface rests the Ego, developed from its nucleus, the *Pcpt*-system. That is, the Ego is essentially a representative of the outside world, reality, over against which stands the Super-ego as "attorney for the inner world." * But as regards the oral and anal, the submissive and aggressive tendencies of—as we may also say—the "individual psychobiological apparatus," these notions, like all of Freud's thought, are based upon the experience and observation of the manner in which people behave. And these modes of behavior must certainly play a role for any genuine anthropology that seeks to ascertain the fundamental meaning matrices of human beings. I have, for example, learned to consider the existential meaning matrix of "oral"—(*movement*) *toward me* and (*movement*) *away from me,* as well as that represented by the slang phrase "having a big mouth"—from an anthropological point of view.†

Our subject matter would be incompletely sketched if, in conclusion, we did not cast one more glance at the relation of Freud's *investigational methods* and *therapy to* clinical psychiatry's Magna Charta. Concerning the first, we may say that it was Freud who raised psychiatric techniques of examination to the level of a tech-

---

higher levels of development. In the living creature, the erotic and death instincts are ordinarily compounded and alloyed. But their disengagement is also possible. Life, then, would consist of the expression of conflict or interference between the two kinds of instincts, bringing to the individual, by means of death, the victory of the destructive instincts, but also the victory of Eros by means of reproduction." "Libido Theory," in *Handwörterbuch für Sexualwissenschaft,* and *Ges. Schr.,* XI, 222 f.

* See *The Ego and the Id, Ges. Schr.,* VI, 367 and 380. That which in *The Ego and the Id* (after *Beyond the Pleasure Principle* the most significant work of Freud's late development), sounds almost unbearably shrill to the ears of psychologists and anthropologists becomes the most valuable building blocks of Freud's biological system.

† See *Über Psychotherapie* and *Über Ideenflucht* (pp. 114 ff.). Of course there are still other meaning matrices that psychoanalysis does not recognize, such as, for example, that of *rising-falling.* See, in this regard, "Dream and Existence," this volume.

nique in the truly medical sense of the word. In the pre-Freudian era, the psychiatric "ausculatation" and "percussion" of the neurotic patient was, as it were, performed through the patient's shirt, in that all direct contact with personally erotic and sexual themes was avoided. Only when the physician was able to make himself into a *complete* physician, to include within the sphere of the examination his total person and the sympathetic, antipathetic, and sexual forces directed toward him by the patient, only then could he create between patient and doctor an atmosphere of personal distance and, at the same time, of medical cleanliness, discipline, and correctness. It was this atmosphere that was able to raise psychiatric technique to the level of general medicine. This, too, was possible for Freud only because his total existence was that of a *researcher*, and because of the quality of his system of thought as I have just sketched it. He saw in the "attitude" of the patient to the doctor only the regressive repetition of psychobiologically earlier parental "object-cathexes" and eliminated what was *new* in the patient's *encounter* with him. Insofar as he did this he was able to keep the physician as a person in the background and allow him to pursue his technical role unencumbered by personal influences —as is the case with surgeons or radiologists. The method of having his patients *free-associate* also goes hand in hand with this necessary and therefore unconscious *repetition* of repressed "situations" and the resistence arising from them. It must not be forgotten that the notion of strict psychic "determinism," which Freud allowed to guide him in this method, was not based on any mere intellectual theory. It was, rather, grounded in the established biological and psychological fact that *every* "experience" down to the simplest perception or even sensation (Erwin Straus, Scheler, and others) has a very definite *place* (*Stellenwert*) in the development of an individual, according to the degree and kind of effect it has. Because of this, a perception, sensation, or "association" must become manifestly discernible *again* when the total situation to which it owes its "origin" and *placing* is repeated.

We come now to our conclusion. Freud once said that psychoanalysis stands to psychiatry "somewhat as histology to anatomy"; "one studies the external form of the organ, the other studies the way it is constructed out of tissues and elementary parts; a contradiction between these two kinds of studies, of which one is the continuation of the other, is unthinkable." [21] As I hope I have shown, Freud is correct with regard to the latter, but not the former claim. In psychiatry, as it were, "histological" and thus "microscopic" examination would correspond to a more detailed "microscopic" analysis of clinical symptomatology and its material substrata, undertaken for the purpose of deepening and enlarging the classification of psychoses with regard to their *general* etiology and course. Here, therefore, what we have is, rather, two points of view that *intersect*. We are faced with the same situation as we were in regarding the doctrines of Meynert and Wernicke. Of the latter, Liepmann has said that it points research in a direction "perpendicular" to that which clinical psychiatry usually takes. All these doctrines attempt—insofar as they are relevant to clinical psychiatry—to move in *one* direction from the "knowledge of psychic phenomena in all their multifariousness" to "a penetration to their roots." Meynert seeks to impress the character of scientific discipline upon psychiatry "by means of an anatomical foundation," Wernicke by means of "anchoring" its charter in neuropathological brain functions, and Freud by extending psychiatric research to the study of the psychobiological developmental history of the organism as a whole.

The psychic object becomes with Meynert an anatomical, with Wernicke a neuropathological, and with Freud a biological theory. But as we have seen, the spirit of the psychiatric charter tolerates the predominance of no *theory* and thus also refuses to have psychiatry founded upon Freudian theory. On Freud's side, however, we have found nothing in his theory that runs counter to this charter. Though his doctrine may be preponderantly materialistic—corresponding in this respect with the intentions of the founders of the psychiatric charter—the direction he sets for psychiatric research is nevertheless the only one that does *not* "leave untouched the actual content of the human psychic life in its whole richness." That this richness of "actual psychic content"—as Dilthey puts it—is projected upon and reduced to a psychobiological apparatus ought to be its least disturbing aspect to the dogmatic proponent of the psychiatric clinical charter. For he, too, leads us merely to an enormous *simplification* of the life of the psyche and to a *reduction* of it to a crude natural scientific schema[22] governed by a few principles. Freud, however, seeks out that rich psychic content in its deepest detail and source, insofar as he pursues the difficult route of transposing and translating psychic content into various biologically functional "systems" and "modes of speech" and then constructs thereof a uniquely encompassing and complex conceptual system. In these respects, therefore, we may say of Freud not only that he builds upon the ground mapped out by Griesinger's reference, in the psychiatric charter, to emotional interests and their connection with insanity—not only, that is, does Freudian theory fill a very pronounced *gap* in this charter —but, in addition, it deepens the very ideas already contained in it by casting light upon things that could never have been seen from within this charter alone. Now man is no longer merely an animated organism, but a "living being" who has origins in the finite life process of this earth, and who dies its life and lives its death; illness is no longer an externally or internally caused disturbance of the substance or function of the organism, but the expression of a disturbance of the "normal" course of a life on the way to its death. Sickness and health, the "alarum" and the "soundless quiet" of life, struggle and defeat, good and evil, truth and error, human nobility and debasement are here—all of them fleeting scenes in the passing drama of the marriage of life and death. But, we must add, here "man" is not yet man. For to be a *man* means not only to be a creature begotten by living-dying life, cast into it and beaten about, and put into high spirits or low spirits by it: it means to be a being that looks its own and mankind's fate in the face, a being that is "steadfast," i.e., one that likes its own stand, or stands on its own feet. Thus, too, sickness, labor, suffering, pain, guilt, and error are not yet, with Freud as we consider him here, (historical) signs and stages; for signs and stages are not merely fleeting scenes of a passing drama, but "eternal" moments of a historically determined being, of being-in-the-world as *fate*. That we are *lived* by the forces of life is only one side of the truth; the other is that *we* determine these forces as our fate. Only the two sides together can take in the full problem of sanity and insanity. Those who, like Freud, have forged their fates with the hammer—the work of art he has created in the medium of language is sufficient evidence of this—can dispute this fact least of all.

Notes

1. S. Freud, *Gesammelte Schriften*, XI, 387.
2. See M. Dorer, *Historische Grundlagen der Psychoanalyse* (Leipzig, 1932).
3. Griesinger, *Pathologie und Therapie der psychischen Krankheiten*, 2nd ed., 6 f.
4. *Ibid.*, p. 73.
5. Freud, II, 98.
6. *Ibid.*, V, 409.
7. Griesinger, p. 48.
8. *Ibid.*, p. 56.
9. *Ibid.*, p. 63 f. Cf. also 72 f.
10. *Ibid.*, p. 9 f.
11. T. Meynert, *Über den Wahn*, p. 85.
12. Cited from Meynert, *Deutsche Irrenärzte*, II, 133.
13. *Monatsschr. f. Psych. u. Neur.*, Vol. 30, 1911.
14. Freud, VI, 223.
15. *Ibid.*, VIII, 426.
16. *Ibid.*, VI, 223.
17. Griesinger, p. 3.
18. Freud, *Zur Auffassung der Aphasien*, p. 32.
19. *Ibid.*, p. 89.
20. Freud, *Gesammelte Schriften*, XI, 223.
21. *Ibid.*, VII, 262.
22. Cf. *Über Ideenflucht*, p. 147 f. where I have thrown into relief the four clinical reduction-principles and brought them under the following formula: "It is everywhere a matter of the transformation of the complex *ego-principle*—with its polarity of *object* and *experience*, of *I* and *you*(*Du*) and its connection with the problem of communicative understanding and culture—into the uni-dimensional *id-principle*."

Heidegger's Analytic of Existence and Its Meaning for Psychiatry

> *And do you think that you can know the nature of the soul intelligently without knowing the nature of the whole?*
>
> PLATO, *Phaedrus*, 270c

Martin Heidegger's analytic of existence is doubly significant for psychiatry. It affords empirical psychopathological research a new methodological and material basis that goes beyond its previous framework, and its treatment of the existential concept of science places *psychiatry in general* in a position to account for the actuality, possibility, and limits of its own scientific world-design or, as we may also call it, transcendental horizon of understanding. These two aspects are quite closely related, and both have their roots in Heidegger's *Sein und Zeit* and *Vom Wesen des Grundes*.

The purpose of *Sein und Zeit* was the "concrete" working out of the question as to the meaning of *Being*. Its preliminary goal was to interpet time as the possible horizon of any understanding of Being. To this end, Heidegger, as we know, gives us the "concrete" working out of the *ontological structure* of the Dasein as being-in-the-world or transcendence. In thus indicating the basic structure of the Dasein as being-in-the-world, Heidegger places in the psychiatrist's hands a key by means of which he can, free of the prejudice of any scientific *theory*, ascertain and describe the *phenomena* he investigates in their full phenomenal content and intrinsic context. It was Edmund Husserl's great achievement to have shown, after Brentano, just what this "phenomenological" method is, and to have indicated what enormous vistas it opened for research in the various sciences. Husserl's doctrine, however, concerns itself solely with the sphere of *intentionality*, considered as the unitary relation between transcendental subjectivity and transcendental objectivity. The shift from the "theoretical" ascertainment and description of psychic processes or events in a "subject" to the ascertainment and description of the forms and structures of "intentional consciousness," consciousness of something or directedness toward something, was a quite decisive shift for psychopathological research. Nevertheless, this consciousness was still suspended in the air, in the thin air of the transcendental ego. The —in the full sense of the word—"fundamental" accomplishment of Heidegger consisted not only in stating the problematic nature of the transcendental possibility of intentional acts. What he did, in addition, was to solve this problem by showing how the intentionality of consciousness is grounded in the temporality of human existence, in the Dasein. Intentionality in general is only possible on the basis of "transcendence" and is thus neither identical with it nor, conversely, does it make transcendence possible. Only by referring intentionality back to the Dasein as transcendence or being-in-the-world and only, therefore, with the inclusion of the transcendental ego in the actual Dasein, was the ("objective-transcendental") question posed as to the *what-ness* of the beings that we ourselves are.* We may thus say, with Wilhelm Szilazi, that *Sein und Zeit* is the first inquiry into our existence "with regard to its objective transcendence."

Since, in "The Existential Analysis School of Thought," [1] I have already sketched the path thus taken, we turn our attention now to the second aspect of Heidegger's dual significance for psychiatry—namely, the question as to the actuality, possibility, and limits of the horizon of understanding, or world-design of psychiatry in general. This problem might also be characterized as concerning the awareness by psychiatry of its own essential structure as science, or, again, as the effort of psychiatry *to understand itself as science*. It goes without saying that in this brief space I can only hint at what the answer to this problem might be.

---

* Here is one juncture where the gap separating Sartre and Heidegger reveals itself. Sartre does not refer back in this manner; indeed, he reproaches Heidegger: "that he has completely avoided any appeal to consciousness in his description of Dasein." *Being and Nothingness*, p. 85.

I

A science does not understand itself simply by being clear as to the "object" it studies and the basic concepts and research methods by which it conducts these studies. Rather, a science understands itself only when it—in the full sense of the Greek *lógon didónai*—accounts for its interpretation (expressed in its basic concepts) of its particular region of being upon the background of that region's basic ontological structure. Such an accounting cannot be executed with the methods of the particular science itself, but only with the aid of philosophical methods.

Science is autonomous with regard to what, in its terms, can be *experienced*. Here it justifiably protects itself against any philosophical "encroachment," just as, for its part, any philosophy aware of its own purposes restrains itself from such encroachment. While, as history has shown, science and philosophy share the same roots, this means that whereas science sets the questions by which it approaches that which is, philosophy poses the question as to the nature of proof as ground and foundation—the question, that is, as to the function performed by transcendence, as such, of establishing a ground. This is simply to repeat—in different words—that a science can understand itself only if it accounts for the original formulation of its question within which, *qua* this particular *scientific* mode of grounding, it approaches the things it studies and has them speak to it. To this extent, and only to this extent, is science to be "referred" to philosophy; to the extent that is, that the self-understanding of a science, considered as the articulation of an actual store of ontological understanding, is possible only on the basis of *philosophical*, i.e., ontological understanding, in general.

II

Whereas physics and biology and the humanistic sciences as well rest upon their own particular "actual store of ontological understanding," [2] the same cannot be said of psychiatry. In its clinical setting, psychiatry views its object, the "mentally ill human being" from the aspect of nature, and, thus, within the natural-scientific—

mainly biological—horizon of understanding. Here psychiatry's object is—as it is in all of medicine—the "sick" organism. But in psychotherapy, it views its object from the aspect of "the human being," and thus within an (either prescientific or systematic) anthropological horizon of understanding. Here the object of psychiatry is the "mentally ill" Other, the fellow man. The incompatibility of these two conceptual horizons or reality-conceptions is not resolvable within science and leads not only to endless scientific controversy, but, also, as the present situation in psychiatry shows, to a split into two separate psychiatric camps. This fact alone shows how important it is for psychiatry to concern itself with the question as to what we human beings *are*.

In actual practice, these two conceptual orientations of psychiatry usually overlap—as one quick glance at its "praxis" tells us. The clinician, too, first "relates himself to" his patient or seeks "an understanding with him." And precisely from this relating or understanding he attains his initial perspective from which to ascertain the *symptoms* of the disease. It was, in fact, Hönigswald who expressed the view that psychiatric symptoms are primarily disturbances of communication and thus refer[3] to a "meaning given to human intercourse." One of the basic demands of medical psychotherapy, on the other hand, is to view the prospective patient *also* as an organism, the demand, namely, that what must first be ascertained is whether the patient is intact "as" an organism—especially as regards the central nervous system—and whether the possibility of such a disturbance of intactness sets up certain therapeutic limitations from the outset.

To the extent, now, that the psychiatrist views the organism as a natural object, i.e., "physicalistically," to the extent that he thus views the fellow man before him, with whom he tries to come to an understanding and who is his partner in the community of man and is another "human soul"—to that extent will his ontological understanding be clouded, at the outset, by the *psychophysical problem*. For, the mind-body problem is not an ontological problem, but a problem of scientific knowledge, a purely theoretical problem. "Theory," therefore, is called in for help in "solving" this problem. No theory, however, can really "solve" it, but can only seek to bridge mind and body with more or less perfunctory theoretical sham solutions ("auxiliary hypotheses"), or immerse the whole problem in a pseudophilosophical (materialistic, spiritualistic, biologistic, or psychologistic) smoke screen.

The problem of mind and body, though it arises out of urgent practical scientific needs, is incorrectly formulated because science —as it must—fails to see that what is involved are two quite different scientific conceptions of reality which cannot be bridged by any theory nor merged together by any amount of speculation. For as soon as I objectify my fellow man, as soon as I objectify his subjectivity, he is no longer my fellow man; and as soon as I subjectify an organism or make a natural object into a responsible subject, it is no longer an organism in the sense intended by medical science. The situation can be put to rights only if we go *behind* both conceptual horizons or reality-conceptions—that of nature and that of "culture"—and approach man's basic function of understanding Being as the establishing of ground—a transcendental function. Our task, then, is to use philosophical rigor in understanding both the power and the impotence of these two conceptions considered as *scientific*, or even as prescientific or "naïve," modes of transcendental grounding or establishment.

III

Scientific understanding is oriented toward fact and factuality, i.e., toward reality and objectivity. Such a project (or design) separates areas of fact and places the various entities in a factual, real, objective, and systematic interconnection.[4] Heidegger has shown that such a project is not simply a demarcation of regions, but is also the establishing of a ground. That is, in such a project a particular sphere "of being" (beings) are "thematized" and thereby rendered accessible to objective inquiry and determination. If this is so, then such a project must be constantly subjected to a critique that concerns itself with the fundamental issues of all scientific inquiry. It is not *only* philosophy that performs this function of criticism. We find it constantly being effected in the way scientific concepts of themselves break down and undergo transformations—in, that is, the various *crises* of science.

Today psychiatry finds itself in just such a crisis. The "Magna

Charta" * or framework that was its guide up to now has been broken down on the one hand by psychoanalysis and by psychotherapy's generally deepened understanding of its own scientific bases, and on the other hand by ever-increasing insight into the game of psychosomatics, and above all by "structural" † and empirical existential-analytic research, which has widened the scope and cast light on psychiatry's horizon of understanding.

Simply as regards this "crisis," Heidegger's phenomenological-philosophical analytic of existence is important for psychiatry. This is so because it does not inquire merely into particular regions of phenomena and fact to be found "in human beings," but, rather, inquires into the *being* of *man as a whole*. Such a question is not answerable by scientific methods alone. The conception of man as a physical-psychological-spiritual unity does not say enough. For, as Heidegger says, the being of man cannot be ascertained by the "summative enumeration" of the rather ambiguous ontological modes of body, mind, and soul. What is needed is the return to (subjective) transcendence, to the Dasein as being-in-the-world, even while constant attention is being accorded its objective transcendence.

It is, of course, true that modern psychiatry also seeks to know the nature of the "soul" by regarding the nature of the whole—as Plato prescribed (see the chapter motto). But psychiatry, as a branch of medicine, primarily views this whole as "life," as a biological whole, and every "consideration" of this whole ordinarily takes place at the level of factual objective "relations." In addition, the soul is understood as something neutrally present (*vorhanden*) in or with the body. But even aside from these considerations, what is meant by the Greek expression *to Holon*—in contrast to *to Pan*—is not the totality of the whole, but—as in Aristotle—wholeness as such. Heidegger's analytic of existence, by inquiring into the being of the whole man, can provide not scientific, but philosophical understanding of this wholeness. Such an understanding can indicate to psychiatry the limits within which it may inquire and expect an answer and can, as well, indicate the general horizon within which answers, as such, are to be found.

---

* [See "Freud and the Magna Charta of Clinical Psychiatry" in this volume.]

† This term is meant to include those psychiatric schools of thought attached to the names of E. Minkowski, Erwin Straus, and V. E. von Gebsattel.

It is incorrect to accuse Heidegger's analytic of existence of failing to deal with nature, for it is through this same analytic of existence that the basis for the problem of nature can be obtained —*via* the approach to the Dasein as situationally attuned (*befindlich-gestimmten*) existence *among beings*. It would be equally incorrect to accuse *Daseinsanalyse* of "neglecting the body." Insofar as a world-design is seen as *thrown*—and this means situationally attuned—then, explicitly or not, attention is being directed to the Dasein in its bodiliness.

In practice, whenever the psychiatrist himself tries to look beyond the limitations of his science and seeks to know the ontological grounds of his understanding and treatment of those placed in his care, it is Heidegger's analytic of existence that can broaden his horizon. For it offers the possibility of understanding man as both a creature of nature, and a socially determined or historical being —and this by means of *one* ontological insight, which thus obviates the separation of body, mind, and spirit. Man as a creature of nature is revealed in the thrownness of the Dasein, its "that-it-is," its *facticity*. "Has the Dasein, as such, ever freely decided and will it ever be able to decide as to whether it wants to come into 'existence' or not?" The Dasein, although it exists essentially for its own sake (*umwillen seiner*), has nevertheless not itself laid the ground of its *being*. And also, as a creature "come into existence," it is and remains, *thrown*, determined, i.e., enclosed, possessed, and compelled by beings in general. Consequently it is not "completely free" in its world-design either. The "powerlessness" of the Dasein here shows itself in that certain of its possibilities of being-in-the-world are *withdrawn* because of commitment to and by beings, because of its facticity. But it is also just this withdrawal that lends the Dasein its *power:* for it is this that first brings *before* the Dasein the "real," graspable possibilities of world-design.

Transcendence is thus not only a striding or swinging of the Dasein toward the world, but is, at the same time, withdrawal, limitation—and only *in* this limiting does transcendence gain power "over the world." All this, however, is but a "transcendental document" of the Dasein's *finitude*. The thrownness of the Dasein, its facticity, is the transcendental horizon of all that scientific systematic psychiatry delimits as reality under the name of organism, body (and heredity, climate, milieu, etc.), and also for all that which is delimited, investigated, and researched as psychic *determinateness*: namely, as mood and ill humor, as craziness, compulsive or insane "possessedness," as addiction, instinctuality, as confusion, phantasy determination, as, in general, unconsciousness. Now, whereas the science of psychiatry not only observes and establishes connections *between* these two spheres, but also erects the theoretical bridge of the psychophysical—*Daseinsanalyse*, on the other hand, shows that it is the scientific dichotomization of man's ontological wholeness that gives rise to this postulate in the first place. It shows that this dichotomization results from projecting the whole of human being upon the screen of that which is merely objectively present [*vorhanden*]. It also indicates the general world-design of science as stemming from one and the same Dasein, from, namely, the Dasein's ontological potentiality of scientific being-in-the-world. Here, too, it is true to say that what lends the world-design its (limited) scientific power is obtained only through its powerlessness to understand the being of human existence [Dasein] as a whole.

It is to Heidegger's great credit that he summed up the being of the Dasein under the all too easily misunderstood title of Care (=caring for), and to have phenomenologically explored its basic structures and make-up. Thrownness, in the sense of the facticity of the Dasein's *answerability* to its that-it-is, is only *one* component ("existential") of this structure, the others, as we know, being existence (project) and fallenness.* Thus what in psychiatry is irreversibly separated into discrete realities of fields of study, namely, the finite human Dasein, is presented here in its basic structural unity. (It cannot be emphasized too often that this presentation signifies something quite different from the approach to man under the aegis of one particular *idea*, such as the idea of the will to power, libido, or any idea involving man as, in general, a creature of nature, or even, indeed, the idea of man as a child of God, as *homo aeternus*, etc.) But where there is structure there can be no dissociation of one structural member from the structural whole. Each, rather, remains implicated in the others, and a change in one structural element involves a change in the others. The Dasein can thus never get "behind" its thrownness and can only

---

* For the significance of fallenness "toward the world"—and not only the *Mitwelt*—see *Schizophrenie*.

project those possibilities into which it is thrown. Only, therefore, as surrendered to its *that*, as thrown, does the Dasein *exist* within the ground of its power-to-be. The self of existence, although it has to lay its own ground, can therefore never have power over this ground. As a being, it has to be "as it is and can be." Its being is a projection of its own power-to-be, and to this extent it is always already in *advance** of itself. This being in advance of itself also concerns the whole of the Dasein's structure. Corresponding to all that we know of its thrownness (as already-being-in-the-world), the being-in-advance-of itself of the Dasein, its futurity, is through and through implicated with its past. Out of both these temporal "ecstasies" the authentic present temporalizes itself. This is what was referred to in the opening pages as the "way" of *Sein und Zeit:* the attempt to understand the basic structure of the Dasein *via* the unitariness of temporality and its ecstasies.

I have elsewhere[5] tried to indicate the significance of this way for psychopathological knowledge and the understanding of the basic forms of human existence. Here, however, we are concerned with pointing out its significance for psychiatry's understanding of itself. The insight into the temporal essence of the Dasein, or transcendence, not only instructs psychiatry as to its "object"— the various modes of "abnormal" human existence—but also instructs it in its understanding of itself in that it compels it to realize that its dissection of human being into various factual regions with their corresponding conceptualizations cannot be the last word. For, as I have already mentioned, it thereby takes *one* level, that of things objectively present [*vorhanden*] "in time and space," here and now, and projects upon that level what makes the understanding of spatialization and temporalization possible in the first place: the Dasein. But if psychiatry realizes—and this is true for all sciences—how provisional its world-designs, its reality-conceptions, are, it will hold on to its basic concepts less rigidly and will find it easier to deepen and change these concepts. It is obvious, after all we have said, that these conceptual changes can be instigated only within scientific research and its particular

---

* Regarding the extent to which the various psychotic forms of manic depression and schizophrenia are rooted in various modes of this being-in-advance-of-itself of the Dasein (be it from the aspect of attunement [*Gestimmtheit*] or "Extravagant" ideal-formation), see my studies *Über Ideenflucht* and *Schizophrenie.*

crises, and therefore only within psychiatry's efforts in its own proper sphere of activity. A "dogmatic" importation of philosophical doctrines as such has almost always been detrimental to science and research.

IV

It is not enough to realize the necessary limitedness of psychiatry's world-design, which, like all world-designs, derives its power from the *elimination* of other possibilities. The analytic of existence can, in addition, show psychiatry *what, materially*, must be "withdrawn," must be neglected, when man is dissected into body, mind, and soul.

I have already cited Hönigswald's essay on philosophy and psychiatry. In it, he also remarks that it must essentially be expected of the organism "that it call itself *I*." The analytic of existence indicates the root of this "expectation," namely, the basic anthropological fact that the Dasein is, in its being, concerned essentially with this being itself, in other words, that its whereto and wherefore is always directed toward itself. This being for itself by no means signifies an attitude of the I to itself that gives it the possibility of calling itself *I*. If this potentiality is to be "expected" also of the organism, it is because we realize that if this power to say *I* (and *me* and *mine*) is lost sight of in the reality-conception wherein man is projected, then the splitting of man into organism and Ego, body and soul, physical and psychic, *res extensa* and *res cogitans*, will never be set aright, and that what will be lost sight of is man as he really is. There may be many "factual" grounds for undertaking this separation. But this should not prevent us from seeing that it is undertaken only "for the sake of the matter" and ceases to be valid once we turn our attention from the particular "circumstances" to the being of the Dasein itself. For, the being for itself also concerns the Dasein *qua* organism or body, the Dasein that *is* organism only as mine, yours, or his, and that, under no circumstances, is purely and simply organism and body as such. It is, consequently, naïve to see the psychophysical problem as a riddle of the universe.

For science, this also means that as biologists, or even as physiologists, we ought not to view the organism only as a natural object, but must keep in mind that the concept of organism results from a natural-scientific *reduction* [6] of man to his bodily existence and the further reduction of this bodily existence to a mere neutrally present, "ownerless," object.

One brief example: the conception of remembering, forgetting, and recollection as Mneme and Exphoresis (Semon, E. Bleuler, among others). Here, memory and recollection are conceived purely as brain functions, as "processes in the brain." As opposed to this, however, it is not hard to show that "the brain," like the organism itself, can still only be my, your, or his brain in its "reality." In other words, the mnemonic "brain-function" can be understood only within the perspective of *my Dasein's* power to be-in-the-world as retentive, forgetful, and recollective. This means, in short, that memory cannot be understood solely within physiology. It means, rather, that retention as well as forgetting involves a retreat by the Dasein to its bodily existence and that recollection means a return of the Dasein from its involvement "in the body" to its psychic existence.[7]

The degree to which both modes of human being are interrelated through their "alliance," through what Plato termed *koinonia,* was recently well shown by Wilhelm Szilazi in his Heideggerian interpretation of Plato's *Philebus.*[8] There we find quite clearly stated that the "elements" of the Dasein's power of being stem from the totality of ontological potentialities (the All), but that corporeality only becomes body *via* the *koinonia* that links "the soul" with that which is corporeal.* Equally clearly drawn is the way in which the Dasein "distances" itself from its bodily involvement, its thrownness, in order first to be fully *free as* "spirit." Wherever one leaves out the *koinonia* of the Dasein's ontological potentialities and their gradations—which Aristotle characterized as *syntheton*—then an understanding of man is unattainable. For then, instead of the facticity of the Dasein, which, though it is an inner-wordly being, differs basically from the factuality of the neutrally on-hand (the *Vorhanden*), in place of this facticity, the "universal riddle" of the psychophysical problem rears its head.

Turning now to the concept of *disease* in psychiatry, we must consider Paul Häberlin's excellent essay "The Object of Psychia-

---

* Thus Häberlin (see below) makes no bones about saying that the isolated body ("body without soul") does not exist.

try." [9] On the basis of anthropology,[10] Häberlin comes to the conclusion that the pathological character of mental diseases is somatically, rather than psychologically, patterned, and that only the so-
called neuroses are really psychic diseases and only they should
really be called psychoses. The extent to which this view approaches the state of affairs in psychiatry is the extent to which it
presupposes a *koinonia* of mind and body that is of a *different kind*
than that which we ourselves are presenting here. Häberlin understands the body as the *image* of the mind, and he characterizes man
as a "mental nation" governed with relative success by its founder,
the mind. These two types of disease are distinguished, according
to Häberlin, in that in one case the mind is "at odds" with *itself*,
while in the other case (what is usually called mental disease), it is
primarily the—*central*—organization of the *body* that is disturbed.
Both kinds of disease necessarily express themselves mentally *and*
physically. In the first case, that of the so-called neuroses, the mind
cannot uniformly carry out its functions, among which is the function of governing the body, and we therefore, to a greater or lesser
extent, find somatic consequences in neurosis. But in the case of
the so-called psychoses, the mind, in turn, suffers from the disturbance in the organism because this disturbance hinders its govern-
ance of the body and, in its receptive aspect, presents the mind
with a distorted image of the world so that it, the mind, reacts ab-
normally. Thus, in *both* cases, the normal *relation* between body
and mind (*koinonia*) is disturbed. Every disease affects both sides,
regardless of where the primary conditioning factors lie.

And *we too*, from the perspective of Heidegger's analytic of
existence, must conceive of both mental disease (Häberlin's soma-
tosis) and neurosis (Häberlin's psychosis) as a disturbance of *koinonia*, of the functional *unity* of the Dasein's ontological potentialities. On this basis it is, for example, understandable that the mental
disease called melancholia can be conceived as a disturbance of the
koinonia between the bodily and mental being of the Dasein, which
manifests itself on the one hand as a "vegetative" disturbance of the
organism, and on the other hand as an "isolated," heightened, and
distorted form of the finite Dasein's inherent guilt. It is not surprising, therefore, that melancholia can arise because of family tragedy, loss of power, or concrete guilt on the one hand, or on the
other hand, in connection with intestinal diseases or even "for no

reason at all." Nor is it surprising, then, that we can "cure" the melancholic with electroshock, or calm him with opium, or comfort him with assurances about his recovery and thus spur him on toward a steadfast endurance of his suffering. In each instance, we seek to restore the *koinonia* of body and mind. That in this case success is easier when the patient is treated from the "physical" side only indicates the nature of the melancholic form of existence that involves the *dominant power* of thrownness as already-being-in-the-world (mood), i.e., pastness (*Gewesenheit*) over existence as being-in-advance-of-itself in the future. It in no way argues against the notion that the mental illness known as melancholia involves the Dasein as a whole. The same, in turn, is true of the "neuroses." No matter how well psychopathology may understand neurosis (in strictly Freudian terms) as "psychic conflict," from the point of view of existential analysis, the neuroses must not *merely* be understood within the perspective of existence. That human beings *can* become "neurotic" at all is *also* a sign of the thrownness of the Dasein and a sign of its potentiality of fallenness —a sign, in short, of its finitude, its transcendental limitedness or unfreedom.

Only he who scorns these limits, who—in Kierkegaard's terms —is at odds with the fundamental conditions of existence, can become "neurotic," whereas only he who "knows" of the unfreedom of finite human existence and who obtains "power" over his existence within this very powerlessness is unneurotic or "free." The *sole task* of "psychotherapy" lies in assisting man toward this "power." It is only the *ways* to this goal that are *various*.

Naturally, the philosophical analytic of existence neither will nor can intrude upon psychiatry's conception of reality, nor doubt its empirically established "psycho-physical" connections. However, what it can do and what it seeks to do is simply to show that what we have cited as psychiatry's dual reality-conception owes its power and meaning to its being limited to particular scientific world-designs and not the being of those beings that it thematizes. All those issues, therefore, that extend beyond the field of this "thematization," i.e., questions as to human freedom, "time and space," relation of "mind and matter," questions of philosophy, art, religion, questions as to the nature of genius, etc.—such questions are not to be answered by the science of psychiatry.

A word, in conclusion, about the psychiatric problem of the *unconscious*. While psychoanalysis, as we know, interprets the unconscious from the perspective of consciousness,* it is clear that a doctrine that does not proceed from the intentionality of consciousness, but that, rather, shows how this intentionality is grounded in the temporality of human existence, must interpret the difference between consciousness and unconsciousness temporally and existentially. The point of departure for this interpretation cannot, therefore, be consciousness. It can, instead, only be the "unconscious," the thrownness and determinateness of the Dasein. A closer examination of this issue would, however, require a separate paper.

From the perspective of psychiatry's transcendental understanding of itself as a science—and only from that perspective—we may now interpret the being of the psychiatrist.† Those whose concern is man's physical health know that they must be not only "medical men," but also physicians. To the extent that diagnostic judgment is rooted not in observations of the patient's organism, but in the "coming to an understanding" with him as a human being, as one who also exists humanly—to that extent what is *essentially* involved is not just the attitude of the "medical man" toward his scientific object. What is involved is his *relation*[11] to the patient, a relation rooted equally in "care" and love. It is of the *essence* of being a psychiatrist, *therefore*, that he reaches beyond all factual knowledge and the abilities that go with it, and that he reaches beyond *scientific* knowledge found in the fields of psychology, psychopathology, and psychotherapy. This swinging beyond or transcending the factuality, objectivity, and reality-orientation of psychiatry can be understood only from the point of view of transcendence itself as being-in-the-world and being-beyond-the-world.[12]

* Whereby there obtains the disproportion between the high methodological esteem given to consciousness—indeed, in this respect the best thing that can be said of the workings of the unconscious is that it approaches consciousness or even excels it—and low esteem accorded its material, psychological significance.

† It goes without saying that what holds true for the physician in general is also true of the psychiatrist, namely: "For him health is the principle of his profession, and wherever he disregards its recognized limits, he makes himself guilty at every step." See the sharp and unambiguous treatment of "Das Prinzip des ärztlichen Berufs" by Paul Matussek in *Festschrift für Kurt Schneider* (Verlag Scherer, 1947).

Not only at the initial interview or examination, but also during the course of the whole *treatment*, being a psychiatrist goes beyond being a medical man (in the sense of knowing and mastering the field of medicine). The being of a psychiatrist—I mean, of course, a psychiatrist, as such, and not what is called a "good" psychiatrist—involves, therefore, the insight that no whole, and thus no "whole man" can be "grasped" with the methods of science. Now, if the psychiatrist is oriented toward encounter and mutual understanding with his fellow man and is oriented toward understanding human beings in their totality, in the *koinonia* of their ontological potentialities and the *koinonia* of this totality with more universal ontological potentialities, then the being of the psychiatrist reaches beyond the purely "theoretical" ontological potentialities of man and is directed toward transcendence itself.

It follows from this that the psychiatrist in his being summons and lays claim to the whole man. Whereas in other branches of science it may, to a greater or lesser extent, be possible to separate one's vocation and existence and, so to speak, find one's "existential center of gravity" in a hobby or in some other scientific activity, or in philosophy, a religion, or art, it is not so in psychiatry. In a certain sense being a psychiatrist also claims the existence of the psychiatrist. For where meeting and mutual understanding furnish the grounds and basis for everything that can be viewed as symptoms or even as disease and health per se, and where, therefore, there can be nothing human upon which—*in a psychiatric sense*—judgment cannot be passed, then hobby, science, philosophy, art, and religion must be capable of being projected and understood from the perspective of personal existence as ontological potentialities and conceptual projects. Where this is not the case—as the history of psychiatry shows—every psychiatric judgment actually is deprived of a solid basis. Consequently, the being of the psychiatrist cannot be understood without understanding transcendence as "the freedom to establish a ground."

This "freedom" now permits us to understand that the scientific concerns and necessities (basic concepts, research methods) of psychiatry must stand not in a rigid, but in a flexible and vital relation to the Dasein as being-in-the-world and being-beyond-the-world. It also permits us to understand why scientific progress in psychiatry is especially bound up with the interaction between research into matters of fact and transcendental reflection upon its nature as science.

Notes

[1. See Rollo May, Ernest Angel, and Henri F. Ellenberger (eds.), *Existence* (New York, 1958), pp. 191-213.]

2. See the (expanded) lecture of W. Szilasi (January 10, 1945) in *Wissenschaft als Philosophie* (Zürich, New York, 1945).

3. See Richard Hönigswald, "Philosophie und Psychiatrie," *Archiv. f. Psychiatrie u. Nervenkrankheiten*, Vol. 87, No. 5 (1929), and Binswanger, Über die manische Lebensform," *Ausg. Vort. u. Aufs.*, Vol. II.

4. See Szilasi, *op. cit.*

5. *Grundformen und Erkenntnis menschlichen Daseins.*

6. See my "Über die manische Lebensform," and above all the excellent treatment by René Le Senne of "La dialectique de naturalisation" in *Obstacle et Valeur*. See further, T. Haering, *Philosophie der Naturwissenschaft* (1923).

7. See "Über Psychotherapie."

8. W. Szilasi, *Macht und Ohnmacht des Geistes.*

9. P. Häberlin, in *Schweiz. Archiv. f. Psych. u. Neur.*, Vol. 60.

10. *Der Mensch, eine philosophische Anthropologie* (Zürich, 1941).

11. See *Grundformen,* Part II.

12. *Ibid.*

Dream and Existence

I

When we are in a state of deeply felt hope or expectation and what we have hoped for proves illusory, then the world—in one stroke —becomes radically "different." We are completely uprooted, and we lose our footing in the world. When this happens we say later— after we have regained our equilibrium—that it was "as though we had fallen from the clouds." * With such words we clothe our experience of a great disappointment in a poetic simile that arises not from the imagination of any one particular poet, but out of language itself. In this respect language is every man's spiritual root. For it is language that "envisions and thinks" for all of us before any one individual brings it to the service of his own creative and intellectual powers. But, now, what of this "poetic simile"? Is it a matter simply of an analogy in the logical sense, or a pictorial metaphor in the poetic sense? To think either is utterly to bypass an understanding of the inner nature of poetic similes. For this nature lies, in fact, *behind* that to which logic and contemporary

[* TRANSLATOR'S NOTE: The idiom in German is *aus allen Himmeln fallen* (to be bitterly disappointed or utterly disillusioned) and *wie vom Himmel gefallen sein* (to be astounded). English contains many similar linkages between falling and disappointment, such as, "The ground gave way beneath my feet," "I came down to earth with a thud," and "The rug was pulled out from under me." The interesting —but for Binswanger's point unessential—difference between the two idioms is that the German locates in the sky any person with deeply felt hopes, while the English reserves this place for a person with exhorbitant or unrealistic hopes. The primary point here, however, concerns the falling itself, which is expressed by the idioms of both languages. The phrase "to fall from the clouds," which I have used here, should not, therefore, be understood as implying anything about the reason-ableness of the shattered hopes.]

theories of poetic expression refer. The nature of poetic similes lies in the deepest roots of our existence where the vital forms and contents of our mind are still bound together. When, in a bitter disappointment, "we fall from the clouds," then we fall—we *actually* fall. Such falling is neither purely of the body nor something metaphorically derived from physical falling. Our harmonious relationship with the world and the men about us suddenly suffers a staggering blow, stemming from the nature of bitter disappointment and the shock that goes with it. In such a moment our existence actually suffers, is torn from its position in the world and thrown upon its own resources. Until we can regain our equilibrium in the world, our whole existence moves within the meaning matrix of stumbling, sinking, and falling. If we call this general meaning matrix the "form," and the bitter disappointment the "content," we can see that in this case form and content are *one*.

There are those who do not concern themselves with man as a whole, but see only one aspect of him, as biologists do when they view man as no more than a living organism. Such observers will say that falling—the high-low vector—is rooted purely in the living structure of the organism. For, they will point out, bitter disappointment is accompanied by a deficiency of muscle tone and tension in the striated muscles so that we are apt to swoon or sink. Language, they will say, is only a reflection of this purely physical circumstance. According to this view, our falling from the clouds or the giving way of ground beneath our feet is a purely analogical or metaphorical transference from the sphere of the body to that of the mind, and within the latter it is simply a picturesque form of expression without genuine content or substance, a mere *façon de parler*.

Klages' theory of expression goes deeper. But with all his emphasis on the unity of soul and body his theory is still based on the presupposition that "the psychic" manifests itself in particular spatio-temporal forms that accord with our psychological organization. For example, a weakly defined psyche manifests itself in weak handwriting, arrogance in our carrying our heads high. And because the psyche manifests itself in such forms, language makes use of expressions drawn from the spatial-sensory sphere to indicate psychic characteristics and processes. This view is not unconvincing. But it nevertheless presupposes agreement with Klages'

underlying theory of expression, which treats the body as the manifestation of the soul and the soul, for its part, as a living body. I, for
one, am far from sharing these theoretical assumptions.

My views are in line with Husserl and Heidegger's doctrine of
meaning, which Löwith first saw as applicable to the particular
problem of language that concerns us here. When, for example, we
speak of a high and a low tower, a high and a low tone, high and
low morals, high and low spirits, what is involved is not a linguistic
carrying over from one existential sphere to the others, but, rather,
a general meaning matrix in which all particular regional spheres
have an equal "share," i.e., which contains within it these same particular, specfic meanings (spatial, acoustic, spiritual, psychic, etc.).
Sinking or falling thus represent a general meaning matrix, a vector
meaning pointing from above to below, which contains a particular existential significance for "our" Dasein, according to the
"ontological existential" of, say, the extending and turning out-
wards of spatiality, the being-thrown of mood (*Stimmung*), or the
interpretation of com-prehension (*Verstehen*). In bitter disappointment, the ground gives way under us or we fall from the
clouds not because disappointment or shock represent, as Wundt
said, an "asthenic affect" that—in the form of physical staggering,
stumbling, or falling—reveals itself as a threat to the upright bodily
posture and thus serves as a real physical model for poetically imaginative language. It is, rather, that language of itself, in this
simile, grasps hold of a particular element lying deep within man's
ontological structure—namely, the ability to be directed from
above to below—and then designates this element as falling. Appeal
to asthenic affect and its bodily expression need not be made. What
does need to be explained is why disappointment, as such, has an
asthenic character; and the answer is that in disappointment our
whole existence no longer stands upon "firm," but upon "weak"
legs—and, indeed, no longer even stands. For because its harmony
with the world has been rent, the ground beneath its feet has been
taken away, leaving it suspended and hovering. Such existential
hovering need not necessarily assume a downward direction; it can
also signify liberation and the possibility of ascending. But if the
disappointment persists as disappointment, then our hovering passes
into tottering, sinking, falling. Language, the poetic imagination,

and—above all—the dream, draw from this basic ontological structure.

Though our way of thinking is not very popular among psychologists and psychiatrists, it is becoming progressively more clearly delineated in the philosophical movement to which I have just referred. From our point of view, the most questionable of the many questionable problems that have puzzled our age is that of the relation between body and soul. We do not essay a solution to this problem, but, rather—by attempting to remove it from its hoary metaphysical and religious rut, by doing away with such formulations as interaction, parallelism, and identity of mind and body—we wish to show that it has been erroneously conceptualized. Only then can the way lie open for the treatment of such individual problems of anthropology as that which concerns us here.

That disappointment is expressed in phrases such as "falling from the clouds" is also, of course, based on further essential connections that are grasped by language, for example, our outlook is said to be "clouded" by passionate hopes, wishes, and expectations, or we say, when we are happy, that it is like "being in heaven." But falling itself and, of course, its opposite, rising, are not themselves derivable from anything else. Here we strike bottom ontologically.

This same rising and falling is to be found in all religious, mythical, and poetic images of the ascension of the spirit and the earthly weight or pull of the body. Thus, to cite one example, Schiller's wondrous image of the transfiguration of Heracles:

> Joyous in the strange, new state of hovering,
> He flows upward, and the heavy, dreamlike image
> Of earthly life sinks and sinks and sinks.

> [Froh des neuen, ungewohnten Schwebens,
> Fliesst er aufwärts, und des Erdenlebens
> Schweres Traumbild sinkt und sinkt und sinkt.]

But if we wish to say who, in fact, this *we* is who happily ascends or unhappily falls, then we find ourselves somewhat embarrassed for an answer. If we are told that this *we* simply means *we human beings* and that any further questions are redundant, then it must be replied that it is precisely here where all scientific questioning should begin; for the question as to who "we human beings" actually are has never received less of an answer than it has in our age, and today we stand again at the threshold of new queries with respect to this *we*. Here, too, the answer has been given by poetry, myth, and dream rather than by science and philosophy. They, at least, have known *one* thing: that this *we*, the existential subject, in no way lies openly revealed, but that it loves to conceal itself "in a thousand forms." In addition, poetry, myth, and dream have always known that this subject must on no account be identified with the individual body in its outward form. With respect to existential rising and falling, for example, poets have always known that it is equally valid to express the subject, the existential "who," by either our bodily form (or by a part or member of this form), or through any property belonging to it or anything that justifies our existence in the world, to the extent that it can serve somehow to express this rising and falling. The question as to the *who* of our existence cannot be answered by reference to a sensory perception of the isolated form, which remains unessential, but only by reference to something that can serve as the subject of the particular structural moment (in this case the moment of rising and falling), and this subject may well be, in its sensory aspect, an alien, external subject. It is, nevertheless, I who remain the primary subject of that which rises and falls. The truth value and much of the effect on us of the presentation of the existential subject in myth, religion, and poetry is based on these correct ontological insights.

Despairing unto death and, in his despair, enraged with himself, Mörike's *Painter Nolten*, "very unexpectedly was shamingly reproached by one whom he dearly respected." At this he suddenly experienced "the most cruel shock" that a person can experience. Reaching this point, the writer breaks off the direct description of his hero's mental state and turns directly to the reader, who then hears himself addressed in the following way: "[In such a state] it is deathly still within you, you see your own pain like a boldly soaring bird of prey stricken by a thunderbolt and now slowly falling from the sky and sinking, half-dead, at your feet." Here the poet speaks, rather than language as such, though at the same time he is drawing upon an essential tendency in language —falling—in the same way that he is "being used" by correspondingly essential tendencies of human existence. It is just for this reason that the simile instantly "reaches" the reader and affects him so that he no longer notices it as a simile, but, rather, straight away pricks up his ear convinced that: "It is I who am involved, it is I who am [or, what comes to the same thing, I who could be] the mortally stricken bird of prey."

Here, now, we find ourselves at the source of dreams. Indeed, all that we have said up to this point applies word for word to the dream that, for its part, is nothing other than a particular mode of human existence in general.

In the above simile, my own pain—that is, something in me, a "part" of me—has become a wounded bird of prey. With this there begins the dramatizing personification that we know also as the dream's principle means of representation. Now "I" no longer fall from the clouds as an individual alone in my pain. It is, rather, my pain itself that falls at my feet as a second *dramatis persona*. This is a most outspoken expression of my ability, under certain circumstances, to keep my "physical" feet on the ground even as I fall and introspectively observe my own falling.

It is true of both ancient and modern literature, and true of dreams and myths of all periods and peoples: again and again the eagle or the falcon, the kite or the hawk, personify our existence as rising or longing to rise and as falling. This merely indicates how essential to human existence it is to determine itself as rising or falling. This essential tendency is, of course, not to be confused with the conscious, purposeful wish to rise, or the conscious fear of falling. These are already mirrorings or reflections in consciousness of that basic tendency. It is precisely this unreflected, or—in psychoanalytic language—unconscious factor that, in the soaring existence of the bird of prey, strikes such a sympathetic note within us.

> Innate in each of us
> Is that rising in the heart
> When the lark, lost in skyey space above us,
> Gives forth his pealing song;
> When above the jagged trees
> The eagle hovers, his wings outspread,
> And when above the flatness of the earth and seas
> The crane compels himself toward home.

[Doch ist es jedem eingeboren
Dass sein Gefühl hinauf und vorwärts dringt,
Wenn über uns, im blauen Raum verloren,
Ihr schmetternd Lied die Lerche singt;
Wenn über schroffen Fichtenhöhen
Der Adler ausgebreitet schwebt,
Und über Flächen, über Seen
Der Kranich nach der Heimat strebt.]

Because of this "innateness," all similes involving eagles and birds—like all existential expressions—are not merely formally, but substantially illuminating. In another example from poetry, Mörike uses the image of an eagle to represent the happiness of love —unreflective, soaring, and fearful of falling:

Deep in the boundless blue the eagle eyes
The sunshine's molten gold with level sight,
Nor is he fool enough to curb his flight
Because he fears his head may hit the skies.

. . . .

So, like the eagle, should not Love be bold?
But yet she fears, and finds her happiness
In hazards ever new and ever sweet.

[trans. by Cruickshank and Cunningham]

It is well-known that in dreams flying and falling often are manifested by the hovering and sinking of our own bodies. These dreams of flying and falling are sometimes thought to be connected with the physical condition, especially breathing, in which case we are dealing with so-called body-stimuli dreams, sometimes with erotic moods or purely sexual wishes. Both are possible and we do not wish to dispute either assumption, since in our case it is a matter of uncovering an a priori structure of which the body-stimuli (and body schema in general) as well as the erotic-sexual themes are special, secondary contents. In these two instances, it is necessary to find certain motives in the manifest and inner life history of the patient in order to understand why at this particular moment this particular "content" comes to be expressed—why, for example, the dreamer at this particular time pays attention to his breathing or why, at this particular time, he is disposed to erotic wishes or fears, etc. Only then can such a dream be understood psychologically. If the wish or fear further clothes itself in a second and third person (or becomes a drama among animals), then a psychological understanding demands, further, the most minute efforts to translate these figures back into their individual psychic urges. I should like here merely to cite a dream that is relatively simple, but thoroughly uniform in its representation of thoughts of death and love. It was dreamed by one of my patients during her menstrual period.

> Right before my eyes a bird of prey attacked a white pigeon, wounded it in the head and carried it off into the air. I pursued the creature with shouts and clapping of the hands. After a long chase I succeeded in chasing the bird of prey from the pigeon. I lifted it from the ground and to my great sorrow found it was already dead.

In the example taken from Mörike's *Painter Nolten,* existential rising and falling found its pictorial content in the image of a bird of prey struck by a bolt of lightning. What we have here, on the other hand, is a struggle between two creatures in which one represents the aspect of victorious soaring and the other of defeated falling. And, as in the *Nolten* example, the person—stricken by the pains of a shocking disappointment—sees the pigeon lying dead upon the ground. In interpreting the dream it makes absolutely no difference whether the drama being played in the deadly silence of the soul is acted by the dreamer's own person or by any combination of the dreamer's own person and derivative *personae.* The theme evinced in sleep by the Dasein—that is, the "content" of the drama—is the important and decisive factor. Disappointment and life in descent is quite often expressed by the image of a bird of prey transformed, after its death, into some worthless thing, or plucked clean and cast away. The following two dreams of Gottfried Keller illustrate this:

First dream:

January 10, 1948

Last night I found myself in Glattfelden. The Glatt flowed shimmeringly and joyously by the house, but I saw it flowing in the distance as it really does. We stood by an open window, looking out upon the meadows. There, a mighty eagle flew back and forth through the ravine. As it flew toward the slope and settled upon a jagged pine, my heart began to pound strangely. I think I was moved by joy at seeing for the first time an eagle in free flight. Then it flew close by our window and we made a point of noticing that it bore a crown upon its head and that its pinions and feathers were sharply and marvelously scalloped, as they are upon coats of arms. We sprang—my Oheim and I—to our rifles on the wall and posted ourselves behind the door. The giant bird came right in through the window and nearly filled the whole room with the breadth of his wings. We fired and upon the floor lay not an eagle, but pieces of black paper piled up in a heap. This vexed us considerably.

Second dream:

December 3

Last night I dreamed of a kite. I was looking from the windows of a house; out front were the neighbors with their children. There, coming toward us, flew an enormous, wondrously beautiful kite. Actually, it merely glided, for its wings were tightly closed and it seemed sick and emaciated by hunger, in that it sank lower and lower and could raise itself only with great effort—but never as high as it was before it began to sink. The neighbors and their children shouted, made a lot of noise, and impatiently began hurling their caps at the bird in order to chase it away. It saw me and seemed—in its upward and downward movements—to want to come near me. At that I hastened to the kitchen to get some food for it. I finally found some and came hurrying back to the window. It was already lying dead upon the ground and was in the hands of a vicious little boy who ripped the magnificent feathers from the wings and threw them aside, and finally, tired of this, hurled the bird upon a dungheap. The neighbors, who had felled the bird with a stone, had, in the meantime, dispersed and gone about their business.

This dream made me very sad.

If we feel ourselves into these dreams—which, in any case, their aesthetic charm invites us to do—it is possible for us to sense the pulse of existence, its systole and diastole, its expansion and depression, its ascension and sinking. Each of these phases seems to present a dual expression: the image and the emotional response to the image; the image of the eagle in its soaring freedom and the joy in contemplating it; the image of the pieces of black paper and the distress that goes with it; the dead, plucked kite and the accompanying sadness. But basically, the joyous image and the enjoyment of it, the sad image and the accompanying sadness are *one*—namely, an expression of one and the same ascending or descending cyclical phase. In this respect, too, what is decisive is the theme supplied by the Dasein in each such phase. Whether the Dasein experiences itself more strongly in the emotive content of the image itself or in the apparent reactive affect is, as we shall see, of secondary (i.e., clinical-diagnostic) significance. By steeping oneself in the manifest content of the dream—which, since Freud's epoch-making postulate concerning the reconstruction of latent dream thoughts, has receded all too far into the background—one learns the proper evaluation of the primal and strict interdependence of feeling and image, of mood [*Gestimmtsein*] and pictorial realization. And what is true of the brief cycles whose thematic reflection we can observe in the image and mood of the dreamer, is, of course, also true of the larger and deeper rhythms of normal and pathologically exalted and depressive "discords."

We may, however, point out in passing that the happy upward cycles of life can be realized other than in images of rising, and that the same holds true *mutatis mutandis* for the unhappy downward cycles of life. Two examples will make this clear.

Gottfried Keller's second dream has an especially charming and, for us, interesting continuation. After the words, "This dream made me very sad," he continues:

. . . however I was very pleased when a young maiden came and offered to sell me a large wreath of carnations. It rather puzzled me that carnations were still to be found in December and I began bargaining with her. She wanted three shillings. But I had only two shillings in my pockets and was greatly embarrassed. I asked her to give me two shillings' worth, or as many as my champagne glass—in which I usually kept flowers—would hold. Then she said, "Look, they do fit," and carefully put one carnation after the other into the slender, shining glass. I watched and began to feel that sense of well-being which always comes when we watch someone perform delicate work with ease and grace. But as she put the last carnation in place I grew anxious again. The girl then looked sweetly and subtly at me and said, "Well, look! There weren't as many as I thought and they cost only two shillings." They were not quite real, these carnations—they were of a flaming red hue and their scent was extraordinarily pleasant and intense.

Thus, after the "wondrously beautiful kite" is shorn of its plumage by the "vicious little boy," and after the rude crowds have heedlessly left the dead bird lying upon a dungheap, there burgeons forth a new wave bearing no longer the image of rising, but the image of intensely colored and fragrant flowers, a sweet, delightfully roguish girl, a brilliant, slender champagne glass—all thematically linked to a happy scene that, despite threats of embarrassment and anxiety, continues to be happy to the end. Here the wave of ascension manifests itself through an orchestration of strongly sensuous and erotic stimuli and, at the same time, through the emotions that correspond to the theme of the scenic image.

At other times the sudden change of a victoriously happy vital current into one that is fraught with anxiety is expressed by the fading or disappearance of brilliantly lit colors and by the obscuring of light and vision in general—as is so well illustrated by Goethe's dream of pheasants in *The Italian Journey*:

> Since I now feel somewhat oppressed by an overwhelming flood of good and desirable thoughts, I cannot help reminding my friends of a dream which I had about a year ago, which appeared to me to be highly significant. I dreamed that I had been sailing about in a little boat and had landed on a fertile and richly cultivated island, which I knew bred the most beautiful pheasants in the world. I immediately started bargaining with the people of the island for some of these birds, and they killed and brought them to me in great numbers. They were pheasants indeed, but since in dreams all things are generally changed and modified, they seemed to have long, richly colored tails, like the loveliest birds of paradise, and with eyes like those of the peacock. Bringing them to me by scores, they arranged them in the boat so skillfully with the head inward, the long variegated feathers of the tail hanging outward, as to form in the bright sunshine the most glorious array conceivable, and so large as scarcely to leave room enough in the bow and the stern for the rower and the steersman.

As the boat made its way through the tranquil waters with this load, I named to myself the friends among whom I should like to distribute these variegated treasures. At last, arriving in a spacious harbor, I was almost lost among great and many-masted vessels, so I mounted deck after deck in order to discover a place where I might safely run my little boat ashore.

Such dreamy visions have a charm, for while they spring from our inner self, they possess more or less of an analogy with the rest of our lives and fortunes.

This dream took place and was written down about a year before Goethe set off for Italy. Its persistence and recurrence in the dreamer's memory affords the psychologist a clear picture of the lability and even the threat involved in Goethe's existence at the time—a danger that, with a sure instinct, he overcame by fleeing to Italy, to the south, to colors, sun, to new life of heart and mind.

Let us, however, turn back to dreams of flying and floating. I should like to illustrate by means of an example that it is often not starkly pictorial dreams that inspire psychiatric concern, but, rather, those dreams whose pictorial content and dynamics retreat before the presence of pure emotion. It is a sign of psychic health when one's wishes and fears are predominantly objectified by the use of dramatic images, out of which, as we have seen, emotional content may then appear to arise. In the following "cosmic" dream of one of our patients, emotional content is so dominant that even the exceedingly strong objectification, the image of the cosmos or universe, no longer suffices to bind it pictorially. Here the patient is not a bystander of the drama, detached from his own body, nor can he completely immerse himself in the drama:

I found myself in a wondrously different world, in a great ocean where I floated formlessly. From afar I saw the earth and all the stars and I felt tremendously free and light, together with an extraordinary sense of power.

The patient himself characterized this dream as a dream of dying. This hovering without a form, this complete dissolution of his own bodily structure (form), is not diagnostically propitious. And the contrast between the tremendous sense of power and the personal formlessness indicates that a deeper disturbance exists in the patient's psychic make-up. It is no longer part of the dream but part of the patient's psychosis when he speaks of the dream as a turning point in his life and finds its emotional content so fascinating that he reverts to it in his daydreams to the extent that he actually tries to remove himself from life. What Jeremias Gotthelf once said of his dream—"I felt the healing power of night envelop me," and "Are not dreams also benign gifts of God and must we not apply them to our spiritual growth?"—cannot be related to our dreamer. How different in style and structure is a dream such as that of our patient from this—also cosmic—dream of flying by Jean Paul:

> Sometimes it would happen that, blessedly happy and exalted in mind and body, I would fly straight up into the deep blue starry skies and sing to the vaulted heavens as I rose.

How different, too, are the wonderful, if somewhat stylized, dreams of his homeland found in the fourth volume of Gottfried Keller's *Grünen Heinrich*. Here the dreamer seems to float above a multitude of wondrous natural forms so that what is below him appears to be a subterranean sky, "save that it was a green sky with stars of every possible color." Compared to this, our patient's abstract cosmic phantasy can only make us shudder. And whereas Keller anxiously saw his dreams as harbingers of a serious illness and tried in every way to remove himself from their thrall, our patient lets himself become more and more captivated by the purely subjective, aesthetic allure of his dream. In the dissolution into the deep subjectivity of the dream's pure mood content, the meaning of life is lost to our patient, something that he himself admits: "We are in the world in order to discover the meaning of life. But life has no meaning and therefore I seek to free myself from life so that I may return to the primal force. I do not believe in a personal life after death, but in a dissolving into the primal force." A complete despair about the meaning of life has the same significance as man's losing himself in pure subjectivity; indeed, the one is the reverse side of the other, for the meaning of life is ever something trans-subjective, something universal, "objective," and impersonal. But we must add that, strictly speaking, as long as man is man there can never be such a thing as a *complete* dissolution into pure subjectivity. Our patient's longing to return to the primal force also points to the desire for an objective grounding and stance. It is only that in this case the striving is, to use a distinction of Bertholet's, fulfilled purely dynamically, or even cosmic-dynamically, rather than, say, theistic-personalistically. A thorough study of our patient's outer and inner life-history shows that this return to the primal, cosmic force corresponds to a strongly erotic oedipal longing, namely the anaclitic need to lean upon a beloved mother (something that was clearly shown in the patient's youth and acted out in reality). Here, then, a strongly subjective personalism emerges from behind an apparently purely objective dynamism, a personalism that again and again jeopardizes the patient's foothold in the objective and impersonal.

II

The image of a bird of prey attacking a dove or some other animal in order to tear at it or destroy it is an image known to us from ancient times. Modern man, however, must build his own personal world, after making himself lord and master of his own life and death; and the external world, ruled by material, economic, and technical powers, can no longer offer him a foothold. Ancient man, on the other hand, neither awake nor in dreams, knew of that primal cosmic loneliness that we have just seen exemplified in our young dreamer. Ancient man would not yet have understood the profoundly wise saying of Jeremias Gotthelf: "Think how dark the world would become if man sought to be his own sun!" The man of antiquity lived in a cosmos that determined even his most private, secret choices, awake or in dreams. For "what, in the moment of decision, appear to us as motives are, for the initiated, acts of the gods. In them, and not in man's bottomless emotions, is to be found the depth and primary ground of everything of great significance which transpires in man." [1] It is not that we seek today to take over for our own the completed forms of ancient Greece. But we can, as does modern humanism, realize that the cultural history of the Greeks involves the erection of a world of forms "in which the natural laws of human nature unfold in all directions," and that in penetrating this world of forms what happens is not less than "the self-understanding and self-development of spiritual man in the basic structure of his being." [2] From this perspective we wish, now, to pursue our particular problem.

When, in Penelope's dream (*Odyssey* 19), an eagle swoops down upon the geese and breaks their necks with his crooked beak, killing them all, neither poet nor reader thinks of this as representing subjective processes in the dreamer's psyche. The dream signifies an external event, namely, Odysseus' slaying of the suitors. (The same is true of a similar dream by Hecuba in Euripides' tragedy: a dream of a wolf attacking the hinds). These dreams, to be sure, are artistic creations. But with the insight we have gained from psychoanalysis, we can follow the famous example of Cicero who, in writing of the prophecies of his brother Quintus (which are constantly exemplified by fictional dreams), puts these words into his mouth: "Haec, etiam si ficta sunt a poeta, non absunt tamen a consuetudine somnorium." [These things, even if they have been made by the poet, are nevertheless not uncharacteristic of the usual form of dreams."]

More often than in the dream itself, however, we find the image of eagle and dove, eagle and goose, falcon and eagle, etc., used to betoken the propitious or unfavorable answer given by an oracle or seer about the prophetic meaning of a dream. Here, too, the image refers to an external event, in accordance with the basic Greek conviction that events of the world are coordinated and predetermined in detail by *Moira* and the gods. (Cf. Heraclitus' pithy saying: "Sun will not overstep his measures; otherwise the Erinyes, ministers of Justice, will find him out.") In *The Persians* of Aeschylus we find an example of just such an oracular pronouncement consequent upon a dream. After Xerxes has departed with intent to lay waste to the land of the Ionians, Atossa, his mother, dreams of two women, one dressed in Persian garb and the other in Dorian attire. They fall to feuding, and Xerxes yokes them both to his chariot. The one bears herself proudly, the other struggles and rends asunder the harness of the car. Xerxes is hurled to the ground and his father Darius stands by his side commiserating him. But Xerxes, when he beholds Darius, rends his garments about his limbs. Deeply disturbed by this and similar dreams, Atossa draws nigh unto an altar with incense in her hand, intending to make oblation of a sacrificial cake unto the divinities that avert evil.

But I saw an eagle fleeing for safety to the altar of Phoebus—and
from terror, my friends, I stood reft of speech. And thereupon I
spied a falcon rushing at full speed with outstretched pinions and
with his talons plucking at the eagle's head; while it did naught but
cower and yield its body to his foe.

[Smyth translation, V. 191-196.]

This image is not viewed as an image stemming either from a
dream or the external world. This indicates the extent to which the
Greek mind effaced the boundaries between the various spaces of
experience, external world, and cult. This is due to the fact that for
the Greeks the subject-source of the dream image, the subject of
cosmic events, and the subject of the cultist pronouncement are
one and the same: the godhead, Zeus, or his direct charges. Here,
then, dream image (the image of the two women harnessed to the
chariot, their quarrelling, and Xerxes' fall), the external event (falcon and eagle), and cultist significance form an inseparable unity.
Where do we hear any talk of an individual subject and where,
then, is the possibility of the ontological grounding of that individual? And who can say here whether truth is to be sought in the in-
wardness of subjectivity or in the outwardness of objectivity? For
here all "inner" is "outer," just as all outer is inner. It is thus of no
consequence whether an oracular event follows upon a dream or
bears no connection with it—just as often a dream alone, without
the oracular, can express the will of the godhead.

In *The Odyssey*, we find two omens of similar form occurring
without being preceded by dreams:

Even as he [Telemachus] spoke, a bird flew by on the right, an
eagle, bearing in his talons a great white goose, a tame fowl from
the yard, and men and women followed shouting. But the eagle
drew near to them, and darted off to the right in front of the
horses; and they were glad as they saw it, and the hearts in the
breasts of all were cheered.

From this omen Helen interprets the future to Telemachus: even
as this eagle snatched up the goose that was bred in the house, even
so shall Odysseus return to his home and take vengeance.

In the same book (XV) of *The Odyssey*, we find an image
quite similar to that which occurred in the dream cited previously:

> Even as he [Telemachus] spoke, a bird flew upon the right, a hawk, the swift messenger of Apollo. In his talons he held a dove, and was plucking her and shedding the feathers down on the ground midway between the ship and Telemachus himself.
>
> [Murray translation]

This bird, too, flying forth upon the right, is sent by the gods to signify good fortune.

We thus find no mention of rising and falling in the sense of the life-flow of a particular individual. It is, rather, the kind, the family, linked as they are by a common, predetermined fate, that ascends in prosperity or falls in misery. The individual, the species, fate and the godhead are intertwined in one common space: x. It is, therefore, even more significant and instructive that we find in this existential space—which differs so markedly from our own—so clear a manifestation of the ontological structural element of rising and falling.

In place of the Neoplatonic, Christian, and Romantic contrast between inner and outer, we find in the early Greeks the opposition of night and day, darkness and light, earth and sun. Dreams belong to the sphere of night and earth; they are themselves demons, occupying their own particular region (*Demos* in Homer), and forming their own tribe (*Phylon* in Hesiod). Their mother is night (Hesiod), who is also the mother of death and sleep. Thus, the close connection between the demons of dreams and the souls of the departed who imploringly or lamentingly appear in sleep—a *motif* that appears in Aeschylus (*Eumenides*) and Euripides (*Hecuba*), as well as in Homer—acquires, in the hands of these poets, a superb artistic form and a deep psychological and aesthetic effectiveness.

It is most significant that while dreams themselves belong completely to the aspect of night in Greek existence, the cultist interpretation of dreams, the oracle, was gradually withdrawn from the sphere of influence of Gaia, the old godhead of earth (and closely related to Night), and was ursurped by the new god, Phoebus Apollo. The dream of Atossa and the omen of falcon and eagle are not distinguished according to inner and outer, or subjective and objective events, but, rather, with regard to the close at hand, constrictive, dark, damp, and obscure realm of night, and the realm of the most awake of gods, the sun-god Apollo, who sees and aims so accurately from afar.

We know, however, that along with this grandly uniform religious world-view of the Greeks there was also a place for sober, empirical observation and for the scientific theory that rested upon it. But above all, we know, too, of their philosophical, metaphysical conception of the world as an organic structure of cosmic events linked together from the most universal down to the most individual and apparently accidental. In his polemic against prophetic dreams, Cicero cites these three conceptions as possibilities for explaining prophetic signs in dreams, and then proceeds to attack all three possibilities and, with them, the whole notion of dream prophecy—with which we, today, concur. He cites (*De divinat.* II, 60, 124) the possibility of inspiration by divine powers (*divina vis quaedam*), by "conventia et conjunctio naturae, "quam vocant (συμπάθειαν)," and by enduring and persistent observation (*quaedam observatio constans atque diuturna*) of the coincidence of dream experiences with later actual events. The new element with which he acquaints us is the doctrine of sympathy. This, however, is a doctrine that we also find in Heraclitus, the Stoics (particularly Poseidonius), and later, in a different form, in Plotinus, and again in the important dream book of Synesius. It is the famous philosophical doctrine of the One, which, wherever we may later encounter it, is bound to recall to us the spirit of ancient Greece. There are various sub-forms of this doctrine: In Heraclitus (following K. Reinhardt's *Kosmos und Sympathie*) what is involved is a oneness of Being (in the sense of ἐν καὶ παν) and its parts, discord and harmony, or, as Poseidonius later formulates it, of "matter and spirit, nature and God, the accidental and the predestined." From this we have to distinguish again the All-one or oneness (in the sense of ἐν τὸ παν), the magical union of the forces of drawing- and calling-towards, of the open and the hidden, the cultist and philosophical evocation, of the "flow from phenomenon to phenomenon," such as we find even today in superstition, and particularly in dream superstitions of all societies. Whereas the religion and philosophy of the early Greeks recognized only a harmonious order of cosmos and world, we find already in Poseidonius a purely dynamistic world-view: in place of the notion of order we find the notion "of an explicative" (*erklärlich*), natural, and yet secret and mysterious force," a notion that is still reflected in much of present-day scientific and philosophical theory. Among the Greeks and the Romans, all this was mirrored in the interpretation of dreams until, upon the collapse of the old world, and as an unmistakable sign of that collapse, Petronius, the fine and free-spirited confidante of Nero, scornfully explained that it was not the instittutions and commands of the gods that sent man dreams from above, but that every man made them himself: "Somnia quae mentes ludent volitantibus umbris, non delubra deum, nec ab aethere numina mittunt, sed sibi quisque facit." (*Anth. lat.* 651 R.)

Just as Lucretius (*De Rerum Natura* IV, 962-1029) before him presented a highly realistic account of the relation between dream experiences and daily activities, fears, wishes, and sexual desires, so Petronius put his finger on the most important aspect of modern dream theory: "sed sibi quisque facit!" Here, not only the history of the problem of dreams, but history itself reveals the caesura between the ancient and the modern: the *hybris* of individuation, the all-powerful and godlike human individual rears his head. Within the context of this unnatural elevation of man in contrast to the *All* of the Greek world of forms ("in which the natural laws of man unfold in all directions"), we should glance again at our particular problem: dream and existence.

III

Who is this *Quisque* of Petronius? Can we really lay our hands on the subject of the dream or even simply on the act of dreaming? The proponents of the *Quisque*-theory of subjectivity forget that they have grasped only half the truth. They forget that man steers his carriage "where he wishes, but beneath the wheels there turns, unnoticed, the globe upon which he moves." This holds as true for the purely scientific-genetic conception of dreams as it does with regard to the ethical significance of the dreams, the problem of man's moral responsibility for his dreams. Freud's distinction between the Ego and the Id, Häberlin's distinction between the Ego and the "universum," Jung's distinction between the individual and the collective unconscious, Schleiermacher's distinction between the individual's consciousness and that of the species, Augustine's distinction between that which merely takes place *in* us and that which takes place *through* us—all these are expressions of the distinction between the carriage and the globe upon which it moves.

There is, however, still another such distinction—an important one—that has played a considerable role in the history of philosophy, and has done so without anyone's recalling that it was originally connected with the distinction between dreaming and awakeenness. I refer to the distinction between, on the one hand, image, feeling, subjective opinion, "doxic form" (Plato, Husserl) in general, and, on the other hand, mind, objectivity, and truth. It is this distinction, again, that is the one drawn between the *Quisque*, the individual, the isolated, the *Hekastos* of the Greeks, and the human-divine community conceived of as mediated by Logos and mutual understanding. But while for Petronius and in every epoch of enlightenment the *Quisque* stands as a completely indeterminate X behind the dream he makes, here man is something more than simply a *Quisque* (though he is that, too, to the extent that he proceeds into the world of dreams, images, and feelings). Here, the individual ceases to be a structure in a naïve realistic metaphysics, and individuality becomes a mode of human being, a type and way of being human—the mode, namely, of nonspiritual human existence. One associates this doctrine with the names—to cite only a few—of Heraclitus, Plato, Hegel, Kierkegaard, Heidegger.

According to Hegel, the beginning of philosophy is to be dated from the time of Heraclitus, the first in whom "the philosophical idea is to be met in its speculative form." His great idea was the shift from being to becoming, his great insight was that being and nonbeing are false abstractions and that only becoming has truth. Heraclitus thereby points to the immanence of the moment of negativity that is, at the same time, the principle of vitality. Hegel and Heraclitus also agree in their deprecation and even contempt for everything individual and isolated, and for all interest in it. To this extent, both find it "senseless" "to take conscious individuality as a singular phenomenon of existence," for "what is contradictory therein is that its essence is the universality of mind." (Hegel, *Phenom. of Mind*).

In Part I, we have already explored individuality (the individual dreamer) with reference to the universal (though, to be sure, only within a small existential segment), with reference, namely, to the picture of the happy or unhappy, harmonious or unharmonious individual life and the dream image of the bird rising or falling from the sky. The universal that concerned us there, the transindividual image content, is not created by each individual, yet each individual sees it in his dreams and is either drawn to it or repelled by it. The individual's images, his feelings, his mood belong to him alone, he lives completely in his own world; and being completely alone means, psychologicaly speaking, dreaming—whether or not there is, at the time, a physiological state of sleep. This, indeed, was Heraclitus' criterion for distinguishing dreaming from awakenness. "Those," he says, "who are awake have *one* and the same world in common (ἕνα καὶ κοινὸν κόσμον); in sleep each (Hekastos, Singularis) returns to his own (world) (εἰς ἴδιον ἀποστρέφεσθαι).

Much has been written concerning Heraclitus' contrast between the communal (the *Koinón* or *Xynon*) and the singular, particular, and private (the *Idion*). Especially instructive, however, is the relationship, in this regard, to Hegel—especially in his *History of Philosophy*. After Anaxagoras, the expression for world, "cosmos," which was used by Heraclitus, signified not the (objective) world, but the (subjective) state of unification (Χοινός) and dispersion (ἴδιος). For Heraclitus, what defines this unification or dispersion is the "Logos," a word that sometimes must be translated as "word" or "discourse" and sometimes as "thought," "theory," "deduction," "rational, lawful relation," etc. It thus refers as much to understanding as it does, so Hegel says, to making oneself understood (communication). Common to both is understanding in the sense of reflective thought (τὸ ρρονέειμ).* Although there therefore exists something in which all might find something in common and communicable, namely the Logos, yet the many live as though they were sanctioned in having their own understanding or their own private thoughts (Fr. 92). This, however, regardless of the physiological state, is dreaming. The dreamers fail to notice what they do after they awaken, just as they forget what they do when asleep (Fr. 1). For Heraclitus, genuine awakenness is, negatively put, the awakening from private opinion (*doxa*) and subjective belief. Put positively, it is life (and not just the life of the mind) that accords with the laws of the universal,

---

* Concerning the main significance of ρρονεῖν and ρρὸνησις in Greek philosophy and what they meant for Socrates, Plato, and Aristotle, see Werner Jaeger, *Aristotle*.

whether this universal be called *logos, cosmos, sophia,* or whether it is considered as a combination of all of them in the sense of a rational insight into their unitary, lawful interrelation and in the sense of action according to this insight. Hegel presents this Heraclitean doctrine by saying that here Reason, Logos, becomes the judge of Truth,—not, however, of truth that is second best, but, rather, of divine, universal truth: "this measure, this rhythm which penetrates through to the essence of the All" (an echo of the ancient συμπάθεια).

Only insofar as we live in awareness of this interconnection—whether we call it understanding, wisdom, or reflection—are we awake. "This is the form of sensibility [*Verständigkeit*] which we call awakenness." "If we do not stand in relation to the whole, then we are merely dreaming." Separated (from the whole), understanding loses, according to Heraclitus, the power of consciousness that it had previously, and loses, according to Hegel, the spirit as an individuation of objectivity: it is not singular in its universality. To the extent that we participate in the divine understanding we participate in the Truth, but to the extent that we are particular and special, we are deceived:

> Nothing truer or more unprejudiced can be said about Truth. Only consciousness of the universal is consciousness of truth; but consciousness of particularity and particular action, originality which results in idiosyncracy of content or form, is untrue and evil. Error, therefore, consists solely in the particularization of thought—evil and error consist in the divorce from the universal. Most men think that their conceptions should be something special and original; this is illusion.

According to Hegel, "the knowledge of something of which only I am aware" is dreaming, and the same is true of imagination (in the sense of phantasy) and emotion, "the mode, namely, in which something is only for me, in which I have something in me *qua* this subject; no matter how exalted these emotions may appear, they are nevertheless still in me and not something separable from me." Just as the object can be nonimaginary, not merely the product of my imagination, only if I recognize it as freely existing, so, too, emotion participates "in the Truth" only when I—to speak with Spinoza—have knowledge of it *sub spaecia aeternitatis.*

Though this may sound too abstract, it is actually quite close to home; for in every serious mental activity, particularly in psycho-analysis, there come moments when a man must decide whether, in pride and defiance, to cling to his private opinion—his private theater, as one patient put it—or whether to place himself in the hands of a physician, viewed as the wise mediator between the private and the communal world, between deception and truth. He must, that is, decide whether he wishes to awaken from his dream and participate in the life of the universal, the *koinòs cósmos*. It would be rather unfortunate if our patients had to understand Heraclitus or Hegel in order to get well; but none can attain to genuine health unless the physician succeeds in awakening in him that spark of mind that must be awake in order for the person to feel the slightest breath of that *koinòs cósmos*. Goethe expressed this better, perhaps, than any of our modern psychotherapists:

> Go into thyself! Shouldst thou there dispense
> With infinity in mind and sense
> There's nought to help thee!

It is not that with the awakening of a sense for infinity as the counter to the limitedness of particularity the individual will be relieved of his images and feelings, his wishes and hopes. These, however, will simply be removed from the context of uneasiness, restlessness, and despair, the context of falling, sinking, descending life, to the context—not of utter, deathlike peacefulness—but ascending, tire-lessly soaring life. This is exemplified in a dream one of my patients had after a therapy session, which shows that the spirit, once awakened, can even kindle the dream into at least an image of the universal life.

> Tired and tormented by a powerful inner unrest and uneasiness, I finally dropped off to sleep. In my dream I was walking along an endless beach where the constantly pounding surf and its never-ending restlessness brought me to despair. I longed to be able to bring the ocean to a standstill and enforce a calm upon it. Then I saw a tall man wearing a slouch hat coming toward me on the dunes. He wore a broad cape and carried a stick and a large net in his hand. One eye was hidden behind a large curl of hair which hung upon his forehead. As the man came before me, he spread out the net, captured the sea in it, and laid it before me. Startled,

I looked through the meshing and discovered that the sea was slowly dying. An uncanny calm came over me and the seaweed, the animals, and the fish which were caught in the net slowly turned a ghostly brown. In tears, I threw myself at the man's feet and begged him to let the sea go free again—I knew now that unrest meant life and calm was death. Then the man tore open the net and freed the sea and within me there arose a jubilant happiness as I again heard the pounding and breaking of the waves. Then I awoke!

This is a most interesting dream in many ways. Notice the trichotomy of thesis (dreaming, tormented life in isolation), antithesis (death by total dissolution of individual life following total surrender to the overpowering objective principle of "otherness"), and synthesis (by "reclaiming objectivity in subjectivity"). The dream thus pictorially mirrors the psychoanalytic process as a progression from the individual's defiant persistence in his isolation, to the humble subjection to the (impersonal) "authority" of the doctor ("transference phase"), to the "resolution of the transference." That such a loosening of the transference bond (about which so much has been and is being written) can come about *only* as a genuine inspiration, an even more lucid wakeness in the sense ascribed to it by Heraclitus and Hegel—otherwise it is a fraud and a self-conceit—is overlooked in interpretations that are either one-sidedly biological or that misguidedly view the spirit as an enemy of life. As psychotherapists, however, we must go beyond Hegel, for we are not dealing with *objective* truth, with the congruence between our own thinking and the reality of objects *as* objects, but with "subjective truth," as Kierkegaard would say. We are dealing with the "innermost passion" by virtue of which subjectivity must work itself through objectivity (the objectivity of communication, consensus, submission to a superpersonal norm) and out of it again (as the third phase of our dream disclosed). Only on the basis of such an insight can the psychiatrist himself turn from a dreaming to a waking spirit, so that what Kierkegaard says of Lessing might be said of him: "In neither attempting an unfree devotion nor recognizing an unfree limitation, he—himself free—enables everyone who approaches him to enter into free rapport with him."

All these problems are dormant in Freud's doctrine of transference and particularly in his theories about the resolution of
the transference. And they remain dormant there because no one
has yet succeeded and no one will ever succeed in deriving the
human spirit from instincts (*Triebe*). These two concepts are,
by their very nature, incommensurable, and it is their incommen-
surability that justifies the existence of both concepts, each within
its own proper sphere. A deeper penetration is achieved, in this respect, by Jung's doctrine of individuation as the liberation of the
self from the "false veils of the *persona* on the one hand, and the
suggestive force of unconscious images on the other." But however
deep the insights may be that Jung gains by seeing individuation
as a "process of psychological development," here, too, the fundamental problem of individuation is concealed by the fact that the
contrast between dreaming and waking, suspension in one's private world and in the common world, is not understood for what it
is: the contrast between image and feeling (which always belong
together) on the one hand, intellect on the other. Since, however,
this contrast is there, it cannot wholly escape an explorer such as
Jung. The attempt to derive this contrast from the compensatory
function of the conscious and the subconsious is unsatisfactory in
that the main problem becomes lost in detailed speculations and
theory. This is especially true with respect to the notion of the
"collective unconscious," which is both a kind of eidetic "race consciousness" in Schleirermacher's sense, *and* an ethical reference to
a universal, to "the world" or "the object." It is clear that in this
"collective unconscious" the contrast continues unmitigated. The
same holds true for Jung's concept of the self, in which conscious
and unconscious "complement" each other to form a whole. The
unconscious processes compensating the conscious Ego are supposed to contain within themselves all those elements necessary
for a self-regulation of the total psyche. It must be borne in mind,
however, that the fundamental ethical agent, the conscious, which
is hidden in that compensation, sets the entire functional dynamism
in motion, and that the total psyche is not, on the contrary, regulated by the compensation mechanism; the problem is not furthered either by shifting it from the whole to its parts. Jung's theory
draws successfully from Eastern sources, from India and China,
and makes good use of knowledge of primitive mentality. We, on

the other hand, with all due respect to these sources, do not think it justified to step backwards—in psychology, psychoanalysis, and psychiatry—from the point reached by the Greeks in their understanding of existence.

We now return to our point of departure. When a bitter disappointment causes the ground beneath my feet to give way, then later, after I have "pulled myself together again," I express what happened by saying, "I didn't know what hit me." Here, as Heidegger tells us, the Dasein is brought before its own Being—insofar, that is, as something happens to it and the Dasein knows neither the "how" nor the "what" of the happening. This is the basic ontological element of all dreaming and its relatedness to anxiety.* To dream means: I don't know what is happening to me. From the I and the Me there emerges, to be sure, the individual, the *Quisque* and *Hekastos;* in no way, however, does the individual emerge as he who makes the dream, but rather as the one for whom—"he knows not how"—the dream is made. And this individual is, here, none other than "the selfsame" in the sense of "personal numerical identity" (Kant): purely formal, without substance, it is the plaything of rising and falling life, the roar of the sea and the stillness of death, the brilliance of sun-bathed color and shadowy night, the sublime form of the eagle in flight and the chaotic heap of paper upon the floor, the splendor of a young maiden, the scent of seaweed, the corpse of a fallen bird, the powerful, terrible bird of prey, and the gentle dove. An individual turns from mere self-identity to selfhood, and the dreamer awakens in that unfathomable moment when he decides not only to seek to know "what hit him," but seeks also to strike into and take hold of the dynamics in these events, "himself"—the moment, that is, when he resolves to bring continuity or consistency into a life that rises and falls, falls and rises. Only then does he *make* something. That which he makes, however, is not life—this the individual cannot make—but history. Dreaming, man—to use a distinction I have drawn elsewhere—is "life-function"; waking, he creates "life-history." What he actually makes is the history of his own life, his inner life-history, and we must not confuse this with participation or nonparticipation in outer or world-history, which by no means

* We view anxiety dreams as the prototype of the Dasein's (as such) primal existential anxiety. See Heidegger, *Was ist Metaphysik?*

lies completely within his power. It is not possible—no matter how often the attempt is made—to reduce both parts of the disjunction between life-function and life-history to a common denominator, because life considered as function is not the same as life considered as history. And yet, both do have a common base: existence.

Our goal here has been to indicate the place of dreaming within the context of this common base. But even apart from this we may point out that dreaming and awakenness have something else in common. Just as the "transition" from one to the other is a gradual one (which is not affected by the leap-character of the individual life-historical decision), so the beginning of life-function (and, with it, of dreaming) and the end of inner life-history (awakenness) lie in infinity. For just as we do not know where life and the dream begin, so we are, in the course of our lives, ever again reminded that it lies beyond man's powers "to be 'the individual' in the highest sense."

Notes

1. Walter F. Otto, *Die Götter Griechenlands* (Bonn: Verlag Cohen).
2. Werner Jaeger, *Die geistige Gegenwart der Antike* (Berlin: Verlag de Gruyter).

Introduction to Schizophrenie

The four studies in this volume are attempts to gain insight into the structural and dynamic order of human existence that is designated in the psychiatric clinic as schizophrenia. The mode of selecting these case studies was in no way based on any special anticipated "outcome." Indeed, the state of the daseinsanalytic understanding of schizophrenia was at that time such that no particular result could have been foreseen. In consequence, everything hinged on the capacity to learn and be guided by an unbiased consideration of the unique aspects of each individual case. In the very nature of things, such instruction could proceed only very slowly, step by step.

Nevertheless, the selection of these case histories had to meet certain conditions. The first and most important was that sufficient material from the life-history and course of illness be available, particularly as much self-description as possible. Otherwise, a daseinsanalytic interpretation of the course of schizophrenia would not have been possible. The second condition was that prime concern not be directed to the so-called end-states in the sense of schizophrenic deterioration. That is, attention was first and foremost to be directed to the existential process, seen both retrospectively and, as much as possible, as represented by the on-going process itself. The third condition consisted of the assumption—which proved to be correct—that the understanding of schizophrenic existence could be facilitated and furthered if "cases" were selected in which the outbreak of the schizophrenic psychosis was, for shorter or longer periods, preceded by certain types of "abnormal behavior." By this is meant types of behavior that on the one hand fit into the life-historical pattern of the patient, but that, on the other hand, already seem to foreshadow the psychosis. With that came, fourthly, the expectation that it would certainly be advantageous to select as many different kinds of cases as possible so that the results would not be bound merely to "one class." If it now appears that three of our five cases concern acute or chronic fears of persecution (*Ilse, Lola Voss,* and *Suzanne Urban*), it means, quite apart from the fulfillment of the previously cited preconditions, that for me the problem of schizophrenia seems to culminate in delusion [*Wahn*] and particularly, delusions of persecution.

So much for the principles that guided the selection of our cases. We turn now to the *basic constitutive concepts of our investigations.* Here, as elsewhere, the most important of these concepts is the principle of *order,* the question, namely, as to how a certain order is to be wrought from the sheer, dazzling, multitudinous plenum of historical, psychological, psychopathological, and biological data that we bring together clinically under the term "case." The clinician, of course, also seeks an order in these cases, an order, however, based on purely clinical concepts and modes of thought that, based as they are on a naturalist-reductionist dialectic, transform all such data into *symptoms of illness.* The order that we strive for in daseinsanalytic communication with the patient is of quite a different sort. It lies on this side of the concepts of healthy and sick, normal and abnormal, and is only attainable by the kind of interpretation that sees all these data as distinct modes of existence, of existential process and determination. We speak, therefore, quite generally of a daseinsanalytic order; it is of a purely phenomenological nature. But such an order would not be ascertainable if the Dasein as such did not exhibit a definite ontological structure. We have Martin Heidegger to thank for revealing to us the a priori of this ontological structure of the Dasein. Only since Heidegger is it possible to speak of a dis-order in the ontological structure of the Dasein and to show of what it can consist, to show, that is, which elements are to be made responsible for the fact that a particular structural order, so to say, "denies," that it exhibits gaps and that these gaps are filled again by the Dasein.

With this we are closer to what is daseinsanalytically the central problem of schizophrenia and its solution. For with the designation of the denying elements in the structural order of the Dasein together with the modes of its disposition, not only are we in a position to bring daseinsanalytic order to the dazzling, superabundant plenum of a clinical case, but we are also in a position daseinsanalytically to compare this "plenum" with the quite different kinds of "plenum" in other cases. While clinical psychiatry strives to make such comparison possible on the grounds of the similarity or dissimilarity of symptoms and syndromes, *Daseinsanalyse* provides us with a different kind of systematic comparison—one based, namely, on certain existential processes and determinations. Instead of a *disease unit* consisting of a small and perhaps also clinically and symptomatically rather varied class, we have here a *unity* of definite existential structures and processes.

Just as the most important constitutive concept of our investigation was that of the general structural order of the Dasein, so we entered upon a genuine investigation of schizophrenia only when we sought insights into the *specific* ontological structure of our cases. That was possible, as we have said, only by approaching them without preconceptions and by allowing ourselves to be guided and instructed by them alone. However, since it cannot be the task of this introduction to recapitulate the progress of our work on the individual cases, let us rather pursue the issues as to constitutive categories or basic concepts that, in the course of investigation, yielded us the perspective from which to speak of a *unity* of the existential processes that were studied. I shall refer the reader to particular cases only insofar as they illustrate these categories.

Since the first basic concept that emerges from our investigations is that of the inconsistency of experience, a few remarks about the consistency of ("natural") experience must serve as preface. Natural experience is that in which our existence moves not only unreflectively, but also unproblematically and unobtrusively, as smoothly as a natural chain of events.[1] This quality of the unproblematic is related, above all, to objectivity. Even when something is unknown to us, this something does not fall out of the self-evident context that is natural experience. The chain of events in experience can therefore be "natural" only insofar as it is *in-*

herently consistent, that is, in our sense of being in harmony with things and circumstances, with others (whom we meet in our everyday intercourse with circumstances and things), and with ourselves: having, in a word, the sense of *residing* [*Aufenthalt*—Heidegger]. The immediateness of this residing among "things" or "circumstances" is manifested in our *letting* beings—all beings—*be* as they are in themselves. This letting-be is, however, in no way a self-evident or easy activity, but, rather—as our case studies all too convincingly and lamentably show—something highly positive and active.

A. The basic concept used in understanding what is called the schizophrenic existential pattern proves to be the notion of a breakdown in the consistency of natural experience, its inconsistency. Inconsistency implies precisely that inability to "let things be" in the immediate encounter with them, the inability, in other words, to reside serenely among things. The case of Ellen West presents us with a clear example of such incapacity. We see Ellen West despotically disposing of "things" about her, as though dictating to them how they should be: the body must not grow too fat, but must remain thin—indeed, she herself must not be as she is, but must become completely different (cf. "Creator, . . . create me a second time, and create me better!"). Human society must not be as it is, but must change. This example shows that when we speak of "letting things be" we are not speaking of the quietist who, as a nonparticipant, leaves everything in the world untouched.

On the contrary, a revolutionary spirit who seeks to overthrow the things of the world actually resides in undisturbed immediacy among them; otherwise he could not overthrow them, could not *subjugate* them. The situation is quite different with Ellen West and our other patients. They persist in suffering because things are not the way they would like them to be and persist in merely dictating the way they should be; which is to say, their mode of behavior is that of mere wishing and chasing after an ideal. Jürg Zünd is an example of an even more drastic inability to reside undisturbedly among the things of this world. His entire comportment, conduct, and interest in others is "inappropriate." Equally grotesque is the distorting and linguistic fractioning of things that is effected by Lola Voss's language oracle. Nor does

Suzanne Urban's excessive concern for her parents represent an untroubled residing among things and people. This arbitrary disposition of things is accompanied by the weakening of every materially consistent existential order. Everywhere experience reveals its gaps, and nowhere can it make peace with itself or unfold freely.

What makes the lives of our patients such a torment is that they are not able to come to terms with the inconsistency and disorder of their experience, but, rather, constantly seek for a *way out* so that order can be re-established. Everywhere we encounter this unquenchable longing to re-establish the disturbed order, to fill the gaps in experience with ever new ideas, activities, undertakings, distractions, obligations, and ideals—the longing, in fine, for "peace and harmony" and "home" (Ellen West), or, indeed, for "death as the sole happiness in life" (Ellen West), for Nirvana (Jürg Zünd) in the sense of a final *ad acta* laying aside of things and, in a "definitely final effort," the laying aside of one's *self*.

This longing for an "end" originates in there being *no way out* of existence and the inconsistency of experience that accompanies it. Ellen West's "simile of the stage" * is a particularly dramatic and tragic representation of this state of having no way out. But before this end appears, be it as suicide, withdrawal from active life, or as insanity, we see the Dasein in fact tormenting itself in the search for ever new ways out, ways that cannot be effective because of the patient's particular life-situation. The last way out manifests itself without exception in the formation of Extravagant [*verstiegene*] ideals that masquerade as a life-stance, and in the hopeless struggle to pursue and maintain these ideals.

But even when it comes to an energetic deed as a way out of the unendurably entangled life-situation—as was the case with Ilse—its futility is easily seen in its inappropriateness to the life-situation. Ilse's act and its inappropriateness must be understood as necessarily foredoomed and as preparatory to another way out that takes the form of (acute) psychosis. The inappropriateness of Ilse's action to the particular situation shows that here the consistency

* See "The Case of Ellen West," in Rollo May, Ernest Angel, and Henri F. Ellenberger, (eds.), *Existence* (New York, 1958), pp. 237-364. Binswanger's book *Schizophrenie* consists of five case studies: "Ilse," "Ellen West," "Jürg Zünd," "Lola Voss," and "Suzanne Urban." Translations of the first two are to be found in *Existence*. The present book contains the fourth, "The Case of Lola Voss."]

of experience, though not yet ruptured, already seems to be threatened. For the Dasein, as it were, "grabs blindly and falsely" in its choice of means, overruns itself in a single experimental possibility that, regardless of *its* own inner consistency, has all the earmarks of the larger inconsistency. This is what we mean when we speak of "inappropriateness to the life-situation." It is manifested not only in the "practical" unsuitability of the means she chooses, but more basically in that the "means" itself bear the signs of experiential inconsistency. The burning of the hand and arm is neither a purposeful action in the technical sense, nor a "proof of love" that is consonant with the "emotional situation." It runs counter to the authentic "logic of emotion"—if we may use such an expression —in that what is involved is not at all an act or gift of *love* that the other can receive as such, but, rather, an *exhibition* of martyred suffering "out of love." As a result, this suffering can forge no bonds, no "bonds of love," and can open no exits from the unendurable life-situation.

B. Even at the time of her act of burning her arm, Ilse's behavior was already being ruled by a particular set of alternatives— the alternatives of either power, victory, and deliverance, or defeat and powerlessness. We thus come to the *second constitutive concept* of our research: the *splitting off of experiential consistency* into *alternatives*, into a rigid *either-or*. This factor is of highest importance for understanding the course taken by that form of existence designated as schizophrenia. The inconsistency of experience now undergoes an apparently new ordering, the apparent taking of a stance amid the disorder of experiential inconsistency. We thus come back to what we have come to recognize in all our patients as the formation of Extravagant ideals. The Dasein now stakes everything on "maintaining" this stance, on—in other words —pursuing this ideal "through thick and thin." The ideal is Extravagant in that it is completely inappropriate to the total life-situation and does not, therefore, represent a genuine means. On the contrary, it sets up an insurmountable and impenetrable wall in the path of existence. The Dasein can no longer find its way back out of this Extravagance and instead becomes more and more deeply enmeshed in it. The effect of this is even more catastrophic in that the formation of Extravagant ideals represents only one aspect of the alternative, while the other embraces everything that contradicts this ideal.

Compared to the severe existential pull exerted by both of these alternatives, the inconsistency of experience was relatively harmless. For now the Dasein is torn by the struggle between both aspects of the alternative into which it is split. Now it becomes a matter of either being able to pursue the Extravagant ideal or of giving it up entirely. But neither the one nor the other is now possible—as we see especially clearly in the case of Ellen West and Jürg Zünd. For Lola Voss and Suzanne Urban the either-or is even more rigid and insurmountable. There can no longer be any talk of Lola's being in a position to give up the Extravagant ideal of absolute safety afforded her by her language oracle because here, as everywhere, giving up the Extravagant ideal means the bottomless *anxiety* of succumbing to the other side of the alternative. Nor, similarly, can Suzanne Urban under any circumstances renounce her overwhelming concern for her family. In both cases a loss of the hold on the Extravagant ideal means that the Dasein becomes anxious—the anxiety of being *persecuted* (delusions of persecution). Instead of a free unfolding of experience we find—in all our cases—an "imprisonment" or "bondage" in the "net" or "fetters" of the rigid alternative (Ellen West). The Dasein can come to rest on neither side of the alternative and is driven from one to the other. And the higher the particular ideal becomes, the more powerful and explosive is the threat posed by the other side of the alternative.

To understand the actual existential meaning of a given patient's alternatives it does not suffice, however, to have them before us in the form in which they appear to the patient himself and in which they communicated to us. These communications must be subjected to daseinsanalytic interpretation. In this regard, let us glance briefly at the alternatives between which the existence of Ellen West is suspended, and those similarly confronting Jürg Zünd. In the former case, we see the alternatives of fat and thin, and in the latter, the alternative is between proletarian and aristocrat.

Ellen West herself speaks of her conflict, of the "eternal friction between the wish to be thin and the inability to control my eating," of the struggle between her "nature" or her "fate" that she must be fat and vigorous, and her "will to be slender and delicate." Even her first psychoanalyst was not satisfied with this formulation and sought to improve it with the equation: slender = higher, intellectual-spiritual type; fat = Jewish-bourgeois. What this equation says is that Ellen West's bodily existence is not the primary or decisive thing. *Daseinsanalyse* cannot rest content with such equations, nor with the notion of psychogenesis, nor the dubious concepts of psychosomatics. *Daseinsanalyse*, too, is convinced that it is not the purely bodily alternative between being slender or fat that is destroying this life; but it goes further in that it points to the perverse[2] and therefore completely unsuitable role with which bodiliness is burdened in this Dasein—the role, namely, of overcoming the basic experiential split between the alternatives of life and death, ideal and reality, "nature" or "fate" and self-will, alternatives that are completely existential. Added to this is the imperative that the consistency of experience, the "mental" and "harmoniously attuned" order of life be thereby restored. Only because of the perversity of this imperative could the building up of ideals "go so far" [*sich versteigen*]. In other words, only because of this imperative could the ideal of being slender assume such inexorable, implacable power over this Dasein. This power does not stem from an equation, nor from some kind of symbolization, but, rather, from the wish to pick up again the lost thread of experiential consistency, a thread that, however, is already irreparably broken. While the thread of experiential consistency can, in fact, be pursued only by accepting Being and leaving things and facts to themselves—the body, nature, fate, and life among them—in the case of Ellen West these things are not left to themselves, but are, rather, "hunted down," "subjugated," indeed negated.

Whereas for Ellen West the traplike existential alternative extended to the bodily sphere, in the case of Jürg Zünd it was socially expressed in, as we have already mentioned, the alternative between the ideal of the noble, aristocratic *grand-seigneur* and the proletarian actuality. Though both sets of alternatives (the bodily and the social) may seem to have little in common, they become quite comparable when we trace them to their existential bases. The role played by physique in Ellen West's existence takes the form here of "belonging," of being-with in commerce or intercourse with others, or, as I have termed it, the *mitweltlich* grasping and being-grasped by something.[3] For Jürg Zünd, "belonging" or social existence is burdened with the role of overcoming the experiential split between the existential alternatives of life and death, ideal and reality, nature (or fate) and will. The imperative, in fact, requires not only that the split be overcome, but also restoration of psychic and emotional order.

When, with reference to Ellen West and Jürg Zünd, we speak of *existential* alternatives and of the carrying over of these alternatives to the bodily and social spheres, it is important to bear in mind that what we are thereby dealing with are *deficient* existential modes. This deficiency arises out of the inconsistency of experience and the experiential splitting off into the particular alternatives. Now, the complete submersion of the Dasein in the particular pair of alternatives also means that the existence can, in general, temporalize itself only in the mode of "deficiency"—in the mode, namely, that we have come to know as *fallenness* to the world, or, in short, as *"mundanization"* [*Verweltlichung*]. This is manifested most clearly in the "concealment" involved in the phenomenon of "protecting" shame[4] (modesty, *pudeur*, *Scham*) by means of the deficient mode of public shame (stemming from one's own reflection thrown upon others—*Schande, la honte*). But the same thing (mundanization) is also manifested in the deficiency of those modes in which we encounter *conscience, regret,* genuine *humor* and, above all, *love* in our patients. We almost always find that the authentic *dual* existential mode of the Dasein is present in the mode of deficiency. Together with this we find—even in the case of Ellen West, and in spite of everything we may say about her ripeness for death—the impossibility of an *authentic* being-toward-death [*Sein zum Tode*] in the sense of the Dasein being ahead of itself in *resolve*, and also in the sense of the ability of the Dasein *to be a whole*, a totality. If Ellen West's suicide points to the fact that she "made an end" to her life, what is thereby implied is not an authentic "dying," but, rather, that her "life stopped."[5] All this serves the more clearly to indicate what it is which differentiates experiential inconsistency and its split into a rigid either-or, i.e. the ontological structure of existence as schizophrenic, from existential process in the sense of experiential consistency.

C. A further constitutive concept for our investigations was the concept of *covering*. By this we mean the sisyphuslike effort to conceal that side of the alternative that is unbearable to the Dasein so that the Extravagant ideal might thereby be buttressed. Jürg Zünd is the classic example of this, and his case provides us with a standpoint from which to understand manneredness and also, to a certain extent, artistic mannerism.[6] What the cloak of elegant manners (which petrified into manneredness) was for Jürg Zünd, the constant efforts to stay thin and the laxatives were for Ellen West, the covering over of anxiety and the buttressing of the ideal of hiddenness by means of the syllable oracle and its "decisions" were for Lola Voss, and the concealment of the horrors of anxiety by means of the hypochondriacally overwhelming concern for the welfare of her family was for Suzanne Urban.

D. In this regard, we made use of a further concept: that of the existence's *being worn away* (as though by friction), the culmination of the antinomic tensions involved in *no longer being able to find a way out or in,* a culmination that is a *resignation* or a *renunciation* of the whole antinomic problem as such, and that takes the form of an existential *retreat.* In this context, a closer look at the particular cases is in order.

1. I have just spoken of Ellen West's retreat from *life.* Her renunciation of life was the most energetic, decisive and self-willed form of retreat from an existence in which the antinomic tension and *no longer being able to find a way in or out* was pitched at its highest. Here, of all our cases, we have the freest decision of which the Dasein has been able to avail itself: the decision to make an end to the hopelessness of experience by annulling entanglement and ensnarement in general.

2. But as soon as we come to the case of Jürg Zünd we can no longer characterize the retreat as completely free. To be sure, he struggles, as he puts it, for one "last effort" that would bring to a final end the torment of the insoluble problem of his existence. In the end, however, he exhausts his strength in these efforts so that he sees himself as "forced" to make an end to this terrible game with what is literally a last effort. He likens his struggles to find a way out from an existence from which there is no exit with efforts of his intention to "dispose" or "take care" of the individual Ror-

schach cards *ad acta*. But with each such "laying aside" of the cards, Jürg Zünd is always taking care of himself, seeking to "close the file" [*ad acta zu legen*] of his own existence in order, ultimately, to have himself forever "taken care of" in an institution. Here, too, we are faced with a "retreat from life"—life, however, no longer as *vita*, but, rather, the life of activity, "social" life, in which Jürg Zünd for so long and so hopelessly has been tossed to and fro. We see in both cases that it is just that existential problem whose antinomic tensions have worn away the Dasein that also determines the mode and form of the retreat from it. This is true of Ellen West, whose whole life from childhood on was "overshadowed" by the problem of life and death, and it is true of Jürg Zünd, whose whole life was similarly permeated by the problem of human society.

3. We come now to the retreat from existence in the *completely* unfree mode of *insanity*, a mode in which the Dasein of its own free will renounces neither life nor social life. What, rather, is renounced is life as independent, autonomous selfhood. The Dasein thus *surrenders itself over* to existential powers alien to itself. What we have here is a particularly radical capitulation of the Dasein. Neither Ellen West nor Jürg Zünd had given up or surrendered themselves, their Selves; what they did, rather, was to withdraw themselves from life as such or from communal life. Now, however, the Dasein removes itself from the autonomy of its own life context. We are forced to say of such a person that he is a victim, a plaything, or a prisoner in the hands of alien powers. Compared to this, both Ellen West and Jürg Zünd, though the prisoners of their own problems, were at the same time their own liberators from those problems.

In this context, we may refer to the case of Ilse. Our point of departure must be her act of burning her hand. Here the Dasein "exhibits itself" as a martyr to other human beings. In insanity this self-exhibition becomes a being exhibited. Such a turnabout from "active" doing to "passive" suffering is something we encounter again and again in insanity. And this is indicative of the fact that activity and passivity, in this case the spontaneity of *making an impression and influencing*[7] and the receptivity of *being* impressed and influenced, are existentially not opposite, but, rather, inseparably bound up with each other.

We may say that, as a martyr, the Dasein was still to a degree capable of self-rule, or that, to put it another way, the Dasein still proceeded (though in a mode inappropriate to the situation) within an experiential consistency—so that, as it were, what was involved was a "leap," rather than a sundering from the world. But in the passage from martyrdom to insanity, from self-sacrifice to being sacrificed at the hands of others, the Dasein progressively loses regency over itself. This first manifests itself in the appearance of "crazy thoughts," in the threat, in other words, to the consistency of experience and, with it, to the continuity of "world." Before the act (of burning the hand), the Dasein had no way out, no exit from the alternatives of victory and defeat, of a "lightning-like" solution to the life situation and its unendurable continuation. In these circumstances, the act of burning the hand, the sacrifice of the hand, offered itself as one possible *way out*, as a possibility, namely, of the patient herself being set at ease by means of a forceful presentation to her father of his "injustice." This way of coping with the situation was so inappropriate that it was bound to fail. The Dasein was at a loss as to which way to turn and was faced for the first time with the total impossibility of allowing the further consistent unfolding of experience. The consistency of experience breaks apart from one of its existential directions, leaving, as it were, a vacuum. This vacuum is filled again: but filled by a mode of experience that, though to a degree related to the experience preceding it, is nevertheless completely inconsistent with it, namely, that mode of experience that we describe as the patient's becoming a victim at the hands of others. The inconsistency shows itself in that the Dasein is now frozen by a *model* in accordance with which all newly emerging experiences are shaped—as references to self, as wrongs perpetrated upon the patient, as torments, as persecutions, and also as persecutions in the sense of being forced to love. All this becomes clearer as soon as we approach the case of Lola Voss, and even more so in the case of Suzanne Urban.

4. Just as the case of Ilse was of special interest in that it presented us with a transitional stage between health and psychosis in the form of a single event and act, so the case of Lola Voss presents an even more instructive example of a transitional stage in the form of a near-psychotic superstitious language-oracle. This "game" allowed Lola Voss, clinging to her ideal of being hidden,

a while in which to find a foothold. However tenuous this foothold might appear to an outsider, it provided a bridge between her anxiety before the unspeakable Uncanny and Horrid and her surrendering of herself to the secret conspiracy of personalized enemies— the bridge, that is, to the Dasein's renunciation of its particular autonomy. What is involved here is neither a solution or, more accurately, setting aside of the antinomic tension of existence by means of the withdrawal of life in the form of suicide, nor by means of the withdrawal of life from society in the form of a "deep concern," but, rather a withdrawal of life from its own decisional context by making all decisions dependent upon another. The Dasein's antinomic tension, the awareness that there is no longer a way out or a way in, culminates here in the Dasein's yielding its power to choose in the face of the decisions of enemies. This is the context in which we may very instructively view Lola's language oracle as a transitional stage.

What it shows us is, in the first place, that Lola has renounced her own particular power to decide and lets herself be advised only by the "things," which, for their part, are not objects or things as they are in themselves, but, rather, things as linguistically modelled and created by her. Production and reproduction, spontaneity and receptivity here engage in a most remarkable union in which spontaneity nevertheless still prevails. To the extent that Lola Voss relies on what the things (which she has, for the most part, herself constituted) "say" to her, everything depends on her attending properly to what they say, or, in other words, her correct understanding or interpretation of the language of things. In this regard it is important to note that the language of things limits itself to commanding or forbidding and that the patient herself sees her whole "salvation" in the strictest obedience to the prohibitions or commands of these products of her own phantasy. Lola Voss's persecution complex is to be differentiated from mere superstition when she begins to feel herself bound no longer by the decisions of her self-created oracle, but by the decisions of her self-created enemies, as is the case with Ilse and Suzanne Urban We need, finally, to note the displacement that consists in the fact that the blind obedience to the commands and prohibitions of the oracle seems, in her psychosis, still to leave room for a freedom either to obey or run away from the demands of her enemies. This freedom, however, is purchased at the price of a complete dependence on the enemies, at the price of a persecution psychosis.

What is common, now, with regard to both the oracle and the psychosis is the necessity to guess or interpret the *words* of the enemies, which, indeed, she herself *has them say*. While with respect to the oracle we might still have spoken of a certain activeness on her part, here there reigns a total and complete passivity. For, in the psychosis, whatever activeness emerges is activity only *within* passivity, within the complete self-surrender of the Dasein to alien forces, within, in other words, the Dasein's complete surrender of itself. Where, however, we thus surrender ourselves, there we become the victim or sacrifice at the hands of others. The retreat from the problems of existence, the Dasein's resignation from its own particular problem, is manifested here in the form of the passivity of victimization and sacrifice.

5. In the case of Suzanne Urban we sought to understand her persecution psychosis by a phenomenological study of the Power of the Terrible (which broke out of the *koinonia* of existential events), and in the life-historical unfolding of that power. Here we draw the consequences with respect to the concept of resignation, the retreat of the Dasein from the antinomic tension, the Dasein's inability any longer to find a way in or out. With Suzanne Urban information supplied by relatives allows us to determine precisely the culmination point of this resignation. It is the moment where, totally exhausted by the efforts at covering that were to support her idealized concern for her relatives and, ultimately, her husband—totally exhausted, she breaks down completely and, instead of dictatorially including the domestic personnel with this concern (as she had done previously), she becomes the victim or sacrifice at the hands of these same domestic servants. Now she is spied upon and betrayed by others.

The case of Suzanne Urban is our crassest example of the culmination of the Dasein's renunciation of its antinomic problem in the form of a retreat into insanity or, in other words, the complete relinquishing of self to that aspect of the alternative that had hitherto been suppressed "with all possible force," an alternative in which the Dasein had long since found itself divided. With this renunciation everything turns into that which was its previously suppressed (or, in Freud's terms, repressed) terrible opposite.

Whereas Suzanne Urban was, like Ellen West, from childhood on a self-willed, obstinate and inconsiderate person who could never subordinate herself to the opinions of others, who never formed real friendships, who had, in general, little trust in her fellow man, and who always sought to rule over her environment, she now, on the other hand, allows herself to be ruled by others, is compelled to subordinate herself to them, suffers now from that same lack of trust in her fellow man and sees herself as completely surrounded by enemies. But the most essential thing in this reversal in insanity is the following. Freud has made us aware that *excessive* concern for others, like every such excess, is a sign of the repression of a painful force that the act of repression attempts to alleviate. At the same time, such excess is always a sign or indication of that which is repressed. The excessive "hypochondriacal" concern for the "idolized" mother is also a kind of wish to master and rule. If, now, we recall the "sadistic orgies" that the Dasein in its persecution psychosis, engages in, then we need not hesitate in speaking, with Freud, of outspoken "sadistic components" in the case of Suzanne Urban. Here, from the point of view of *Daseinsanalyse*, is the basis for the inconsistency of experience and its splitting off into a fixed either-or; here is the real basis for the antinomic tension of the Dasein, and the particular *content* that the Dasein imposes after the reversal and the victory of the hitherto suppressed aspect of the alternative. Here, in a word, lies the basis of the "psychotic content."

But in all this we have still not yet understood the daseinsanalytic significance of psychosis in general and persecution psychosis in particular. What it signifies, as we have seen in the case of Ilse and, especially, in the case of Lola Voss, is *one* of the forms of existential resignation with respect to the Dasein's antinomic tensions, a resignation that takes the form of a retreat from Dasein's own decision, the complete renunciation of the Dasein's own ability to decide and, with this, the complete *self*-surrender to the power of others. That, in this case, it is other people to whom the Dasein surrenders itself, and not, say, to demonic forces, is related to the basic sadism that is dominant in this Dasein—and sadism is, at root, a mode of being in the *Mitwelt*. In this *self*-surrender to the will of others, however, we also find the reason why the others must become *enemies*, must, that is, become those "upon whose will I am dependent, who can do with me as they wish"—in other words, "whose victim I am." If, now, the Dasein "senses the enemy" everywhere, if in every event and act it not only suspects, but sees hostile intentions, the reason lies not in an alteration of the Dasein's sense of reality or meaning, its perception or psychic functioning, nor does the reason lie in a "physiognomic" alteration of the world and "sympathetic relationships" in Erwin Straus's sense. All these alterations are, rather, secondary and tertiary consequences of the resignation of the Dasein in the form of its self-withdrawal from its own decisional frame of reference.

It should be clear now that the content of the psychosis (in this case the sadistic orgies of the enemies) also represents nothing primary. It merely indicates to us the mode in which the Dasein fills "with phantasy" the experiential gaps or vacua that its retreat from the antinomic tension has left. The purely positivistic judgment that psychosis in general has to do with "mere phantasy" and "phantasms," and that in it "nothing is real," but only "psychotically imagined": none of this furthers the understanding of psychosis. The decisive element lies, as has been said, in the particular, individual nature of the *resignation* or final capitulation of the Dasein, culminating in the withdrawal from the Dasein's decisional frame of reference—in other words, the Dasein's surrendering of itself to the will of "alien" forces or "alien" persons. In the place of an antinomic tension (arising from the inconsistency of experience) between two irreconcilable alternatives, what emerges now is a more "one-sided" and thus more consistent, "incorrigible," "unproblematic" experience in the sense of a psychotic experiential model according to which all new experience is fashioned.

Notes

1. See W. Szilasi, "Die Erfahrungsgrundlage der Daseinsanalyse Binswangers," *Schweiz. Archiv. f. Neur. u. Psych.*, Vol. 67 (1951).
2. See Binswanger, *Drei Formen Missglückten Daseins*, Chapter 2.
3. See Binswanger, *Grundformen, Das mitweltliche Nehmen-bei-etwas*, pp. 300-375.
4. See Rollo May, Ernest Angel, and Henri F. Ellenberger (eds.), *Existence* (New York, 1958), pp. 331-341.]

5. See Heidegger, *Sein und Zeit*, p. 247.
6. See Binswanger, *Drei Formen*, Chapter 3.
7. See Freud, "Psychoanalytische Bermerkungen über einen autobiographisch beschriebenen Fall von Paranoia (Dementia paranoides)," *Gesammelte Schriften* VIII.

᪥᪥᪥᪥

The Case of Lola Voss

[The reader should note that, in Dr. Angel's translation of this study, the term *Dasein* is generally rendered as "existence."]

First published in *Das Schweizer Archiv für Neurologie und Psychiatrie*, Volume 63, Zürich, 1949.

TRANSLATED BY *Ernest Angel*

Report

HEREDITY / Lola's father is a blue-eyed Germanic type, very quiet, somewhat stiff and formal but friendly and simple. The mother, offspring of a German father and a native Spanish-South American mother (and therefore considered a half-caste) is "nervous," always excited, easily frightened, but enjoys life; she likes company, loves to talk and laugh, and displays a Southern temperament. Her thyroid condition is obvious. A brother, one year Lola's junior, is gay, cheerful, and thoroughly "normal."

Unfortunately, further data are missing from Lola's case history.

ANAMNESIS / Information received from the father: Lola is now [at the time of Lola's admission to Dr. Binswanger's sanatorium in Kreuzlingen, Switzerland] twenty-four years of age.

[266]

Breast-fed in infancy, she was always healthy during childhood and had no problems in her early development. She was an extremely spoiled child, used to doing or not doing whatever pleased her at a given moment. When her father told her to do something, she would be excused by the mother; when an order came from her mother, it was Grandma who offered her refuge. "There was always someone who offered her a haven," remarks the father.

At the age of twelve, she suffered from a serious attack of typhoid fever with high temperatures and had to spend fifty-two days in bed. During that period the first indications of an anxiety state occurred. She would, for instance, refuse to sleep at home because "it was not safe enough" and stayed overnight in Grandma's house.

At thirteen, Lola—who was born in South America—was placed in a boarding school in Germany, where she behaved in a markedly boyish manner, denied that she was a girl, was domineering and quarrelsome and could not get along with her peers. At fourteen, she returned to South America. During those first years she was still completely inconspicuous and pleasure-seeking, liked to dance and to attend dances. She did needlework, occupied herself with painting and reading and, in general, was rather active. But a certain tendency to be by herself and lock herself up in her room was observable. She was quite religious; under the influence of Catholic friends, she turned against her Protestant father.

At twenty, she met a Spanish doctor at a dance. He fell in love with her and made his serious intentions known to her family, although he had not yet attained a solid position and did not have the means to support a family. He was described as a very serious, reasonable, quiet, if somewhat calculating man. Her father's hesitant and rejecting attitude toward this suitor caused Lola to become somewhat rebellious: she began to fast frequently, appeared joyless and depressed, and announced her intention to marry—or take the veil. During this entire period, the mother sided with Lola against the father.

At twenty-two, Lola accompanied her mother on a trip to a German spa. Shortly before the departure she refused to go aboard the boat unless a certain dress was removed from the luggage. Only after her wish was fulfilled did she join her mother on the boat.

Subsequently, the Spanish doctor came to Germany to see his

fiancée. During their two-weeks' meeting she was calm and re-
strained and appeared somewhat more interested in her wardrobe,
which she had previously neglected. She showed more pleasure in
entertainment, theatres, etc., and altogether made a different and
much more cheerful impression. The correspondence between
Lola and the doctor continued. In May of the following year he
wrote that now he had a secure position but could not yet think of
marrying Lola; he had to take care of his sick mother and his situation would not yet permit him to marry. At that point Lola
"collapsed."

She became melancholic and peculiarly superstitious: she would
look for four-leafed clovers and display an irresistible aversion to a variety of objects, particularly umbrellas and rubber
shoes, which, she said, brought her bad luck. When she noticed
that her chambermaid in the hotel was a hunchback, she immediately left the place. Hunchbacked men she considered lucky, however, and even tried to touch them.

Most of the year before entering the sanatorium Lola had
spent with her elderly aunts in Germany. These women had al-
legedly turned her against her mother, who meanwhile had left for
home. So intense did Lola's resentment against her mother grow
that upon the latter's return Lola would not enter her room any
more. Anything connected with her mother she considered "bewitched," and everything coming from her mother had to be destroyed: clothes, underwear, toothbrushes. She discarded them by
hiding them, giving them away, or packing them in small bundles
that she later "lost" or sold in the streets. She even refused to wear
garments that had come from the laundry along with her mother's
underwear. She threw away a pen and ink that had been used by
her mother; she would not even write a letter at the same table at
which her mother had written. Repeatedly she cut up her own
clothes.

During the preceding year a great many physicians had been
consulted, all of whom observed certain peculiarities, and recommended marriage. Lola received injections of various sorts, such
as ovarial substance and thyroid extract. Subsequently, an endo-
crinologist found the thyroid gland in perfect order and recommended a specialist for nervous diseases. When this specialist (who

was not introduced to her as such) touched upon her superstitious ideas, she refused to have anything further to do with him.

A trip to Switzerland was agreed to by Lola without any difficulty since she thought she was going there to meet her fiancé, who had started to write her again and had suggested a meeting in Europe.

The essentials of the father's report were confirmed by information supplied by the mother. She added that Lola had always impressed people as being tired; even as a child she had reminded them of an old woman. Photographs disclosed that Lola's face had changed a good deal over the last few years; it had become coarser.

OBSERVATIONS DURING LOLA'S STAY AT THE SANATORIUM / Lola Voss is a pretty girl of medium size, in her twenty-fifth year, with an animated facial expression, but somewhat stiff in her gestures. Her manner is vivacious and open, but her speech is labored and foreign. The shape of her face is regular and oval, the shape of the skull slightly pyknic rather than leptosome. The total constitution is slightly asthenic.*

The patient did not bring with her any underwear, not even a nightgown. She does not seem to resent her father's placing her in a sanatorium, even though this was contrary to what he had told her was the purpose of the trip. Although she does not consider herself sick, she accepted the nurse without demur.

Psychological Report† Lola has a good mind and is verbally astute; she is also a master of the art of lying. She twists everything to her own advantage; cunningly and slyly she arranges her complaints and requests to suit her own purposes. While it was easy for the physician to establish rapport with her, she would—at meals—not utter a single spontaneous word to her fellow patients and, when spoken to, would respond merely with "yes" or "no" or "don't know," accompanied by a vacant smile.

[* TRANSLATOR'S NOTE: The latter observations show the influence of Kretschmer's anthropometric theories typical of the pre-World War II period in Europe.]

† No systematic analysis of the case was contemplated at the time of this report.

The impression she makes is that of a rather stiff and affectless person who is extremely careless and indifferent, has no interests, and finds no satisfaction in work. She is very spoiled and shows a childish stubbornness, symptoms of a general disproportion between her age and mental development. In all her behavior she is unpredictable: e.g., she would promise to attend an evening party and would leave to dress, but suddenly decide to go to bed because she was tired. On the other hand, she would stay for hours on end without tiring if she liked a party. Or she would take a medication once or twice and then refuse it, explaining that it had done her harm, or taken her breath away, etc.

On the very first day she ran away to her father's hotel and had to be brought back against her vigorous resistance. She stayed four weeks in the closed ward before she could be retransferred to the open ward. During the first few weeks she was afraid she would be hypnotized. To the nurse she said, "Don't look at me this way, you are trying to hypnotize me." Again and again, she had to be reassured. After a few days she was more at ease. Hypnosis was not mentioned any more, and when someone brought up the topic, she asked, "Do you know how to hypnotize? I would like to be hypnotized." All she knew about hypnosis was that she had once read about it and had seen a movie showing a hypnotic scene. Sleep and nourishment were satisfactory so that the patient gained 1½ pounds within the first 10 days.

Lola always wears the same dress, has only one pair of shoes, and no hat. But she refuses to do any shopping: she does not want to retain anything that might remind her later of her stay in Kreuzlingen. Her superstition breaks through constantly although she tries hard to cover it up: e.g., after a movie in which superstition is ridiculed she manages to join in the laughter. Otherwise, she is reticent, lacking in affect, resentful, irritable, and suspicious. With tremendous stubbornness she continuously opposes treatment by way of passive resistance. Over and over again, she has to be urged to do some gardening. She likes to be by herself, paints a little, reads novels, but excludes any serious literature as too difficult. In view of her growing opposition to her physician—she falsely accused him of having lied to her—a new physician took over at the end of the year.*

* Lola's attitude toward the new doctor (this writer) is much friendlier and

Furthermore, she said she had experienced something else, something so terrible that she could not possibly talk about it. On a day when she might mention it or even merely hear of some-

---

more outgoing. She now agrees to wear new dresses, gives much more of herself, and gradually, despite great inner inhibitions, finally talks about her anxieties. She confesses to having been superstitious for the past six years. Her superstitions started while she was staying with her grandmother and other relatives in New York. At that time, an aunt of hers died unexpectedly after an illness of nine days. Previously, a fortuneteller had predicted to Lola that something unexpected was about to happen. After her aunt's death, Lola told her relatives that she had known her aunt was bound to die. This event reinforced her belief in such phenomena. Her superstition regarding male and female hunchbacks also began in New York. While there, she saw a woman hunchback just prior to receiving a letter from her friend reproaching her for not writing to him. This was not the only instance when something unpleasant had happened to her after she had seen a hunchback. Her stay in New York also marked the beginning of her superstition regarding clothes. She became afraid that something might happen to her friend if she wrote to him while wearing a particular dress. This fear prevented her from writing to him at all for a long period of time. It took a great deal of effort to induce Lola to disclose this information, meager as it was. She constantly found new excuses, such as, that it would take her too long to explain things, the doctor would laugh at her, etc. At the same time, however, she added that these experiences had, indeed, been hard to bear.

Subsequently, she reported that her obsessive ideas had grown worse after she had seen her fiancé. She became utterly exhausted by the effort involved in concealing her compulsions—all of which were associated with fear that bad luck might befall him—from her fiancé. Bit by bit, her superstition extended to a multitude of situations. For instance, if she happened to see four pigeons, she interpreted this as a sign that she could receive a letter, since the number four (*cuatro* in Spanish) contains the letters *c-a-r-t* (as in *carta*—letter). She loved her fiancé but was afraid he would not marry her if he knew the state she was in. On the other hand, she felt she should not be with him at all, so as not to be overwhelmed by her obsessive ideas. She explained that it was the compulsion to *"read" something into everything* that made her so exhausted, and the more so, the more she was among people. Reluctantly, and with an embarrassed laugh, she reported that, among other things, canes with rubber ends had a special significance for her. She would always turn back when she saw a gentleman with such a cane, since she "read" into it the following: "cane" in Spanish = *baston;* "on" in reverse = *no;* "rubber" in Spanish = *goma;* the first two letters in English = "go." When put together, this equals "no go," which stands for, "Don't go on! Turn back!" Whenever she had not obeyed this portent, something had happend to her. When she was very anxious inside and saw someone supporting his face with his hand, she felt reassured. Why? "Hand" in Spanish = *mano* (second syllable *no*); "face" in Spanish = *cara*, which reminded her of the English word, "care." From this, she arrived at: "no care," i.e., no reason to worry or, in Spanish, *no cuidado.* Any word beginning with "car" in Spanish or German (*cara, carta, Kartoffel*) and connected with something that means "no" signifies luck. Anything containing the syllables "si" or "ja" implies "yes" to an inner questioning: e.g., *nar-iz* (nose)— "is" is "si" in reverse; *ore-ja* (ear); *si-lla* (chair); *go-ld* stands for "go," etc.

thing connected with it, she could not wear anything new because she was afraid the memories of that experience would contaminate what was new and bring her bad luck. After many weeks of preparations and protestations on her part we finally succeeded in bringing the facts to light. By way of mere guessing, as in a social game, we found that the experience in question centered around an umbrella (she herself avoided uttering the word). Umbrella [*Schirm*] contained *si*, an affirmation. When her father had bought a new umbrella two years ago, she met a woman hunchback on the street. She had been afraid of hunchbacks before; but now all the bad luck emanating from that hunchback was displaced onto the umbrella. "It was *in* the umbrella" because the bad luck was confirmed through the meaning of the *si*. Shortly thereafter, her mother had touched the umbrella. From that moment on, she was set against her mother and against traveling with her to France where she was supposed to meet her fiancé. Why? Because her mother would transfer the bad luck from herself and the umbrella to her boy friend. On that same day she had had still another "terrible experience" of which she really could not talk. She saw an old man who was not exactly a hunchback but nevertheless somehow crippled; she categorically refused to talk more about this experience.

After eight months, Lola's situation became more complicated when her anxiety focused upon a certain nurse (Emmy), a particularly pretty and delicate girl. Lola provided the following information: The nurse (whose name Lola never used in speaking or writing—she just called her "she," or "that one") owned an umbrella similar to her father's. It had been lying about in various places, all of which now made her feel very frightened, and was the cause of her feeling so much sicker. While disclosing this, Lola was very upset. She got worse in the course of the following weeks and looked more worried and tortured. She was particularly fearful of everything that could possibly be connected with the closet in which she had seen Emmy's umbrella. She asked people to swear that this or that had not touched anything that was in that closet. She refused to use the towels because they could have been close to a brush that might possibly have been in contact with the umbrella and, to be on the safe side, she called for her towels at the office herself. She abstained from drinking water because the glass might have been in the closet. The cleaning brush might have been left lying on the sink, so she cleaned her sink herself. Again she wanted to give away her clothes, refused to change her dress, and wore soiled underwear. When she learned that "that one" was on duty on her floor, she got so upset that she had to be transferred to another building at once. She insisted she would "go crazy" if she were to meet "that one" again.

Lola found ostensible relief when she got permission to describe her fears in writing to the physician. Ten months after her arrival, she expressed her feelings as follows:*

I realize that you didn't understand me. But what I have suffered here I don't want to suffer again. I would like to make it more clearly understandable to you, but I can't, and this is the saddest thing on earth. Everything I gather from the signs always happens—so I believe in this superstition. What I went through in the closed ward I shall never forget, and later in Villa Roberta the most terrible because I thought if I didn't say anything I would get out sooner, but because of that it got worse, that superstition. When I think of my father who touched that, this is the saddest thing on earth, and then I imagined how it would feel to see him again, therefore I don't even want to think of going home. Because of all this, and not because of anything that happened to me, my life is in complete desperation. Now, after I have struggled so much to get away from these thoughts and after I left in Villa Roberta what reminded me of them, I feel better the first time since all that happened. But the great fear never leaves me, that she could come here, if only in passing by, and even if I wouldn't see her, the mere idea makes me despair. I believe that the moment she would enter the house she would bring the worst bad luck with her, where she steps she leaves bad luck, and I cannot help this idea, and I see that it is very difficult and think that it would be better to leave here before such a thing could happen. I am very sorry to tell you this, but with the terror I am in day after day I cannot possibly change.

And all this is only because I love him more than anything and want to forget it above everything, to see if I can be different, be-

[* TRANSLATOR'S NOTE: Lola's letters are written in a foreign and more or less confused style. Wherever feasible, some of the original touch has been preserved.]

cause I feel that without it, maybe, I am almost healthy—the only thing is this.

Some weeks later, she wrote to her physician that again "something terrible" had happened to her, and that she could not possibly stay. While she was resting on the terrace, "she" had passed. Lola could not stand the fear any more, didn't know what to do, how to protect herself, and she was afraid the bad luck would catch up with her. She felt that she had something frightful in herself.

Lola refused to go out because she could never be sure where "she" had gone. She stopped taking books from the library since "that one" may have read the same book. She wanted to return a new dress because she had worn it when she had seen the nurse downstairs. Two months later, Lola again got into a state of excitement, at one time because she was afraid she had seen the nurse from a distance, at another because she had seen another nurse bringing Emmy's bicycle into the kitchen wing. She planned to go on a hunger strike because the bicycle had infected all the food. Finally, she merely refused to eat butter, which she believed was most strongly infected (without revealing her reasons). Another time, she objected to using a blanket any longer because a lady had touched it with a dress that in some way seemed to be related to the nurse. In the early morning she sent a letter to a matron asking her to call her immediately on the phone and to tell her whether she was right yesterday when she believed she had seen the nurse. Actually, that day she had run after an elderly woman whom she had mistaken for the nurse. When she had lost sight of the woman, she started to brood over the question of whether the woman really had been the nurse. The situation grew untenable, so much so that the physician threatened Lola that he would bring the nurse into her room himself if she continued in this way. Thereupon Lola became very upset, turned furiously against the doctor, screaming loudly. Nevertheless, she put up with having the clothes, of which she was so afraid, returned to her room. She also put on a new dress.*

* On other cases, too, I would break the "terror" of such "compulsive" patients by a counter-terror, whenever there was no other way out. The precondition is, of course, something of a relationship of trust between patient and doctor.

On the day the bicycle incident occurred, Lola wrote her doctor about it and reported a new experience:

I was lying downstairs on the deckchair, and saw two figures in the corridor who watched me; when I turned toward them, they ran away, so I stayed downstairs. But it was very uncanny. Then the girlfriend of . . . you know who . . . returned, took the bicycle out, and took it to "that one."

About the same time, Lola took an overnight trip to Zürich with another nurse to replenish her wardrobe. The day before, she had asked the nurse to have a young gardener work in front of her window on the morning of the day they were to leave. She wanted to guarantee a lucky day by arranging to see a young man first thing in the morning. Naturally, this request was not complied with. When the nurse called for her, she first had to put her hat on the table: the hat, said Lola, was a warning that something might happen, and one had to be on guard. On the way to the station and while changing trains she covered her eyes and ears with her hands. Shortly before they arrived in Zürich, she became alarmed and explained she couldn't buy anything today because she had "seen something." Since the day was "lost" anyway she felt happy and at ease as long as nobody spoke to her about shopping, or pointed out stores where she should shop tomorrow, or took her to streets in which she was to walk tomorrow; otherwise, stores and streets would be "lost" again tomorrow. She would not enter any hotel but a cheap one, and never one with a doorman. If everything else seemed to click, she would then "see" a "no." Eventually a suitable hotel was found. In the evening Lola stood happily by the window and listened to the unwonted noises of the street. Next morning she visited a cheap department store with her eyes closed, guided by the nurse. She actually purchased a dress, but ran out in horror when she noticed that the saleslady was squint-eyed. In another store, books were exhibited in the entrance; on the cover of one of the books Lola saw the picture of a nun; the effect was that this store was "lost" for her, too.

There was no other department store left, so she finally agreed to visit a regular store but everything had to be cheap and should not be pretty. She would tolerate only female sales personnel, and not the slightest bit of red on a dress, because her last summer dress had been red. Shoes she could not buy because men would wait on her in ladies' shoe stores. On their return trip, Lola insisted on carrying all her packages herself and on the way home avoided meeting anybody. Back in her room, she made the nurse put all her old things on the table before she permitted her to hang up the new ones.

When Lola refused to let the nurse dust her room, the girl replied, "What do you think the doctor would say?" Whereupon Lola remarked, "The doctor knows about it anyway; I know it is just superstition." On the other hand, in her many written complaints and descriptions, often scribbled on scraps of paper, she told the physician again and again of her "indescribable fear," of the "most horrible possibility" that in years to come she would have to remember "all that," which was too frightening ever to name:

> It is worse than what you said—that I think something could happen to me—such a thing would perhaps only last a moment, but this is such a horrible feeling that it will never be finished as long as the thing is present.

All over again, she tried to explain her situation to the doctor, time and again she promised to do everything he advised, in the hope that he would help her "to find a solution." Later events proved that she did have confidence in her physician. One day she implored him not to mention the word "nurse" any more: "The mere sound of the word hurts me because it will always be the saddest of all my memories."

Another time she wrote:

> I feel such a sadness in me and wonder if it means that something even worse could come, and therefore I cannot rest and am asking you, please, to tell me whether it could come from "her." . . . I don't want to write it down. . . . For I see in the signs constantly that I should be cautious, and so many things, so that I don't know what may happen.

That Lola is by no means as empty of emotions and affectless as she appeared to the first physician is illustrated by the following lines:

In order to tell you everything quite frankly I shall explain to you how it really is and was, so you will understand me, I hope. What had happened was something so horrible beyond all description that it is now for me the saddest thing on earth, because after this, I am now lost forever to my fiancé. I love him so much that I got sick only for that reason. Since I met him first I haven't forgotten him for one single second and what makes me most sad is that I feel that he always thinks of me.

Unfortunately, I know of only one of Lola's dreams. Here it is in her words:

The dream was that my grandmother had sent her bed here. And suddenly—comes and lies down on that bed, and then on mine which was next to it. It was terrible. I was so afraid when I thought that my grandmother would lie down there that I had to go and see you to tell you about it, and you said you had another one for my grandmother. I felt very reassured by this. Later the dream continued with something else. But this is what disturbs me most because I see it in the bed because it is also called "cama" and the sound "cam" in English, and because all this was together, I don't know if it means something bad.

Lola had been in Bellevue a little longer than fourteen months when an aunt called for her and explained that Lola's family was now ready to permit her to marry the Spanish physician, and that a meeting with him in Paris was planned.

Lola was overjoyed and immediately joined her aunt in her hotel without even letting her enter the sanatorium and without ever entering it again herself.

CATAMNESIS / The material for this chapter consists primarily of letters from Lola to her physician, to whom she still turned for advice and help; of letters by her relatives who time and again asked him to exercise his influence with the patient, and of a report from her doctor in Paris. This material extends over a period of four years.

Eight days after her departure, Lola reported that the trip to Paris had gone well and that she was returning her passport because the photograph reminded her too much of "everything un-pleasant" she had experienced here. After another two days, Lola was feeling wonderful. She enjoyed her reunion with her grand-mother and cousin, did a lot of shopping, and everything went very well. She even went to a hairdresser's. "Imagine, a hunchback cut my hair." She asked that her cordial regards be given to all those to whom she had not said good-bye.

October 17: She had attended a theatre and a movie, still felt much better but could not forget "the things the doctor knew about. . . ." She often dreamed of them, and felt somewhat re-lieved on awakening, when she realized she had been dreaming and that she was "so far away." She felt nostalgic when thinking of the sanatorium, but a great number of diversions were help-ing her to get over it. "You must have wondered at my sending you my passport, I got so upset at the idea of arriving in Paris with it since 'she' had touched it so often and I thought that everything else could get infected by it, so I don't want to have it any more."

October 29: "I feel fine. On the surface I seem full of joy, only because I have no such fears as I had in the sanatorium and there-fore feel relieved, but the only thing which worries me is that I feel I am infected, mainly with what you know." She asked the doctor for advice because she felt that it was wrong not yet to have informed her fiancé of her move to Paris. It was so difficult for her to write. She was certain that the doctor would advise her to do the right thing "so as to know better what he (the fiancé) would answer." But the doctor should write his answer personally, because "I am afraid that 'her' girlfriend might do it." (The secre-tary who was a friend of the nurse in question.)

November 2: She did not want to write the letter to her fiancé herself but wanted it to be done by her aunt or cousin, but, in any case, would like to know what her fiancé thought of her. "I know that I can't think of marrying, and that I would become different in that I won't have to feel infected, I find it difficult." * She tries "to forget herself in diversions," attends the theatre often, finds everything wonderful, but afterwards feels infected and fears the future. Maybe, the only thing left was to take the veil, but she would like to let "him" know ahead of time. "All this I have in me and I don't know how to go about it."

[* TRANSLATOR'S NOTE: Confusion is in the original.]

December 7: She felt the same way, not quite all right, a little tired. Should she go to a Sanatorium? Preferably one known to the physician. "I remember everybody at Kreuzlingen."

December 24: Christmas and New Year wishes. The doctor's letter had brought her joy and reassurance. She had had a look at the sanatorium he recommended; its park had reminded her of Bellevue's. She liked the doctor there; was looking forward to going there in the beginning of the new year, being "very much in need of rest."

February 3: Lola's entrance into the sanatorium had been post-poned for external reasons. This letter was her first in Spanish, obviously written hastily and with many corrections. She wrote of her great anxiety, emphasized her confidence in the physician and asked him to write her again. She wrote in Spanish, she told him, because of an obsession: her fiancé, whom she loved so much and who was the object of so many of her obsessions, had been in Paris and had learned that she, too, was there, but had not known that she was staying in an institution. . . . Terrible fear that he would ask to see her. Since she was still "contagious," she had asked her doctor to ask her fiancé to leave Paris that very day. To be quite sure that he would actually do it, she had let him know that she was doing everything to be cured and would see him in a month. "But this is impossible and I am so afraid he might come to the sanatorium." Should she stay there?—

February 14: She seemed to have forgotten her previous letter, since she reports as news her entrance into the sanatorium. The building in which she was placed reminded her of the closed ward at Bellevue. Her nurse in the new place* had told her that she knew the Bellevue ward. But that girl was French so it didn't mat-ter too much. She had soon moved to another building and liked it a great deal. But although the doctor was *sympatisch*, she could not "tell him anything," as she did not believe she could change. Should she stay any longer?—

May 1: Her doctor had left for some weeks, and a strange doc-tor had arrived who was "sent by her relatives." She did not see him because she did not like him. Would I write to her aunt asking her to leave her alone and not send "that other one" any more.

[* TRANSLATOR'S NOTE: The German word for "nurse" is abbreviated from *Schwester* to *schwes.*]

On June 2 her aunt wrote that her niece's ailment had deteriorated lamentably. She appeared to be hallucinating. For a month she had been in the ward for the most agitated patients. Her begging to be transferred could not be complied with as she was in a state of terrific anxiety. The doctors had little hope for her recovery. Lola's relatives' only hope had been Professor Janet; he had diagnosed her case as serious but assured them that Lola was not *irrémediablement perdue* [incurably lost]. But after Dr. Janet's second visit, she had stubbornly refused to receive him, giving as her reason that she knew he was "sent by her relatives." Since her entrance into the French sanatorium she had developed an animosity against her entire family, and the fact that someone or something came from them sufficed to make her not receive him, or accept it. Professor Janet had recommended another sanatorium; would I—her first doctor—please endorse this advice? She would not leave the present place because I had recommended it; she acted only on my orders.

On June 15 Lola, too, mentioned Professor Janet; she believed that I knew him, he was said to be "very good," but she could never have him as her doctor (no explanation). She was somewhat better, having "less of the earlier idea," and having "nothing new for three months either."

> But my relatives cannot believe it and think that I have not improved here; because they think one can be cured faster, and all this upsets me so much.

The first doctor, who was *sympatisch*, had not yet returned. Should she stay there or go to some other place?

December 8: She often wanted to write, but it was impossible for her. She had had an unpleasant time from September to November. She wanted to leave, go to the country; but the nice doctor had advised her to do something else, at the request of her family, because she did not want to live with them. The doctor had prevented them from visiting her because he knew "that I would manage to get away without them." She was now in another sanatorium but wanted to go back to the first one since she believed that the nice doctor could cure her, "because he understands me as well as you do."

Five weeks later, she wrote from the original place that she was doing better. Three months later, her doctor wrote: "Elle ne va pas mieux; la manie du doute, les phobies, les idées superstitieuses persistent, aggravées par des hallucinations, des idées d'influence, et un véritable délire de persécution. Cette psychasthénie délirante menace d'évoluer vers la chronicité, ce que je n'ai pas caché à la famille."

Enclosed was a letter from Lola. Her fiancé had written he would have to know within eight days what her intentions were or else he would have to make other plans. It seemed to her that all this was put into his mouth by her family. She was very upset when she learned that her family had written to him. Her fiancé must not write to her family either. I should write him that she felt even better than last year and would be able to see him "in a few months." If he agreed and promised not to write to her family, she would recover sooner.

October 25: Her handwriting is much better and larger. Constant upsets "caused by her family." In June, her mother arrived unannounced although Lola had said that she could not see any member of the family because of her ideas.

> One should never surprise me with something unexpected because I get a certain idea from it which stays forever.

Her fiancé had come to Paris, too. She was very angry for he knew she did not want to see him. If she, herself, had wanted him to come, the situation would have been different. She had made him leave immediately and did not even feel like writing him yet. She asked for advice, and inquired elaborately about the nurse who had been in Zürich with her.

Several days later, her aunt reported that there was no change in her niece's condition; she lived a secluded life in her room, did not want to see any member of the family, and was "full of manias." She inquired about Professor Wagner von Jauregg, who had been recommended to the family.

The next letter came four months later, still from Paris. Lola seemed to have left the sanatorium. She deplored the death of her nice doctor who had understood her so well. For the first time she, herself, wrote about her ideas of reference and persecution (in a tremorous, unsteady handwriting):

Unfortunately, I haven't written you sooner to tell you what horrible people were after me and spread all kinds of bad things about me. I knew that they came into my room and watched me from outside with greedy curiosity.* I don't know them. I shall tell you about them. They are South Americans,† and most of them are not admitted there; they are so false and, as I observed, only out to kill. I feel so sad to be seen and watched for so long a time by these strangers. My family is influenced ‡ by them to believe that I am sick. Perhaps I can tell you more about it some other time. I would never have believed the things I have discovered about these people. I am only writing you to explain everything I have gone through, and without being able to talk to anybody; they are always listening and planning evil things, so I have to be very cautious. I planned to go to . . . for some time, or do you think it would be better to go directly to South America from here? I have had no diversions for such a long time. Please give your wife my regards and many thanks for her card. I was not able to write her. Please tell her that as soon as I am freed from these people I shall write to her, and hoping that all are well, many regards to all and to you, Yours sincerely.

The last letter, dated nine months later, came from the patient's home town in South America. Its content and style reveal still more of her delusional system than the preceding one:

. . . that my parents are under the influence of all the doctors who arrange to have me treated with such insolence and watch me [neugieren mich] in the house and make everybody believe that I am sick. It is like having made an invention to heal the sick and to find out who is right. I am writing you this letter because I received a signal from other persons that I may write, and because I want to be free of all that, so I thought of asking you to help me to get away from here. Maybe I could say that there is a cheaper sanatorium in Z., or if you could free me from here without my going into a sanatorium, this is what I want. Furthermore, if these doctors have other interests to watch me and find out

[* TRANSLATOR'S NOTE: neugierten—a neologism as a verb, derived from the noun Neugier.]

† Lola's original letter shows names of her fellow countrymen.

[‡ TRANSLATOR'S NOTE: suggestioniert, another neologism.]

whom I write to and whether I tell what terrible crimes they have directed, after they let me talk to you in this letter. For three years they are after me and have been so successful that I wasn't able at all to get rid of them. When they kept me in . . . like a prisoner before I came here, because I had noticed that the president's son while being very ill was murdered by a governess—I would say this aloud during the time I stayed there to see whether someone would hear me and help me to get away from there. Some days later it was in the papers that Mrs. Wilson of North America was murdered. I was informed of it several days before through certain words of the nurses. Everything I said which was similar to these words they murdered her with, and let me know it before through signs that it would happen. After all I am saying, and even after I have said it and they know that I did, about their crimes, they calmly act as if they hadn't done anything, and this way they get away with it. Because they are so evil, I try again and again to tell somebody what they did, as I'm afraid that further crimes could happen. These doctors in . . . are their friends, as I wrote you, and the service is dispatched from there in order to kill, they are used to doing it. Already in the sanatorium in Paris they watched me and had me treated quite unfairly when they saw that I was in a good mood. It was terrible how they had them treat me, this was at the time when they wanted me to forget what I had discovered about them in London—about all those who went so far as to pursue me on the streets.

October 8:

I wrote this some days ago because I have difficulties with writing letters and going out; for my relatives have become like sick people through these guys or doctors who say that they are from . . . and who want to make them believe that I am crazy. Because of all this I have made up my mind to get away from here as a maid and would only like you to help me to get away from here, or else there would be further crimes. I noticed that they planned to feed something to me or to give me an injection, something which makes one sick or makes people believe that one is sick. When I recently wanted to mail a letter at the post office I noticed that they made me notice . . . because there was a very good doctor here, his name was H., and a car ran against him and killed him.

After they let me see from signs that this meant the same, his nephew who is also a doctor passed me and greeted me in a strange way as if this should happen to me, too; and with all this they want to make me sick with my nerves. I am still very sad about something that happened recently, and I am sure that they are behind it. It is that accident of the pilots. On October 3, they had someone take something from me which I needed legally, and you should know that they are the only ones who can take it away and do something evil, also one of the pilots came here, and I overheard him say something about something evil that was going to happen . . . that was a message. And when I asked my brother several times to take me out, he told me that the car was out of order, and it was they who did it, and they put it in the newspaper as a caricature so that he did not know where it came from. I think you will understand that for some time I shall not be able to stay with my relatives. With cordial regards, Yours sincerely . . .

Existential Analysis

In the case of Lola, we could observe in an extreme degree the phenomenon of what we call mundanization [*Verweltlichung*], a process in which the Dasein is abandoning itself in its actual, free potentiality of being-itself, and is giving itself over to a specific world-design. In all these cases, the Dasein can no longer freely allow the world to be, but is, rather, increasingly surrendered over to one particular world-design, possessed by it, overwhelmed by it. The technical term for this state of being surrendered over is: "thrownness" [*Geworfenheit*].

I have shown the important part played by the formation of an ideal in the process of being increasingly overwhelmed by a specific world-design. Far from widening or deepening the ability of being-oneself, the Extravagant [*verstiegene*] ideal restricts the possibilities of being-oneself, so much so that the existence is only able to be itself within quite specific, ever narrower limits; outside these limits it becomes more and more dependent and bonded, that is, squeezed in the vise of a single world-design or world-model. This is what we called "thrownness," absorption of the existence by "world." * What all such cases have in common is that, to express it in everyday language, they are not able to harmonize ideal and reality; or, in terms of psychopathology, they represent schizoid types. Their schizophrenic states have then to be seen only as a more advanced stage of this process of thrownness as the existence gets more and more overwhelmed by one single world-design. Becoming overwhelmed in this sense finds its extreme expression in the phenomenon of delusion.

In contrast to earlier cases, Lola does not verbalize her ideal. Nevertheless, it can be easily recognized. Her ideal is being alone, and being left alone by the world. From the very beginning, she preferred being by herself. She liked to lock herself up in her room and flirted with the idea of taking the veil. We could also say that her ideal was to let no one and nothing come close to her. This calls for a world-design in which beings in general and, particularly, the coexistors [*Mitdaseinenden*] are accessible only by way of a predesign of unfamiliarity, of the Uncanny, or—alternatively—of the expectation of the Threatening. Just as Ellen West pursued the ideal of slenderness, of having an ethereal body, Jürg Zünd, that of societal security, so Lola was after the ideal of security of existence in general. And as Ellen foundered ("went to the bottom spiritually") due to the overwhelming "claims" of her body or those of her environment, so Lola foundered through the "claims" of the disturbing world at large. While Ellen sought cover against getting fat by fasting, Nadja against becoming "conspicuous" by hiding, and Jürg tried to be "inconspicuous" by wearing a protective overcoat, appearing harmless, and mixing with upper-class company, so Lola sought cover from the world, which disturbed her security and peace of mind, by the continuous interrogation of "fate." Thus, everything unfamiliar or threaten-

---

* This falling-to and being-thrown was analyzed by Heidegger in *Sein und Zeit* primarily with regard to the "they," (i.e., to gossip, curiosity, and ambiguity), in other words, to the everyday being-in-the-world. These analyses were extended in Heidegger's review of the second part of Ernst Cassirer's *Philosophy of the Symbolic Forms: Das mythische Denken* (Deutsche Literaturzeitung, Neue Folge, 5. Jahrgang, 21, 1928, pp. 1000-1012). What makes this extension significant for the case of Lola is the replacement of the being overpowered in the sense of being thrown into the "they," by being overpowered (mana) in the sense of the "thrownness" of the mythical existence.

ing was to be kept away or removed. All these are attempts to maintain and defend the thoroughly unfree (because once and for all determined) "ideal" self against anything contradictory. What is new in the case of Lola is, therefore, not the process of mundanization as such, that is, the ever increasing being-given-over to the overwhelming power of a specific world-design and the being-possessed by it, but the fact that Lola feels threatened by an existence becoming uncanny [*Verunheimlichung*].

Lola's entire being is, as we have seen, used up by attempts to protect herself from anything that could disturb her existence and call it in question. She is only reassured if she can protect herself from the Uncanny by means of certain rituals, just as Ellen West was reassured only when she thought herself protected through the practices of fasting and purgation, Jürg Zünd through his overcoats or his ostensible harmlessness.[1] Where the person fails in controlling that ever-lurking fear, that tightrope walk over the abyss of existence, there existence plunges into the abyss, and panic and anxiety attacks follow. In this case, the Dasein is steeped in anxiety, but not in intrinsic or existential anxiety, which consists in being submerged in nothingness as the source and ultimate test of existential maturation, but in an extrinsic, derived anxiety, fear of something *definite*, of a specific catastrophe.* And yet we must recognize that already the formation of the ideal as such stemmed from a secret existential anxiety, from that of having to accept the existence as being such and such. And so, because the ideal had already originated in anxiety, the threat to it had necessarily to lead to the anxiety attack. This we must always keep in mind. Kierkegaard has pointed out that willing not-to-be-oneself (or, better, not-to-be-myself) while at the same time clinging stubbornly to willing to-be-myself in the sense of mere personal identity, already implies despair in the sense of anxiety. (It should be remembered that in all these cases *love*, the dual mode, had already been abdicated earlier as an important mode of being.) In Lola's case, however, despair is not only, as in the other cases, despair at having to be in the world in a particular way and no other; it is despair at being-in-the-world at all!

Before we turn to the existential analysis of Lola's case, we

* I shall point out later in what way we can still speak of existential anxiety in the superstitious stage.

must focus more closely on the conflict between the ideal and the resistance from the dull world ("reality"). This conflict is most clearly and simply expressed in the case of Ellen West; there the ideal was slenderness and the resistance appeared in the form of hunger. Thus the ideal was contradicted by a vital need, an irresistible force arising from the bodily sphere. The more the need was suppressed for the sake of the ideal, the more voracious it grew. More and more the ethereal world became a grave world, a world of the hole. This overgrowth and hypertrophy of the hunger-theme proves in itself that the Dasein must originally have felt threatened from the direction of the vital sphere, that of the body, and that already the ideal (of slenderness) must have represented a dam, a defense against the threat. Where the dam was not quite "tight" or had "gaps" (acute feeling of hunger at the sight of tempting food), anxiety poured freely through, and an anxiety attack occurred. Fasting and purging were attempts to close the gaps. But eventually the entire dam threatened to collapse, and existence threatened to be reduced to voracious greed; Ellen West escaped this peril by way of suicide.

In another case, that of Jürg Zünd, things were not so simple. It was said before that objections to the ideal and resistance to it were offered by the world of fellowmen. Against this, it could be argued that Jürg Zünd's fellowmen had done no harm to him, and that their "resistance," their scorn, their criticism existed largely "in his imagination." But not only had Jürg Zünd actually suffered in his childhood from the scorn of "the street," and not only had this suffering become "fixated" in him, but also—and more important—the world of one's fellowmen is, in itself, a power that every existence comes to feel, in whatever way it may come to terms with it: by suffering from it, or even breaking down under it, by defying it, ignoring it, or scoffing at it. This is the power to which—in the case of Jürg Zünd—anxiety is predominantly tied. Here the ideal of social elevation is the dam, the safeguard against existential anxiety focused upon the world of fellowmen. The more closely the dam encircles the existence, the more intensely anxiety breaks through its gaps. Here, too, attempts at covering up are attempts to fill in the gaps all over again. But eventually here, too, the dam proves insufficient. Existence escapes anxiety into inactivity, the mental death. Jürg Zünd can no longer come to terms with life and wastes himself in ever-new "last efforts." Again, the idea has to capitulate to reality, to the anthropological fact that existence does not exist in isolation but shares its existence with others. Existence, which is always co-existence, conquers the Extravagant wish not to be bothered by one's fellowmen and to be absorbed only by one's own existence.

Anticipating the argument that the Dasein eventually does prevail in its singular, isolated, "autistic" form, the answer is that it is erroneous to consider the extremely autistic existence as a solipsistic one; in complete autism, the Dasein does not exist any more as *solus ipse* at all; it does not exist any more as a self.* When it retreats from the world of fellowmen, from its coexistors, the Dasein also forgoes itself, or rather forgoes itself as a self. This only applies to complete schizophrenic autism. Where man merely shuts himself off from the world, where he just retreats in grudge and anger, suspicion or scorn, he still exists—as a grudging, laughing, distrustful, or scornful self.

It is precisely this kind of thinking that lets us see in schizophrenic autism not simply a higher degree of a psychological peculiarity (e.g., of introversion), but helps us to understand it Daseinsanalytically as a mode of being that is essentially different from any psychological category. Where Dasein no longer temporalizes and spatializes, where it has ceased to be a self and to communicate with others, it no longer has a "here" (*da*). For it has its "here" only in the transcendence [*Überstieg*] of Care [*Sorge*]—not to speak of the exaltation [*Überschwang*] of Love —or, in other words, in its accessibility [*Erschlossenheit*], which is only a comprehensive term for temporalization, spatialization, being a self, etc. This also explains why we do not experience an extremely autistic schizophrenic as being "the like of us," but as an automaton. We do not consider him a fellowman who is responsible for his behavior toward us and from whom we generally expect a meaningful [*sinnvolle*] answer, but an irresponsible, nonresponsive "mere creature." (This, of course, does not touch upon the purely humane medical attitude toward the patient, which still "sees" the fellowman in the "creature.") All

---

* For this reason the term *autism* (autós-self) is far too "psychologistic" and, in any case, misleading in regard to the final autistic states.

this is illustrated by the case of Lola Voss, whose autism, though not complete, surpasses that of all the other cases.

THE UNCANNINESS OF THE DREADFUL / As in earlier cases, the report on Lola Voss points at the outset to existential anxiety. Her initial childish obstinacy obviously is not an expression of existential richness but of existential weakness, of fear of being overwhelmed by "the others." At the age of twelve, Lola developed a serious case of typhoid fever; it was then that she first felt insecure in her own home and fled to the house of her grandmother. In her twenty-second year, Lola felt anxious about a dress and refused to wear it when going aboard ship. Gradually, her phobia of clothes developed into her predominant symptom. But while psychopathology is concerned with the genesis of this phobia, existential analysis is concerned with the "world-design" of such an existence, which always means *with the mode of its being*. Hence, we immediately focus upon the "world" in which Lola presents herself to us already as a very sick person; we do this without bothering in the least about the purposive biological judgment that pronounces Lola as "sick."

When Lola entered the sanatorium she was already completely obsessed by the superstitious delusion (or delusional superstition) that "something dreadful" might happen to her, something against which she had to protect herself by purely superstitious practices. Already her existence was at the point where it could only move by balancing on a swaying rope across an abyss. Any "wrong step" was bound to cause the plunge into the "dreadful chasm," or, as Jürg Zünd called it, into catastrophe. Superstition is always an expression of fear of the demonic power of fate. The "civilized Westerner," who publicly touches the table or wall, or just exclaims "touch wood" when someone mentions his good health or success in business, thus hopes to entreat fate to remain good to him.

Such conjuring of fate springs from the fear of having challenged fate by the mere verbal affirmation of prosperity. Hence this act represents at the same time an apology for the affirmation. The act of conjuring or the "touch wood" formula contains an appeal to fate not to consider that affirmation as *hybris*, as an overconfident presumption [*Übermut*]. The person who uses the "touch-wood" formula feels the power of fate to be present, and at the same time believes that he can influence it in his favor. Such belief in one's dependency upon a fate that is at once blind and yet can be influenced or conjured, betrays the "primitivity" of "civilized" modern man or, in Daseinsanalytic terms, the "gap" in his "structure," * his existential weakness. By existential weakness we mean that a person does not stand autonomously in his world, that he blocks himself off from the ground of his existence, that he does not take his existence upon himself but trusts himself to alien powers, that he makes alien powers "responsible" for his fate instead of himself. All this applies in an extreme degree to the case of Lola Voss.

Earlier we compared Lola's mode of existence to walking on a swaying rope. We may be forgiven for using still another metaphor: Lola's existence can be likened to walking on the thin ice-cover of a lake; she knows that at every step the ice may break, and she catches desperately at every "straw" that offers itself. Such metaphors are more telling than any abstract description. They clarify more precisely the fundamental meaning of a phrase to which we often refer: to stand with both feet firmly on the ground. It signifies the mode of a secure existence, confident of itself and the world, in no need of any aid or props "from the outside." † Only where existence moves on a swaying rope or a thin ice-cover does it need such props. We call them props of superstition, regardless of whether the entire existence moves on thin ice (as in the case of Lola), or whether it gets onto thin ice only now and then, as with most people. Standing on the ground means indisputable protection of existence from falling, sinking, breaking through into its abyss. Walking on the thin cover of ice means suspension in constant fear of such falling, plunging, sink-

---

[* TRANSLATOR'S NOTE: *Bildung*, which has the double meaning of education and structure.]

† Hence, the phrase "to stand with both feet firmly on the ground" denotes more than the phrase "to stand with both feet in reality," since the first also expresses confidence in the existence as being firmly grounded in the earth. What we call "reality" in everyday language as well as in psychology and psychopathology should not be used in an absolute sense, for that reality is but a particular world-design, that of practice, of the practical intercourse with people and things, and of the confidence on which it rests.

ing. In Ellen West, the "walking on ice" is expressed by the fear of submersion in animalistic voracity; in Jürg Zünd, by the fear of a demotion to a proletarian level and falling into social disrepute; in the case of Lola, we deal with a fear of immersion in the Dreadful per se, in what we have called "the naked horror." [2] He who rests with both his feet firmly on the ground does not need any crutches or any external support, but he who walks on thin ice exists mainly in seeking some protection. Such an existence appears strange, or indeed ridiculous, to the one who stands on secure ground; he cannot understand it and tries to explain it to himself, on the basis of a "weak will," or of sickness. We, however, intend to understand such an existence anthropologically, that is, in its existential structure.

It is self-evident and follows from the total mode of existence that, in the case of Lola Voss, her existence had deserted itself and had succumbed to an alien power in a much higher degree than in any of the earlier cases. It does not maintain itself any more in designing its own authentic potentialities, but is constantly sucked into the whirl of inauthentic possibilities of being, that is, such as have not been chosen by it but imposed upon it by a power alien to the self. In other words, it exists only as something "thrown," or in the state of thrownness. But thrownness is still part of existence. Hence the "alien power," although alien to the self, cannot be considered as alien to existence, as something outside or above it. Thrownness means, rather, the seduction and temporary reassurance, the alienation and entanglement of existence in general. It is, in our case, definitely distinguished from thrownness in the sense of constant addiction, an addiction to the everyday power of the "they," of being possessed by it. While Jürg Zünd's existence was completely possessed by the coexistence of the others, by the preponderance of public opinion and judgment, Lola's existence is possessed by and exposed to a very different, still more anonymous, still less tangible superpower that seduces existence time and again, reassures it temporarily, alienates it more and more from itself, and completely prevails upon it. Existence in this case is "tossed around" in a way quite different from the way it is tossed around by the "they." Here it is not immersed in "public gossip," in the curiosity and ambiguity of mere opinion. True, it is interested in getting reassurance, but this time it is not the seeming reassurance to be found in the bottomlessness of the "they," but the seeming reassurance to be found in the bottom-lessness of bargaining with "fate." Here the others do not play the same decisive part as in being "they"; the decisive part is played by a superior, uncanny, even dreadful *it*, confronted with which the Dasein feels completely forlorn, abandoned by the others (and even more so by the thou), and left to its own devices.

Here the existence of the others is only the main *occasion* for the disturbance, for the existence turning uncanny, with the physician representing the one and only exception. He is, at least to some degree, the post to which existence clings while adrift in the whirlpool, from whom it expects aid and protection as a sign that some interhuman relationship is still possible.

Since existence in this case has totally surrendered to the Uncanny and the Dreadful, it can no longer be aware of the fact that the Dreadful emerges from itself, out of its very own ground. Hence there is no escape from such fear; man stares fear-stricken at the inescapable, and all his happiness and pain now depend solely upon the possibility of conjuring the Dreadful. His one and only remaining desire is to become as familiar as possible with the Dreadful, the Horrible, the Uncanny, and to make himself at home with it. He sees two alternatives: the first is to "capture" the Dreadful and anticipate its "intentions" with the help of words and playing on words; the second, which interferes more seriously with living and life, is to put spatial distance between himself and the persons and objects struck by the Dreadful's curse.

The Word-Play Oracle Lola's first type of defense strikes us immediately as extremely playful. It impresses us as a very thin net* with which Lola tries to protect herself against the onslaught of the Dreadful and by which she seeks to guess its intentions. In the oracle of syllables, Lola looks for indicators of what to do and what not to do; hence both are no longer subject to her decision but depend on constellations in the outside world,

* Owing to this "thinness," however, Lola is in a position to receive an answer from fate in any event, be it positive or negative. We can say about this net what Freud said in reference to one of his phobic patients (and which, incidentally, holds true of any phobic system): "The net of conditions was far enough extended to catch the prey in any case; it was, then, up to her whether she wished or did not wish to pull it in." (*Totem und Tabu, Gesammelte Schriften,* X, 118.)

determined by objects and words. As Lola, in her interpretations, resorts to various languages, compositions of syllables, and inversions of letters, she reveals the basic features of all superstition: fixation upon the most inconspicuous, unimportant, and innocent details, and their elevation into the sphere of the decisive majesty of fate.

The modern man who, despite his alleged culture, knocks on the table or contents himself with exclaiming, "touch wood," proceeds very much as Lola does, except that he is satisfied with one single formula of defense against the "envy" and fickleness of "fate." In any event, his "structure" [*Bildung*] discloses the same gap that we know from Lola's "structure." What is important in and characteristic of the superstitious mode of her being-in-the-world is, we remember, the faith in the omnipotence of words. This proves only that in the state of superstitious thrownness anything that is and is revealed in some way, has the existential character of a superpower (of the "mana" in mythical thinking). For, in being dependent on and delivered to the Overpowering, the Dasein is "possessed" by it and hence, as Heidegger has shown, can only experience itself as belonging to it and related to it. Therefore, everything-that-is and has in some way been revealed, has the existential character of the Overpowering. While words constitute an area that has always and everywhere been preferred, they are only *one* form of that-which-is.

The "Taboo" In the inquiries made to the oracle of fate we are dealing with a "net of conditions" designed by the inquirer himself that in any event guarantees an answer; but the net becomes an imposed one as soon as persons and objects are involved. The meshes of the net are formed by contamination of an object through contact with, or mere spatial closeness to, a person or thing already avoided as taboo. Spatial closeness replaces any context of psychological motivations or objective logic. The complex and multi-stratified context of reference to the world is reduced to the category of the spatial-beside-each-other, which, of course, involves that of simultaneity.

The spatial-temporal proximity forms the clue to the propagation of the mishap, of the danger, of the Dreadful, of the anxiety-stimulus. Sometimes contiguity or temporal contingency prevails, as when Lola believed that something would happen to her friend if she wrote him a letter while wearing a certain dress (the spatial togetherness of dress and writing utensils might have played a part); or when her father had bought a new umbrella and she subsequently met a woman hunchback. In this case, the *si*-meaning of the word "umbrella" confirms retroactively the bad-luck meaning of the hunchback. But once something is afflicted with the bad-luck meaning, it propagates the bad luck indefinitely. To the spatial-temporal contact is added similarity, which turned the umbrella of nurse Emmy into a symbol of catastrophe. All this pertains only to the net per se. But since it is so far flung that it can meet almost all conditions, we have to observe where and when the patient closes the net to catch her prey. Considering the "boyish" character of Lola, it is not surprising that she chose for prey the prettiest and most attractive of all the nurses! The closing of the net is largely determined by specific motives with regard to the world [*weltliche Motive*]. But this belongs in the sphere of psychopathology. What we are interested in here is the image of the world that underlies such a "taboo pathology" (Freud).

Since the world-design is dominated by the fact of having surrendered to something overpowering, we should not be surprised that "superficial" categories such as spatial-temporal contact and similarity are so prominent in it, that the frequent sequence of meeting a hunchback and "bad luck" becomes the basis of a compelling process of induction, or that even psychic facts like memories produce a contagious effect ("enter the new things") and no longer fade out.

We should wonder rather that categories and conclusions are still brought into play at all, since being possessed by the overpowering Dreadful signifies "a specific being-driven-about" that is of itself open everywhere to the new and thus can be waylaid by anything and everything, just as it can establish relations between anything and everything.

Being "delivered to," "possessed by," "having surrendered," "thrownness"—all these expressions imply, in terms of time, the bare inauthentic present; "bare" insofar as this present is not temporalized out of the future and the past into a genuine present. The bare present, in contrast to the actual moment, can only mean a nondwelling [*Unverweilen*], a lack of location. Where, as in the case of Lola, existence has surrendered in so large a measure to the Overpowering, it remains totally closed to itself. It may again and again be at rest for a moment, only to be "driven about," disturbed, harassed anew.

With this, we are touching again, as in the case of Jürg Zünd, upon the Urgent and the Sudden, upon the "negation of temporal continuity." As Kierkegaard puts it:

> At one moment it is present, at the next one it is gone, and as it is gone, it is again totally and completely present. It can neither be worked into a continuity nor worked through to one.

In Heidegger's words, it is an "expression of non-freedom," of being at the mercy of the world," or, as we call it, of "mundanization" of existence. To quote Kierkegaard again:

> In superstition, objectivity is granted Medusa's power to petrify subjectivity and unfreedom does not want this magic to be disturbed.[3]

Inasmuch as continuity is tantamount to freedom, to existence, or to formation of an authentic self [*Selbstigung*] and hence also tantamount to communication (without which authentic existence is not possible), negation of continuity means unfreedom, being-possessed by the overpowering Sudden and, at the same time, lack of independence and of communication. Indeed, existence as it is "thrown" into uncanniness is destined to be isolated. That Lola was still capable of opening herself to the second physician to the degree she did, and that she lovingly clung to her fiancé for so long a time, only go to show that in her state of existence she was not yet completely lacking in "self" [*entselbstet*], had not yet completely surrendered to the Uncanny and Dreadful. Authentic communication, however, was no longer possible. "Walls" of taboolike fears and prohibitions, produced by the Overpowering, constantly slid between her and the physician and, even more, between her and her fiancé.

The spatialization of Lola's "world" is, as is customary, determined by temporalization. To the assault of the *sudden*, to the restlessness and locationlessness, corresponds the discontinuous, jerky, changing character of spatialization and its dependence on the respective source of "contamination." The boundaries of the space within which the Dasein moves are extremely shiftable. They are determined neither by the "oriented," nor by the geographical, nor by attuned [*gestimmten*] space,[4] but conform merely to a space which is determined by the respective carriers of Mana, the Dreadful. More specifically, this space is fixed on the basis of visual distance and tactual closeness. It can be artificially extended by closing the eyes (avoidance of sight). But here, too, the process is one of increasing narrowing of the life space, leading to the occupation of all exits of the life stage by "armed guards" (Ellen West), and to anxious groping about in a vault. Here, too, less and less moves, and nothing new happens any more. Everything rotates around the old, well-known—and yet so unknown—Uncanny that, a priori, makes every situation into an anxiety-provoking one, and pre-empts the possibility of entering and seizing it in accordance with its own meaning. The statement "Nothing moves any more" is only another expression for the phenomenon that whatever has once made its appearance does not leave the existence any more but—having existential anxiety as its source—remains fixated, which is the reason why there is nothing more dreadful than being burdened with "memories." Thus, Lola's environment, world of fellow men, and personal world [*Umwelt, Mitwelt, Eigenwelt*] are equally ruled by *Mana* so that the distinction among them has lost its meaning: their meaning is Mana! And since there is no longer a distinction between the memory of an object and the object itself, the burden of memories is just as narrowing and oppressive as the proximity of the respective objects themselves. The memories block the road into the future, future here meaning the being-ahead-of-oneself, just as the respective objects block the "space." Instead of mastering the memories, of being able to shake them off, or to work them through existentially for the sake of regaining freedom, the afflicted objects, as such, have to disappear (must be sold, given away, burned or remitted). The place of existential progress or maturation, of achieving the self [*Selbstgewinnung*] has long since been taken by a mundane [*weltliche*] restitution whereby existence was *verweltlicht*. Lola's mode of existence, as can easily be seen, is much more deeply and completely delivered to "the world" than that of Ellen West or Jürg Zünd. Nowhere do we notice any trace of such existential phenomena as shame, guilt, conscience, and anxiety stemming from conscience; inner-world threats, oppressions, and defensive measures against them prevail throughout. What might be a matter of existence has become a matter of mundane care. This will be illustrated again in connection with an analysis of the superstitious questioning of the oracle and compliance with its answers as though they were the answers of fate.

In Lola's "fate" theme, primal existential anxiety [*Urangst*] combines with the Uncanny and with superstition. Kierkegaard in his ground-breaking investigations of the meaning of anxiety recognized fate as "the nought of anxiety" that later assumed a central position in Heidegger's ontology. There the nought of anxiety is interpreted with deep insight as being-in-the-world per se: "The 'of-what' of anxiety is being-in-the-world *per se*." (*Sein und Zeit*, p. 186.) In anxiety, the world is reduced to insignificance so that existence cannot find anything through which to understand itself, "it reaches into the nought of world; but, encountering world, understanding through anxiety becomes aware of being-in-the-world *per se;* the 'of-what' (*wovor*) of anxiety is simultaneously its 'what for' (*worum*)." "Anxiety is concerned with the bare Dasein as existence thrown into uncanniness." *

But whereas anxiety also reveals the possibility of an authentic or existential being-able-to-be (how it does so is irrelevant in this context), Lola remains thrown into anxiety without any possibility of regaining herself, or even of becoming aware of herself. Instead, she stares at the nought as if it were an uncanny *objective* power; but she never manages to focus upon or come to grips with it, however painstakingly she tries to "read" its intentions "into things." It is the "compulsion to read something into everything" that prevents her from coming to rest and that drains her strength.

This reading of meaning into objects, as we have noticed, is tied in with their verbal symbols and with their accidental constellations in space and time. It is not the "four pigeons" that spell good luck for her, but the word *cuatro*, in which she finds the letters *c-a-r-t;* since *carta* stands for "letter," she reads in it that she will receive a letter from her fiancé. It is not the walking sticks

---

* It should be mentioned here again that existential anxiety is possible only where *love*—the dual mode that "eternalizes" the existence as home and shelter—shines not yet, or not any more.

with their rubber bases that alarm her, but the syllables "no" (read in reverse from *baston*—stick) and *go-ma* (rubber) that convey to her "no go!"="do not go on!"

From such "signs" she "reads" that she "ought to be cautious," for, "I never know what may happen. . . ." Lola consults "fate," just as the Greeks consulted the Oracle, obeying it "blindly," even though she recognizes its ambiguity. But while the Greeks accepted their system of signs as an inherited tradition, Lola had designed her own, but treated it as if it were objectively valid, or the message of an objective power. Lola's attitude is reminiscent of some people's attitude toward astrology. In neither case is there any realization that what they are practicing is just a "fetishism of names projected onto the skies." But again, in contrast to astrological superstition, which is rooted in tradition, Lola's superstition is a purely private one. What is common to both is the clinging to an alleged, blindly operating, power and evasion of the opportunity to retrieve *oneself* from thrownness and return to being one's real self or to accept genuine religious faith.

The compulsion to "read" significance into things by means of a system of verbal symbols, which results in certain Do's and Don't's, is closely related to the compulsion to evade, and even flee, from the ominous things themselves and from anyone who has been in contact with them. The connection with the verbal expression is mostly very clearly indicated, as in the case of the ominous meaning of the umbrella that originated from the letters *s-i* and the temporal coincidence of this *s-i* with Lola's meeting the woman hunchback. The hunchback herself—but only the female hunchback—draws her ominous portent (just as does the squinting salesgirl) from the "abnormality" of these life-phenomena, an abnormality in the sense of a "descending life" ("The Case of Ellen West"), namely, of deformation, crippling, disfigurement. These forms of "descending life" figure so prominently in all superstition because superstition "springs" from the anxiety of being-in-the-world per se, of the naked existence thrown into uncanniness. These symbols of descending life can have an uncanny effect only for one reason: because the existence that persists in uncanniness is in itself descending life! Or, differently expressed: being continuously suspended in existential anxiety and staring at its uncanny nothingness makes existence "clear-sighted" with respect to all those phenomena that deviate from the "reassuring" existential norm and indicate its frailty.

That contact—tactual as well as associative, in the sense of association by proximity and similarity—becomes so important here can be understood when we consider the leveling down of the world-design from a highly complicated interrelated whole reference-context to a merely spatial beside-each-other and sensory or abstract with-each-other.

We see in operation here a tremendous simplification and impoverishment of the "world," which naturally is an expression of the simplification and impoverishment of existence. As existence becomes simpler and poorer, so does the "world" which, at the same time, grows more overpowering in its simplification; for "behind" it stands, and through it stares the Medusa head of the "nothingness of anxiety." It is anxiety that makes the world appear ever more insignificant, ever more simple, because it "petrifies" existence, narrows its openness, its "here," down to ever smaller and smaller circles, forces it into ever more difficult and ever rarer possibilities. What is true of spatialization, is even more true of the temporalization and historization [*Geschichtlichung*] of existence. Genuine historization—an authentic history in existential terms—is replaced by a mere "coincidence" of circumstances and events, an indication not of having a genuine fate, but only of worldly "objective" happenings.*

It is a symptom of such mundanization [*Verweltlichung*] or externalization of fate, that the place of fears and memories is taken by the actual objects and persons with whom the former were connected. But the memories not only become connected with objects and persons, they "enter them." Hence, "a terrifying feeling never ends as long as the thing is present." Thus the world-spatial distance from the things replaces the existential (truly life-

---

* See this distinction in G. Simmel, *Lebensanschauung*, p. 127: "That someone's father is murdered and that his mother marries the murderer would certainly be an overwhelming occurrence for anybody; but that it becomes Hamlet's *fate* is determined by Hamlet's character, and not by the fact that this occurrence has hit him as "someone." The single "fates" are essentially determined by external events, that is, the objective factor appears to outweigh all others; but their totality, "the fate" of each person, is determined by *his* character. If one only steps back far enough, one sees in it a unity that does not stem from single causes, but whose center lies rather in the a priori forming power of the individual life."

historical) overcoming of the terrifying feeling that has entered them. We can recognize here a universal human trait—the "pushing away," locking up, hiding away of things connected with unpleasant or sad memories; in Lola's case, however, a feature of convenience, cowardice, or "self-protection" turns into a need, a "must." In psychological terms one could say that, in this instance, the place of intentional acts or of psychic phenomena (in the sense of Brentano) is taken by the "intended objects." But this is only a different formulation of what in existential-analytic terms we have described as mundanization. What we are dealing with here is a transformation of life-historical spatiality into mundane space and its orientation-potential of closeness and distance. That which can no longer be treated in existence-historical terms has now to take place in "world-space." Thereby existence escapes its actual task and its actual meaning, but it does not escape anxiety. What it gains through mundanization—displacement of its own responsibility and guilt onto an outside "fate"—has to be paid for with the loss of freedom and compulsive entanglement in the net of external circumstances and occurrences.

But why do just garments—clothes, underwear, shoes, hats—play so prominent a role in Lola's case? To answer this question we would have to conduct a biographical investigation. Unfortunately, we do not have any historical points of reference at our disposal. But the question of how it is possible that garments *can* play so prominent a part is, indeed, a problem for existential analysis.

While certain utensils, like umbrellas or canes, assume their unlucky connotations via verbal symbols, others, like soap, glasses, towels, food, through accidental contact with an inanimate or human "source of contamination"—garments become actual representatives of persons, and particularly of the mother. Lola's own garments, too, attain a commanding fatal meaning; we remember that she could not go abroad unless certain garments were removed, that she was afraid to write to her fiancé when wearing certain clothes lest something happen to him; that she cut up her clothes, continuously wore the same old dress, hated her underwear, and used all possible means to resist the purchase and wearing of new clothes. From what we know about Lola, it would seem that her garments became invaded by memories. For Lola, clothes and underwear seem to play a role similar to that played by fat for Ellen, and by all the physical and psychic clothes in the case of Jürg Zünd. In all these cases, the focus is on some sort of hated garment, on an unbearable covering. But while Jürg Zünd tried to hide or to fortify himself behind some other cover (overcoat, higher social milieu) and Ellen West tried to avoid the acquisition of a "fat" layer in all possible ways, Lola's problem is much less difficult since it deals only with the cover provided by clothes, so she discards them, cuts them up, removes them, and contents herself for a long time with one and the same "old rag." But all these cases have one feature in common: the mundanization of the total existence and the transformation of existential anxiety into the horrible fear of a "worldly" shell. Furthermore, all these garments and shells are experienced as threats and restrictions, either coming from the world of fellow men (Jürg Zünd), or from the world of one's own body (Ellen West) or, as in Lola's case, from the world of garments. And, in each case, the pseudo-existential ideal is contradicted by the respective shell. Lola's mode of existence impresses us as even stranger than that of the other "cases." What we feel to be "our world" consists predominantly of our physical and psychic world as well as the world of our fellow men, whereas we assign much less significance to the world of our garments. In Lola's case, however, it is the latter world that assumes prime importance. This is reason enough to make Lola appear "sicker" than the other patients.

The world of garments, as such, seems to be "part" of the "outside world," but the "as such" cannot be understood here in a philosophical sense but in a very unphilosophic-rationalistic or, if one prefers, a positivistic sense. For, just as the body is not only "part" of the outside world but, at the same time, "part" of the inner world; so, the clothes are not just things but, also, personal shells. "Clothes make the man" expresses their significance within the world of fellow men.* But one can also say that clothes make *us* because their anthropological significance is based on more than our belief that we attract attention and are judged by our clothes.

* See Roland Kuhn, *Über Maskendeutungen im Rorschach'schen Versuch*, pp. 27 f.: "Clothes cover . . . clothes give away . . . clothes disguise."

We experience them not only as something that exposes us to the eyes of others and, at the same time,* protects and hides us from them, but also as something that belongs to us, that lends us a feeling of elation and well-being, or of discomfort and depression; something that is not only "carried" by us but that also carries us, helps or hinders us (in our own eyes and in the eyes of others), extends or restricts us, and shrouds and conceals from us our own body.

Small wonder that the world of clothes can also represent ourselves to others. And because this is so, a "curse" with which we are afflicted can be felt as directly adhering to our clothes. How much more can this be expected in a world in which everything is regulated by nearness and distance, as is Lola's world! For what, except our skin, is "nearer" to us than our clothes? And how gladly would Ellen and Jürg give away, dispense with, sell, cut up their bodies if this were only humanly possible! Instead, they beg fate to let them be born again with another body or another soul —while all Lola needs is to discard a dress that she does not like, or to put a distance between herself and it. And while the other patients implore fate to save them from their tortuous or trite existence, Lola believes that she is able to "read" fate's intentions. What does this mean? It means, in the last analysis, that she succeeds in wresting from the intangible, uncanny Dreadful a personlike character, namely the personification of a fate that proceeds according to predictable intentions, that warns or encourages her and thus saves her from being totally delivered to the Dreadful in its naked uncanniness.

This is shown not only by Lola's casting a large net about fate that she believes will enable her to interpret its intention and escape the Dreadful, but also by her behavior toward the actual

* Nowhere, except maybe in the Rorschach test, does this "expressive" significance of clothes play a greater role than in dreams. There they are the most frequent and most explicit exponents of our experience of self-evaluation. One has only to think of the torn, worn out, ill-fitting, sloppily carried, or badly matched "dream" clothes on the one hand, and of the elegant, conspicuous, or neat ones, of the officers' and diplomats' uniforms on the other. One also remembers dreams of being half-dressed or dressed in inappropriate garments. But such "mistakes" occur in wakefulness, too. I myself appeared once at an academic anniversary celebration in black tuxedo trousers and a tuxedo vest, but in a yellow pajama jacket. There the motive was not self-deprecation, but depreciation of someone else; I had only reluctantly attended and felt a definite "resistance" against the person to be honored.

carriers of the Dreadful, the clothes. When Lola wears the same dress for a long time, enters the sanatorium without underwear, and surrounds the buying and wearing of a new dress with a network of safeguards against the breakthrough of the Dreadful, we gather that she has to "guess" the intentions of "fate" in order to ward off *her* fate. The fewer garments she wears, the less "contact" she has with the Dreadful; the longer she can do with her worn-out dress, the less she feels endangered by a new "horrible" catastrophe, implicit in the new dress. However, the new as such, newness per se, is, as we know, the Sudden as such, Suddenness per se. Definitely thrown into uncanniness, Lola lives in anxiety lest the Sudden break through, the Sudden against which she tries to protect herself in every possible way. (See her remark: "One should never give me something unexpectedly because that gives me an idea that stays forever.") Since the Sudden is the negation of continuity, indeed, the "complete withdrawal of continuity from the Preceding and the Succeeding" (Compare the fear of catastrophe in the case of Jürg Zünd), we again see that Lola has neither a genuine future nor a genuine past but lives from one Now to the next, in the mere (inauthentic) present. Her existence, too, no longer extends steadily and continuously, i.e., unfolding in the three "ecstasies of temporality," but has shrunk to the mere present, the mere being-at-something. Existential continuity, the authentic becoming in the sense of authentic historicity, is replaced by the uncannily sudden jump from one "now-point" to the next. It is not difficult to see now that the wearing of the same dress, the external mundane continuity, replaces the missing inner or existential continuity and preserves existence from total dissolution.

That the new dress is not permitted to be pretty or expensive betrays the ascetic trait in Lola's existence—an atoning quality that, however, is not "lived" as atonement but merely as a precaution, so as not to provoke the dreaded power by anything conspicuous (Lola is by no means stingy by nature). But it would also mean such provocation if she were to accept the dress—the carrier, par excellence, of the Dreadful—from the hands of a squinting and, therefore, "ominous" saleslady. And when the new dress must not be red because last summer's dress was red, then this, too, proves the mundanization of her existence; for while genuine existential continuity rests precisely on repetition,* we are dealing here with the worldly category of recurrence of sameness. At this Lola also shudders. To be sure, she would prefer no change at all; but if she has to accept something new, then it ought to be different from the old. We must remember that to Lola "things" mean *memories*, since "memories enter things." Hence, the "horrible," "ghastly" feeling "never ends as long as the thing is around." Things, therefore, are not just carriers of memories, they *are* the memories. We thus perceive the most tangible sign of the process of mundanization, of the transformation of existence, and of genuine fate into "world" and "worldly" destiny. But even the memories and feelings themselves are no longer mobile and dirigible; they can no longer be worked through into continuity, but are congealed, impervious to influence, fixated in a mere sham-continuity, and are overpowering to existence. The memories, too, become, in some sense, clothes, shells of existence, carriers of mishap but, in no way, past and repeatable existence. Hence the gap between existence and such "congealed" memories is far greater than the gap between the thing-memory and the memory-thing. Having to retain or wear the old dress that is not afflicted with horrible memories means being obliged to remain in having-been-already, that is, in the state of thrownness. To buy and to have to wear a new dress means risking an uncanny adventure, a step into the future. But to have to remove a "contaminated" dress or thing means, I repeat, to get rid of the thing-memory through removal of the memory-thing. In other words, the inability to integrate the memories into the continuity of existence is replaced by the placing of world-spatial distance between oneself and the memory-thing.

THE SURREPTITIOUSNESS OF THE ENEMIES AND THE UNCANNI-NESS OF THE DREADFUL† / The nosological system of psychopathology has to maintain a clear distinction, descriptively as well as substantively, between the symptom of compulsive superstition

* Cf. Kierkegaard's *Repetition*.

[† TRANSLATOR'S NOTE: The play on words, *Heimlichkeit der Feinde—Unheimlichkeit des Furchterlichen*, is untransferable but dispensable. What this section deals with is the close relation—from the existential viewpoint—between compulsive superstition and delusions of persecution, and how the latter evolves from the former.]

and that of delusions of persecution. *Daseinsanalyse,* on the other hand, tries to reveal precisely what is fundamental to both these descriptive symptoms and to explain how one evolves from the other.

Lola herself uses in both conditions of her existence one and the same expression:

> I see in the signs all the time that *I ought to be cautious* (since I don't know what may happen).

> I never imagined something like that, all the things I discovered these people have done—because they always eavesdrop and plan to do evil things, that's why *I must be very cautious.*

Cautiousness, in the first statement, refers to the breakthrough of the Dreadful; in the second, to the hostility of "the people." The uncanniness of the Dreadful has turned into the surreptitious acts of the people: "suggesting," being curious (*beneugieren*), eavesdropping, betraying, treating insolently, murdering. But then, again, the two are similar in that caution in relation to either of them is only practicable if one has the key to, and pays accurate attention to, a *system of signs.*

In the first mode of existence, there is still confidence in an authority—"fate"—that provides warning signs whose interpretation enables the existence to protect itself against the invasion of the Dreadful; in its second mode of being, however, the existence lacks the protection of a superordinate power in which it can still believe. Being defenseless, it is now delivered to its enemies. This finds drastic expression when Lola, in the first instance, says that she *"ought to be* cautious," in the second, that she *"must be* cautious." Here the signs are no longer warnings of *a* danger, but an expression of *the* danger itself, of something that is present. The last authority in which the existence was still able to believe, its last remaining foothold (however thin, even threadbare, the net had been in which it tried to catch the Dreadful) is now gone. Only now has the existence completely abandoned itself and given itself up to the world. In the first stage, Lola "reads" (interprets) fate's commands and prohibitions by means of a superstitious system of verbal signs that she still employs more or less "independently," but in the second phase, she now *feels*, *sees*, and *hears* the enemy's signs in perceivable forms that have taken on the aspect of reality.*

From the viewpoint of existential analysis, this does not signify an *essential* difference but only a difference with respect to the form in which the Overpowering and the "being delivered to it" are manifested. The same applies to the distinction between the two phases (that of the impersonal overpowering, and of the personal overpowerer). Already in the first stage, "fate" was a quasi-godlike person having "intentions with regard to us" that could be "read"; moreover, the nurse Emmy was—over and beyond being a carrier of bad luck—already a "personal enemy" whose proximity made Lola expect the unspeakably Dreadful. Hence, the nurse Emmy forms a connecting link between the Dreadful as a fateful, uncanny power and the surreptitious acts of the enemies. The only remaining difference is that Emmy is the uncanny carrier and conveyor of the Dreadful, while the "persecutors" are no longer conveyors of intentions and carriers of the Dreadful, but are, themselves, dreadful persons. We are thus confronted with the phenomenon of personification and, therefore, of pluralization of an uncanny power into several, nay, many surreptitious persecutors. This reminds us of the "technique of magic," which involves the "allotment of carefully graduated magical powers to strange persons and things (*mana*)." †

Freud has devoted a very instructive study to the kinship between the Uncanny and the Secretive, based on Schelling's definition of the Uncanny: "Anything which ought to remain in secrecy and obscurity and has become manifest is known as uncanny."

This, however, is not the context in which to discuss Freud's psychoanalytic elaboration of "the scope of factors which turns anxiety into fear of the Uncanny." I prefer to return to Schelling's definition, adding to it that what was supposed to remain in secrecy and hiding is the original existential anxiety, which now "has emerged." The feeling of uncanniness is aroused by anything

* It is well to consider that these signs are still largely based upon verbal phenomena (similarities of words).

† See Freud, "Das Unheimliche," *Sämtl. Schriften*, X, 393. I wish to emphasize that I don't by any means identify this pluralization with the magical interpretations of the "primitives." What is common to both is merely being at the mercy of an uncanny power that extends to persons and things.

that causes that anxiety to emerge, anything that is apt to shock us out of our familiarity with "world and life," as the (unwonted) recurrence of the similar, the Wraith [*Doppelgänger*], as well as all symbols of declining life: a hunched back, squinting, madness, and, finally, death. The more overwhelming the existential anxiety, the weaker the confidence in world and life, the wider the scope within which it may emerge. In Lola's case, a network of precautionary and defensive measures is interposed between the existential anxiety and the Uncanny, the latter being caused to emerge by the former. This process, though more dramatic, is essentially the same as that which occurred in the cases of Jürg Zünd and Ellen West. Through defensive measures, the existence tries to protect itself against the emergence of the Uncanny. Through them, it still finds some foothold in "care" [*Sorge*], worrying [*Besorgen*], bargaining, being cautious, even though this caution serves exclusively to ward off the Uncanny, and completely spends itself in the service of the Uncanny. Yet it is still the self that defends itself against the "naked horror," against the break-through of the Dreadful into the existence.

But then, in the second phase, we discover something very peculiar. Here, the defense measures have proved inadequate, and the Dreadful can no longer be banned by questioning the oracle, or be "removed" by way of spatial distance. At this point, the Dreadful is no longer felt as naked horror, as an "indefinite" threat to, or even, underminer of, existence; it is felt, rather, as a "definite," concrete threat arising from the world. In losing its uncanny character, the Dreadful turns into something secretively threatening and, simultaneously, the real self is threatened with annihilation. Now the self no longer stands with both feet "firmly planted on the ground," either in practice or practical reality, but has surrendered to a phantasy world and is completely under its spell. We are dealing here with that world which is, itself, marked by secretiveness, intangibility, and incomprehensiveness, with the world of the others, with the historic "being-taken-by-the-others," and with the reputative image [*Rufgestalt*] established in the process.[5]

The continuous feeling of being overheard and being threatened is only a special case of the inescapable, uncanny-secretive being-taken, being-judged, and being-condemned, of being-impeded and being-attacked by the others ("the people"). Since the intentions of "the others" are never completely transparent, there always remains a margin of incalculable secretiveness. Those who "stand with both feet firmly on the ground" do not worry about that margin and even ignore, more or less justifiably and securely, the "reputative image" that represents their existence in the eyes of the others. On the other hand, existential anxiety, once unshackled, can nowhere succeed with a break-through more easily than in this "region" of our world that, in itself, is incomprehensible, unsurveyable, inscrutable, and incalculable. The secretiveness perceived in the actions of "the people," the perception of their evil intentions through "signs," the compulsion to derive intentions from those signs—all these point to the secret emergence of the uncanniness of the world of fellow men. Whatever emerges quite "openly" is no longer uncanny.*

While in the superstitious phase, "all exits of the life-stage" (to use Ellen West's metaphor) "were occupied by armed men," now, in Lola's case, the men actually converge upon her. The "life-stage" itself has changed. In the first phase, Lola could still, in some way, hold at bay the Threatening that "burdened her soul"; now she must at any moment expect to be murdered. While before the salvation of her soul was at stake, now the threat is to life and limb. And this leads not only to a pluralization of the Threatening but also of the Threatened. The crimes† occur everywhere, and the entire world now consists only of murderers and the murdered. On the one side, we find the innocent victims, on the other, the villains. The uncanny "world" has turned into a world of secret crimes, a world in which everything has its un-

---

* Of course, it is no counterargument against my statement that in this mode of existence the "intentions" of the "enemies" come openly to the fore and thus can be fought; for even behind the "openly emerging" intentions of the "persecutors" lurks the uncanniness of the "puzzling" fate of being persecuted as such—of being treated unjustly, being incriminated, being impaired. Thus the torturing questions of the persecuted: Why must just *I* suffer so much, Why was this destiny assigned just to *me*, Why do I have to stand alone against my enemies, Why does nobody believe my reports about my suffering, etc. All these are questions posed to fate which are then passed on to be answered by the explanatory delusions. What matters here is the uncanniness of the delusionary fate felt by the patient himself, and not by the observor; for *him* the source of the uncanniness lies in the relation of insanity to the "descending life."

[† TRANSLATOR'S NOTE: *Krimen*—again a neologism.]

canny omens [*Vorbedeutungen*] into a world of secret meanings [*Bedeutungen*].

Thus the life-stage has become the scene of drama, even of tragedy. Lola, herself, has become a helpless tool of the stage action, compelled to say what the enemies want her to say (in order to "direct" their crimes). She is nothing but a machine [*Erfolgsapparat*] that must reproduce whatever words or thoughts are fed into it. Not only is she a helpless, but also an innocent tool. The existential guilt is transformed into a mundane being-held-guilty: "they" consider her bad.

In the first stage, uncanniness clung mainly to clothes. Hence, one could have expected clothes to be of importance in the second stage, too, as is sometimes observed in advanced cases. (We shall return to this point in our psychopathological analysis.) It may be due to the gaps in our material that in the case of Lola we find almost nothing of this, apart from her plan to escape her enemies *disguised* as a maid. Otherwise, the clothes motif has undergone a change: the spatial contact with garments and with persons clad in them is replaced by the "make-believe" disguise of the enemies. Although their crimes are obvious, Lola is in no position to "grasp" her enemies, due to their "disguise" and secretive practices. Earlier, she could evade the persons whom she felt to be threatening since she *knew* them; now she is groping in the dark. Earlier, the dreadfully Threatening was intangible, but its carriers were "tangible"; now the Threatening (the persecution) is close at hand, but its executioners are intangible. Such are the peculiar dialectics of the Uncanny of which we psychiatrists still know so little.*

If, in the second stage, Lola appears still "sicker," still "crazier" than in the first, we can explain this by recognizing that the process of mundanization has advanced, that the fear of the un-cannily Dreadful and the superstitious questioning of fate (which to some degree is shared by most people) has been replaced by fear of the executers of evil and by the fight against them. This

---

* This is not offered as an explanation for the "delusions of persecution" in general. We do not even know so far how many possibilities exist. We are satisfied if we succeed in gaining insight into the dialectics of *one* case, to provide some guidance for other cases, particularly those in which insanity occurs so rapidly that its stages can hardly be observed or separated from each other.

may impress us psychopathologically as an enormous "qualitative" difference; but in terms of existential analysis it is but an expression of the progressive conquest of existence by "world," of still the same drainage of the Dasein in the sense of its being delivered to world, of still the same process which von Gebsattel calls "dis-becoming" [Ent-werden]. It is a manifestation of the highly complex dialectic of existence that in psychopathology we have simply named *autism* and that we diagnose by way of clinical psychopathological symptoms.

The "transition" from the superstitious mode of existence, from the feeling of being threatened by the Uncanny, to the certainty, the evidence of being threatened by the world of fellow men, can be still more clearly illuminated by a discussion of: a) the verbal mode of communication; b) the temporalization (historization); c) the spatialization of both modes of existence.

Verbal Communication In Lola's verbal communications —not with the Dreadful per se, but with the communicative authority established between her and it—she follows consistently the mode of "taking-it-at-its-word." She takes fate at its word, which means she communicates with it as with a person, one that is not only responsive but also responsible, i.e., on whose response one can rely and with whom one can conclude an oral agreement.* Within these limits, there still exists a certain relation of confidence, hence a relation of confidential closeness. In "taking-something-at-its-word," we know something about the other that we can hang onto, that can be grasped. In such a confidential relationship, therefore, the one who takes the other at his word gains a secure standpoint, a "point" where he can take a "stand" in relation to the other (in this case, in relation to fate) and from which he can regulate his own conduct. By believing that she can take fate at its word, Lola, to some degree, makes the Uncanny familiar to herself and, as far as possible, familiarizes herself with it.

All this is still within the "normal" limits of the anthropological

---

* See Binswanger, *Grundformen und Erkenntnis menschlichen Daseins*, pp. 322 ff., 361 ff. All this is only a specific variation of the dialectics of the locked-in-ness or, according to Kierkegaard, of the Demonic: "The demoniacal does not shut itself up *with* something, but shuts *itself* up; and in this lies the mystery of existence, the fact that unfreedom makes a prisoner precisely of itself." (*The Concept of Dread* [Princeton, 1946], p. 110.)

mode of taking-someone-at-his-word. But it becomes evident that this mode is being transgressed when we see that it is the Dasein that makes fate talk, and that it uses an artificial system of verbal communications. What we call mental disease comes about when the self is no longer able to distinguish between "inside" and "outside," between existence and world or, more precisely, when a need of the existence is perceived as an actual occurrence in the world. Nevertheless, or, rather, because of this, we are still dealing here with an assertion of the self, however emptied and drained of power that self may be. It is true the self has relinquished its power of *free* resolution and decision, yet it still maintains itself in its subjugation to the authority that it—the self itself—has vested in fate, and in its obedience to fate's commands. Existential anxiety is still channeled; it has not yet overflowed the dams artfully constructed around it.

In "delusions of persecution," however, these dams have burst. Existential anxiety floods the world of fellow men; the Dasein is threatened from everywhere, a prey to all. Intimidation and threats are only exceptionally interrupted by permissions. All this is communicated through secret signs, that is, mainly through verbal manifestations: Lola hears something being said, which "they" have caused to be said; "they" let her know through the words of the nurses that Mrs. Wilson has been murdered; "they" tell bad things about her. But even her own words are overheard and used for "evil" purposes; that is why she has to be so cautious. And finally, the "others" murder other persons "through the words they put in my mouth," and "with everything I said which was similar in words." Unfortunately, we possess no further information on the connections between words and acts, and on the nature and consequences of that "similarity of words." In any case, here we observe not only the "magic omnipotence of thoughts," but also of words. The "bad consequences of the similarity of words" appear to apply to similarities between what Lola says and what others say, possibly in reference to the net of verbal combinations that she throws over the Uncanny.

However that may be, we see that Lola uses every possible means to get her enemies to talk in order to gather their intentions, just as she had previously got fate to talk. But while fate permitted her to wrest from it a definite "yes" or "no" and, thus, clearly and distinctly reveal its intentions, the enemies remain, as a rule, veiled or disguised. Only exceptionally do they betray themselves and, expressly or surreptitiously, announce their intentions. Their main activity consists in secret eavesdropping, veiled inquisitiveness, clandestine pursuit. The actual, tangible and removable garment is replaced by the intangible, no longer removable, psychic disguise. The world of fellow men now assails the existence bodily, with the intention of physical threat, namely murder. The place of the indefinable, hence ineffable Dreadful (in expectations and memories), has been taken by the definite, dreadful menace to life and limb. The "Naked horror," the dread of loss of existence, has turned into the definite dread of the loss of bodily life. Existential anxiety, the fear of annihilation [*Nichtigung*] can now only manifest itself as fear of wordly destruction. Verbal manifestations no longer warn: "You may do this, you must avoid that" (in order to escape the Dreadful); they now bluntly state: "Your fate is decided, you will be put to death." Thus, existential anxiety that, in the superstitious phase, was still genuine *anxiety*, turns in the persecution phase to *fear* of something definite, of being murdered (viz. Freud's conception of the Schreber case). By no means do we see a healing process in the metamorphosis of the indefinite Dreadful into a definite fear (i.e., into delusions).

In this context, we must state that the disease has progressed enormously. Whereas, previously, the self was still able to preserve itself to some modest degree, now it is completely delivered to the superior power of the world, and benumbed by it [*benommen*]. What previously, in some measure, could still be addressed as a self is no longer an autonomous, free self, but only a dependent Ego in the sense of being a mere plaything of "the others." The threat of what existence conceals from itself, which is felt as anxiety, is no longer seen as the authority of "fate," but is now disguised as the superior power of the enemies. This "disguise" is a form of Mundanization, that is, a dressing of the world with those "clothes" with which existence had dressed itself and, finding them "unbearable," * had torn them off and thrown them over to the world of fellow men. In Lola's clothes-phobia the throwing off was still expressed by tangible discarding of the actual clothes

[* TRANSLATOR'S NOTE: In German, "unbearable" and "unwearable" are the same word.]

(giving them away, selling them, cutting them up) and by avoidance of the persons who then wore them. In her delusions of persecutions, the clothes cling, as it were, to "the others" or, more precisely, the Dreadful spreads from the discardable clothes and their carriers to *all* men, to everything that is human.

Thomas Carlyle, in his profound *Sartor Resartus*, has made the "philosophy of clothes" his topic. He tries to show that "all symbols are actually clothes," and he embarks upon the "long and adventurous journey from man's external common, tangible woolen covers through his miraculous covers of flesh and his miraculous social clothes down to the clothes of his innermost soul, to Time and Space." One could call the book an attempt at a "philosophy of symbolic forms," reaching far beyond Cassirer's scope of verbal, mythical, and knowledge forms. Like the German idealists, Carlyle recognizes that essence or inside, and symbol or cover, are interdependent; he believes he can recognize the essence in the symbol and find the key to the former in the latter. But, again following the pattern of German idealism, he neglects the dialectical movement from the one to the other that corresponds to the existential relationship between freedom and nonfreedom, nonfreedom and freedom. Hence, his book, like all philosophies of symbolic form, while it is helpful for existential-analytic and life-historic clarification, is sterile with regard to that dialectical movement itself. But if we wish to arrive at an anthropological understanding of clothes, Carlyle's theories must be borne in mind.

Our discussion of the secretiveness of the enemies has carried us to the analysis of verbal safeguards, and the latter to the analysis of safeguards against clothes—because all these topics rest on a common denominator: the conjuration of the Dreadful. Through her complicated system of verbal oracles, Lola takes the Dreadful at its word—by conjuring it—while through clothes and enemies she takes it at its weak spot. By means of clothes and enemies the Dreadful can be most safely grasped, and thus fought. But since in the Dreadful Lola has to deal not with another person but with an uncanny, superior, demonic power, the taking-at-its-word as well as the taking-at-its-weak-spot must assume the nature of conjuration. Conjuration, however, means perpetual invocation, adjuring, incessant emphasis, never-ending repetition.* Conjuration is the

* Conjuration is *Ahmung* as used by Leopold Ziegler (cf. *Überlieferung*

expression of subjugation that has made itself a prisoner and now desperately beats at the walls of its prison. What sort of imprisonment and prison we have to deal with is of secondary importance. While in earlier cases we encountered only one kind of imprisonment, in Lola's case there are two, imprisonment by fate and imprisonment by the enemies. Since what Kierkegaard called "the mystery of existence"—that unfreedom makes a prisoner of itself—is valid for all human existence, schizophrenia merely represents a particularly intensive and peculiarly constituted variation of that change of freedom into unfreedom or, as we express it, of existence into world.

Temporalization As stated earlier, the transition from the superstitious mode of existence, from the vague "feeling" of being threatened by the Dreadful, to the certainty of the threat by fellow men can be illuminated by way of verbal communications, of temporalization (historization), and of spatialization of the Dasein. We shall now turn to the second task.

We may immediately refer to the conjurational nature of intercourse with the Dreadful. Where we hear of perpetual invocation, untiring conjuring, and continuous repetition, we deal with the temporal mode of urgency (which we know so well from the case of Jürg Zünd) and hence with that of the sham-continuity of the Sudden, and of the mere nonactual present. This is the mode of temporalization that we also find in the case of Lola. Here, too, the existence is continuously on the alert for a danger that may suddenly break in, a danger that now no longer threatens simply from the Dreadful, but from "people." Vague anxiety about the Dreadful has turned into fear of the Criminals. Thus, the existence is still farther removed from itself, still more mundanized [*verweltlicht*]. True, Lola seems to be closer to us than in the first stage insofar as she is more "active" and beyond the stage of mere "active passivity" (Kierkegaard) of superstition. When she defends herself against the enemies and tries to avoid their ambushes, to discover and to "sue" them, the procedure does not appear so

[Leipzig, 1936], pp. 23 ff.), though not in the form of pantomime but in that of the verbal oracle. What lies at the bottom of all *Ahmung* is the conviction that "nature" (or "fate") can be persuaded to respond to human claims as desired. (P. 25.)

different from that of a healthy person. Again, when she seems to "stand with both feet on the ground," to gather observations, make plans "for the future," to look for a "way out," one might be tempted to believe that the existence temporalizes itself [*zeitigt sich*] here in a fashion no different from that which is required for ordinary activity, for normal "acting."

But then, it is of decisive importance to remember what temporalization actually means: temporalization should not be confused with world-time which is only a derivative mode of the former. Temporalization is not merely one existential phenomenon among others; it *is* existence (Dasein). In this case, the Dasein is already mundanized to such a degree that we can no longer speak of genuine existential temporalization, nor of historization, nor of the self as "becoming." But where we no longer find a genuine self behind industriousness, where the existence has become the "plaything" of demonic powers, there it no longer stands with both feet on the ground (which always implies an existential, or "self-stand" [*Selbststand*] but "hangs in mid-air." Existence has, as Kierkegaard puts it, detached itself from its (historical-temporal-spatial) "fundamental conditions" that, now, become its enemies.

The difference between the temporalization in the first and in the second stage can, in accordance with Heidegger (see *Sein und Zeit*, pp. 341 to 345), be interpreted as that between temporalization of anxiety and temporalization of fear. While *anxiety* is concerned about "the naked existence as one which is thrown into uncanniness," *fear* is caused by worries [*Besorgen*] concerning the world of fellow men. But even in the first stage, anxiety "loses itself to something worrisome" (Lola's anxiety about clothes), which shows that here, too, fear is involved. Furthermore, although, in the second stage, fear does have its root in worries about the intrigues of "people," these people do not become accessible to Lola through the world design of practical action, but through that of being subject [*verfallen*] to an overpowering Dreadful. Hence, the temporality [*Zeitlichkeit*] of the fear cannot be understood through the interpretation of practical activity, but through the state of surrender, of the "being-thrown-into-the-world." Temporalization, in this case, takes the form of being-driven about, of the whirlpool (see my "Über Ideenflucht"). Not only is the existence open to the startling Extraordinary (Heidegger); the being, as such, has assumed the character of the ever-startling Extraordinary!

Let us keep in mind the fact that, in the second stage, the existence has been caught in that "being-driven-about," in that whirlpool, even more than in the first. It is true that in both stages we are dealing with a fixation of the (dreadful) Extraordinary—dictated by existential anxiety—on a definite, worldly meaning: *danger*. In the first stage, the danger could be averted through "reading" from the objects, through a complicated system of questioning fate for a "Yes" (you may) or a "No" (you must not)—and thus for an indication of a possibility of escaping the danger. In the second stage, however, this court of appeal is out. Now, no alternative is left—only a "No." Now, in all signs, one reads the "No," the "Turn about!" the "Beware!" the "Trust no one!" A still mobile structure of temporalization, in which the future is now open, now closed, is replaced by the unreal omnipresent determinate evil. The only way in which the future still appears is in the expectation of the worldly emergence of the ever-present evil in the form of "crimes." But whereas, in the first stage, the Dreadful was still of an existential nature in its threatening of the existence, in the second stage, it has shed all of its existential character and has become merely a worldly danger to life and limb. The issue is no longer "peace of mind," but life itself. Where we had formerly seen existence in its historicity, in its potentiality of becoming and maturing, we now see only the unfolding of threatening events "in time." Obviously, such a "world without grace" [*Gebsattel*] cannot be penetrated by any ray of love. It lacks not only existential communication, but also loving communion, since the existence has long since isolated itself in anxious seclusion and insulation.

As a result of this investigation, let us remember that along with the transformation of the temporal mode of existential anxiety into merely worldly fear, the uncanniness of the Dreadful has retreated into the secretiveness of the enemies. Without knowledge and understanding of the first stage we could not possibly understand the second stage, the secretiveness of the enemies. At the same time, we are struck by the paradox that the uncanniness of the Dreadful could still be taken at its word as it manifested itself openly in the "yes" and "no" of fate's voice while the uncanniness of the enemies expresses itself only by way of secretiveness. But the paradox disappears as soon as we realize that uncanniness and secretiveness are not opposites but of one and the same order. They both represent anxiety about a demonic superpower and fear of being delivered to it. The different ways in which this super-power manifests itself (from our point of view: the ways in which it is interpreted and deciphered) are closely related to the process of pluralization of the *"Thou."* With fate, as personification of the Dreadful, one can still be a "pal," one can still "take it at its word"; but the unsurveyable many, among whom the *One* Dread-ful has distributed itself, can no longer be "taken at their word," but can be recognized, by words and other signs, only as enemies.

Hence the delusions of persecution prove to be a further phase in the controversy of the existence with the dreadful Overpowering that rose from it; a "further" phase, because the Overpowering has progressed from the uncanniness—which is closer to existence —to the secretiveness of the enemies, which is more removed from the existence but so much nearer to the world. The Overpower-ing has descended from the heaven of fate to the bustle of the earth; it has developed from an extra-worldly demonic superpower into a superpower of fellowmen. Anxiety about the uncanniness of the extra-worldly superpower has turned into immediate evi-dence of the worldly evil, into delusions of persecution.

Spatialization Our next step will be to clarify, in terms of spatialization, the transition from the superstitious mode of exist-ence to that of being threatened by the world of fellowmen. Again we must refer to the existential difference between anxiety and fear. And again we must remember that the first stage was by no means determined *only* by the "dreadful" anxiety, but also, at the same time, by the fear of actual clothes and individuals. Hence, the clothes as environmental stuff, and the carriers of these clothes as fellowmen, are already on the same worldly-level as the "people" in the second stage. The differentiation we made between the temporality of the still existential anxiety and that of the world-fear applies equally to spatiality.

We may start with spatialization as related to anxiety. In this state the world has sunk into insignificance. The worrying ex-pectation [*besorgendes Gewärtigen*] does not find anything to help it understand itself: "it reaches into the nothingness of the world." What makes this anxiety so dreadful is that it is completely "incomprehensible," since it is the "Dreadful" per se (as so drastically demonstrated in the case of Lola) and that in the Dreadful both self and world are being nullified [*genichtet*]. And yet, even in anxiety there must be an "of what." As we have emphasized repeatedly, the "of what" of anxiety is the Dasein itself.

By perpetually asking fate for its opinion, Lola tried to let some *light* (which always means some space) enter into the uncanniness of her existence.

To us, this shows the struggle of the existence to create space even in the nothingness of anxiety, a space in which it can move freely, breathe freely, act freely—free of the unbearable burden of the Dreadful. Even if the answer is "no," space is nevertheless opened through that negation; and although it is a limited, imprisoned space, nonetheless it is space. Hence spatialization, in this case, bears the mark of superstition. Through superstition the existence salvages whatever remainders of "world," and thus of the self, can be salvaged from existential anxiety. Without the foothold of superstition, the existence would sink into the night of naked horror or lose itself "head over heels" to the world, as subsequently happens in the second stage. The third alternative—the genuinely existential one—of a recall of the conscience into the authentic being (self-being) has long been buried. No longer can the existence perceive the call, "back to the self!"

The second alternative—losing oneself to the world—does not contradict the hypothesis that the existence in anxiety grasps at the nothingness of the world; because in losing itself to the world the existence does not grasp at the world at all and so finds nothing through which to comprehend itself, but feigns world to itself. This means that the existence no longer spends itself in worrying expectation [*im besorgenden Gewärtigen*], in unlocking and controlling the everlasting world situation, but that it now spends itself only on the present situation, which is once and for all determined by the Dreadful—in the situation, that is, of the ever-present danger. Delivered to that constant threat from the mundanized Dreadful and benumbed by its superior power, the Dasein actually no longer finds anything through which to comprehend itself. When the Dasein is no longer able to comprehend the world as danger, genuine free comprehension of self also ceases. Being-in-the-world no longer involves worrying as a form of resolute action but only in the sense of a self-abdicated dreaming of danger (we should not forget that even in our dreams we *mean* to act).

On the other hand, the fear of a danger also implies an unburdening on the part of the existence of its dreadful anxiety, for while man can face or dodge danger, neither of these can be done in the face of anxiety. It is in this context that we come to admire Freud's profound interpretation of dream anxiety: either the dream turns the vague ("free-floating") anxiety into a fear of something, or else we awake from the anxiety dream, because, above all, the existence strives to escape existential anxiety. The delusions, too, are a mode of striving to escape this anxiety.

In relation to the "danger," the existence spatializes itself in the first stage in a way not so different from the second. "Space" is opened and closed not only through the answers of the oracle, but also through the carriers of the superpower in the environment and world of others, through the clothes and their wearers, the "bad-luck" persons such as the hunchbacks or the squinters, the hotel-clerks, the nuns, etc. But since the oracle does not always negate but sometimes also affirms, we find in the young gardener an affirming, or good-luck-promising representative of fate. Like the oracle, these characters codetermine the spatial dimensions and directions, and advance and retreat within them. This is possible only because spatialization, as such, is in this case a "magic" one, i.e., it is determined not primarily through the situation and through comprehension, but through subjection, the surrender of the existence to a power alien to the self. Naturally, even "mythical thinking," even the "delusionary" interpretation of the world is still a form of comprehension—is still a "View of the World" ["*Weltansicht*"] (W. von Humboldt). But both are world-designs —the one historic-traditional, the other purely individual—in the sense of the thrownness of the existence, not of authentic self-being.

All that was said of spatialization in the first stage applies to it in the second stage, too, with one exception—that the place of certain clothes and their wearers is now taken by "the people" at large. Almost all fellow men are "no-sayers"; rarely do we hear of an exceptional permission. The "No," the "Turn about," the "Beware!" can now no longer be "read" from a reply by the oracle, from a dress, or from a person (by way of his being infected). It has become "ubiquitous," or—to remain with the image of infection—"endemic." The widespread dissemination of the poisonous Dreadful is an expression of the progressive "expansion" of bondage to the world of fellow men. This expansion is accompanied by a shrinking of the Dreadful, which had threatened the Dasein, and its investment in the "Criminals," which are now threatening life and limb. Both the expansion and the shrinking are expressions of the total possessedness of the existence by the Dreadful, or to express it differently, of total existential drainage.

Hence we find that spatialization now opens up the "there" of existence ("da" of Dasein) as a disproportionally larger hostile space and a disproportionally smaller friendly space (the latter still contains the "second doctor" of the first sanatorium and the "sympathique" doctor of the second, in addition to other unidentified persons).* This again may give the impression that Lola "had reduced the distance between her and us." We are tempted to say that Lola behaves exactly as the normal person does when he faces his real enemies, namely, suspiciously, cautiously, slyly, self-protectively, accusingly, etc. The reason is that she again seems to be moving "in-the-world," which is more "comprehensible" to us than the dreadful fear of the Dreadful. We can once again "understand" her fears and defensive measures. What we tend to forget is that this "understanding" applies only to Lola's reactions to the enemies as such, and not to her anxiety about a world governed by the Inimical! Thus, the impression that Lola's behavior is now more understandable, is deceptive. To be sure, she is not so autistic in either stage as to prevent her from preserving some modes of conduct from her earlier world. But these modes of behavior lack what would make them comprehensible in the full sense of the world, namely, continuity of the self. Because of the self's surrender to an alien power and the accompanying loss of self

* We may remember from the report that the first doctor had completely replaced the oracle: he alone was now consulted to make for her the "yes" or "no decisions" ("I do nothing without your advice,"). She was now infiefed to the doctor the way she had earlier been infiefed to the oracle.

in general, the total structure of being-in-the-world is so different that psychological "empathy" is no longer possible, merely phenomenological description and understanding. Thus, existential analysis still permits a methodical-scientific understanding where so-called empathy has failed.

As to the emergence of the Criminal, we unfortunately know too little about the prehistory of our case to account for it in life-historical terms. In any case, Lola's anxiety, at the age of twelve, when she felt "insecure" at home after an attack of typhoid fever, and her subsequent flight to her grandmother's house, seem to have been caused by fear of burglars rather than of apparitions and could probably be traced to "infantile roots." Fear of the "crimes" would, in this case, have to be considered an upshot of an infantile anxiety and, therefore, a symptom of regression. But in this context this is of no interest to us. What attracts our attention is the circumstance that the world seems to have closed in upon Lola at all times. This is indicated not only by her defiance and quarrelsomeness, but even more so by the reports that she was "always" inclined to be alone, that she enjoyed staying in her locked room, thus secluding herself from the crowding world, and that she often thought of taking the veil. I mentioned this earlier in discussing her life-ideal, the ideal of being-left-alone, and of security. Hence, it is safe to assume that the fundamental feature in Lola's existence is the same as that disclosed in other cases and called by Kierkegaard "the mystery of existence," namely the phenomenon that "unfreedom makes a prisoner of itself." In schizophrenic existence, this phenomenon reveals itself much more drastically than in ordinary life. Freedom consists in the commitment of the Dasein to its thrownness as such, nonfreedom in denying it autocratically and violating it on the basis of an Extravagant [*versteigenen*] ideal. Such wrong-doing to existence is most cruelly punished in schiziphrenic existence. We are by no means attempting to "moralize." What we are facing here is not a moral guilt—which would be far more harmless—but the lack of existence as such, due to Extravagance. Extravagance, however, is man's ignoring of the fact that he has not himself laid the ground of his existence, but is a finite being, whose ground is beyond his control.[6]

The Materiality of the "World" / When we finally ask in what element or material aspect the Dasein, in Lola's case, materializes as "world" [*sich weltlicht*], we are, initially, embarrassed for an answer because nowhere do we find a direct reference to any of the four elements, neither to Air and Water, nor to Fire and Earth. This is so because our closer acquaintance with Lola dates from a time when she was already cut off from all "elemental" existence—when she was almost a "burned-out crater." This mode of speaking, which obtrudes itself upon us in such cases, can guide us toward the answer to our question. If an existence gives us the impression of a burned-out crater, it implies that the life-fire, the life-glow, even the life-warmth have left it. Such an existence is "ashened" and "earthened" [*verascht und vererdet*] —in the sense of *dead* earth! In the case of Ellen West, we could still follow this earthening process step by step . . . from the ethereal, bright, beaming region to that of vegetative decay and, thence, to the swamp and the discarded husk. In Lola, we see before us almost the end-product of the process, although under the ashes there still glow a few sparks (of love, of confidence).

If we ask, further, on what the existential fire, the existential warmth has spent itself, we must answer—as we did in the cases of Ellen West and Jürg Zünd—on existential anxiety. It was existential anxiety that drained this existence of its "inner warmth" (*la chaleur intime*),[7] that forced all its resources into the service of the war against anxiety. It threw the existence into misery and placed it under compulsion, the compulsion to ward off anxiety at any cost, even at the cost of the life-fire.

This means that existential anxiety has cut off the existence from its deepest roots, from its original "free" key (in the existential sense of the word, from the capability of being keyed). The existence is, in this case, pressed into the perpetual unfree key of anxiety, and of its offspring, wordly fear. With this, the existence has started on the road to death (as we so clearly observed in the case of Ellen West). Existential anxiety bespeaks not life-fire and life-warmth, but an opposing principle—chilling and destructive —the principle of death. To this extent, but only to this extent, one may rightly say that any anxiety is anxiety about death. To be sure, the Dreadful, the Unbearable in all our cases is *death;* but not an "exogenous" death, not the destruction of life, but the "nihilation" [*Nichtigung*] of existence in naked horror. Seen from this angle, the subsequent mundanization of existential anxiety— the fear of life-destruction as it occurs in the delusions of persecution—is actually a "relief" for the existence. We must admit that Lola's descriptions of "persecution" no longer impress us as something unbearably dreadful to which existence has been delivered in naked horror, but rather as a threat by the world (of fellowmen) against which one can defend oneself with worldly means, such as precautions, tricks, accusations, etc. To be sure, the superstitious practices and the spatial removal of clothes also represented worldly defense measures but, mind you, not measures with which to battle the enemy (that is, the world of fellowmen) but with which to dodge existential anxiety! So we face again the peculiar dialectical process that turns the unbearable anxiety of nihilization of existence into the more easily bearable fear of a threat to life and limb.

It is this increased ease in bearing anxiety that gives the impression of a "healing process" although it should, from a biological view of health and disease, on the contrary invoke insight into the *progress* of the "disease." What, to the suffering patient, means a mitigation of his suffering from and in existence, means in medicobiological judgment an increase in a totally different kind of suffering, in terms of the disease.

The being-burned-out, the loss of *"chaleur intime,"* helps us to understand the mode and means by which Lola tries to penetrate the intentions of fate and of her enemies. If Bachelard is right in stating that "le besoin de pénétrer, d'aller à l'intérieur des choses à l'intérieur des êtres" is a "séduction de l'intuition de la chaleur intime," then this temptation is, in Lola's case, no longer a "sympathetic" phenomenon, no longer a phenomenon "de la sympathie thermique," but a warding-off and defense phenomenon, and thus a practical one.* The penetration into the "inside" of fate and of "the others" no longer occurs by way of sympathy and antipathy, but by means of rationally interpretable signs. Hence, it is no more a "feeling" but, in keeping with Lola's own expression, a

---

* In contrast to the case of Lola, in the far less advanced and very acute case of Ilse this "desire to penetrate" was still a phenomenon of warmth.

"reading." The compulsion to read something into all things (and persons) is no longer a temptation of the intuition *de la chaleur intime*, but a temptation motivated by fear or, more precisely, by the anxiety-driven compulsion to decipher and interpret superstitiously, at all costs.

Psychopathological-Clinical Analysis

Since the available material is not sufficient for a psychoanalysis of the case, we shall continue our report with a clinical-psychopathological analysis. We may, however, call attention to the fact that Lola in puberty behaved like a boy and asserted that she *was* a boy. If one relates this to the undeniable predominance of the (negative) mother complex, to the "elevation" of the pretty nurse to an actual carrier of bad luck, and to the fear of women hunchbacks and nuns, one may consider a (repressed) homoerotic component in Lola's sexual constitution. Accordingly, one would have to deduce—in line with Freud's theory of paranoia—that Lola's later enemies, too, would be of the female sex, a hypothesis that is not confirmed by the data. Furthermore, Lola certainly shows some normal, heterosexual tendencies; she appears to have genuinely loved her fiancé; she regards the sight of a young gardener as a lucky prospect for her trip, and seems to have enjoyed balls and dances. Her narcissism showed itself clearly in her naughtiness, stubbornness, defiance and quarrelsomeness, and later in the tendency to stay alone and lock herself up. We know only one of her dreams, the one about the nurse who lies down on the bed sent by Lola's grandmother, as well as on Lola's bed, and about Lola's fear lest her grandmother should also lie down on one of the beds. Lola's special love for her grandmother is further expressed by the child's flight to the grandmother's house, after her typhoid fever. But these meager references by no means suffice for a psychoanalysis of Lola's superstition and her delusions of persecution.

Lola's childhood provides some information of psychopathological interest. We remember that she was an "extremely spoiled" child, did not tolerate any authority above her own and, like Jürg Zünd, used to seek and find protection with some person. Hence, one cannot speak of any disciplined training [*Erziehung*]. Lola can be called "neglected" in terms of being prepared for adulthood [*im pädagogischen sinne*].* She neither knew nor learned anything about the possibility of an "inner support" but only of external retreats and protection. As we have seen, this trend pervaded her entire life and also dominated her illness. Already as a child, Lola was "not normally developed" in a psychic sense, by reason of both constitution and training. Her intelligence seems to have been rather below average. In any case, the entire report shows no signs of a well-developed intelligence.

Lola's lack of inner support intensified after the serious illness (typhoid fever) in her twelfth year and grew into anxious insecurity in her own home. Since we do not find a reference to fear of ghosts, the feelings of "insecurity" at home might be seen as a fear of burglars that, in turn, could be traced to concern with respect to masturbation. On the other hand, such fear could just as well be explained by a "post-infectious state of nervous weakness." This could tempt us to assume that the anxiety that emerged in that state had pathoplastically influenced the later psychosis and greatly determined its "content." But I do not share this opinion. I believe that, conversely, the post-infectious state of weakness merely offered the occasion for the "insecurity" inherent in the constitution to break through and to grow into acute anxiety; and that it was Lola's constitution, perhaps aggravated by lack of moral training, which can account for her first anxious insecurity as well as for her later fear of fate and enemies. Since this polymorphous form of schizophrenia usually appears at an early age we are justified in interpreting that first emergence of anxiety as an early symptom of an incipient schizophrenic process.

When Lola, during her thirteenth year, stayed in a German boardinghouse she was, according to the case report, boyish, domineering, bellicose, and quarrelsome. In immediately succeeding years, however, she was apparently quite inconspicuous, pleasure-loving, and fond of dancing; at the same time, she showed a tendency to stay alone and lock herself in her room. This may have coincided with the onset of her morbid superstition that, by her own testimony, emerged between the ages of seventeen and nineteen. All this is bound to renew the suspicion of an incipient schiz-

[* TRANSLATOR'S NOTE: This does not refer to school learning. Significantly, no English word for *Erziehung* exists. *Erziehung* comprises parental upbringing plus school learning.]

ophrenic process. True, Lola's defiant attitude toward her father because of his objection to her engagement, her frequent fasting, her joylessness and depression, and her threat to take the veil, can still be seen as a purely "psychogenic" reaction of a schizoid psychopath; but all these symptoms tend rather to reinforce the indication of incipient schizophrenia.

When Lola's case history reaches age twenty-two, we hear for the first time of her peculiar behavior regarding clothes, apparently her own clothes: she refuses to board a boat unless a certain dress is removed. Here again, her will prevails. On a visit to Germany where she met her fiancé, she is reported to have become more interested in clothes and to have opened up somewhat. But from her own report we know that, already at that time, she was "most severely" tortured by her obsessive ideas. Only during the following year—her twenty-third—was her illness noticed by the persons around her. After the marriage was postponed by her fiancé, she "collapsed, became melancholic and peculiarly superstitious." Hence, there is no doubt that Lola's so-called "compulsion neurosis" was already fully developed when she was twenty-two, perhaps even earlier, and only much later noticed by her relatives (except for the observation of her objection to going aboard with certain clothes). That the "compulsion neurosis" was a further manifestation of the schizophrenic process is thus no longer a suspicion, but a scientific conviction. . . . Now the "aversion" against her mother assumes such morbid forms that Lola regards as bewitched anything that comes from her; she hides these objects, gives them away, "loses" or sells them in the streets, wrapped in small packages. Experience tells us that such behavior goes beyond the symptoms displayed in a mere compulsion neurosis.

THE SUPERSTITIOUS STAGE: THE "READING COMPULSION" AND THE "CLOTHES PHOBIA" / Already in this stage we can observe, if only on one occasion, a definitely delusional perception. During her distraught period when Lola's anxiety about the pretty nurse emerged, she felt that she was being watched by two men: "I was lying downstairs in a deck-chair when I saw two figures in the corridor who watched me; when I turned toward them, they ran away, so I stayed downstairs; but it felt very uncanny."

To this we must add Lola's fear of being hypnotized. Although "delusions of hypnotic persecution" were not yet present, we nevertheless see in her fear of being hypnotized, in her request "not to look at her this way" and to promise her solemnly not to hypnotize her an expression of "feelings of hypnotic influence."

But there were other sure symptoms of schizophrenia that could be observed in the institution. Lola at first gave the impression of a stiff and affectless person, sloppy and indifferent in every respect, very reticent, revengeful, sensitive and suspicious, extremely stubborn and even negativistic, without any interest or joy in work, and retarded in her mental development. We must include her unpredictable behavior and decisions, her vacillation, and her hyprochondriacal reaction to medications. Furthermore, we must take into account her sudden change—within a day—from a definite fear of hypnosis to the avid wish to be hypnotized; such striking ambivalence, added to all the other symptoms of instability, permits us to speak of a dissociation of personality in a schizophrenic context.

That the picture changes somewhat when Lola finds a physician who is agreeable to her, should not impress us as astonishing. Lola is still emotionally receptive, and her need for support and direction is by no means extinguished. She now becomes more manageable, much more open, even trustful. Hence it is now possible to gain deeper insight into her psychic life. Thereby, the impression of the patient's total personality grows definitely more favorable, particularly as it now becomes obvious how intensely she suffers.

Turning to Lola's "compulsive phenomena," we have again to distinguish between the "reading compulsion" (compulsive interrogation of fate) and the compulsive "tabooization" of her environment and the world of fellowmen. How closely the two are interrelated we have already shown. The psychopathological problem that poses itself is the following:

Are we dealing here with genuine compulsive ideas as in a compulsion neurosis, or are the ideas already delusional? The diagnosis of schizophrenia per se does not necessarily represent a decision since in the course of schizophrenia we quite frequently observe genuine phobias, compulsive ideas, and compulsive acts (in my experience, most frequently these consist of fear of germs and compulsive washing). Hence, in each case of mixed schizophrenia we must investigate precisely whether we are facing genuine and pure symptoms of compulsion neurosis based on the mechanism of substitution, or merely abnormal psychic phenomena that impose themselves upon the patient against his will and are felt and judged by him as a "compulsion." We know that there is hardly a psychopathological symptom that has not been called "compulsive." [8] In our case, we have to ask and decide whether Lola's "compulsively superstitious" ideas and acts are compulsions at all, or already represent delusions. And supposing we do want to speak of compulsive ideas, we are still facing the alternative that they might be much closer to delusion than to compulsion (viz. Kretschmer's admonition to search much more for the distinction between compulsion and delusion than for that between delusion and delusion). Here we meet again the much discussed but, in my opinion, very vaguely formulated problem: can delusional ideas originate in compulsive ideas? What should be asked and investigated is, I believe, whether and to what degree compulsion and delusion are only different stages or periods of one and the same anthropological "change of form" [Gestaltwandel]. This question has not yet been answered by psychopathology, which is primarily interested in a strict distinction between compulsion and delusion as psychopathological *symptoms*. The main criterion for this distinction has, since Westphal, been the insight or lack of insight into the nonsensical and ego-alien quality of the morbid event. From a symptomatological point of view, this criterion is valid, although such insight is frequently subject to vacillation so that the criterion often fails in a particular case. But the question is, whether psychopathology can content itself with this descriptive psychopathological viewpoint and its purely "functional" interpretation, which will always form the directive for the clinical and particularly for the forensic judgment. But should not psychopathology, in the interest of pure research, be directed by other and deeper perspectives? Heeding the latter view, we believe that psychopathology, through anthropological investigation and research, can indeed gain "deeper" perspectives.

The "Reading Compulsion" Lola, as we have seen, experiences her "reading" as a "must," as a compulsion and, as all genuine compulsive neurotics do, feels a terrifying, unbearable anxiety if she cannot yield to the compulsion. But in contrast to the compulsion neurotic, Lola not only obeys a compulsive impulse by way of thinking, feeling, or acting (as, e.g., the impulse to repeat, to think things through to the very end, to count, to wash, to destroy, to curse, to pray, etc.), but beyond that, yields to the "nonsensical" compulsion to gather a sensible answer from "the things." Thus, the "reading" and interpreting, experienced by herself as an intruding ego-alien "must," results here in a solution that does make sense to her personality, a solution on which she depends for her bliss and happiness, while in compulsion proper, bliss and happiness depend only on the obedience to the nonsensical compulsive command as such, which has to be executed endlessly or in definite sequences of time. Hence the meaning of the genuine compulsion, if we consider it merely descriptively, lies in the execution of an act that is completely meaningless or drained of meaning—quite independent of what "meaning" may be found in or behind that act by psychoanalysis. The meaning of the pure compulsion lies, in our case, quite outside the act, namely, in avoiding the anxiety that occurs as soon as the act (interpreting is also an act) is omitted.

No doubt, Lola's "reading" compulsion is also of that anxiety-avoiding type but, in addition, it is given the very meaningful task of reading the "yes" and "no" out of things, particularly out of words or names signifying things that coincide spatio-temporally. In this case, we can actually speak of a "compulsion to extract the meaning" [*Sinnentname*].[9] Things don't function any longer according to their own "objective" meaning, but exclusively to express a "higher" meaning, one pregnant with fate. Are we still dealing here with compulsion or already with delusion? In my opinion, with both: compulsion, insofar as the reading imposes itself as an ego-alien "must"; delusion, insofar as it is based on the no longer ego-alien, delusional idea that "fate" speaks through the objects and provides compelling hints as to the "reader's" future conduct. One could reply that every superstition is founded on such a "delusional idea," without deserving the name "delusion." But we are dealing here (as most investigators since Westphal, Bleuler among them, have emphasized) with graduated shades of psychic structures; moreover, Lola's reading compulsion would have to be termed a delusion if for no other reason than that she unshakeably "believed" not only in the "omnipotence of fate" but also in each one of her interpretations, and that she ascribed reality-character to them. We may add that her questioning and reading system as such represents a logically motivated "delusional system." The fact that her "logical motivation" is extremely skimpy and superficial, even nonsensical, rather supports than contradicts our opinion.

To be sure, we expect to observe the most extreme nonsensical acts in genuine compulsion neuroses; but there the nonsense is recognized as nonsensical by the patient, whereas Lola identifies with the nonsense, which indicates that she experiences and comprehends it as something that does make sense!

Hence we have to understand that the signs from which she reads the intentions of fate are interpreted in just as delusional a manner as the signs from which she "reads" the intentions of the "enemies." On both occasions she "projects" (as we would put it in psychopathology—not phenomenologically, to be sure, but merely theoretically) "something" onto objects and people "that is not in them at all." We shall, however, neglect this common feature for the time being, because the reading from the objects is still to some degree experienced as a compulsion, in contrast to "reading" from people; furthermore, the reading from objects calls for a special system of interpretation while the reading from people seems to be independent of any artificial reading system but guided only by the natural human phenomena of expression. But if we could learn anything from the anthropological analysis of our case, and particularly from a juxtaposition of the two stages, it would have to be the realization that underneath the reading from facial expressions, words, and other "signs" of "the people," there must be an artificial, self-produced system of interpretation of which the reader is no longer aware. With the simple statement of a "delusional interpretation" nothing is accomplished. (We shall return to this point in the discussion of Lola's delusions of persecution.)

To what degree the questioning of fate is the expression of "infantile regression" must remain unanswered, for lack of any findings about Lola's inner life history. I wish, however, to point to the possibility that Lola's seeking and finding protection, particularly from her grandmother, might be connected with a similar relation to the "person" she saw in fate. Undoubtedly, this early seeking and finding of protection was propagated in the "reading" compulsion, which lends additional support to our view of its infantile quality.

"The Clothes Phobia" While the "answers" of fate had certain taboolike characteristics, these characteristics became much more marked with respect to certain garments and their wearers as well as other objects mentioned by Lola. Here again, the question becomes Phobia or Delusion?

That Lola's behavior in these areas displays phobic symptoms is almost self-evident; but her clothes phobia extends beyond the psychopathological content of a phobia of the merely compulsive neurotic type. This is indicated by the very close connection between the phobia and the delusional system of reading and interpretation as well as by the fact that this very phobia is no longer felt as ego-alien but as ego-syntonic.

Lola perceives her phobic symptoms not as a "must," alien to her personality, but as something quite meaningful, namely, again, as "fateful" in the earlier sense. Here, too, the decisive factor is the delusional feeling of being delivered to an overwhelming power of fate. Indeed, to Lola fate manifests itself not just through verbal oracles, but also in material form. We have found sufficient purely existential grounds as to why clothes were the primary objects through which fate manifested itself, but we lack the individual life-historical "explanatory" grounds for this phenomenon.

Since the will of fate expresses itself in the material form of garments and other utilitarian objects, the ensuing defensive measures are also purely "material." They consist in the elimination of the "contaminated" material. This removal of the "fateful or taboo-laden" clothes expresses drastically the basic pattern of Lola's battle against fate: by discarding, disposing of, giving away, selling, cutting up these clothes, she wards off her fate as long as possible. "Her" fate is, as we know, the sinking into the anxiety of naked horror, from which she is actually freed—if we consider the degree of her subjective suffering—by her delusions of persecution. Here, the "phobia" expresses the fear of complete subjugation by the overwhelming power of that fate and, thus, of the "nihilation" of existence in general. That the phobia is not felt and judged as alien to the personality is, therefore, not its only delusional component; another is its incorrigible delusional conviction that fate manifests itself in material forms.

Unfortunately, we also lack material that could elucidate the psychopathological genesis of these delusions. We do not know to what degree abnormal somatic feelings, or even somatic hallucinations, or feelings of being influenced have played a part (which does not affect our purely anthropological understanding of the case, since change in anthropological structure must be understood as a priori to the ways and means of its a posteriori forms of expression). However, we know from the case history of another patient (Rosa), that the putting on and taking off of garments was related to delusions of being psychically or sexually stripped, drained, deprived, exposed, and that psychic pressure and a "heavy heart" were identified with the pressure and weight of clothes on the body. In German, the verbal analogy is undeniable: "ausgezogen . . . ," "entzogen . . . ," "seelisch ausgezogen . . ." etc.* Of course, the patient did not have to be conscious of that analogy, since language "thinks" for us. Ever since Luther it has been German usage to say of a man that he would have to "doff the old Adam" in order to become a "new man." On the other hand, I am reminded of idioms like that of the person "who changes his convictions like his gloves." The concept of external habiliments as a symbol of the inner man—as offered by Carlyle in his *Sartor Resartus*—does not suffice. The common ground for the possible "co-incidence" ("symbol" is derived from *symballesthai:* to be thrown together) of the intended object and the word used has to be demonstrated. It is the common ground that permits the interchangeability. An additional factor is, of course, the intimate affinity of clothes and wearer, within his own world as well as in the eyes of his follow men (viz., "Clothes make the man").†

In Rosa's case, to which we have just referred, the content of the verbal metaphor was, as is so often true in schizophrenia, rendered absolute, that is, severed from the mutually interrelated links of comparison. Hence, no difference exists any more between be-

[* TRANSLATOR'S NOTE: The case history referred to above is more fully treated in an extensive footnote in the German original.]

† Strangely enough, "clothes" have rarely been considered in psychopathology. Cf. R. Kuhn: "Über Kleider," *Die Irrenpflege*, 21. Jahrgang, No. 8 (1942); and: *Über Maskendeutungen im Rorschach'schen Versuch*, 1944, pp. 71-74.

ing psychically stripped or covered, and the taking off and putting on of clothes; between psychic pressure and weight on the soul, and the pressure and weight of clothes on the body. This phenomenon is related to the simultaneity of seeing and feeling and to the elimination of the boundaries of the personality (viz. the draining of thoughts). When this patient *sees* the others do this or that, she *feels* it on her hair, on her arm, and on her dress. She is particularly exposed to pressure while sewing. The dress "belongs," like her soul and body, both to her *and* to the others, and vice versa. She becomes invested with vulgarity when she puts the dress on, with goodness when she divests herself of it, until eventually the dress, itself, becomes personified and turns into an enemy that threatens to leave the suitcase and torment her. A change of clothes is identified with a change of persons.

It is regrettable that we know nothing about the last stage of Lola's psychosis. But even so, we can see analogies, although in Lola's delusions the clothes were not personified and the enemies acted much more like actual persons. What Rosa's case more impressively demonstrates is the carrying of the delusions of reference and encroachment into the clothes. This may arouse a suspicion that in Lola's clothes phobia, delusions of reference and of encroachment were more markedly involved than the report discloses. That such "ideas" were already present at the time of the clothes phobia has been definitely established. Hence, Lola's phobia can in many respects be seen as a prelude to a "clothing" delusion —as a prelude only since she, herself (i.e., as a self), does not yet permit the clothes "to get at her," but still "takes them off," "does away with them . . . ," whereas Rosa actually feels dressed or stripped *by* the clothes.

But we must not forget that what we are here observing are only different degrees of the "secondary elaboration" of anxiety. Thus, the "of what" of anxiety is in both cases essentially the same, namely: the Threatening, Damaging, Hostile, which in Lola's case use the garments only as carriers through which to manifest themselves while, for Rosa, the garments, themselves, *are* the Threatening, Damaging, Hostile. To us, these two attitudes indicate only differences in degree regarding the possibilities of warding off the threat. For Lola, the threat can still be warded off by removal of the clothes, or by keeping away from their wearers. For the other patient, Rosa, it can only be done through a wall of space or abuse. Lola's terrible fear of the nurse Emmy and of other wearers of clothes forms a link between both cases. True, Lola still differentiates here between the garment and its wearer; but the person has already become an enemy—although not an outright murderer— yet an enemy as a carrier of everything evil and horrible. So far, only an emotional—not a logical—motivation is given for the hostility; but in either case the motivation is incorrigible, and inaccessible to logical counterarguments. The only remaining difference is that Lola, in contrast to the other patient, still understands us in our attempts to change her ideas. And although this understanding does not save her from the delusional fear of the Dreadful, it nevertheless preserves communications between her and "us" to some degree, whereas they were completely disrupted in the other case.

All this leads to the conclusion that Lola's clothes phobia, while phobic in character, is closely related to delusions, another confirmation of the often-observed fact that the mixed form of schizophrenia is typified by the ambiguity of its psychopathological symptoms.

THE DELUSIONS OF PERSECUTION / The appearance of delusions of persecution marks the end of the mixed form of schizophrenia and its transition to a paranoid syndrome. The scene that is permeated by compulsive and semiphobic symptoms, ambivalence, delusional perceptions, and feelings of hypnotic influence, dissolves into a picture *dominated* by delusions.

Already in the superstitious stage we discovered manifold delusional components:

1. A single delusional *perception of being watched,* a forerunner of what Lola later called being *beneugiert,* being seen, observed, eavesdropped upon.

2. *The feeling of being hypnotized:* ("You want to hypnotize me, don't look at me this way!") Already this could be seen as a delusional fear of being influenced.

3. *The delusional component in the "reading compulsion:* the attempt to learn the intentions of fate through a self-designed system of verbal symbols and the incorrigible submission to these "experiences." Already the compulsion is merely an auxiliary. The "compulsion" to question fate continually protects Lola from the

break-through of the Uncanny-Dreadful, but does not yet represent its transformation into the secretiveness of the enemies—the delusions of persecution. The imperative of having to "read" is the whip that drives Lola on so that she may avoid the Dreadful that threatens her entire existence.

4. *The delusional component in the clothes phobia:* this has been recognized as identical with that of the "reading" compulsion. One could call it a kind of persecution mania if this expression were not reserved for delusions of persecution by one's fellowmen. Lola feels actually that she is pursued by the Dreadful, which is ever and everywhere close at her heels, which threatens her and lurks about her. She is, in what Jaspers most fittingly describes as a "delusional mood not to be confused with psychasthenic moods and feelings. In the delusional mood there is always 'something' which, however vaguely, has in it the seeds of objective validity and importance. A general delusional mood without definite content must be quite unbearable." [10]

Hence, the clothes phobia, too, enables us to understand that the delusions do not "originate" in the phobia, just as they do not "originate" in the "reading" compulsion, but that the phobia is already the expression of a delusional mood, of a "being keyed" [*Gestimmtheit*] by the "unbearable" Dreadful. *What the case of Lola demonstrates is that there are phobias and compulsive ideas based on delusions, on a delusional mood.*

Jaspers agrees with Hagen, who states that there emerges in the patient "a feeling of rootlessness and insecurity which drives him with the force of an instinct to search for something stable to hold on to and cling to"; and that "he can find this completion and consolation only in an idea, in a way very similar to that of the healthy person under corresponding conditions." This explanation of the process, however, contains such heterogeneous elements that it calls for closer examination. The analogy with the healthy does not appear valid. It is true that in sadness or desperation the healthy, too, may search for a *definite* idea and grasp it in order to find something stable to hold on to. But while this is a valid description of what happens in less seriously ill patients, it does not hold true in Lola's case. Considering the genesis of delusions of persecution, we must be particularly cautious in accepting this explanation, as far as phenomenological facts are concerned. It is correct only theoretically if we focus upon the effect: Lola in her delusions of persecution did not suffer as terribly as in the superstitious stage. But neither has she "herself" brought about these delusions nor does she experience them as "completion, strengthening, or consolation." There we are thinking strictly in terms of "normal psychology." As we found in the existential analysis, in Lola's case, the more or less "active" resolve of the self to search for a hold is replaced by the process of mundanization of the existence, which follows its own norms and course. We must not impute to the self something which the self, in its delusions, no longer is able to perform! To expect the self still to make decisions or at least render some help contradicts the anthropological phenomenon of delusions as such, since where there is delusion there can no longer be any genuine self. To speak of a "delusional self" would be a contradiction *in adjecto*. The fact that Hagen, however vaguely, states that a feeling "drives the patient with the force of an instinct" (which in any case suggests a relative lack of participation on the part of the self), demonstrates, in itself, the degree to which, in psychopathology, we still miss firm fundamental concepts and basic premises. Two approaches are mainly responsible for psychopathology's failure in the area of delusions. Either the oft-criticized attempt was made to understand and explain the delusions in terms of normal psychology, or they were declared scientifically "ununderstandable," and stared at as an incomprehensible enigma that could at best be explained in terms of cerebral pathology.

In my opinion, the Daseinsanalytic case studies have at least demonstrated that there is a road to the scientific understanding of the delusions (not to be confused with empathic and psychological understanding), and that this road is that of phenomenological-anthropological investigation.

As already shown here, we can approach the scientific understanding of the delusions only if we recognize that we are dealing with a certain mode of existential decapacitation [*Entmächtigung*] or, to use a synonym, with a certain mode of mundanization. We say expressly, "a certain mode!" Therefore, it is our task to demonstrate and describe precisely each stage of this process of decapacitation while considering all possible structural links in the structure of the existence or of the being-in-the-world.

In an earlier chapter I have shown that, like the genuine phobias, delusions can only be understood in terms of existential anxiety (and by no means through the "affect of anxiety"). "World" now no longer means a totality of conditions that the existence has taken in its stride, but a condition definitely determined by the being as something frightful, a condition of hostility, of something that is, once and for all, hostile or threatening. It is a world design that is no longer carried by nor bears any traces of *love* and *trust*, or of the closeness to humans and things that results from these feelings.*

AUTISM AND ANXIETY / "Autism"—as emphasized in earlier studies—is neither a "being keyed" nor a mood and thus must not be interpreted as such in existential analysis. The case of Lola confirms this view. We have only to recall what we said about the lack of materiality or consistence of her world design. Where the "world" no longer shows a material vesture, where the "life-fire" is burned out and only "ashes" are left, the "key" [*Gestimmtheit*] of the existence, its "keyability," has suffered or has altogether disappeared. We described Lola as a "burned-out crater," that is, as a person in whom almost all freely flowing, immediate feelings were extinguished. Instead, the existence was dominated, even consumed (*ashened*) by *anxiety*. But this anxiety (as I have emphasized repeatedly) is basically not feeling or affect, but an expression of *existential* anxiety, that is, of the draining of the existence, and of its progressive loss of "world." Of course, loss of world is accompanied by loss of self. Where the existence is no longer in a position to design the world freely, it also suffers the loss of the self. This was clearly realized and expressed by Schopenhauer. He was the first to mention the possibility that we "could become conscious of ourselves through ourselves, independently of the objects of cognition and will," although he subsequently adds, "but, alas, we cannot do it, and as soon as we try it and direct our cognition inward for complete contemplation, we lose ourselves in a bottomless vacuum

---

* The present paper was concluded in 1945. In 1946 W. Szilasi published his "*Macht und Ohnmacht des Geistes* (Francke, Bern) in which the author, following the interpretation of Platos *Philebos* points out with unsurpassed clarity and conciseness the essential unity of anxiety and confidence as "the original transcendental power. . . ."

and find ourselves resembling a hollow glass sphere with a voice sounding out of its emptiness, a voice whose source cannot be discovered within; and by thus trying to grasp ourselves, we shudderingly grab nothing but a contentless apparition." *

This (psychological) presentation of the mutual relation of world and self can perhaps more clearly demonstrate to the psychopathologist what we mean, than can the Daseinsanalytic presentation. When we speak of a "burned-out crater," we speak of losses both in existence and in world, even though they can be traced to a single root. The "about what" of anxiety and of the shudder of which Schopenhauer speaks; the "at what" of the naked horror, as we call it, is no object and no enemy, but the ghostliness or "contentlessness" [Bestandlosigkeit] of the existence (deprived of "world") as such. Consequently, in terms of existential analysis, we no longer speak of a mood or of an affect (as in the case of fear), but of a loss of world and self.

Hence, when we talk about *autism*, we must first of all think of existential analysis and of losses of world and self (or at least of a reduction of the potentialities of world and self); and we must be aware of the fact that this "reduction" manifests itself first of all in a reduction of "keyability." Small wonder that this fact had already attracted the attention of E. Bleuler, the originator of the concept of autism, although he thought primarily of the increasing barriers to *positive* feelings.†

It is this reduction of the potential "keyability" caused by existential anxiety that explains the "lack of contact with reality," the reduction of the *fonction du réel* (Janet), the lack of attunement to the environment and world of fellowmen, of syntony (Bleuler) or synchronism (E. Minkowski), which accounts particularly for autistic thinking. That autistic thinking is "directed" by strivings,

---

* Cf. *The World as Will and Representation*, Book Four, Paragraph 54. The same situation is tersely expressed by Szilasi (in reference to Heidegger) as follows: "The existence perceives as external world that which is originally it (the existence) itself."

† See "Das autistische Denken," *Jahrbuch Bleuler und Freud*, IV, 24: "It appears that the process of Dementia praecox as such renders difficult the formation of such positive affective tones [Gefuehlstöne] or else the 'pleasure mechanism' would have to result much more frequently in ecstasies or in feelings of extreme joy; on the other hand, one must admit that to produce for oneself a perfect hallucinatory paradise calls for a certain creative ability which not every one possesses who turns schizophrenic."

that "thinking occurs in terms of the strivings without consideration of logic and reality," all this is psychopathologically not a primary cause, but the effect of existential anxiety, and of the reduction or elimination of the keying potential which accompanies the
latter.

THE HALLUCINATION PROBLEM / Our knowledge of Lola's hallucinations is too skimpy to allow for a detailed discussion. Nevertheless, this case may yet throw some light upon the problem posed
by hallucinations.

The fact that hallucinations are associated with autism, that is,
with a certain state of existence, has already been emphasized by
Bleuler. But I know of only one paper that explicitly explained the
problem of hallucinations on the grounds of "structural-analytic"
considerations. I am referring to a brief paper by E. Minkowski: "À
propos du problème des hallucinations" (1937).[11] In it, Minkowski
clearly states that the hallucinations must no longer be investigated
as isolated disturbances but "en fonction . . . du fond mental qui
les conditionne. . . ."

What Minkowski, in his discussion, calls the phenomenon of
"desocialization" consists in the fact that the patients are not at all
surprised when they notice that others do not perceive what they
themselves think they are perceiving. But all this still does not help
us to progress beyond autism in the usual sense. We can do so only
if we, with Minkowski, realize that the perceptions, in general,
have a significance that by far transgresses their sensory and cognitive function—as can be demonstrated by the "sensory metaphors"
(to "have tact," "flair," etc.)—and if we focus on them not from a
merely spatial (measurable) distance, but rather from the "experienced distance." Hallucinations and, particularly, "voices" cannot
be understood through a "rational" concept of closeness and distance, presence and absence, but only by understanding them in
terms of dynamics and living (I would say "through phenomenological-anthropological understanding"). Without going further
into Minkowski's paper, I only want to point out that in the case of
Lola, too, the delusional perceptions (the perceptions of hostile
signs, hostile intentions, hostile voices) by no means represent isolated phenomena, and that it would be hopeless to attempt to
understand them merely on a sensory basis. They have to be under-

stood as partial phenomena of a special world design—a design of the world, and particularly of the world of fellowmen—under the (unfamiliar, purely anxiety-conditioned) aspect of the Threatening and the Hostile.* They are the strongest expression of the hostile closing in, that is, of bodily closeness (viz. especially the feelings of hypnotic influence and the bodily hallucinations possibly connected with the former or with the clothes phobia).

Considering Lola's flight from the world, we may assume in her case, too, that the world "has closed in on her" and has "weighed too heavily on her soul" (Jürg Zünd). In the stage of superstitions, she was still able to keep away from that closeness and pressure; this she could not do any more in the phase of the delusions of persecution and during the hallucinations that accompanied them. To put it more correctly, the delusions of persecution and the corresponding sensory illusions are the very representation of that "experienced" hostile crowding of world and of that hostile world pressure. It is true that these delusions helped her to overcome the ghostliness and bottomlessness of the existence (Schopenhauer), the existential anxiety as I have elaborated it here, but only at the price of a recurrence of world closeness and pressure in a particularly intensive way. True, the delusions helped the existence to a tenure or content [*Stand oder Bestand*]; once again it had something through which it could comprehend itself—but at the expense of its *freedom!* What we have called delusional perceptions or hallucinations are nothing but isolated bridges or links "between" an unfree subjectivity and a corresponding "imaginary" objectivity; they are only isolated aspects of a deeply changed existential structure.

With all this, I intend nothing more than to point to the position and method from and by which the problem of hallucinations can, in my opinion, be attacked by means of existential analysis.

* Obviously, where the transcendental unity of anxiety and confidence has been torn apart in favor of the superiority or tyranny of one or the other, we are dealing with what is clinically known as *psychosis*.

Notes

[1. See Binswanger, "The Case of Ellen West," in Rollo May, Ernest Angel, and Henri F. Ellenberger (eds.), *Existence;* and "The Case of Jürg Zünd," in *Schizophrenie.*]

2. Binswanger, *Grundformen und Erkenntnis menschlichen Daseins* (Zürich, 1953), p. 445 ff.

3. Kierkegaard, *The Concept of Dread.*

4. See Binswanger, "The Spatial Problem in Psychology," *Zeits. für Neurologie,* Vol. 145, Nos. 3 and 4 (1933), p. 598 ff.

5. See Binswanger, *Grundformen,* pp. 328 ff. and 375 ff.

6. On the problem of Extravagance, compare the analysis of *The Masterbuilder* in my *Henrick Ibsen und das Problem der Selbstrealisierung in der Kunst* (Heidelberg, 1949).

7. See Gaston Bachelard, *La psychoanalyse du feu* (Paris, Gallimard, 1939), pp. 84 f.

8. See also Binder, *Zur Psychologie der Zwangsvorgange* (Berlin, 1936), and "Zwang und Kriminalität," *Schweizer Archiv für Neurologie und Psychiatrie,* Vols. 54 and 55.

9. See Erwin Straus, *Geschehnis und Erlebnis* (Berlin, 1930), and my own paper with the same title in *Monatsschrift für Psychiatrie,* Vol. 80, Nos. 5 and 6 (1931).

10. K. Jaspers, *Allgemeine Psychopathologie,* 3rd ed. (1922), p. 63.

11. From *Annales Médico-Psychologiques,* No. 4 (April, 1937).

Extravagance (Verstiegenheit)

Human existence projects itself in breadth, and in height;[1] it not only *strides* forth, but also *mounts* upward. In both respects, therefore, it is possible for human existence to go *too* far, to become Extravagant. If, now, we are to understand the anthropological meaning of Extravagance, we must seek what it is that makes possible the change from existential rising into a mode of existence that is Extravagant. Anthropology can never limit its investigations to only one existential direction, but, rather, being *anthropological*, must always have before it the *total* structure of human beings. The basis, therefore, of this change or conversion from existential rising into Extravagance will, from the start, be viewed not merely as upward movement, but will be understood as part of the *koinonia*[2] or community of other basic potentialities of human existence. As I have attempted to show elsewhere,[3] Extravagance is, in fact, rooted in a certain disharmony in the relation between

TRANSLATOR'S NOTE: There is no one word in English that adequately conveys the meaning of the German *verstiegen*. The verb, *sich versteigen*, means to climb too high so as not to be able to return, to lose one's self among precipitous mountain peaks, to fly high, to go too far, etc. As an adjective, it is, therefore, inaccurately rendered by such words as "extravagant," "eccentric," "queer," "odd," or "high-flown," none of which convey the sense of one's climbing into a *cul-de-sac*. The term "extravagance," capitalized, is used here because, despite the fact that its common English usage is not adequate to the German word, its Latin roots (*extra*, beyond, and *vagari*, wander) taken together, give the meaning of wandering beyond a limit. To feel the full sense of the word, imagine a mountain climber trapped on a narrow ledge such that he can neither descend nor ascend, and from which he must be rescued by others.

[342]

rising upward and striding forth. If we call such a relation "anthropologically proportionate" when it is "successful," [4] then we must speak of Extravagance as a form of anthropological disproportion, as a "failure" of the relationship between height and breadth in the anthropological sense.

The rising upward of human beings is not to be understood within the context of its being-in-the-world [5] and its corresponding spatialization and temporalization. It is, rather, to be understood in the context of its being-beyond-the-world in the sense of the at-homeness and eternalness of love, [6] in which there exists no above and below, no near and far, no sooner and later. If, nevertheless, human existence, as a finite being, still remains "consigned" to height and breadth, it can "go too far" only where it has broken out of the home and eternity of love and is completely contained in "space and time." For only where the *communio* of love and the *communicatio* of friendship is missing and where mere intercourse and traffic with "others" and with one's self has taken over the exclusive direction of our existence, only there can height and depth, nearness and distance, present and future, have so much importance that human existence can *go too far*, can attain to an *end* and a *now* from which there is neither retreat nor progress. In such a case, we speak of conversion into Extravagance. It may be an Extravagant "idea," an ideology (ideologies are by their very nature Extravagant), an Extravagant ideal or "feeling," an Extravagant wish or plan, an Extravagant claim, opinion, or viewpoint, a mere "whim" or an Extravagant deed or misdeed. In all these instances, "Extravagance" is conditioned by the fact that the Dasein has "gotten stuck" at a certain experiential locus [*Er-Fahrung*] from which it can no longer, to use a phrase from Hofmannsthal, [7] "strike its tent," from which it can no longer break out. Robbed of *communio* and *communicatio*, the Dasein can no longer widen, revise, or examine its "experiential horizon" and remains rooted to a "narrow minded," i.e., sharply limited, standpoint. In this respect, the Dasein is "stalled" or ob-stinate, but not yet Extravagant,* for

---

* Of the languages familiar to me, only German clearly draws this distinction. In English and the Romance languages, corresponding expressions are drawn almost exclusively from the worldly sphere (*aller trop loin, andar troppo lontano,* or *troppo oltre, to go too far* or *so far as* to maintain). Spanish is an exception. It recognizes both an *irse demasaido lejos* (too far or too wide) and a *tomar su vuelo demasiado alto* (to fly or swing *too high*).

an additional precondition of Extravagance is that the Dasein rises *higher* than is appropriate to the breadth of its experiential and intellectual horizon, that, in other words, breadth and height are not proportional to each other.

The classic clinical psychiatric example of this is Bleuler's concept of a certain kind of mental deficiency as a "disproportion between striving and understanding"; the classic example from dramatic literature is Ibsen's master-builder Solness,[8] who "builds higher than he is able to climb." * In no case, however, should this disproportion between breadth and height be understood as a relation between particular "abilities" or characteristics, and least of all as a relation between "intelligence and the need to be admired"; what we must look for, rather, are the anthropological conditions that make such disproportionate relationships possible. We do not consider Extravagance as something applicable to particular groups (parties, cliques, sects, etc.) that patently embody a lopsided collection of "traits" or "identifying characteristics." Nor, therefore, is it to be understood in general as a character trait or as some kind of ascertainable psychological, psychopathological, or sociological event or "symptom." It is, rather, to be approached "daseinsanalytically" [9]—i.e., as something to be understood within the total structure of human existence—as, in short, an *anthropological*, ontological possibility. Only when this approach is understood can we reach a genuine understanding of the richly extensive "symptomatology" of Extravagance. Only then shall we, for example, be able to see how and to what degree we can differentiate anthropologically between the (incorrectly) so-called "extravagant ideas" of the manic,[10] the "extravagant" ("screwy," "bizarre") gestures, language, or actions of the schizophrenic,[11] and the phobias of the neurotic—even while as psychopathologists or in our everyday life we speak of them all as "extravagant." Even schizophrenic insanity can, in my opinion,

*That Ibsen clearly *saw* ("seeing" is his own word for poetry) the significance of the relation between height and breadth for the success or failure of human existence is indicated by the fact that in his *Little Eyolf* he presents a figure in clear contrast to the masterbuilder Solness. The road builder Bergheim is a figure who does not seek to "build higher" than he can actually climb. Indeed, as his profession indicates, he does not, like Solness, build towers soaring into the sky only to lie one day shattered upon the ground. Bergheim builds pretty roads on the earth. He does not strive after an unattainable "happiness," nor desire more than he is capable of. He thus attains to that which he seeks and *grows* thereby.

be understood[12] only if it is taken initially as an *existential mode* of Extravagance. The same holds true for "mass phenomena" of Extravagance.

Let us, however, turn our attention back to Extravagance considered as a structural displacement of anthropological proportions. The horizontal, as a vector of meaning, the "going out into the wide world," corresponds more to "discursivity," to the experiencing, traversing, and occupying of "world," to the "broadening of the field of vision," the broadening of insight, perspective, and vista with respect to the "hubbub" of outer and inner "world." Similarly, the vertical, as a vector of meaning, the rising upwards, corresponds more to the desire to overcome the "earth's gravity," the desire to be *elevated* above the pressure and "anxiety of the earthbound," as well as the desire to gain a "higher" perspective, a "higher view of things," as Ibsen says, *from which* man may shape, master, or, in a word, appropriate the "known." Such an appropriation of the world in the sense of a becoming and realizing of the self is termed *choosing oneself*. Choice, be it of a particular action or of a whole life's commitment, presupposes a rising or lifting of oneself *above* the particular worldly situation and thus *above* the ambit of the known and seen. But what does this "above" * mean? As Nietzsche so eloquently described in the preface to *Human, All Too Human*, it does not mean the adventurer's "circumnavigation of the world" in the sense of worldly experience; it means, rather, the strenous and painful scaling of the "rungs on the ladder" of the *problem of evaluation*,† i.e., of establishing an order of preference.

Rising upward is thus not simply mere learning, knowing one's way about, knowledge in the sense of *experience*, but involves, rather, "taking a stand," choosing oneself in the sense of *self-realization* or *maturation*. We must, however, be careful not to confuse this rising upwards with mere *will* in the sense of the *psychological* distinction of understanding, feeling, and will.‡ Rather

---

* This lifting of oneself above a worldly *situation* must not be confused with the "beyond" of the being-beyond world as such in the sense of love.

† Gaston Bachelard makes the same point (see *L'Air et les Songes*) when he characterizes vertical rising as *valorisation*, as the apprehension and lending of *value*. Recall, for example, the *decision* of Antigone.

‡ I am in complete agreement with E. Minkowski when he (see "La Triade psychologique" in *Vers une Cosmologie*, pp. 57 ff.) disputes this "triadic" classifica-

we must realize that (as is hinted by Bleuler's term "striving") in rising, the fact of being *carried* (by the "wings" of moods, wishes, passions—by "fantasy" or imagination) passes smoothly into the fact of decisively* "taking a stance." Nevertheless, we must clearly distinguish, anthropologically, between the dispositional state of *being carried* by wishes, ideas, ideals, and the strenuous, toilsome act of *scaling* the "rungs on the ladder," which allows these wishes, ideas, and ideals to be weighed against each other in life, art, philosophy, and science and to be translated into words and deeds.

This conception sheds light on the height-breadth disproportion that underlies the possibility of "manic ideation." We shall soon see that this mode of disproportion is so different from that of Extravagance that we cannot even speak of it as "extravagant ideation," but rather as a "flight of ideas," a term that is also used in psychopathology. The height-breadth disproportion of the type of being-in-the-world represented by the flight of ideas is completely different to that exemplified by Extravagance. In the *former*, the disproportion consists in the fact that striding forth is replaced by a leaping and jumping-beyond "into the infinite." The horizon or circle of vision is "endlessly broadened," but at the same time the rising upward remains solely a *"vol imaginaire,"* a being-*carried* on the wings of mere wishes and "fantasies." The result is that neither an *overview* in the sense of experiential wisdom, *nor* a *penetration* of the problematic structure of the particular situation (elevation is, at the same time, also basically a penetration, since *altitudo* refers essentially to both height *and* depth) is attained, and thus no decisive stance is taken. This height-breadth disproportion is rooted in an "excessive" expansion of the manic's pervasively *volatile* world; excessive, that is, in that the sphere of the *authentic* undergoes a simultaneous process of *"leveling."* [13] By "authentic," we refer to those heights (or depths) which can be attained only insofar as the Dasein undergoes the *arduous process* of choosing itself and growing into maturity. The disproportion evidenced in the manic pattern of life[14] is spoken of daseinsanalytically as *flightiness*. It signi-

---

tion of psychological phenomena and, indeed, argues against the very possibility of such a classification.

* Consequently, we must unreservedly agree with Bachelard when he writes: "Il est impossible de faire la psychologie de la volonté sans aller à la racine même du vol imaginaire."

fies the impossibility of obtaining a genuine foothold on the "ladder" of human problems and, in this respect, thus *also* signifies the impossibility of authentic decision, action, and maturation. Detached from loving *communio* and authentic *communicatio*, all too far and hastily driven *forward* and *carried upward*, the manic hovers in fraudulent heights in which he cannot take a stand or make a "self-sufficient" decision. Love and friendship have, in these *airy* heights, lost their power. Human intercourse is reduced to the level of psychiatric treatment.

The Extravagance of the *schizoid psychopathic personality* and the countless forms of *schizophrenic* being-in-the-world are quite different.[15] Here the anthropological disproportion is no longer rooted in an excess of breadth (of "leaping") and of the heights of mere *vol imaginaire* that outweigh the (authentic) heights of "decision." It is rooted in the excessive heights of decision that outweigh the breadth of "experience." Disregarding for the moment the essential difference between the psychopathic schizoid and the schizophrenic, we may say that their mode of "going too far" differs from that of the manic precisely in that they are not *carried* into the "airy heights" of optimistic moods, but that, alone, and "without regard to experience," they *climb up* to one *particular* rung of the "ladder of human problems" and *remain there.* The height involved in this climbing upwards bears no relation to the narrowness and inflexibility of the experiential horizon ("experience" being understood in the widest sense of ex-perience, i.e., "discursivity" [16] as such). Here Extravagance means more than merely "being stalled" in that what is involved is not only the impossibility of experiential progress forward, but rather the strict attachment or bondage to a *particular* level or rung of human experience (*Problematik*). The widely flexible human "hierarchy of height" is, in this case, basically "mis-taken" and one particular idea or ideology becomes fixed or made absolute. Insofar as "experiences" are still realized at all, they are no longer valued or turned to account, for their "value" is inflexibly fixed. Extravagance signifies, therefore, the *"absolutizing"* of a single *decision.* Again, such "absolutizing" is only possible where the Dasein is "despairingly" exiled from the home and eternalness of love and friendship, where, therefore, it no longer knows or senses the "relativity" of the "above" and "below" seen against the background of an unquestioning *trust* in Being, an unproblematic ontological security. It stands isolated from this security, and from intercourse or traffic with others, and is thus barred from the challenge and correction that can only be derived from such intercourse. Thus, withdrawn into intercourse or traffic with itself alone, such a process can only "wear itself out" until it becomes a mere staring at a Medusalike, psychotically rigidified problem, ideal, or "nothingness of anxiety." [17] Consequently, rescue from the Extravagant position becomes possible only by means of "outside help," as is true of a mountain-climber who has climbed too far out upon a precipice.*

The neurotic, too, can be "rescued" from the Extravagance and confinedness of his existence (for example, in cases of phobia) only by outside help, in the sense of collaboration and communication with someone else. For this very reason, it is perhaps true that the example of neurotic Extravagance shows more clearly than any other that Extravagance (in the physical or the psychic sense) is always based upon a failure of insight or circumspection with regard to the particular meaning-context or "region of the world" *in* which the Dasein overextends itself. In mountain climbing, one goes too far only if the over-all structure of the precipice is hidden from view or unknown. Similarly, one goes too far mentally or psychically only when one lacks insight into the over-all "hierarchical structure" of human ontological possibilities and, in ignorance thereof, mounts ever higher and higher. Thus, Extravagance can never be understood solely from a subjective point of view, but only from the combined perspective of (transcendental) subjectivity and (transcendental) objectivity. What we call psychotherapy is basically no more than an attempt to bring the patient to a point where he can "see" the manner in which the totality of human existence or "being-in-the-world" is structured and to see at which of its junctures he has overreached himself. That is: the goal of psy-

---

* At this point it may not be superfluous to suggest that, as Heinrich Wölfflin formulated it in his highly important dissertation "Prolegomena zu einer Psychologie der Architektur," *Kleine Schriften* (Basel, 1946), p. 23: "The image of our bodily existence" everywhere represents the "standard" according to which we judge every other appearance. This is true first of all of the "standard" according to which *language* grasps and names "all other appearances." Language is able to do this because, unlike analytic understanding, it sees our existence in its unity and togetherness. This is not to say that language "corporalizes" the noncorporal "phenomenal modes" of our existence. What it does, rather, is to see the psychic and the spiritual as already inherent in the corporal appearances, and vice versa.

chotherapy is to bring the patient safely back "down to earth" from his Extravagance. Only from this point is any new *departure* and *ascent* possible.

I have attempted merely to sketch out an understanding of the anthropological meaning of Extravagance. In so doing, I have stressed the interpretation of spatial aspects and have allowed the even more important aspect of temporality to remain in the background. But it has obviously been implied in such expressions as "maturation," "decision," "discursivity," "leaping," "being carried upwards," "climbing the rungs of the ladder," "being brought to a standstill," and, finally, in the expressions "anthropological proportion" and "disproportion." Existential height and breadth signify, ultimately, two different "spatial" schemata of one temporal direction of finite human existence; they are, therefore, only conceptually separable.

Notes

1. Binswanger "Dream and Existence" [in this volume]; Gaston Bachelard, *L'Air et les Songes: Essai sur l'imagination du mouvement* (Paris, 1943). For an introduction to phenomenological cosmology in general, see E. Minkowski, *Vers une Cosmologie* (Paris, 1936). For a theory of lived space, see also Erwin Straus, in *Nervenarzt*, No. 11 (1930), and E. Durckheim, "Untersuchungen zum gelebten Raum," *Neue psychologische Studien*, Vol. 6, No. 4 (1932).
2. W. Szilasi, *Macht und Ohnmacht des Geistes*, p. 46.
3. Binswanger, *Henrik Ibsen und das Problem der Selbstralisation* (Heidelberg, 1949).
4. Szilasi, p. 19.
5. Martin Heidegger, *Sein und Zeit* and *Vom Wesen des Grundes*.
6. Binswanger, *Grundformen und Erkenntnis Menschlichen Daseins* (Zürich, 1953).
7. Binswanger, "Über das Wort von Hofmannsthal: Was Geist ist, erfasst nur der Bedrängte" (*Festgabe für R. A. Schröder*), *Schweizer Studia philosophica*, Vol. VIII (1943).
8. Binswanger, *Henrik Ibsen*.
9. Binswanger, in *Schweiz. Arch.*, Vol. 57 (1946), p. 209.
10. Binswanger, "Über Ideenflucht," *Schweiz. Arch.*, Vols. 27-30.
11. Binswanger, in *Mschr. Psychiatr.*, Vol. 110 (1945), pp. 3-4.
12. Binswanger, in *Schweiz Arch.*, Vol. 63 (1949).
13. Binswanger, "Über Ideenflucht," especially the second study.
14. Binswanger, in *Schweiz. Med. Wschr.*, No. 3 (1945).
15. Binswanger, *Schizophrenie* (Pfullingen, 1957).
16. Binswanger, *Grundformen*, Chapter 1.
17. Binswanger, *Schizophrenie*.

INDEX